VEILED VALOUR

Tom Frame AM has been a naval officer, Anglican Bishop to the Defence Force, a member of the Australian War Memorial Council and numerous ethics oversight bodies, and a theological college principal. He became Professor of History at UNSW Canberra in July 2014 and was appointed Director of the Public Leadership Research Group in July 2017 with responsibility for establishing the John Howard Prime Ministerial Library. He is the author or editor of more than 50 books, including *HMAS Sydney: Loss and controversy*, *Stromlo: An Australian observatory*, *The Life and Death of Harold Holt*, *Evolution in the Antipodes: Charles Darwin and Australia* and *Gun Control: What Australia got right (and wrong)*.

VEILED VALOUR

Australian Special Forces in Afghanistan
and war crimes allegations

TOM FRAME

UNSW PRESS

A UNSW Press book

Published by
NewSouth Publishing
University of New South Wales Press Ltd
University of New South Wales
Sydney NSW 2052
AUSTRALIA
https://unsw.press/

© Tom Frame 2022
First published 2022

10 9 8 7 6 5 4 3 2 1

This book is copyright. Apart from any fair dealing for the purpose of private study, research, criticism or review, as permitted under the *Copyright Act*, no part of this book may be reproduced by any process without written permission. Inquiries should be addressed to the publisher.

A catalogue record for this book is available from the National Library of Australia

ISBN: 9781742237633 (paperback)
        9781742238371 (ebook)
        9781742239279 (ePDF)

Design Josephine Pajor-Markus
Cover design Phil Campbell
Cover images iStock / KaninRoman and jacekbieniek

All reasonable efforts were taken to obtain permission to use copyright material reproduced in this book, but in some cases copyright could not be traced. The author welcomes information in this regard.

CONTENTS

Introduction   1
Map of Afghanistan and Uruzgan Province   11

PART I: THE CONTEXT

1. From Gallipoli to Uruzgan, 1915–2020   15
2. Downfall of a nation: Afghanistan's journey, 1747–1979   27
3. Collapse of a state: The Soviet occupation, 1979–1992   47
4. Disintegration of a military: The Soviet 40th Army, 1979–1989   67
5. Implosion of a society: Taliban extremism, 1992–2001   89

PART II: THE PLAYERS

6. Advent of Australia's Special Forces, 1957–2003   111
7. Evolution of a commitment: The Taliban revival, 2001–2005   139
8. Drafting a story: Selling the Afghan war, 2005–2013   165
9. Searching for solutions: Australia's longest war, 2005–2013   194

PART III: THE DRAMA

10. Rumour and reform: The Crompvoets and Irvine reports, 2014–2018   227
11. Revelations and allegations: Media reporting, 2016–2020   252

PART IV: COMPARATIVE EXPERIENCES

12 Media and misinformation: The New Zealand experience   285

13 Historical legacies and public opinion: The United
    Kingdom experience   306

14 Shameful shadows and superior standards: The Canadian
    experience   331

15 Facing the future by acknowledging the past: The French
    experience   355

PART V: DISCORDANT NOTES

16 Towards a reckoning, 2016–2020   381

17 Asking questions   402

Acknowledgments   415
Notes   417
Index   445

INTRODUCTION

Reputations take years to establish and decades to enhance. Unsurprisingly, they are strenuously guarded, given they are demanding to build and can readily dissolve. The Australian Defence Force (ADF) is one of the nation's revered institutions. It is also numbered among the world's respected militaries. The ADF's standing is the source of considerable social, political and strategic capital for the Australian Government, which recognises its value as a vital asset in the management of domestic and diplomatic affairs. It is esteemed for its discipline and leadership. When there are difficult jobs to be done, such as humanitarian assistance and disaster recovery, peacekeeping and counterinsurgency, the Commonwealth looks to the ADF for its wide-ranging expertise, which it knows will be delivered efficiently and effectively.

Having secured an enviable status for its competence and professionalism, anything detracting from the ADF's position at home and abroad attracts immediate attention and usually elicits a swift response. Mistakes and misconduct are always serious because they damage reputations. Mistakes imply a lack of ability or lapses of judgment; misconduct a lack of leadership or lapses of discipline. Given the importance of ability, judgment, leadership and discipline to the effective performance of any military force, the nation faces a serious problem when the public begin to have doubts and politicians start to distrust, the capability of the defence force and the reliability of its members. Goodwill and confidence are integral to a sound relationship between the people and their defence force, and between politicians and senior commanders. Misgivings and suspicion not only erode the morale of uniformed men and women, they detract from the military's overall capacity to promote national security and protect the national interest.

Apart from being accused of incompetence or negligence, the most damning charge that can be levelled at an officer or soldier is involvement in war crimes. The Rome Statute of the International Criminal Court defines war crimes as 'grave breaches' of the 1949 Geneva Conventions. The very long list of actions deemed war crimes includes 'wilful killing' (murder); 'torture or inhuman treatment'; 'wilfully causing great suffering, or serious injury to body or health'; 'extensive destruction and appropriation of property, not justified by military necessity and carried out unlawfully and wantonly'; 'wilfully depriving a prisoner of war or other protected person of the rights of fair and regular trial'; 'intentionally directing attacks against the civilian population as such or against individual civilians not taking direct part in hostilities'; and 'killing or wounding a combatant who, having laid down his arms or having no longer means of defence, has surrendered at discretion'.[1]

These crimes are odious because they usually point to the collapse of discipline and failure of leadership. They are collectively referred to as 'atrocities', insinuating they are born of cowardice and cruelty. Most Australians could not have imagined that Australian soldiers sent to a troubled land among oppressed people to restore order and revive hope would ever be accused of wrongdoing. War crimes are utterly inconsistent with the public's perception of Australian soldiers and a complete abrogation of Australian Army values. The mere suggestion that an Australian soldier would assault an innocent civilian or execute an enemy detainee would be met with righteous indignation from many sectors of society: how could anyone accuse the representatives of a civilised nation like Australia, and the members of a disciplined organisation such as the ADF, of this kind of barbarism? Australian soldiers are just not like that. Larrikins yes, murderers no.

On 19 November 2020, the findings of a long-running inquiry conducted by a superior court judge into the conduct of Australian

Special Operations Task Group (SOTG) personnel during their deployment to Afghanistan between 2005 and 2013 were released to the public.[2] The Inspector-General of the Australian Defence Force (IGADF) Afghanistan Inquiry was prompted by allegations that members of the Special Air Service (SAS) Regiment and 1st and 2nd Commando Regiments – men considered the ADF's elite and worthy recipients of honours and awards for courage and gallantry – had committed serious crimes while fighting the Taliban. The mere utterance of such allegations damaged Australia's standing as a good international citizen and devastated the Australian Army's reputation as a model military institution.

This book examines the context, explores the operations, and traces the events that led to Australian soldiers being accused of war crimes in Afghanistan. It does not canvass the contents of the Inquiry's findings or cover reactions to its public release. The narrative intentionally ends the day before the report's public release. My aim is to describe the complicated journey that led to this day of reckoning. It is impossible to perceive the nuances of the report and the effect of its recommendations without an appreciation of why this particular form of inquiry was necessary and why its conduct was far from straightforward.

There are five parts to this book. After the opening chapter, which explains the place of armed conflict in Australian history, the prominence of soldiers in the national story and the community's unwillingness to accept they are capable of war crimes, Part I sets the scene. Chapters 2 to 5 describe the modern history of Afghanistan; its faltering transition from decentralised tribalism to nationalised democracy in the 1960s; the Soviet Union's military intervention in 1979; the decade-long foreign occupation undergirded by the Soviet 40th Army's widespread violations of human rights; the civil war among rival militia leaders that engulfed the country in 1989; the rise of the Taliban in 1994 and the subsequent proliferation of religious extremism across the country; and, lastly, Australia's interactions with

Afghanistan prior to 2000 and its involvement in the multinational invasion in 2001. I will contend that the desire to achieve military success in one of the most intractable political conflicts of modern history increased the possibility there might be breaches of the Law of Armed Conflict and violations of Rules of Engagement (ROE) (which are described in chapter 9).

Part II deals with the evolution of Australia's Special Forces capability since 1957 and the deployment of Special Forces personnel to Afghanistan in 2001. Chapter 6 describes the maintenance of two Commando companies after the Second World War, the raising of an SAS company in 1957 and its early experiences in Borneo and South Vietnam. It also looks at the journey of the 4th Battalion, Royal Australian Regiment (4 RAR) from its designation as a Special Operations unit in 1997 to being renamed the 2nd Commando Regiment in 2009. I will also touch on the decisions that led to the formation of a separate Special Operations Command (SOCOMD) in 2003. Chapter 7 recounts Australia's participation in the invasion and initial occupation of Afghanistan in 2001; the ADF's withdrawal in late 2002 ahead of the invasion of Iraq in 2003; the subsequent return of Australian Special Forces to Afghanistan in 2005; and the Commonwealth Government's decision to send a Provincial Reconstruction Team in 2006. These chapters will also focus on the character and commitments of the adversary – the Taliban. I will outline the changing shape of Talibanist belief and allegiance before and after 2001, and the complex ethnic, social, economic and political features of Uruzgan province, where the Australians were based. Chapter 8 outlines the Australian Government's objectives in joining the International Security Assistance Force (ISAF) in Afghanistan after 2005, and how it explained the deployment, then justified the continuing presence of Australian personnel in Uruzgan. Chapter 9 is an overview of the missions undertaken by the SOTG between 2005 and 2013, including a series of operations in which civilians were mistakenly killed and non-combatants were allegedly harmed.

Part III covers the end of Australia's involvement in combat operations in Afghanistan at the close of 2013 and the slow spread of rumours that SOTG personnel had allegedly committed and then concealed serious misconduct. Chapter 10 explains why several studies were launched into the organisation and culture of Special Operations Command (SOCOMD) after 2014, and assesses the reports submitted to the Special Operations Commander (SOCAUST) by consultant sociologist, Samantha Crompvoets,[3] in 2016 and to the Chief of Army by former intelligence head, David Irvine, in 2018[4] and 2020.[5] Chapter 11 deals with the inquiry initiated in May 2016 by the IGADF into rumours of wrongdoing in Afghanistan, and the subsequent proliferation of media stories accusing Special Forces soldiers of indictable offences, including threats of violence against their former colleagues.

Part IV is devoted to comparative analysis of alleged and actual breaches of the Law of Armed Conflict and violations of the ROE by military personnel from New Zealand, the United Kingdom, Canada and France. In this part, I will contrast the varied military traditions of each nation; the nature of the allegations made against their conventional and Special Forces; political and public reactions to revelations of misconduct; and how senior officers and political leaders dealt with reports of wrongdoing. These chapters will demonstrate that the officers and soldiers of every nation deploying its forces to Afghanistan after 2005 faced legal and ethical dilemmas in the field. Australia was not the only nation whose personnel may have made mistakes or engaged in serious misconduct.

Some readers may wonder why the United States has been excluded from this comparative exercise. Allegations of American misconduct in Afghanistan have ranged from excessive force during arrests; arbitrary and indefinite detention; mistreatment (torture) of detainees and mass murder.[6] They have exceeded the number and severity of allegations made against other ISAF partner nations in Afghanistan. For all the similarities between the two nations and their militaries, and the United States apparently being the 'gold standard' of Special Forces capability, Australia and America had different reasons for being in Afghanistan. Their respective forces conducted different operations and their soldiers imbibed a different spirit of service. Despite the occasional suggestion that Australian Special Forces soldiers aspired to be like their United States Army Delta Force and United States Navy SEAL counterparts, there remain many more similarities between the Australian and British armies and their respective Special Forces regiments than with those of the United States; the United Kingdom chapter delivers sufficient valuable contrasts and comparisons.

Part V contains the closing chapters. Chapter 16 looks at the conduct of the IGADF Afghanistan Inquiry and criticism of its length and processes. I will also consider the efforts that were made by competing stakeholders to create the most favourable circumstances for its reception, predictions of what the Inquiry was likely to find and tentative early explanations of why alleged misconduct had occurred. The final chapter does not resemble a conventional conclusion, although it does draw together the threads that linked the earlier chapters. Its objective is to prepare the reader for an informed and insightful appreciation of the publicly available redacted version of the Inquiry report which was released on 19 November 2020.

I have tried not to anticipate any of the report's findings, conclusions or recommendations in my handling of the preceding two decades of military operations. This book does not speculate on whether any Australian officer or soldier committed war crimes or had knowledge of their commission. I have, however, mentioned the spate of allegations featured in media stories that have appeared since late 2016. The allegations in these stories, which have not been critically examined, are included because they have become part of the public record. Press reporting shaped expectations about what the IGADF Afghanistan Inquiry might find and influenced the receptiveness of the Australian parliament, press and people to the report's findings.

Allegations of serious misconduct should be deeply concerning to all Australians. Claims that Australian military personnel are the best in the world, that Australians have greater natural fighting aptitude than their military allies, and that Australians have deeper respect for civilised values than their operating partners, cannot be sustained in the face of so many allegations of grievous offences. If only a handful of the incidents described in the Inquiry report are substantiated in the nation's courts, Australia faces national humiliation not unlike the British experienced over the killing of 14 unarmed Irish civil rights campaigners on 'Bloody Sunday' in 1972 and the Canadians felt after the murder of two civilians during the 'Somali Affair' in 1993 (both of which are described in subsequent chapters). The conduct of the nation's elite fighting forces in Afghanistan continues to be a national concern. Judgments on their behaviour have the potential to change how we view the past, as well as what happens in the present and the future. Australian soldiers allegedly did what many thought they could not do. Those soldiers now stand among us as people we do not recognise. Further, Australia has relinquished the high moral ground and cannot presume the trust and goodwill of its friends and allies.

The need for this book reflects the magnitude of the topic and the complexity of the issues, most particularly the rapidly changing strategic situation that confronted the Australians in responding to Afghanistan's intricate human terrain. Coming to terms with the many complications associated with the multinational Coalition military operations conducted in Afghanistan is crucial in understanding how and why Australian soldiers were allegedly drawn into the darkness where misconduct usually occurs.

Readers will also note that the SAS Regiment features more prominently in the discussion of misconduct than the Commando Regiments, although SOTG force elements drawn from both the SAS and Commando communities served together in Afghanistan. My explanation for the preponderance of attention on the SAS Regiment has two parts. First, more in-theatre inquiries and most media reports of alleged misconduct concern SAS soldiers. Second, as the majority of adverse findings in the Inquiry report relate to the SAS Regiment and its members, this is where I have concentrated my energies. Foregrounding the SAS Regiment should not imply any lack of interest in the Commando Regiments or any disinterest in the particular challenges its members faced in Afghanistan.

Nothing in this book has been drawn from classified sources or relies upon privileged access to official information. Where possible I have tried to avoid naming current or former serving ADF members, even when an individual's identity has been disclosed publicly in relation to an incident I have mentioned. The ADF has not commissioned or endorsed this book. The views presented are entirely my own. They do not represent the views of the ADF, the Department of Defence or any Commonwealth Government agency or official.

This is the first work to consider the context in which the alleged offending occurred and the events that led eventually to the release of the Inquiry report in November 2020.[7] There are four related works that deserve mention. Chris Masters' *No Front Line: Australia's Special Forces at War in Afghanistan*, released in 2017, hints at questionable conduct but does not mention war crimes or the IGADF Afghanistan Inquiry.[8] Mark Wales' *Survivor: Life in the SAS* is an autobiography that briefly describes combat operations in Afghanistan and even more briefly (less than a page) mentions war crimes allegations without explaining their causes or consequences.[9] Samantha Crompvoets' essay *Blood Lust, Trust and Blame* refers to war crimes and the IGADF Afghanistan Inquiry, but is mainly preoccupied with whether corporate culture was the cause of individual misconduct.[10] Mark Willacy's *Rogue Forces* is an amalgam of previously published media stories based on personal conversations with former and serving ADF members who claimed to have witnessed misconduct in Afghanistan. It does not canvass the wider context in which the misconduct occurred or offer a detailed account of why it occurred.[11]

In preparing this work I have been conscious that rumours of misconduct and allegations of wrongdoing involve at least five different groups of people with a significant stake in establishing their truthfulness. The first are the Afghans who were allegedly assaulted or murdered by Australian soldiers. They and their families are entitled to know whether there is any substance to these rumours, and to justice as well as compensation if the courts decide that serious offences have been committed.

The second are those who intentionally spread rumours or made allegations. They knowingly impugned the reputation of comrades and risked the censure of colleagues in drawing attention to behaviour they believed was wrong, and possibly criminal. These soldiers deserve to be heard, given the seriousness of their claims and their willingness to suffer opprobrium.

The third group consists of those who have been the subject of rumours and allegations. They are entitled to have the air cleared of innuendo, and their innocence or guilt established by formal legal proceedings. Their reputations and possibly even their liberty are at stake.

The fourth are members of the ADF, whose standing in the community has been eroded by rumours and allegations. The vast majority of those who deployed to Afghanistan do not want their achievements undermined by lingering doubts about the alleged conduct of a small minority.

Finally, there are the Australian people who feel let down by the rumours and allegations. They are entitled to a defence force that is worthy of their confidence and an assurance that uniformed men and women will continue to exemplify the highest Australian values.

Rumours of military misconduct and allegations of war crimes are always serious. They are never minor nor inconsequential, because they relate to behaviour that has blighted human civilisation for centuries. Even when it is possible to demonstrate that rumours have no substance or that allegations are without foundation, mere mention of war crimes causes reputational damage. The harm is never readily overcome nor easily reversed. Coming to terms with the origin of the rumours and allegations is an important first step. Dealing with them conscientiously and impartially is a necessary second step. This book is an attempt to examine whether the steps taken by the Australian nation and the ADF were sure-footed and in the right direction.

MAP OF AFGHANISTAN

MAP OF URUZGAN PROVINCE

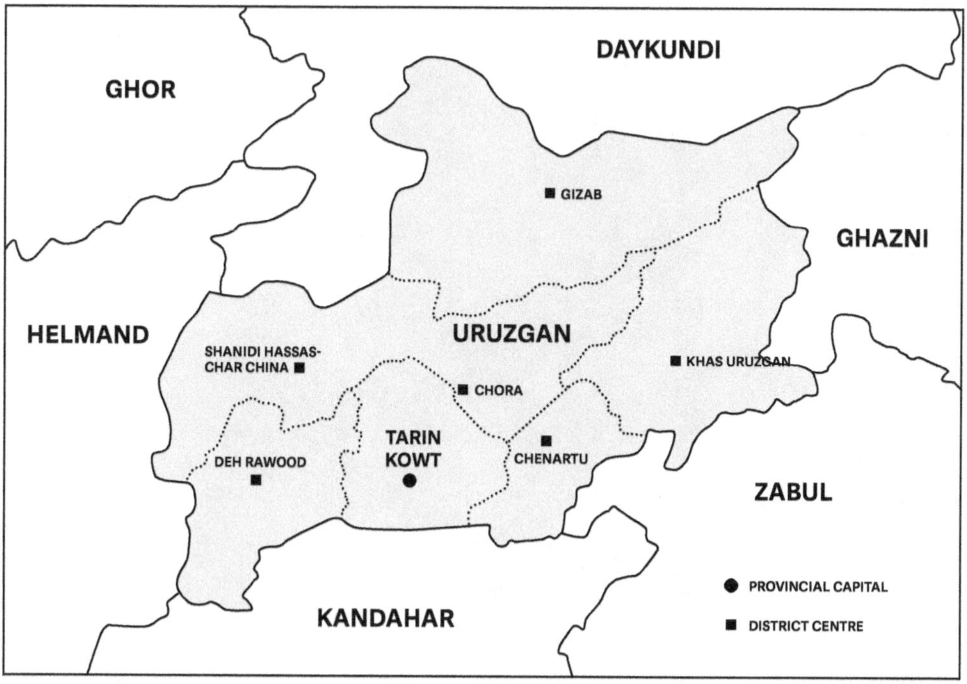

● PROVINCIAL CAPITAL
■ DISTRICT CENTRE

PART I
THE CONTEXT

1
FROM GALLIPOLI TO URUZGAN
1915–2020

The Australian War Memorial is a shrine to nationhood. It faces the Federal Parliament as a reminder that the exercise of political power has lasting human consequences. Its design and ambience are reminiscent of a cathedral, albeit a secular one, laid out in the shape of a Byzantine cross. The domed Hall of Memory conveys a sense of the sacred and the transcendent. The stained-glass windows feature images of Australian servicemen and women. The central feature, the Tomb of the Unknown Soldier, symbolises the selfless spirit of those who perished in war. The Memorial is meant to be much more than bricks and mortar. It is a serene place eliciting reverence and awe, contemplation and gratitude; the antithesis of the battlefields upon which thousands of Australians fell. They become mystically present when their deeds are recalled. Those who have worn the uniform and faced an adversary have been set apart and now hold a special place in the life of the nation. The ordinary have become the iconic and their exemplary deeds promoted as worthy of emulation.

Built originally to honour those who fought and died in the Great War of 1914–18, the commemorative areas have been extended to honour Australians who served in the earlier Boer War, the Second World War, the Korean War, the Malayan Emergency, the Confrontation in Borneo, the Vietnam Conflict, peacekeeping missions such as East Timor, and more recent campaigns in the Middle East – Afghanistan and Iraq. It is one of Australia's most popular destinations for domestic and international visitors and a place of pilgrimage for many. One million people every year, including school-aged children and revered heads of state, travel to Canberra and pay their respects.

The Memorial does not offer a static presentation of history. It reaches out to visitors and tries to touch their affections. Since opening in 1941, its galleries and exhibitions have conveyed evocative messages to successive generations of Australians who are obliged to remember and to reflect. The consistent theme is the prevalence of the 'Anzac spirit' which emerged among those fighting in the trenches at Gallipoli in 1915. The men of the Australian and New Zealand Army Corps, the 'Anzacs', who fought and died in that campaign, are credited with establishing a tradition of service that has provided an enduring benchmark that uniformed men and women aspire to attain. The Anzacs exemplified the national character and embodied the values and virtues for which the young Australian nation wanted to be known.

A slideshow in the Great War gallery concludes with the statement: 'Every nation has its story, this is ours'.[1] It is a tale of courage, ingenuity and creativity, sacrifice and honour. Like the Memorial, the Anzac story has a quasi-religious tenor with its own sense of the divine and the eternal. The *Protection of the Word 'Anzac' Act*, which was passed by Federal Parliament in 1920, means 'Anzac' cannot be associated with any commercial purpose without the government's consent.[2] The concern is that something sacred might be profaned. Clearly, this epic story is to be received and respected rather than challenged and contested. Its self-appointed and well-meaning defenders consider it impertinent to doubt its authenticity or question its veracity. As the Anzacs and their successors are men and women of hallowed memory with saint-like status, criticising them has been likened to blasphemy. Iconoclasts are unwelcome. Those who have asked hard questions about these legends have been chastised for their temerity.

In the early 1980s, David Kent, a University of New England

historian, was researching the origins and contents of the publications produced by Australian soldiers embarked in troopships who were deploying to the trenches during the Great War.[3] He located a file at the Australian War Memorial containing material that did not appear in *The Anzac Book* edited by the official war correspondent, Charles Bean, and published in 1916.[4] Reading the file led Kent to conclude that Bean had been highly selective in the material he accepted for inclusion, in order to produce a rather pristine image of the Australian soldier for recruiting purposes.[5] Bean confessed: 'the tender Australian public, which only tolerates flattery and that in its cheapest form, would howl me out of existence'. Kent noted that 'the rejected material contained references to cowardice, drunkenness, malingering, friction between the men and their officers, personal suffering, the waste of life and the de-humanising effects of warfare'. Kent decided the file would serve as the basis for a journal article on Bean's role as editor or, perhaps more accurately, censor of *The Anzac Book*.

The first draft was presented at the annual Australian War Memorial conference in 1984. Kent read one of Bean's reflections on the challenges facing the war correspondent:

> There is horror and beastliness and cowardice and treachery, over all of which the writer, anxious to please the public, has to throw his cloak – but the man who does his job is a hero … Well, this is the true side of war – but I wonder if anyone would believe me outside the army.[6]

A summary of his presentation later featured in the *Sun-Herald* newspaper, unleashing a barrage of abuse from its readers, although Kent had simply reported Bean's comments. In personal letters, many of them anonymous, Kent was berated for being a 'knocker' and accused of 'smearing the deeds and memory of wonderful men'. His research was considered 'unnecessary and hurtful'; he had produced 'an indecent ... macabre and unsubstantiated treatise' which was 'an exercise in futility'. Detractors called him 'a traitor and treason-monger' whose ideas were 'vile, filthy, distorted'.

Thirty years after the controversy, Kent wondered whether reactions to this kind of writing 'would be repeated today or whether it might be even more hysterical?'[7] Was the enthusiasm for remembrance eroding Australians' capacity to accept difficult, even painful, critiques of the nation's military tradition? Did respect for the Anzacs preclude frank, even forthright, appraisals of contemporary wars and assessments of those who fought them? Indeed, could the Anzac aura be used to conceal attitudes and actions that deserved censure, if not condemnation? As war is the most destructive of all human endeavours, recalling heroic deeds might be used by an opportunistic government to shield its decision-making from scrutiny. Bravery does not transform failures into successes or elevate folly to wisdom. These were not unreasonable fears unless, of course, they were accompanied by polemical intent.

The centenary commemoration of the Gallipoli landings in 2015 was accompanied by movies, documentaries, books and articles. Inevitably, there was a debate about whether some of the claims being made about the enduring legends of the campaign and those who fought it were exaggerated or even polemically motivated. In *Anzac and Its Enemies: The History War on Australia's National Identity* published in 2015, Mervyn Bendle argued this debate was generated by political sentiment. He claimed:

> While the vast bulk of the Australian people attempt to honour the promise made a century ago – Lest we forget – we witness a sustained new round of attacks on the Anzac tradition from determined ideologues on the far-Left; pampered, well-resourced and influential academics, disgruntled politicians and junior military officers; and their media camp advocates. This campaign began with the historian Manning Clark and the 'New Left',

given fresh energy by former Prime Minister Paul Keating and academic historians in elite institutions including the Australian National University, and (incredibly) the Australian Defence Force Academy, and the Australian War Memorial.[8]

His book was not a rebuttal of flawed scholarship but a denunciation of partisan scholars.[9]

As Bendle counselled the need for eternal vigilance, rumours were circulating among the uniformed and younger veteran community that had the potential to inflict more damage on the standing of the Australian Defence Force (ADF) and the exalted status of the nation's military tradition than an army of left-wing activists and ill-informed academics could ever have achieved, if they tried. Unbelievably, the rumours involved the conduct of Australian Special Forces soldiers, principally members of the Special Air Service (SAS) Regiment based in Perth and the 1st and 2nd Commando Regiments headquartered in Sydney. These 'elite' units and their achievements in Afghanistan had been the subject of many complimentary, if not laudatory, books, articles, profiles and documentaries.

These regiments had provided the main fighting elements of the Special Operations Task Group (SOTG) that was deployed to Uruzgan province in Afghanistan after 2005.[10] The SAS had specialised in strategic reconnaissance and long-range patrolling; the Commandos were experts in cordon and search tasks and ground clearance operations. In Afghanistan they were used to neutralise insurgent leaders, uncover hidden weapons, disrupt enemy supply lines and debilitate illicit drug production. Much of what they did was 'close quarters battle' with Taliban fighters and their civilian sympathisers. SOTG members had received the nation's highest decorations for bravery and ascended to the most senior command positions in the ADF. They provided the Australian Government with world-class capabilities that had advanced the national interest. It was beyond belief that these men could have engaged in serious misconduct, although there had been criticisms of Australian behaviour and protests about inadequate follow-up.

There were many media stories between 2006 and 2013 of Afghan villagers and local government officials complaining that Australians were using excessive force, and killing unarmed civilians and captured insurgents. These stories had been the subject of inquiries instigated by the ADF and the United Nations' mandated International Security Assistance Force (ISAF). Each of these claims was investigated and, some thought predictably, no evidence of war crimes was found and no disciplinary action was taken against any soldier. Officials told reporters that claims of misconduct were either enemy propaganda or motivated by opportunistic Afghans seeking financial compensation. Australian accounts were deemed more reliable because they were detailed, objective, supported by evidence including photographs, and provided by Australia's best soldiers, who deserved to be trusted. Rules of Engagement (ROE) and tactics, techniques and procedures (TTPs) could be reviewed to reduce or remove either uncertainty or confusion but nothing the Australians did had led to any criminal conviction. Every nation deploying its personnel to Afghanistan as part of ISAF dealt with similar allegations. Taliban insurgents were responsible for more than 98 per cent of civilian casualties but those attributed to ISAF were thoroughly exploited for their propaganda value. If nothing else, Taliban leaders knew that investigating claims of alleged misconduct would be a distraction from Coalition counterinsurgency operations and consume ISAF resources.

Rumours involving Special Forces personnel breaching the Law of Armed Conflict and violating ROE in Afghanistan eventually reached the Special Operations Commander, Major General Jeff Sengelman, who tried to gain a sense of the scale and severity of the alleged misconduct. The 'rumours' could no longer be discounted as gossip or tall stories. There was too much veiled chit-chat hinting at dark deeds for those in responsible positions to remain idle. Convinced that the prevalence and persistence of rumours was corroding morale and diminishing confidence, even if the rumours proved to be unfounded and any allegations baseless, Sengelman referred his suspicions to the Chief of Army, Lieutenant General Angus Campbell, early in 2016. Campbell asked the Inspector-General of the Australian Defence Force (IGADF) to conduct an inquiry. The public soon sensed there might have been another dimension to the Afghan war.

The first intimation of wrongdoing was Chris Masters' substantial work, *No Front Line: Australia's Special Forces at War in Afghanistan*, published in 2017.[11] In 2010, Masters was the only journalist to have access to Camp Russell, the SOTG compound within the Coalition base at Tarin Kowt in Uruzgan. Over several weeks the award-winning journalist spoke with soldiers who were willing to share their stories and allude to a little of their uneasiness about the conduct of Australian and ISAF operations. Masters noted inconsistencies in personal accounts of significant engagements with the Taliban; the ugly tensions that existed between SAS soldiers and Commandos; the understandable desire for revenge that was felt after the loss of comrades; the closing of ranks and the stifling of inquiries when unarmed men and civilians were killed; the inadequacy and uncertainty of ROE in many tactical situations; annoyance with the 'catch and release' policy that returned many insurgents to the battlefield; the gap between theoretical responsibility and its practical application; anger that the enemy was not constrained by the laws, morals and public expectations to which they were obliged to adhere; frustration with the overall Coalition counterinsurgency strategy and debatable measures of success; suspicion that the leaders of Afghan partner forces were participating in operations for personal gain; and the acute difficulties of managing local ethnic tensions when they reached fever pitch. Masters detected the feeling among Australian Special Forces that they were operationally hamstrung at every point (although no more so than the forces of other ISAF partner nations), and that additional rules and revised regulations only served to assist the insurgent cause while increasing the risk of Australians being wounded or killed.

The book did not contain any specific allegations of misconduct and no Australian soldier was accused of war crimes. There were, however, a series of unanswered questions and veiled hints that 'a gap between what some in Special Forces considered justified and their commanders knew to be intolerable had never quite closed'.[12] It seemed to Masters that within the SAS, 'mateship became more important than leadership and hubris trumped accountability'. By 2010, 'a low-pressure system of rumour about Special Forces behaving badly in Afghanistan swept Defence precincts in Canberra, Sydney and Perth'. Masters had been told about 'episodes of heavy drinking, drug taking, domestic violence, insubordination and undermining of senior officers'. He assumed ADF commanders must also have heard about these things.

Concluding that the prospects of success in Uruzgan were always marginal and noting the rapid return of Taliban insurgents to places Australian forces had earlier 'cleared', Masters was critical that few with political power and military authority were concerned with 'the neglected battleground of public opinion'. Public *relations* and public *education* were very different activities. The Australian people were not told of the myriad difficulties and dilemmas facing their soldiers and were then, unsurprisingly, shocked when they heard, without any context, that unarmed men and civilians had been killed. He concluded with a plea:

> Given the finely tuned requirement for ethical conduct and scrupulous discipline, anger rightly settles on all who surrendered moral authority. For all that, I hope fault can rest more broadly than on those who carried the most weight of this long and losing war.[13]

These were foreboding words. Over the next three years, a small number of journalists that included Masters and Nick McKenzie of Nine Newspapers, Rory Callinan and Ben Packham at Newscorp, and the ABC's Dan Oakes, Andrew Greene, Sam Clark and Mark Willacy, filed a succession of stories that relied upon the recollections of unnamed former SOTG members and leaked classified documents to persuade the Australian people that serious offences had been committed in Afghanistan, and that the IGADF Afghanistan Inquiry was completely justified. The accusing finger pointed predominantly at SAS members rather than Commandos. The reasons were not apparent. Although possessing distinct traditions and specific skill sets, they were constituent units of Australia's Special Operations Command (SOCOMD) and subject to the same laws, rules, directions and discipline. Those who spoke with journalists 'believed these crimes needed to be exposed, the perpetrators punished and the [SAS] regiment's honour restored'.[14]

It was difficult for anyone to diminish the gravity of media reporting between late 2016 and 2020. It would take a good deal of counter-evidence to ameliorate the reputational damage that the publication of so many adverse stories had inflicted on the ADF. The media was hardly responsible for the poor publicity the SAS and Commandos were receiving. It was difficult to blame journalists for being negative. Their reports were drawn from the recollections of soldiers who were volunteering the opinion that their former colleagues had wilfully breached the Law of Armed Conflict, intentionally violated the ROE and knowingly committed war crimes. These words were usually uttered more in sorrow than in anger because every Australian soldier was diminished by allegations of war crimes, the dishonesty that was associated with concealing the crimes, and the deceitfulness that kept investigators from the truth. When taken together, revelations of extreme violence and criminal conspiracy were hard to hear and difficult to believe. Units that had been commended for meritorious service, and men decorated for heroic deeds, were being accused of serious offences. If the allegations were proven, the consequences for Australia and its Army would be substantial and lasting.

Despite the succession of detailed allegations, there remained staunch resistance to even the thought that Australian soldiers could possibly be guilty of such wrongdoing. The former Minister for Defence Industry, Science and Personnel, Bronwyn Bishop, lamented in November 2020 that:

> we as a people, our governments, both Labor and Liberal, sent those men to fight for our principles in a foreign land. We eulogised and spoke of them, I even attended ramp ceremonies when their bodies were returned to Australia. Yet this same government that sent them, we sent, to fight for us, is now attacking our own people, our own soldiers.[15]

These were, she claimed, unnecessary and self-inflicted wounds. Bishop was appalled that the IGADF Afghanistan Inquiry 'actually advertised in Afghanistan for Afghans to come forward and testify and give evidence against our soldiers' while the despicable Taliban were being invited to the negotiating table. After doubting whether the Inquiry could determine whether the Afghans 'tell the truth or tell lies', she was critical of the Inquiry's duration because 'those men have now lived with it for four years'. Without any knowledge of the report's findings, which were yet to be released, Bishop was still able to conclude: 'we are hanging these people out to dry'.

The former minister's remarks echoed the response to David Kent's article on Charles Bean and *The Anzac Book* published 35 years earlier. To claim that good men might have done bad things was seemingly to question a legend and darken a tradition from which Australians had drawn collective pride and individual comfort. In a dark world that was blighted by so much evil, the Special Forces were a ray of light and a beacon of hope that Australians would always be safe while such men stood guard. But were they worthy of such confidence? Had the nation been misled by their mystique?

The letters pages in the daily newspapers showed that many Australians still wanted to believe the stories were nothing more than media hype and journalistic exaggeration. More troubling, a section of the community thought the illegal killing of Afghans was a regrettable by-product of counterinsurgency warfare and no further action was needed. After all, civilians were caught in crossfire and prisoners were killed in every war. Afghanistan was, they suggested, no different. There was clearly more at stake, however, than the fate of perhaps a dozen Australian soldiers and the grief of a few Afghan families.

The controversy triggered by war crimes allegations demonstrated that the ADF's social and political roles were nearly as important as its defence and security responsibilities. It was an institution that Australians wanted to revere, comprising women and men they wanted to respect. There remained a spontaneous desire to elevate uniformed women and men to quasi-hero status because, the rhetoric continued, they had freely offered to promote the common good and protect the innocent from harm. This desire was understandable and even laudable. The civilian population, encouraged by its elected leaders, still pointed to sailors, soldiers, airmen and airwomen as exemplars of service from which every Australian girl and boy might draw inspiration and find encouragement. ADF service continued to be praised as noble and ennobling. But allegations of misconduct had the potential to change all that. No one was, and no one should be considered, above the law or beyond reproach.

The public were entitled to know whether these allegations were indicative of deep-seated problems that existed across the ADF or aberrations that were limited to SOCOMD. Did these allegations reflect the complexity and the intractability of the conflict in the country where they occurred? Would these soldiers have been accused of committing war crimes in any other circumstances, anywhere else in the world? These were difficult questions to ponder for a nation with a proud military heritage. They would prove even harder to answer given the alleged misconduct had occurred in a small landlocked country on the other side of the world where everyday life could not have been more different from that known, and taken for granted, by ordinary Australians. Afghanistan had belatedly become a place of pressing interest to Australians with no previous investment in its past and no particular stake in its future. A sense of its deeply troubled history helps to explain why Australian soldiers might have lost their way.

2

DOWNFALL OF A NATION: AFGHANISTAN'S JOURNEY

1747–1979

Few countries in modern history have suffered more in the quest for nationhood than Afghanistan. Although it has recognised borders and a permanent population, it possesses few of the other attributes associated with being a nation. There is no unifying story, common language or shared identity to unite those who live within Afghanistan's arbitrarily drawn geographic boundaries. Little else brings the people together. As the Afghan–American scholar Shaista Wahab has remarked: 'In some ways, the country just does not make sense ... what unites the Afghans are the things they are not.'[1]

To outsiders, the economy appears to be weak and most citizens are poor. Revenue raising is insufficient to fund services. Education is limited and available to few. Roads and infrastructure are inadequately maintained. The government is fractured, the judiciary is erratic and policing is unreliable. For much of the 20th century, Afghanistan might have been an independent country but it was far from a sovereign nation. It was only foreign military interference that imparted a sense of being Afghan to much of the population. Family, clan and tribal affiliations took precedence in the formation of personal identity. Ties of blood and ethnicity elicited much deeper loyalties than did calls for patriotic spirit or pleas for national solidarity.

Afghans appeared to be locked in endless war with each other over the basic necessities of life and competing visions of the future.

Civil strife was both the cause and effect of Afghanistan being a fractured country and a weak nation. Its domestic affairs were of little concern to outsiders until the 1970s, when they unsettled the stability of Central Asia. By 1998, a growing tide of anti-Western extremism within Afghanistan, fuelled by the global terrorist organisation al-Qaeda, had attracted closer attention. Following the '9/11' terrorist attacks in 2001, an international coalition entered Afghanistan, pursued those responsible for the outrages in Washington DC and New York, empowered a replacement national government and dissipated the structures supporting violent extremism. A fanatical minority would not be allowed to threaten the peace and prosperity of any nation beyond their own borders. Afghanistan was a country that foreigners struggled to imagine, let alone interpret, when the aim was to fix the problem it represented to outsiders. As University of London political scientist Nivi Manchanda has argued, the way Afghanistan was perceived and portrayed by outsiders generated its own sense of what the solutions should be.[2]

With little sense of the immensity of what would follow, Australia was among the first nations to pledge support for the American-led invasion. Despite being primarily a show of solidarity for the United States, the Australian Government expected its military personnel to embody the values of a modern, liberal, democratic state and to exemplify the standards of a well-trained, highly disciplined, professionally led and constitutionally apolitical army. Fulfilling the Australian Government's expectations and adhering to the Army's values would be challenged by the harsh realities of Afghanistan, including the vestiges of past conflict and enduring resentment of foreigners.

This chapter, and the three that follow, chart Afghanistan's faltering progress towards nationhood in the 18th and 19th centuries, and end with its eventual unravelling in the late 20th century. A consistent theme is the struggle to discern a form of government and a framework for public administration that can embody the hopes and fulfil the aspirations of a majority of the population. The institutions and processes that undergird the common life of any group of people involve fundamental political questions. The citizens of every nation must answer these questions for themselves or risk deep division and continuing conflict. Over the past 50 years the Afghans have failed to find a way to resolve their differences of opinion over competing claims, let alone settle on persuasive answers and then to implement them. The consequence has been violence and brutality, suffering and death. Decades of external interference and the abject failure of Afghan politics has left a destructive remnant of resentment and bitterness that foreigners were likely to exacerbate by their well-meaning but often ill-informed intervention in the affairs of people who ultimately needed to find their own solutions to problems that were mostly of their own making.

In 2001, Australian soldiers found themselves embroiled in Afghanistan's existential crisis with little understanding of its dynamics and nuances. Despite their determined efforts, peace and prosperity would remain second-order concerns until crucial questions about Afghan nationhood were answered satisfactorily. These questions went to the heart of being Afghan and how social, political, economic and ethnic differences could be managed creatively and constructively. Ending armed conflict and reasserting civil order depended on resolving expansive issues, such as the distribution of authority and the exercise of power. By the turn of the millennium, three decades of profound disagreement had blighted the country and produced the worst possible conditions for nation-building. The legacies of those decades, and they were subtle in form but substantial in nature, were part of the complex daily reality for Australian soldiers sent to Afghanistan. It was hard to imagine a more fraught operating environment and one with less potential for mission success, however progress was to be measured. Indeed, there were few places to which Australians could have been sent after 2001 that were more ethically demanding and morally degrading.

Coming to terms with the substructure of the conflict required much more than pre-deployment briefings on Afghan culture and customs. Afghanistan has a complicated history that was easier to describe than to interpret. The land contained within the country's modern borders straddles strategically important trading routes between India and Iran, Central Asia and Russia. Between 500 and 1500 CE, a series of non-resident powers sought to control or influence the movement of people and goods through Afghanistan for military and economic purposes. Each power left behind traces of their cultural conventions and religious traditions. As Afghan–American commentator Tamim Ansary has observed: 'Afghanistan is not really impossible to conquer. It's just that all the successful conquerors are now called "Afghans".'[3]

Between the 7th and 12th centuries, Islam gradually became the dominant religion, although Muslims and non-Muslims, mainly Buddhists, Hindus and Zoroastrians, continued to live side by side in an ethnically diverse society. The physical terrain, which features high mountains and deep valleys, contributed to the regionalised character of Afghan society. The Hindu Kush mountains run through the centre and south of Afghanistan, making the journey from Kabul in the east to Herat in the west a long and arduous adventure. Travellers are obliged to go around rather than over some of the world's highest peaks in a country whose climate shifts between bitterly cold winters and blazing hot summers.

After more than four centuries of Mongol and Mughal rule, during which the Afghans gained a reputation in some Western eyes for being 'an intractable race' that was 'high-spirited and warlike',[4] its territorial borders were not settled until the 18th and 19th centuries under the leadership of Ahmad Shah Durrani, who was appointed *emir* (ruler) by a *loya jirga* (grand assembly) held in Kandahar in 1747. Although others had failed to seize control of the land and subdue its people, the British, who believed themselves to be the world's most accomplished colonisers, thought they could succeed through superior weaponry and better tactics. In 1839 they attempted to occupy the country, intending to bar the expansion of Russian influence in the direction of India, which was then under British control as well.

With British forces blockaded on the edge of Kabul, an agreement was signed to grant all British personnel safe passage to Jalalabad (150 kilometres away). After leaving Kabul and heading east in January 1842, 4500 British and Indian soldiers, and more than 12000 camp followers, were killed by Afghan tribesmen. The remnants of the retreating force, 20 officers and 45 soldiers of the 44th East Essex Regiment, were slaughtered on a hill near Gandamak on the road to Jalalabad. There was only one British survivor, Dr William Brydon, the assistant surgeon of the British East India Company Army. The Afghan way of war was uncompromisingly brutal. It was usual for non-combatants to be killed and prisoners to be executed. Massacring enemies left fewer embittered adversaries to hamper the next generation.

The capitulation at Gandamak has been described as the worst defeat in British military history.[5] Six months later a British 'Army of Retribution', commanded by Major General Sir George Pollock, fought its way from Jalalabad to Kabul and exacted revenge on Afghan tribesmen despite being directed to show restraint. There were hundreds of unnecessary killings as the British slaughtered every living being in their path. Pollock arrived at Kabul on 15 September 1842, where his troops were joined by another British force marching from Kandahar to the south. Afghan cities were laid waste as military discipline among British troops deteriorated and soldiers engaged in looting and wanton destruction of private property. The lessons were clear. The Afghans would resolutely oppose an unwelcome administration and political considerations could not be allowed to overrule military judgments. The British had also learned something about the potential for savagery among their own troops.

The British were less interested in what Afghanistan might yield in exploitable natural resources. The aim was to close a potential access route to India to competitors. But observers and participants were not convinced the objective of the mission made sense or was even achievable. The chaplain of the First Bengal Brigade stationed at Jalalabad (and later Chaplain-General to the British Forces), the Reverend George Gleig, noted in his diary that the conflict was:

> a war begun for no wise purpose, carried on with a strange mixture of rashness and timidity, brought to a close after suffering and disaster, without much glory attached either to the government which directed, or the great body of troops which waged it. Not one benefit, political or military, was acquired with this war. Our eventual evacuation of the country resembled the retreat of an army defeated.[6]

It was difficult for British forces to see any point or purpose to their mission. The lack of a compelling explanation influenced their behaviour towards the Afghans.

After returning to Kabul, the British eventually managed to reassert their influence and use Afghanistan as a buffer against the Russian Empire for the next few decades, despite fighting another bloody war with the Afghans in 1878–1880. Remembering the painful lessons of Gandamak, the British never sought to make Afghanistan one of its colonies. It was more of a vassal state whose rulers realised the futility of working against an empire with interests that did not necessarily conflict with its own, if managed with tact and diplomacy. While Afghanistan kept its distance from Russia and stayed away from India, it was largely free to order its own affairs.

Afghanistan's transition to nationhood was accelerated after 'Abd al-Rahman Khan became the emir in July 1880. According to historian (and later President of Afghanistan) Ashraf Ghani, the supremacy of 'local power-holding families' who had 'managed to reproduce themselves socially and politically' since 1747 was superseded by the new emir's exertion of 'state sovereignty' throughout the country.[7]

Islam was used as an 'ideology of state-building' to raise the profile of the courts and jurisprudence, and the authority of administrative institutions and officials. Shari'a became the supreme law of the land, and state-appointed courts replaced local means of settling disputes. Hasan Kawun Kakar explains that the 'overall effects of these laws were that for the first time the inhabitants of Afghanistan began to learn how to obey a sole monarch and a uniform set of laws'.[8] Controlling the legal system was a tool for centralising authority and promoting nationhood.

With the focus on internal reforms, relations between Britain and Afghanistan remained cordial, with London having 'oversight' of Kabul's foreign policy to ensure there were consistent and compatible objectives for the next 30 years. Although Afghanistan declared its neutrality during the Great War of 1914–18, it resisted overtures from their fellow Muslims in the Ottoman Empire to side with Imperial Germany against Britain and its allies. Following the war's end, Emir Habibullah Khan was assassinated. He was succeeded briefly by his brother, and then by his son, Amanullah Khan, in March 1919. To strengthen his position, and conscious that Britain was wearied by the human and financial cost of the war, Amanullah ordered an invasion of neighbouring British India beginning on 3 May 1919. The British responded by declaring war on Afghanistan three days later. This was a conflict Britain did not want but seemed unable to avoid.

To reduce their own casualties, the British contemplated using chemical weapons against the Afghans in the perverse belief that poisonous gas might be 'more merciful' than using high explosives. Winston Churchill, then Secretary of State for War, thought that:

> If it is fair for an Afghan soldier to shoot down a British soldier behind a rock and cut him to pieces as he lies wounded … why is it not fair for a British artilleryman to fire a shell which makes the said native sneeze?[9]

A poisonous gas attack did more, of course, than cause its victims to sneeze. But was resorting to gas an offence against the prevailing code of chivalry in frontier warfare? The wartime Director of Gas Services, Brigadier Charles Foulkes, had no hesitation in recommending the use of gas against Afghan tribesmen. British officers considered them 'vermin fit only for extermination'.[10]

After three months of fighting that left more than 1000 Afghan and 236 British troops dead, it was clear the British had secured a tactical victory while the Afghans had achieved a strategic success. The British repelled the Afghan invasion force and obliged Amanullah to accept the location of the 1893 'Durand Line' separating Afghanistan from British India (a divide that remains contested); the Afghans negotiated the Treaty of Rawalpindi, which ended British supervision of Afghan foreign policy. There were, however, ethnic Pashtuns living on both sides of the Durand Line. Some looked to India for political autonomy (rather than national sovereignty) while others wanted the reunification of 'Greater Afghanistan' or the formation of a separate Pashtunistan.[11] As political science scholar Amin Saikal notes: 'it sowed the seeds of an enduring border dispute between Afghanistan and Pakistan which emerged upon the creation of the latter as a majority Muslim state out of the Hindu-dominated India in 1947'.[12]

Despite discontent with boundaries, Afghanistan was again independent and was later admitted to membership of the League of Nations. It also became the first nation to recognise the newly created Soviet regime in Russia, with Moscow acknowledging the restoration of Afghan nationhood in 1920, signing a non-aggression pact the following year. The Bolshevik Government remained anxious about British support for its counter-revolutionary opponents. To secure its southern border from incursions, the Soviet Union could either consider invading British India or prepare to repel a British attack from Afghanistan. In evaluating the options, the Red Army's foremost scholar of Central Asian affairs, Lieutenant General Andrei Snesarev, delivered a series of lectures in 1919–20 that dealt with all aspects of Afghan political, economic, social and military life, examining its principal geographic features and strategic lines of communication.[13] Snesarev was an outstanding linguist and highly observant traveller. He was adamant: the Red Army needed to stay out of Afghanistan. The land was of no geo-strategic or economic value to the Soviet Union other than as a transit route. He explained that:

> the country is extremely well-adapted to a passive resistance. Its mountainous nature and the proud and freedom-loving character of its people, combined with the lack of adequate roads, makes it very difficult to conquer and even harder to hold.[14]

The Soviet Union neither invaded British India nor entered Afghanistan. Afghan leaders sought to preserve their diplomatic neutrality and avoid any involvement in distant conflicts. Internally, Afghanistan's domestic political affairs were relatively stable given the tumultuous state of European politics at the time. In contrast to the political and economic upheavals that followed the Great Depression and the onset of global war in 1939, Afghanistan was perhaps the most peaceful nation in the region for nearly four decades. Squabbles between competing political factions in the cities never spread to Afghans in the rural areas.

There were modest attempts at modernisation but progress beyond Kabul was slow in a traditional society with a large agrarian base. With the rise of mass communication and rapid transport in the 1950s and 1960s, it was clear that Afghanistan was slipping behind its neighbours, Pakistan and Iran. The principal source of development funding was the Soviet Union, which provided more aid (on a per capita basis) to Afghanistan than any other nation. The road to material progress seemed to lie with political reform but this depended on Afghans embracing national sentiment ahead of tribal affiliations.

With his rule effectively thwarted by political factionalism, tribal loyalties, declining state revenues and rising infrastructure costs, the Afghan king after 1933, Zahir Shah, consented to a form of power-sharing with the introduction of a new constitution in 1964. Afghanistan would become a democracy with free elections, universal suffrage, an independent parliament and legally protected civil rights.

Before legislation was presented to the newly established Afghan parliament legalising political parties (with the notable exception of the Communist Party, which was deemed un-Islamic), the People's Democratic Party of Afghanistan (PDPA) was formed on 1 January 1965 without any active assistance from Moscow. Although it embraced Marxist ideology, the PDPA essentially pursued an anti-government program. Within a decade, the Communists were attracting supporters in Afghanistan's few cities and gaining political confidence, although the party itself was split between the dominant 'Khalq' and the rival 'Parcham' factions. *Khalq*, the Pashto word for 'masses', drew on Pashtun tribal loyalties and was stronger in the rural areas. It advocated violently overthrowing the government followed by pursuing a proletarian revolution and rapidly introducing a Soviet-style command-and-control economy. *Parcham*, the Pashto word for 'flag', built its support base among intellectuals and the middle class in Kabul. It felt that Afghanistan lacked industry and infrastructure, and needed to be prepared gradually for a transition to socialism, and that a national democratic and patriotic movement was needed before a proletarian revolution was even attempted. Neither faction managed to attract a large following. The country was, however, at a turning point with modernists gaining ground over traditionalists. The new constitution had unintentionally created an unstable political system while Afghanistan's non-aligned standing was being challenged by those whose sympathies lay with Moscow.

Known for moderation and compassion, Zahir Shah was overthrown by his cousin and former prime minister, Mohammed Daoud Khan, while he was visiting Italy in July 1973. In conceding 'the will of my compatriots' and abdicating the throne, the deposed king effectively legitimated the mostly non-violent coup that led to his exile. The king's action gave Daoud, and whoever wanted to replace him, the licence to use undemocratic means to secure political power. Daoud declared Afghanistan a republic and proclaimed himself its first president. The new government could claim no greater political legitimacy than the one it supplanted. The country's elites were divided on whether the coup would bring progress or result in chaos. This was uncharted territory for a people without a developed democratic tradition and a test for Afghanistan's standing as a nation. In attempting to seek a form of democratic mandate, ordinary Afghans were drawn into political turmoil for the first time.

As Daoud's efforts to reform the country's political system and reshape its popular culture floundered, he steadily concentrated power in his own hands. By 1978, he had antagonised both leftist politicians and the religious establishment. He was also unpopular with the nation's intellectuals and Afghan military officers. Economic growth had stalled and Afghanistan defaulted on foreign loans; this was attributable in large part to a protracted drought but nonetheless blamed on Daoud. After the assassination of a Parchami leader and a crackdown on political dissent following his well-attended funeral, a group of Afghan Army officers aligned with the PDPA launched a military coup on 27 April 1978 and initiated what they called the 'Saur Revolution' ('Saur' being the zodiacal symbol – 'Taurus' – for that month). In an attempt to erase the past and prevent any revival of hereditary rule, Daoud Khan was assassinated by members of the Afghan armed forces loyal to the PDPA. His extended family were also shot and buried in mass graves. Their murder was not unlike the fate of Russia's entire ruling Romanov family, who were killed by the Bolsheviks in July 1918.

The military officers leading the coup handed power to the PDPA's Revolutionary Council. Daoud was replaced as president by Nur Muhammad Taraki, the General Secretary of the PDPA's

Central Committee and leader of the Khalq faction, who established the pro-Soviet Democratic Republic of Afghanistan (DRA). As the pioneering British commentator on the country, Anthony Hyman, observed, the Khalqis had an almost messianic faith in their quest to modernise Afghanistan.[15] As the party attracted no popular support beyond its own narrow membership, its opponents, together with those considered to be nationalists or middle-class bourgeoisie, were rounded up and taken to the Pul-e-Charkhi prison in Kabul. The commandant of the prison explained: 'A million Afghans are all that should remain alive. We need a million Khalqis. The others we don't need, we will get rid of them.'[16] The 18 000-strong membership base of the PDPA was rapidly expanded by another 28 000 members eager to gain a share of the political largesse. The few bonds that held Afghanistan together as a nation were being tested to breaking point.

The PDPA's position was not, however, materially secure. Had it known of the PDPA's intentions in advance, the supreme policy-making body of the Communist Party of the Soviet Union, the Politburo, would have counselled against removing Daoud. The Politburo believed genuine Communist uprisings were much more difficult to provoke in religious societies than in secular ones. The notion that a conservative Muslim society could be made to embrace modernity and socialism by force was utterly mistaken. In the 1960s the Soviet Union had been unwilling to assist the PDPA, concerned with provoking an Islamic revolt in Afghanistan and damaging its evolving détente with the United States. It was only after pressure from other socialist states that Moscow embraced the new regime in Kabul, which the Politburo considered politically incompetent and mindlessly violent. Killing the population into submission – making people 'disappear' – would not succeed as a political strategy. Indeed, it would alienate the very people that the party needed to attract.

The PDPA leadership thought otherwise. Anyone could be killed by a Khalqi member with absolute impunity. Inspired by the 'Red Terror' that followed the Bolshevik Revolution in 1917, Taraki reminded the Soviet Ambassador to Afghanistan, Alexander Puzanov, that 'Lenin taught us to be merciless towards the enemies of the revolution, and millions of people had to be eliminated to secure the victory of the October Revolution.'[17] He regarded Afghanistan's 300 000 mullahs (mosque leaders) as the foremost obstruction to 'the progressive movement in the homeland'.[18] Many were imprisoned, tortured and shot. Afghanistan was becoming acquainted with the terrors of arbitrary detention, political violence and mass murder.

Taraki was determined to pursue the Khalq agenda, transforming Afghanistan from a feudal society into a socialist one while claiming the party's program was a shortcut to 'the destiny of the Afghan people'. Many of Afghanistan's social structures were soon collapsing with the forced removal of community leaders who exercised authority and exerted influence on everyday life. The PDPA's aim was to ensure Afghanistan could never return to pre-modern conditions.

The principal opposition to Taraki's regime came in the form of a loose alliance of anti-PDPA forces known collectively as the *mujahideen* (Islamic fighters) engaged in *jihad* (usually rendered in English as 'holy war', although in Arabic it is literally translated 'extended struggle'). Support for anti-government activity in the major cities had come from Pakistan during the 1970s and increased dramatically when the PDPA seized power. Despite the absence of a coordinated strategy, the mujahideen started attacking Afghan Army columns using classic guerrilla tactics and encouraging villagers to resist a government that clearly depended on foreigners. Soon there were uprisings in all 29 provinces, with almost every element of Afghan society defying PDPA rule. At Herat in western Afghanistan, government officials and Soviet advisors were killed after an entire division of the Afghan Regular Army mutinied on 15 March 1979. The deserting soldiers distributed weapons to the local population and waged a determined offensive that led to the deaths of 30 000 people in five days. The PDPA controlled very little territory beyond Kabul. The regime's fate was in the balance. Its already limited support base contracted as oppression of the population widened. The one thing uniting its opponents was religious commitment and shared abhorrence of the PDPA's disrespect for Islamic customs. In neighbouring Iran, Ayatollah Khomeini had become the supreme ruler after its Islamic revolution had driven the Shah, Mohammad Reza Pahlavi, into exile in February 1979. It was possible an Islamic revolution might also gain ground in Afghanistan.

Taraki appealed to Moscow for a 'discreet intervention' against the escalating Islamist rebellion. The Chairman of the Soviet Council of Ministers, Alexei Kosygin, was unpersuaded by the case for direct Soviet action and remained so. An intervention on any scale could not be hidden from the watching world. Inevitably, it would be interpreted as an invasion and prompt sanctions that would hurt the Soviet Union and Afghanistan. Rather than trying to increase local support as Moscow had counselled, the PDPA extended the crackdown on opposition and appointed 1500 political instructors to the armed forces in June 1979. There were also reports of government troops killing civilians suspected of supporting the mujahideen. The slaughter of 1170 unarmed men at Kerala, a town not far from the border with Pakistan, was one of the first atrocities to make world headlines.

By October, the Afghan taskforce attached to the Politburo in Moscow was making policy decisions for the PDPA. The number of civilian advisors increased to between 3000 and 4000 with the Soviet intelligence service, the KGB, directing most of the country's daily affairs. The Politburo believed that Afghanistan could be absorbed into the Soviet sphere of influence in the same way as many of the poor and illiterate Central Asian territories had been drawn into the Soviet Union, and then developed and modernised during the 1920s. Invasion was the least attractive option. Moscow preferred to make Afghanistan a vassal state.

Shortly after returning from a meeting of so-called 'non-aligned' nations (many of them Soviet allies) in Cuba and a personal meeting with General Secretary Leonid Brezhnev in Moscow, Taraki was assassinated on the order of his party colleague and prime minister, Hafizullah Amin, in September 1979. Taraki had been advised by Brezhnev to remove Amin from his positions of power and returned home intending to do so. Taraki was unaware, however, that word of his intentions had been conveyed to Amin, who struck first. After Taraki was strangled and suffocated, his supporters were either imprisoned or executed. Moscow was angered by this unexpected and unwelcome development. It was reckless and self-serving on Amin's part. Brezhnev's public assurances of personal support for Taraki a few weeks earlier now seemed empty and hollow. Brezhnev referred to Amin as 'scum' and a 'bastard' for murdering Taraki.

From the day he seized power, Amin proved to be even more dictatorial and destructive than the man he deposed. He remarked: 'we have ten thousand feudal lords. We eliminated them and the problem was solved. The Afghans recognise only force.'[19] He deployed combat troops and attack aircraft against the rebellious civilian population. With thousands of people fleeing to Pakistan and Iran, he also created a refugee crisis that made his regime even more unpopular in Islamabad and Tehran. When Soviet advisors criticised his aggressive tactics, he replied: 'You don't know our people! If any tribe takes up arms it will not lay them down. The only solution is to destroy them all, from big to small! Such are our traditions.'[20] Amin insisted that terror was needed: 'Comrade Stalin showed us how to build socialism in a backward country. It's painful to begin with, but afterwards everything turns out just fine.' It appeared to Moscow that Amin was eroding the PDPA's ability to rule and destroying his country. He had become a serious liability. A report to the Politburo concluded: 'in the person of Amin we have to deal with a power-hungry leader who is distinguished by brutality and treachery'. For the Soviets to be repulsed by Amin's behaviour indicated how extreme he had become. Amin had no hesitation killing fellow Afghans for the sake of an objective whose difficulty he grossly underestimated.

Events in Kabul continued to alarm the Politburo. After assessing the state of the Afghan Army and believing its preparedness and morale were low, Moscow was told the PDPA regime was facing imminent collapse. There were now 4500 Soviet military advisors in Afghanistan. Their job was to further the socialist revolution and prevent an Islamic rebellion. The Soviet military leadership in Kabul was, like the Politburo, opposed to an invasion. Several senior Soviet generals thought the presence of their troops:

> would provoke the initiation of combat operations and lead to a strengthening of the rebel movement, which would be directed against Soviet troops, and the poor knowledge of local customs and traditions, especially Islam, and national ethnic relations would force us into a quite difficult position.[21]

In the second week of December the Politburo decided to replace Amin with someone Moscow believed it could control. With Afghanistan on the brink of implosion, four senior members of the Politburo – Leonid Brezhnev (General Secretary), Yuri Andropov (the KGB chief), Andrei Gromyko (the Foreign Minister) and General Dmitry Ustinov (the Defence Minister) signed a recommendation, subsequently endorsed by the Politburo, to deploy the Soviet Army to Afghanistan to 'restore order'. They would end Amin's 'terrorist regime', save the Afghan people from genocide, help the PDPA to extend its influence (given that it controlled so little of the country), preserve an ideological ally on the Soviet Union's southern border, prevent potential uranium reserves in Helmand province being exported to a hostile power, and avert any annexation of Afghan territory by Pakistan.

Drawing on his military experience and knowledge of insurgencies, Ustinov did not think highly of the mujahideen. He expected many resistance fighters would drop their weapons and that most would flee when the Soviet Army rolled into Afghanistan. The

Chief of General Staff, Marshal Nikolai Ogarkov, was incredulous on being told to mobilise 75 000 to 85 000 troops for an operation he deemed 'reckless'. He thought many more personnel were needed to stabilise the situation and urged a political settlement. He cited all of the arguments outlined by Snesarev in his lectures of 1919–20 to no avail. These 'measures' were to last no more than six months. Although the decision to intervene was neither irrational nor without justification, it was based on some serious political miscalculations and poor strategic judgment. The Soviet Army was entering Afghanistan. A minor decision was to have major consequences.

In two years, Afghanistan went from being a relatively peaceful nation with stable social structures supporting a rich and varied culture to a country damaged irreversibly by political adventurism. The life most Afghans had known was at an end. Power struggles among political rivals had spread to distant towns and remote villages, where the people were dragged into a fractious dispute over what Afghanistan would become. Decentralised governance, which reflected the importance of provincial affiliations, district associations and local loyalties, had been unilaterally discarded by an urban elite who lacked sympathy and respect for their fellow citizens, and the ability to administer an impoverished country with little infrastructure and poor communications.

The 'new' Afghanistan seemed less attractive than the 'old' to those who were oppressed by Kabul. In refusing to accept the PDPA's legitimacy, the sources of authority and power in Afghanistan were starting to shift. The decentralised political system was assaulted by an expression of nationhood with which few Afghans had any affinity. They also resented its close companion: centralised government. The rising class of political bureaucrats dominating Kabul would soon be challenged by a coterie of provincial and district strongmen. Aside from ridding the country of Communist apostates, the emerging strongmen saw an opportunity to fulfil their own ambitions for position and prestige. They might be able to rid the country of the

PDPA, but what then? The principal threat to Afghanistan was the absence of any vision for the future. There was little consensus on what kind of nation Afghanistan might become. Indeed, was it a viable and sustainable nation at all? No-one possessed the political legitimacy or could claim the mandate to create the structures necessary to deliver a holistic vision for the future. The conditions had been created for a long-running conflict that would determine the character and culture of Afghanistan or whatever was left of the country after the fighting ended.

The contours of this struggle would change little in the coming years. The government in Kabul lacked authority, credibility, support and influence beyond the capital. It was considered beholden to foreign interests, susceptible to external interference, compliant with outside values and unsympathetic to religious sensibilities. Violence would become an accepted feature of public life and the armed forces were partisan players. Political opponents and their families were physically eradicated with excessive force as a warning to future contenders. National institutions were weak (or non-existent) and respect for the rule of law throughout the country was minimal. There was little faith in the competence of the judiciary and the impartiality of the courts. The security services and the domestic police largely operated without ethical oversight or judicial control. Arbitrary detention and torture were also intended to crush dissent. Large numbers of people would simply 'disappear'. Human life appeared to have little value when so many people were being mistreated and murdered with apparent impunity. Intimidation and brutality seemed to be without consequences for the perpetrators. There were no charges, no trials and no convictions. The PDPA government was at war with people it had pledged to liberate from political subjugation and practical hardship. The population had been hardened as hopes of non-violent social change and economic development evaporated when its leaders seemed incapable of finding creative ways to resolve their differences.

By the end of 1979, Afghanistan was a deeply conflicted society with few accepted processes for dealing with its many internal conflicts. Afghan politics had rapidly descended into barbarism and the pain was felt well beyond Kabul. National leaders showed no hesitation in murdering their political rivals; collective punishments were used to coerce mass compliance. Afghanistan could not go back to halcyon days when things were better. It could not go forward either because of its deep internal divisions. The differences between Afghans were now profound. The animosities between people were entrenched. The turmoil would not end while violence continued to prevail over negotiation. As so many people had died and so many livelihoods had been disrupted, the cycle of recrimination and revenge would take decades to overcome among a people with long memories and embittered hearts.

The particular difficulty facing Afghanistan was the weakness of national identity and the fragility of provincial cooperation. Those who possessed political power could not fashion an inclusive system of government animated by a commitment to shared aspirations that were sufficiently compelling to unite the disintegrating body politic. Most Afghans saw the government as an adversary and not an advocate. A nation that had struggled for a decade to deal with its complex social relations and the complications of shifting political arrangements was about to face a long, dark night. Afghanistan had slid into an existential crisis that would eventually provoke the involvement of distant powers with a poor grasp of its problems and a limited appreciation of its potential. Their involvement would be consistently unhelpful. While armies had been used effectively elsewhere to end disputes and create conditions conducive to peace and prosperity, resorting to the 'military option' in Afghanistan would obscure the principal challenge facing its citizens: the utter failure of its politics to address problems and advance possibilities.

The Soviet Union was about to demonstrate the tragic consequences of misunderstanding Afghanistan and misjudging its people. Its many mistakes would provide lasting lessons. An island nation some 9000 kilometres away at the foot of South-East Asia, with which Afghanistan had few dealings over the past century, showed little interest in learning them. No-one in Canberra could have predicted that the overthrow of the Afghan king in 1973 would lead to the brutal internal conflict into which Australian soldiers were dragged three decades later. The conflict had its origins in a life-and-death struggle these soldiers had little chance of understanding and no hope of containing.

3

COLLAPSE OF A STATE: THE SOVIET OCCUPATION 1979–1992

In democratic countries, politics is often portrayed as a contest of ideas. In totalitarian states, politics is usually considered the projection of power. The People's Democratic Party of Afghanistan (PDPA) was determined to use whatever power it could project to transform Afghanistan into a modern socialist state. Fulfilling this ambition would come at the expense of Afghan sovereignty and self-respect. The leadership of the new Democratic Republic of Afghanistan (DRA) in Kabul consisted entirely of PDPA members but power resided within the Political Bureau of the Central Committee of the Communist Party of the Soviet Union (Politburo) in Moscow. The PDPA, a fringe party, could not claim democratic legitimacy or political authority. It was completely reliant on Moscow to sustain the Afghan revolution and maintain its hold on power. Long-term social and economic objectives would necessarily take second place to short-term political and military imperatives. Civil strife in Afghanistan was about to become more intense.

More than 280 transport aircraft conveyed Soviet commando units to Kabul, where they seized a number of airfields on 24 December 1979. They were soon followed by the Soviet 40th Army, which had re-formed in Turkmenistan two weeks earlier. It was based on three motor rifle divisions and airborne regiments, which would secure the districts around Kabul, the other larger cities and the major roads. Hafizullah Amin welcomed the arriving Soviet troops, believing their presence fulfilled the Soviet–Afghan Friendship Treaty which was signed the previous year. Rather than neutralising anti-PDPA opposition, their actual mission was to remove Amin from the presidency.

After a Soviet attempt to poison him earlier in the day failed, Amin took refuge in the Tajbeg Palace, a former royal residence more recently serving as an Afghan Army headquarters. The palace was stormed by Soviet Special Forces on the night of 27 December 1979 and Amin was killed in the ensuing gun battle. Amin's son was killed, as were 350 Afghan soldiers and palace guards. Amin's three-month rule had ended abruptly and violently. Few mourned his passing. The former president was described by the country's education minister, Anahita Ratebzad, as a 'cruel and criminal murderer who had made terror and suppression and crushing of every opposition force part and parcel of his way of rule, and started every day with new acts of destruction, putting opponents of his bloody regime, group by group, to places of torture, jails, and slaughterhouses'.[1]

With Amin gone, the Soviets installed the more moderate Babrak Karmal, leader of the Parcham faction and one of Amin's party rivals, as president of Afghanistan. For those living beyond Kabul, Karmal seemed a weak man whose ascendance could not be attributed to ability. He was widely considered a puppet of the Soviet Union. Karmal was instructed to unite his party, foster a closer relationship with the people, develop the Afghan Army and revive the economy. He released 15 000 political prisoners, included non-Communists in his government, portrayed himself as a devout Muslim, restrained unpopular reform programs initiated by his former colleagues, promoted nation-building alliances and reinstated the former national flag. The Soviets told the PDPA it needed structure and discipline to attract women and young people to the socialist cause.

Within weeks, the Soviets realised the PDPA regime was on the verge of disintegration and needed protection while its position was stabilised. Afghanistan was clearly not, the Politburo realised, in a 'socially developed state ripe for Socialism'.[2] Because the PDPA government was weak and the rebels seemed stronger, the Soviets would need to build a modern state but it would require some traditional Afghan structures to be abandoned or abolished for socialism to succeed. This would take more than a few months. Moscow was obliged to send additional civil and military advisors and increase material assistance and munitions.

As a marginal political organisation with minimal presence beyond Kabul, and even with substantial Soviet investment across the country, the PDPA struggled to win Afghan hearts and minds. The rural population displayed little interest in a socialist revolution, although most villagers welcomed aid and development programs, many of which began prior to the invasion. The advisory effort was more than mere tokenism. There were sustained attempts to build infrastructure and to link Afghan roads to Soviet transport networks. The emphasis was on material improvements to the way of life. Preoccupied with survival, there was not much scope for political indoctrination among either the PDPA's membership or within the general population. The slogans propagated by political cadres to generate Communist sympathies were denounced as symbols of Western secularism. The invasion was easily depicted as an affront to Islam. The conflict was quickly internationalised.

The Palestinian insurgent leader and Islamic scholar Abdullah Azzam travelled to Peshawar in north-west Pakistan and began recruiting foreign fighters, including a young and wealthy Saudi, Osama bin Laden, as he promoted the cause of global *jihad*.[3] Bin Laden would establish the militant al-Qaeda organisation in 1988.[4] Azzam's extreme views, which prescribed jihad as a first-order duty for Muslims throughout the world, significantly left no room for negotiations, conferences or dialogues. The mujahideen were fighting a noble cause that demanded utter self-sacrifice. Azzam fused religious convictions with political aspirations to create a paramilitary structure that was intended to radicalise a generation of Muslims who were implored to pursue an undivided Islamic community worldwide.[5] Although physically and philosophically fragmented, the mujahideen resistance would have continued without external assistance from Pakistan and Saudi Arabia. Foreign aid coming across both the eastern and western borders made a material difference nonetheless. For their part, the Soviets were helped by Iraq's invasion of Iran in 1980. The ensuing conflict would preoccupy the government in Tehran for the next eight years and make Iranian intervention unlikely.

The radical Afghan militias, particularly that led by the anti-American extremist Gulbuddin Hekmatyar, attracted the strongest support from Pakistan, whose Inter-Services Intelligence (ISI) Directorate had become increasingly sympathetic to militant Islamists who saw their religion as a political ideology as well as a belief system.[6] Hekmatyar was a ruthless autocrat who lacked any principles beyond the relentless pursuit of power. He was prepared to assassinate mujahideen rivals, betray those entitled to his loyalty and make whatever deals were necessary to strengthen his own position. To the Americans, he was strongly anti-Soviet and that mattered most. Ironically, Hekmatyar was later (2003) deemed a 'global terrorist' by the State Department in Washington.[7]

Another warlord, Jalaluddin Haqqani, would become the third-ranked terrorist on America's 'most wanted' list after the terrorist attacks in September 2001. Haqqani was a pre-eminent guerrilla commander among the eastern Pashtun tribes of Paktia. He commanded a large following and was skilful at uniting different tribes and political factions. Democratic Congressman Charles Wilson, whose advocacy of the mujahideen cause in the 1980s was depicted in a Hollywood movie starring Tom Hanks, was so taken by Haqqani that he referred to him as 'goodness personified'.[8] Haqqani was, however, one of Osama bin Laden's closest associates in the 1980s and supported the Taliban in the 1990s. A British photojournalist, Ken Guest, who travelled into Afghanistan 36 times and spent more than three years in total with the mujahideen, including bin Laden, watched the ISI groom Haqqani and turn him from a noble freedom fighter into an ignoble political zealot.[9]

Within 12 months, the Soviet invasion force had turned into an army of occupation of 50 000 troops. The number would rise to 108 800 by 1984.[10] Unlike the Americans, whose personnel strength in South Vietnam eventually ballooned to 549 500 troops in 1968, the Soviets intentionally limited their troop numbers because they wanted the Afghans to carry their share of the fighting. The strategy was clear: the Soviet 40th Army would secure the population and transport hubs and leave Afghan troops to consolidate in districts beyond major cities and towns.[11] But the invasion, and now the occupation, had taken a heavy toll on the Afghan Army, which declined from 100 000 men in 1978 to fewer than 30 000 men in 1981, mostly because of mass desertions, defections and the lack of fighting spirit. Weapons and ammunition went with many government troops to the mujahideen. The Afghan Army was slowly rebuilt, although finding sufficient officers willing to leave their homes in Kabul to command troops in rural areas remained a challenge. The Soviets had more success with the Afghan State Intelligence Agency (KHAD). It would be closely mentored by the Soviet KGB and soon flourished, increasing in size from 5000 members in 1980 to 90 000 a decade later.[12]

By the end of 1980, decades of goodwill between the Soviet Union and Afghanistan was rapidly dissipating. Moscow desperately wanted a political solution rather than a military one but it also knew the PDPA would not survive without the 40th Army. Between 1982 and 1986 and with two changes of party general secretary in Moscow, the 40th Army persisted with its efforts to crush the mujahideen while telling Karmal not to presume their presence was permanent. In early 1983, the KGB reported to Moscow that 'no substantial improvement has taken place in the past year. The process of social reform and strengthening of revolutionary power by the regime is slow and protracted.'[13] Further, disagreement within the PDPA 'could lead to uncontrollable consequences' while the Afghan Army was incapable of 'the independent performance of missions to defeat the counter-revolutionaries and normalise the situation in the country'. Soviet forces were not, however, making much lasting progress either.

The Soviets held the major centres of communication and transport: the capital Kabul, Mazar-i-Sharif and Qunduz in the north, Herat and Farah in the west, Kandahar in the south, and Jalalabad in the east. Their major air bases were located in Jalalabad, Bagram, Kabul, Kandahar, Herat, Shindand and Farah. The insurgents managed to hold much of the countryside with low-intensity operations and occasional bursts of aggression. The Soviets operated mostly during the day; the insurgents conducted their operations at night. The pursuit of 'migratory genocide' had made certain areas uninhabitable. After burning crops and destroying infrastructure, the inhabitants were forcibly evacuated from 'free fire zones' which rendered every remaining person a legitimate military target. The British had adopted a similar strategy during the Boer War. To prevent insurgents from reinforcing an area, the country was littered with landmines. In as many as 15 provinces, chemical weapons were used against insurgents. There was no mention in official communications of misconduct or atrocities. The Soviet troops were praised by their commanders for being 'selfless and brave'.

In parts of the country, such as the Panjshir Valley, where Ahmad Shah Massoud's forces had led an effective resistance, ceasefires were quietly agreed. The Soviets thought these agreements were a sign of success because they looked like local capitulation; the mujahideen saw them as opportunities to regroup ahead of the next armed engagement. Senior Soviet military officers wanted the government in Kabul to be more active and engaged in projecting its civil authority. When the mechanised infantry brigades of the 40th Army proved to be less than ideal for the conduct of a 'counter-revolutionary' conflict, Soviet 'Special Forces' units operated by the Directorate of Military

Intelligence (GRU), known as Spetsnaz, operated in areas adjacent to the Pakistan border.[14]

The Afghan secret police acquired human intelligence in collaboration with Soviet military intelligence, the GRU. Intimidation and torture proliferated as allegiances were often questioned. But there was little prospect of these efforts ever 'pacifying' either the urban centres or the countryside. Killing more people would not eliminate opposition to the PDPA government, it would merely restrict insurgent activity temporarily. By 1985, the insurgency was fading as Soviet military supremacy took its toll on the mujahideen's resources and personnel, but it was far from finished. Resisting Soviet oppression would persist until the last mujahideen had perished. Fighting foreigners was a sacred duty.

Afghanistan was enjoying neither peace nor prosperity as a Soviet vassal state. For most Afghans, it was a time of ever-increasing fear. The country's future was uncertain. The PDPA had become accustomed to terrorising the population and showed few signs of internal reform. Despite being warned, Karmal mistakenly presumed the 40th Army would remain in Afghanistan indefinitely. The Politburo was conscious of the immense diplomatic and geo-strategic problems the continuing occupation had created. The Soviet Union could not withdraw without losing face domestically or damaging its international standing. The war dragged on without an end in sight. The mood among Soviet citizens began to change as the bodies of young soldiers were repatriated in regulation zinc containers. Although it had never needed to rely on popular support, the Politburo was nonetheless conscious that rising casualties would provoke dissent at home. After telling the people the occupation would be brief and refusing to hold public ceremonies to honour those who died, it was clear by 1985 that the occupation had brought no honour to the Soviet Union.

In Moscow, the famous dissident and Nobel laureate Andrei Sakharov published an open letter criticising the Politburo for taking sides in Afghanistan's civil affairs, committing the nation to an unjust war and killing many innocent civilians.[15] He wrote that 'these actions are a terrible mistake that it is necessary to correct as soon as possible, even more so because to do so becomes more difficult with every day that passes'. Western commentators were by now referring to the occupation as 'the Russian Vietnam'.[16] To outside observers, the PDPA's failure to gain popular support and the rising tide of violence across the country demonstrated that the Soviet Union was stuck in a military and political quagmire, not unlike the unpopular and ultimately unwinnable war into which the United States was drawn in South Vietnam in the early 1960s.

Soviet attitudes changed appreciably with the election of Mikhail Gorbachev as Communist Party General Secretary in March 1985. Gorbachev was not involved in the initial decisions to invade and occupy Afghanistan, and he had no personal political commitment to either the objectives or the outcome. The occupation was, he said, the Soviet Union's 'bleeding wound'.[17] After deciding to bring Soviet forces home, would the draw down occur rapidly or gradually? He decided the withdrawal would be gradual, not for the sake of the PDPA but because he needed to manage Moscow's relations with other client states carefully.[18]

Disappointing Moscow with his continuing over-reliance on the 40th Army to undergird his rule and protect his regime, the reportedly 'unwell' Karmal was replaced by Mohammad Najibullah, the head of Afghan state security, as the PDPA General Secretary in May 1986.[19] In a dossier prepared for the Politburo, Najibullah was said to be 'an intelligent, clever, and a vicious politician. He is vain and ambitious.'[20] He was behind the 'Pashtunisation' of Afghan society and promoted 'colleagues not for their professional qualities but for their personal devotion to him, predominantly relatives and fellow-villagers'. Entirely lacking an inclusive spirit, Najibullah enjoyed even less support within the PDPA than Karmal and was the focus of protest rallies that were soon dispersed by government forces. A ruthless party apparatchik whose readiness to use violence had initially brought him to the KGB's attention, Najibullah was instructed to bring more moderate opposition elements into the government and to promote national reconciliation.[21]

Two months later, Moscow announced the beginning of a gradual troop withdrawal, referring to the mujahideen not as 'bandits' but as 'internal opposition forces'. At a meeting of the Politburo on 13 November 1986, a clearly frustrated Gorbachev claimed the continuing occupation was 'casting doubt on our military capability. Our generals are not learning their lessons. It could be that they just cannot apply themselves fully there! But we do have the past experience from Angola, Ethiopia, and Mozambique. There must be a learning curve'.[22] There was no acknowledgment of the 40th Army's counterproductive efforts to obliterate all opposition or the hardships endured by many within the population because of the often senseless destruction of roads and infrastructure. The Politburo was caught on the horns of a dilemma. Andrei Gromyko, the foreign minister, was adamant: 'our goal is to make sure that Afghanistan is not a hostile nation, but rather a neutral state. We must salvage what we can of the social situation. Most importantly, we need to end the war and get our troops out'.[23] Rapid withdrawal had been rejected but there was little point in remaining beyond the short term.

Sergei Akhromeyev, the chief of the Soviet Army, offered a grim account of the prevailing situation:

> After seven years in Afghanistan, there is not one square kilometre left untouched by a boot of a Soviet soldier. But as soon as they leave a place, the enemy returns and restores it all back the way it used to be. We have lost this battle. The majority of the Afghan people support the counter-revolution now. We lost the peasantry, who has not benefited from the revolution at all. 80 per cent of the country is in the hands of the counter-revolution, and the peasant's situation is better there than in the government-controlled areas.[24]

Gorbachev was exasperated: 'we got ourselves into this mess – we did not calculate it right, and exposed ourselves in all aspects. We weren't even able to use our military forces appropriately. But now it's time to get out ... We've got to get out of this mess!'[25] After Gorbachev advised Gromyko he should not be 'hasty with the withdrawal of advisers: everyone will see that we're running away', he predicted the end of the Soviet presence would be followed by a bloodbath 'for which we would not be forgiven, either by the Third World, or by the shabby Western liberals who have spent the last ten years lambasting us for occupying the place'. There was no turning back. A political solution would be pursued irrespective of its practical merits.[26]

Najibullah held a *loya jirga* to endorse a new constitution and elect a new president. As the only candidate on the ballot paper, he was elected for seven years. Those outside the process – scholars, religious elders and mujahideen leaders – doubted his ability to change. Despite publicly re-embracing Islam and conceding that the PDPA needed to correct past mistakes by relaxing its monopoly on power, Najibullah was too deeply committed to PDPA ideals and the Soviet alliance to embrace a new philosophy. Najibullah claimed the insurgents' 'social base is dwindling, which is largely the result of their irrational, mad policy of terror. This will only increase their isolation. There are great disagreements among the opposition inside the country.'[27] Afghanistan had improved relations with Cyprus and Zimbabwe, while he conceded Pakistan, Iran, China and the United States were providing 'assistance to the extremists'.

In February 1988 after long-running talks in Geneva, Gorbachev formally committed the Soviet Union to withdrawing its troops from May 1988 and pledged to have the withdrawal completed within 10 months if a satisfactory agreement were signed.[28] The word 'satisfactory' denoted a dignified exit for the Soviet Union not unlike the Paris Peace Accords signed in January 1973, which had allowed the United States to leave South Vietnam having achieved 'peace with honour'. An agreement was reached in April 1988 that the Afghans and Pakistanis would not interfere in each other's affairs; refugees would be allowed to return safely to Afghanistan; the United States and the Soviet Union would both guarantee Afghanistan's future non-aligned status; and Soviet forces would be withdrawn from 15 May 1988 and completed within six months.[29]

The agreement was, however, all symbol and no substance. There were no detailed plans and no provisions for handling disagreements between the signatories. The last Soviet soldier departed on 15 February 1989. A total of 620 000 Russian military personnel had served in Afghanistan over the previous decade. Their departure was ignominious; their achievements were ignored. These disheartened men would later play a decisive role in the dissolution of the Soviet Union. The Afghan Communists and the mujahideen were left to fight for the future of Afghanistan.[30]

The PDPA continued to battle against the insurgency, helped by substantial supplies sent from Moscow. But with the end of the Soviet Union in December 1991, material support rapidly dried up and the regime continued entirely on its own.[31] Najibullah created regional militias to defend roads and urban fringes. These militias were led by warlords who were paid subsidies and given substantial autonomy. It was clear that the central government had been unable to control the major cities and regional centres without Soviet weaponry and support. Najibullah's regime clung to power without direct Soviet assistance for almost four years because of the deep divides and bitter rivalries that existed between the opposing factions. Their loathing of each other was only surpassed by their hatred of the Kabul government. When the United Nations proposed a political settlement in Afghanistan, Najibullah was alone in being willing to accept its conditions.

Eventually, his regime was completely surrounded by hostile forces. No-one came to his aid. Najibullah's party colleagues eventually defected to the militia groups that most closely represented their ethnic identities and which best suited their self-interests. Sensing the end of his rule, and with each of the mujahideen factions controlling different parts of Kabul, Najibullah resigned in March 1992.³² A new wave of violence was unleashed. Throughout Afghanistan, mujahideen fighters proved themselves to be little better than the PDPA, killing their fellow Afghans in revenge attacks and fighting among themselves for the spoils of so-called 'victory'. The warlords seized stockpiles of Soviet weapons and ammunition as they prepared for the next battle. It was said that Kabul belonged to everyone but was controlled by no-one.

A largely unrepresentative group of 51 stakeholders attended a conference at Peshawar in Pakistan in April 1992. Ignoring the United Nations and its proposals, they agreed to form the Islamic Republic of Afghanistan and approved the installation of an interim government.³³ The symbols and structures of national unity were a cover for escalating internecine violence. Afghan politics was completely fractured. There was no acknowledged strongman to unite them. Although the country had been at war for more than a decade, the principal belligerents were determined to fight on.

The Soviet occupation had ended in calamity. Its many legacies were profound. Embedded Russian journalist Artyom Borovik reflected:

> we bombed not only the detachment of rebels and their caravans, but our own ideals as well. With the war came re-evaluation of our own moral and ethical values. In Afghanistan the policies of the government became utterly incompatible with the inherent morality of our nation.³⁴

In a rare admission of government error, Gorbachev referred publicly to the 1979 invasion as a 'tragic mistake'. It was certainly costly in terms of human lives. There were initial estimates of between 1.2 and 2 million Afghan civilian deaths in addition to 90 000 mujahideen,

18 000 government troops and 14 500 Soviet soldiers. There were 1.5 million people permanently disabled, according to the World Health Organization. A further 6 million people became refugees. For the Soviets, losing fewer than 15 000 soldiers was tolerable. Public opinion had not, of course, determined the length of the campaign. By way of comparison, 80 000 soldiers and 5000 officials were killed during a 10-year campaign to crush a CIA-supported Lithuanian resistance to Soviet rule that ended in 1956. The Americans had lost 57 000 soldiers in South Vietnam. In its reckoning of the costs, the Politburo placed greater emphasis on the financial drain of combat operations and the diplomatic cost of invading, occupying and then withdrawing from Afghanistan.[35]

The occupation did lead to an improvement in the living standards of some Afghans in some parts of the country. There were positive benefits in terms of new roads, enhanced infrastructure and improved agriculture. But Soviet civil advisors understood neither the people nor their problems. Afghanistan was not modernised, liberalised or secularised. Could the population ever have accepted the PDPA and its revolutionary aspirations? Even with a more creative and nuanced program of aid and development, too much change was attempted over too short a period within a conservative society among a traditional people. By 1989, the country was more fractured, its politics more fraught and its future more tenuous than a decade earlier. One Soviet colonel predicted what would occur:

> most of the rebel gangs, which are squabbling here for zones of influence, cover their banditry with a lot of talk about fighting [the Soviets]. It's all a smoke screen that lets American politicians pour dollars into the furnace of the Afghan war with a clear conscience. When the Soviet troops leave, internecine war will break out all over the country. The rebel leaders, however, will no longer be able to disguise their terrorism with talk of 'holy war'.[36]

Of the three main objectives the Politburo articulated in 1979, only one was achieved and that was the easiest: the removal of Amin. Despite Moscow's efforts, the PDPA was no more politically or militarily secure than it had been a decade earlier, while the integrity of the Soviet Union's southern border remained a frontier of potential instability. The Soviet intervention in Afghanistan had begun with a series of serious political mistakes and practical miscalculations that were apparent by 1982 when Moscow first started looking for a way out. In addition to backing an ineffectual regime that failed to attract majority support, the PDPA and the Soviets had attempted to nullify the central organising pillar of Afghan society – Islam. They were wholly unsuccessful.

Communist hostility to Islam inadvertently contributed to the popularity of what became known as 'Salafist Jihadism', which inspired and sustained an influential minority within the insurgency. For Muslims drawn to this interpretative tradition, Islam was less a spiritual struggle for purity of heart and mind, and more a physical struggle against irreligious temporal authority in the guise of the godless secular state. Salafists in Afghanistan believed they had a duty to God and to the dignity of their religion to protect its place and to promote its virtues within a nation that had begun to encourage an unacceptable degree of liberalisation.[37] Any readiness to consider compromise ended when the 40th Army was deployed. Afghan traditionalists saw the cultural freedoms promoted by the Soviet-backed regime as malignant influences that would corrupt the rising generation of young Afghans. Western secularism would not only damage Afghan popular culture, it would inevitably weaken commitment to Islam. Soviet economic aid and technical assistance, which was designed to improve the quality of life Afghans enjoyed, was portrayed as godless materialism. The only acceptable help came from Pakistan. Afghanistan remained among the world's least developed countries and therefore among the poorest, with low levels of education and high levels of illiteracy. It was ranked 170 out of 174 in the United Nations Development Programme's *Human Development Index* in 1989.[38]

By 1990, Afghan society was fractured, its population cleaving to tribal identities and regional ideologies that were claiming a greater significance than a decade earlier. The Soviets had tried to turn the various tribal groups and political factions against one another in the hope of rewarding those willing to support the central government. This policy left lasting ethnic enmities that a future central government would struggle to resolve. There was no common negotiating language and no shared commitment to a set of values or principles around which Afghan national life could be arranged. The structures and institutions of the state were so weakened by the Soviet presence that the Kabul government exercised authority over less than one-quarter of the country. The Soviets tried to strengthen a poorly performing government and left Afghanistan without a viable central administration. Afghanistan was a nation lacking the necessary structures within which political authority and military power could be exercised to advance the common good and defend the public interest. The security services routinely violated basic human rights and lacked credibility. The machinery of government was beset by corruption and inefficiency. By concentrating on fortifying border crossings and consolidating garrisons in population centres, the Soviets weakened the Afghan Army's already limited capacity to operate in rural areas – a capacity it would not regain.

The Soviets also ignored the destabilising effects of the lucrative narcotics trade. Indeed, their presence encouraged its proliferation, as more arable land was diverted from growing vegetables and grazing animals to cultivating poppies to produce opium resin. The resin could then be sold to generate funds to support the mujahideen. Grain production declined by an average of 3.5 per cent during the 1980s, albeit hastened by prolonged drought.[39] As the war damaged the little infrastructure that existed and crops were destroyed to prevent the harvest feeding the mujahideen, the traditional agrarian economy was disrupted and many found working for the mujahideen an attractive source of income. The manufacture of bombs and improvised explosive devices proliferated as farmers sought income supplements or, in extreme cases, income replacement.

The conflict also led to a proliferation of privately held weapons ranging from anti-air and anti-tank missiles to mortars and personal firearms, including the ubiquitous AK-47 assault rifle, which had replaced the old Lee Enfield bolt-action rifle from the British period as the firearm possessed by most rural households. During the 1980s, these weapons had come from several sources including: the Afghan National Army prior to mass desertions in 1979; deserting Afghan Government soldiers who sold their weapons to whoever would buy them (a rifle sold on the black market was worth at least two months' wages); those captured from the Soviet military after an insurgent attack; and the Pakistani ISI as part of its material support for the insurgency. None were manufactured in Afghanistan. With the Soviet withdrawal in 1989, much of the country was armed, if only for self-defence against nearby criminals or greedy ex-mujahideen.

The Soviet Army's lack of concern for the civilian population also left a legacy of substantial long-term physical harm. Afghanistan was now strewn with landmines and infested with unexploded ordnance. The total number of mines was initially estimated at 10 million although government records put the actual figure at nearer to 270 000. Over the next 15 years, an average of four Afghans would be killed every day by landmines.[40] Much of the unexploded ordnance, such as artillery rounds and mortars, was recovered and repurposed for use in a future conflict. The remaining detritus of the Soviet era was neither dismantled nor removed. Damaged tanks, decaying trucks and twisted artillery stood adjacent to the main thoroughfares and alongside main roads. They were a constant reminder that the 40th Army had failed to bend the will of the Afghan people. Rusting Soviet armaments were symbols of their triumph against yet another foreign invader. After a decade of oppression, most Afghans were even more distrustful of foreigners and their habit of intruding in local affairs. Afghans in rural areas with little formal education had no grasp of superpower politics or the social, economic and political convictions that distinguished their erstwhile allies, the Americans, from their former adversaries, the Russians. If the foreigners were Westerners, they were almost certainly not Muslims; their motives were suspect and they were likely to interfere.

These important messages were conveyed to children, either orphaned or refugee, who received their formative education at *madrassas* – religious schools – in Pakistan, where they were inculcated into conservative, if not extreme, interpretations of Islam that led to deep dislike of Westerners.[41] Over the next decade, graduates of the madrassas travelled to contested Muslim homelands, such as Bosnia and Chechnya, to free their oppressed brethren. Others returned to Afghanistan, where they were intellectually and emotionally susceptible to overtures from violent extremists. Foreigners were the enemies of God; defeating them was God's work. Networks to establish alliances and systems to generate funds raised the profile of jihad and made its promotion a personal obligation. To resist the call to jihad was effectively to resist the will of God. 'Islamism' was providing a potent political motivation.

Anti-European, anti-Christian and anti-Semitic sentiment was conveyed through extreme violence across theologically inconsequential national borders. Ironically, most jihadist training and equipment was funded and supplied by the United States as part of its support for anti-Soviet forces. America's most important ally in the Arab world, Saudi Arabia, had also done more than any nation to promote Islamic fundamentalism through its own embrace of Wahhabism – an austere form of Islam insisting on literal interpretations of the Qur'an. President Najibullah had earlier told the *International Herald Tribune* that 'if fundamentalism comes to Afghanistan, war will continue for many years. Afghanistan will be turned into a center of terrorism'.[42] Iran was similarly wary of its predominantly Sunni Afghan neighbours, preferring political stability over religious conformity. It did not want another flood of Afghan refugees from the region around Herat crossing its borders. The conditions were right for interminable war.

In failing to understand their adversary – one of the first principles of warfare – the Soviets had unintentionally encouraged and equipped a generation of tough and tenacious fighters. The mujahideen increased from 45 000 fighters in 1981 to 150 000 five years later.[43] As the distinctions between combatants and non-combatants in Afghanistan had slowly dissolved during the 1980s, all adult males were considered legitimate targets. Military skills were effectively civilianised among the Afghan population. Every boy learned how to use a rifle; every man was taught to conduct an ambush. Dispossessed farmers joined deserting government soldiers in the ranks of private armies led by warlords, many of whom relied on the narcotics trade to finance their operations. Rather than protecting the Afghan state, they were defending the honour of Islam. Something much greater than national pride was at stake.[44]

The third objective prompting the Soviet invasion in 1979 – the fear of another Islamic revolution in Central Asia – was now more likely. Afghanistan was blighted by poverty, sectarianism, distrust, instability, violence and warlordism. The Afghan state was in pieces. When Najibullah resigned, there was no functioning state, no viable administration and no commitment to acting in the national interest. Afghanistan was tearing itself apart and little could be done by external parties to prevent it. Political anarchy led to social chaos as the rest of the world was preoccupied with the rebuilding of Kuwait following the short-lived Iraqi occupation in 1990, Saddam Hussein's attacks on the Kurds in the north of Iraq and the enforcement of a 'no fly' zone in 1991, and the worsening humanitarian crisis in Somalia in 1992.

First World nations, such as the United States, the United Kingdom, France and Germany, had abandoned the long-suffering

Afghan people to whatever fate awaited them as chaos and criminality took hold. The United States and its allies were, of course, complicit and partly to blame. Robert McFarlane, the National Security Advisor in the middle years of the Reagan Administration, said bitterly, we left 'a country in ruins, 1 million dead, 3 million maimed, 3–5 million refugees'. He added: 'It was a shameful betrayal of the Afghan people, an outrageous betrayal.' The United States had exploited the Soviet occupation as a Cold War stratagem but felt no continuing obligation to the Afghan people. It looked to Pakistan to manage the consequences and the possibility of reviving the Afghan state.

The Soviet Union was, of course, directly responsible for the existential crisis that had enveloped Afghanistan in late 1979 but could point to some mitigating factors. Had the PDPA regime collapsed, there was no alternative government; no representative parliament and no democratically elected officials. A viable administration might have emerged although it is difficult to imagine from where it might have come. Political chaos and social anarchy were more likely. The 'model revolution' had upended the Afghan nation and left little that was desirable or functional in its place. The political crisis that precipitated the Soviet invasion in 1979 was compounded by a decade of cruelty and callousness. The Afghans had been brutalised and traumatised. They had no reason to trust anyone – especially foreigners – who had brought only death and destruction, aided and abetted by advanced technology and aggressive tactics. Afghanistan was now a failed state and whatever remained of Afghan society was headed for implosion.

Although they entered the country as 'revolutionary comrades', the 40th Army was responsible for killing thousands of civilians and non-combatants in defiance of the Law of Armed Conflict. Apart from international indifference to the wanton death and destruction inflicted upon the Afghan people, no-one seemed to be asking why Soviet personnel had engaged in such widespread criminal conduct. Was leadership adequate and discipline satisfactory when the

40th Army first deployed in 1979? Did standards slip once its members encountered an implacable enemy? Was there effective constraint on reprisals and restraint on revenge when Soviet personnel were killed and property was destroyed? Were those who killed Afghans illegally brought to justice or did military personnel believe they could act with impunity?

The Soviet experience had the potential to yield important lessons and insights about moral principles and legal requirements in counterinsurgency warfare. It also said something about the manner in which Afghans would oppose foreign forces. The difficulty was discerning whether these lessons applied to all foreign forces in Afghanistan or only those conditioned to concede they would never do anything wrong.

4
DISINTEGRATION OF A MILITARY: THE SOVIET 40TH ARMY
1979–1989

Armies are tools of state that advance national interests. Ideally, they embody and reflect the standards of the nation and the values of the people from which its officers and soldiers are recruited. In Western societies, armies are controlled by elected civilian politicians and accountable to legally constituted tribunals. When deployed, uniformed personnel are bound by national and international law, influenced by military customs and conventions and constrained by mission parameters. In terms of individual freedom of action, officers and soldiers are influenced by everyone they meet and everything they encounter. These interactions might make departing from acceptable conduct or defying organisational values more tempting. It is also possible for an army deployed far from home to develop a mind of its own, overlooking government directions and disregarding national expectations. Hence, the abiding importance of leadership and discipline.

The resentment generated among the Afghan people by the conduct of the Soviet military was not a factor the Politburo considered when it decided to send the 40th Army into Afghanistan in December 1979. Soviet troops were despised by dissidents in the Soviet republics and detested in Soviet satellite states, such as Hungary and Czechoslovakia. The presence of the Soviet Army was not only oppressive, its personnel were known for their bellicosity and brutality. Its officers and soldiers were often angry and aggressive. The 40th Army was not chosen because it had a reputation for professionalism or restraint. In November 1979, it did not even exist. Initially raised in 1941 following the German invasion of the Soviet Union, the 40th Army was disbanded after the Nazi defeat in 1945. It was re-formed in early December 1979 for the invasion of Afghanistan specifically because it was untrammelled by traditions and unconstrained by conventions.

Despite the propaganda peddled by the People's Democratic Party of Afghanistan (PDPA) about the warmth of the Afghan–Soviet friendship, the relationship between the Afghan people and the 40th Army was always fraught. Before being sent south, Soviet soldiers were told their adversary consisted principally of 'bandits' and 'mercenaries' from Pakistan, China and the United States. They were also told the Afghan people would welcome them as socialist comrades. It was soon apparent to the 40th Army that they were not peacemakers. Few Soviet soldiers encountered a single Afghan Communist beyond the 'few thousand' in Kabul. The 'lies' they heard before leaving for Afghanistan – that they might be fighting their arch-enemies, the Americans – made many think the entire war was one big lie that no amount of propaganda could ever turn into truth. Being misled about the essential character of the conflict had a direct influence on the morale of individual units and on the outlook of individual soldiers. Whatever happened in Afghanistan had no direct or demonstrable bearing on their homeland. The Politburo either did not understand what was happening on the ground or did not seem to care. The differences between the official version promoted by Moscow and the unofficial version pursued in Kabul added to the unreality of the war and the artificiality of the patriotism that was expected of Soviet soldiers. Their own expert on Afghan affairs, Yuri Gankovsky, thought the 40th Army was 'provoking a conflict that could go on for centuries'.[1]

After securing Kabul and the surrounding districts, military operations were stepped up towards the end of 1980. The Soviets feared the likely election of Ronald Reagan to the American presidency might lead to the insurgents receiving more support from the United States via their friends in Pakistan. By then, however, the 40th Army believed it had rendered the capital safe from insurgent attacks and entrenched the PDPA government. They also thought the mujahideen and a restless civilian population had been taught a lesson about the futility of resistance. After the winter season when fighting was curtailed by the weather, the 40th Army concluded it could neutralise any remaining defiance. The Soviets were mistaken on every count. Attacks on the outer suburbs of Kabul continued and isolated tank troops in the rural areas were constantly threatened by rockets and bombs.

As the countryside refused to be pacified, Soviet military advisors had little success with remnants of the Afghan National Army. Former KGB general Leonid Shebarshin asked in his memoir: 'How did it happen that 2,000 advisers, including colonels and generals, failed to create a single fully combat-capable and reliable unit in the Afghan army?' He attributed a large part of the Soviet failure to organisational rigidity and individual attitudes, noting:

> we did teach something to Afghans, no doubt. But mainly we ordered them around and commanded them, 'stitching them on' to our operations, imposing our decisions, while loudly shouting about the weak fighting capacity of the ally.[2]

Fearing they were not going to succeed on the battlefield and would eventually be left to face the mujahideen alone, thousands of Afghan soldiers deserted to avoid the revenge and recrimination they knew would follow their inevitable defeat. Soviet soldiers deeply resented the Afghans' unwillingness to fight for their own country, and most of them could not see the point of fighting and dying for a revolution that few Afghans supported. There was a clear failure of political narrative in Kabul and in Moscow.

General of the Army Makhmut Gareyev was critical of the sparse official explanation for the initial deployment of Soviet troops because it gave soldiers little reason to face danger and fight courageously.[3] He observed that Directive 312/12/001, signed by the Defence Minister Dmitry Ustinov and the Chief of the General Staff Nikolai Ogarkov, stated that Soviet troops were being sent into Afghanistan for 'fulfillment of international duty' but the lack of detail meant 'what that duty constituted was to be decided by each commander and soldier themselves'. Nor had Soviet commanders aligned the mission's objectives with any relevant or binding Rules of Engagement (ROE). He lamented: 'the inadmissibility of the use of weapons against the civilian population is stipulated by international legal norms, but what about the "civilian" armed with an automatic rifle or a grenade launcher? Wait till he shoots?' Gareyev recalled that 'as strange as it may sound, from the very beginning of the introduction of troops and until the end of their stay in Afghanistan there was no clear line on whether our troops in this country should fight or not'. Consequently, some Soviet commanders displayed 'covert resistance to attempts to force the troops to fight'. This resistance also influenced how they fought.

Recognising the close relationship between political will and military morale, the mujahideen tried to sap the 40th Army's fighting spirit in the hope the Soviets would give up and go home. Although the mujahideen could never defeat the 40th Army on the battlefield, it was constantly wearing down the Politburo in Moscow. The commitment of Afghans to their own country was prevailing over the transient interest of foreigners, albeit in this instance a close neighbour. Killing more and more people produced a statistic, it did not deliver a victory. With little faith in the competence or the longevity of the Karmal and Najibullah regimes, Soviet officers and soldiers alike were not persuaded they were fighting for a worthy cause. The 40th Army might not have been doomed to fail but it was certainly not destined for success. By 1985, Soviet political and military resolve was waning and talk of withdrawal inevitably followed.

Unsurprisingly, the 40th Army's problems started with leadership. Afghanistan was considered a backwater posting by officers of genuine ability. Those who volunteered were attracted by the chance to experience active service and improve their promotion prospects while being much better remunerated. Wages paid in Afghanistan could be spent at more exclusive foreign currency shops in Moscow. The need to offer inducements was a measure of the unpopularity of the war among military personnel and the thin veneer of socialist spirit, even among officers. Within the ranks of the 40th Army the commonly held view was that only greedy, self-interested officers deployed to Afghanistan.

Most young soldiers accepted the reality of compulsory military service as part of their 'patriotic and internationalist duty' but took exception to the physical beatings they received from officers and non-commissioned officers (NCOs) over minor disciplinary matters. As most soldiers spent two years in Afghanistan, those in their first six months were at the bottom of an unofficial 'pecking order', whereas those about to depart were at the top. First-year soldiers were required to perform menial, domestic chores for second-year soldiers. Enduring cruelty and even sadism at the hands of their seniors drove many junior soldiers to alcohol and drugs. The majority of Soviet soldiers used hashish, opium and marijuana on a regular basis because vodka, the preferred intoxicant, was more expensive to buy and difficult to acquire. Drugs were purchased using the proceeds of stolen military supplies and hardware. Afghans were willing to trade a steady supply of opium and marijuana for food, ammunition and weapons. Most officers turned a blind eye to their soldiers' drug use unless it actually affected their operational performance. That many soldiers were slowly becoming addicted to a range of substances was ignored. Any dependency could be treated when they returned home.

The standard of Soviet military catering and barracks accommodation in Afghanistan was consistently poor and contributed to deteriorating discipline. Healthcare and measures for controlling infectious diseases were substandard.[4] Around 73 per cent of personnel serving in Afghanistan returned home wounded or sick, including 115 308 who suffered from infectious hepatitis and 31 080 from typhoid fever. Heatstroke and frostbite were common complaints because the uniforms issued to soldiers were inadequate. Sanitation and laundry services were appalling. There were no chaplains and no pastoral care. The Soviet Army did not think psychologists were needed. It was the task of political officers to inspire and encourage. Soviet training and tactics were ill suited to the task at hand and when they failed to produce the expected results, desperation and despair turned into bitterness and barbarism.

The 40th Army gave up trying to win over the Afghan people or defeat the insurgency; they wanted only to punish the people and hurt the mujahideen. Looting and theft were rife. One soldier explained:

> It was quite common to take things from the Afghans. We called it *bakshish* (bribe), but it was really robbery. You would see something in the house like a cassette recorder and just take it. You just need to point to what you want and they would give it to you, because they are afraid that you will kill them.[5]

The atrocities perpetrated in Afghanistan – murder, torture and reprisals – were partly a function of the 40th Army deriving from a society in which the state routinely turned on the citizenry and regarded individual rights as subordinate to collective interests, and partly a reflection of the Afghan Government itself using every conceivable means of coercion against its own people. Soviet commanders overlooked the fragility of the Afghan Army despite the outward pretence of preparing it for independent operations. If forced to fight the mujahideen alone and unaided, the Soviets were convinced the Afghan Army would crumble. The 40th Army was also disintegrating. None of its leaders sought moral ascendancy; most had even lost sight of moral decency.

There is considerable difficulty determining either the frequency or the severity of the atrocities committed by the 40th Army. There are no publicly available records on the incidence of war crimes or the conduct of investigations, possibly because no such records were ever generated by commanders in the field. The Soviets did not authorise press reporting of military operations in Afghanistan and tried to prevent journalists and reporters entering the country.[6] As most of the atrocities were carried out by whole units rather than isolated individuals, it was impractical to court martial an entire battalion of nearly 1000 men for misconduct. Accusations of war crimes were presumably either ignored or dealt with internally. In the absence of official records, contemporaneous reporting and formal inquiries, assessing the extent of misconduct relies largely on personal recollections and educated projections.

The total number of Afghans killed during the invasion and occupation is not easy to determine. Most estimates range between 1.2 and 2 million. The Afghan demographer, Noor Ahmad Khalidi, puts the figure of 'unnatural deaths' at 876 825, noting that the population declined from 13.36 million in 1980 to 12.41 million in 1990.[7] After making an allowance for the number of Afghans killed by Afghans and the number of local mujahideen killed in combat, the 40th Army was responsible for well over 500 000 *civilian* deaths. With a large number of variables involved, the total figure can never be known but between half and three-quarters of a million people would be a reasonable estimate. Whatever the actual number, the death toll was nonetheless staggering, with many more civilians dying than combatants. The Soviets frequently ignored the requirement to distinguish combatants from civilians. Believing every Afghan was complicit in the insurgency, they plainly felt justified in killing everyone despite the heavy burden imposed on all military forces to respect non-combatant immunity.

In defiance of international law, the Soviets also directed the mass deportation of civilians. They expelled people from their ancestral lands and destroyed everything that was left behind including food supplies, irrigation canals, wells and dwellings. This de-population program was most aggressively pursued in the provinces of Nangarhar, Ghazni, Laghman, Kunar, Zabul, Kandahar, Badakhshan, Logar, Paktia and Paktika. The Soviet 'scorched earth' policy was intended to prevent villagers from supporting mujahideen while separating the insurgents from the local population. They destroyed religious schools and mosques, encouraged the forced removal of children from their parents to indoctrinate them in Marxist–Leninist theory, and publicly ridiculed Afghan cultural practices and spiritual beliefs. There were countless reports of girls and women residing near Soviet garrison towns being abducted and raped. Of all Soviet soldiers charged with offences in Afghanistan, 11.8 per cent were indicted for sexual assault.[8]

The first reports of widespread unit-level misconduct coincided with the realisation that the invasion force would not be withdrawing within six months as planned. To reduce the number of Soviet casualties associated with insurgent 'clearing' operations, massive aerial attacks would be followed by sustained artillery barrages before ground troops entered an area supported by tanks and armoured personnel carriers. As a consequence of these tactics, the civilian population would almost always suffer higher casualties than the insurgents. In late May 1980, at least 30 civilians who had taken refuge in an irrigation canal during an engagement between Soviet forces and mujahideen were killed by chemical weapons at Waghiz in Ghazni province. During the following month, heavy artillery and mortars were fired without warning or provocation from the major Soviet air base at Bagram, killing civilians in the Kohdaman, Gul Dara and Farza valleys. In July, up to 60 villages in districts around

Kabul were damaged or destroyed to create a cleared buffer zone around the capital.

As the mujahideen did not wear uniforms or distinguishing attire and drew their support largely from local villagers (whether freely or coerced), Soviet commanders readily dismissed claims they had targeted the 'civilian' population. The local Afghan forces were often enraged by the indifference of the Soviets to the welfare of their fellow Afghans. University of Kabul academic Mohammad Hassan Kakar noted in his diary:

> In this way the defenceless, tyrannised people, women, the old, and children alike, fell like leaves in the autumn in their own homes, mosques, hamlets, and villages. The operations were so ruthless that an Afghan regiment in Maidan clashed with the Russians until the regiment was recalled to Kabul.[9]

Soviet forces were quick to mount revenge operations, which were notable for their devastation. On 28 July 1980, a Soviet tank troop was ambushed by mujahideen after a house search in the village of Turani near the city of Baghlan. A larger ground force arrived the next day and, after bombarding the city with mortars, killed around 50 people in a revenge attack. Three months later, Soviet forces returned to Baghlan in response to insurgent attacks in that city and at Kunduz. After rounding up the civilian population and looting their houses of valuables, the Soviets spared PDPA members but shot the remainder. Their bodies were dumped into pits dug by Soviet bulldozers. The estimated death toll ran into the hundreds. Social events were also targeted, sometimes mistakenly, as insurgent gatherings. In mid-September several hundred villagers had come together to celebrate a wedding at Ganjabad in the Bala Buluk district of Farah province. They were targeted by helicopter gunships which fired rockets and small-calibre rounds at the crowd, reportedly killing 150 people and wounding many others. There were many similar stories.

In seeking to control the main roads between major population centres, 40th Army forces ejected villagers from homes it deemed were too near the road or too attractive as potential staging posts for mujahideen attacks. This was sometimes done in an orderly manner, with the inhabitants evacuated prior to their homes being burned. It was sometimes done in a chaotic manner, with artillery bombardments, gunship attacks or poisoning of water supplies. In certain parts of the country, especially along the Salang and Jalalabad roads, trucks were looted by Soviet troops and buses were fired upon to deter the movement of people across the country. Truck drivers refused to transport food and other essential commodities to Kabul until the Soviets agreed to review their tactics. Bus drivers complained to the Afghan Interior Ministry and refused to convey passengers until their safety was assured. Unsurprisingly, the Soviets never won the allegiance and the goodwill of the civilian population. The 40th Army fuelled resentment and generated local support for the mujahideen, although this support was always tempered by the fear of reprisals. For every 40th Army soldier who was killed the Soviets were determined to kill 100 Afghans.

The 40th Army committed every crime prohibited by the Geneva Convention, although both the Soviet Union and Afghanistan were signatories to the 1949 conventions. The offences were individual and collective. Whole units engaged in atrocities ranging from the forced deportation of entire villages to the deliberate mass killing of unarmed non-combatant civilians. Few people were safe from the savagery of the 40th Army. While it was in the propaganda interests of the mujahideen to exaggerate Soviet misconduct, a Tajik defector from the 40th Army reported that when his 'drunk commander found out that his brother and three soldiers were killed by mujahideen, he took the whole commando unit at night. He went to the village and butchered, slaughtered all the village[rs]. They cut off the heads and killed perhaps 2,000 people'.[10]

Among the worst reported mass killings was an operation

conducted from 11 to 18 March 1985 in the villages of Kas-Aziz-Khan, Charbagh, Bala Bagh, Sabzabad, Mamdrawer, Haider Khan and Pul-i-Joghi. A Soviet ground force that included 200 tanks and armoured personnel carriers rolled into the Kharga district of Laghman province (east of Kabul). Two Western diplomats in Kabul told foreign news organisations that the Soviets described the operation as 'a search for rebels'. A request by Afghan officials to allow Afghan troops to participate in the hope of reducing civilian casualties was apparently denied. When no insurgents were captured, the Soviets turned on the 'sympathetic' local population without mercy. Bodies were left lying in the decimated villages. Survivors were expelled from their homes, which were looted and then burned. The Soviet commander later gave permission for families to bury their dead. When the rebels reappeared in the area, a second clearing operation was staged on 22–26 March 1985 in which more civilians were killed. Another diplomat was told that 900 villagers were massacred in northern Kunduz province on 26 March. The survivors spoke to appalled Afghan officials, who secretly conveyed the news to Western diplomats who then spoke with foreign media.[11]

The first detailed, systematic report on human rights abuses and war crimes was compiled by Felix Ermacora, an Austrian human rights advocate and Special Rapporteur on the Situation of Human Rights in Afghanistan, who reported to the United Nations General Assembly for the first time in 1985.[12] He outlined four types of actions directed against the civilian population: 'i) acts of brutality committed by armed forces; ii) bombardment and massacre following reprisals; iii) use of anti-personnel mines and booby-trap toys; iv) other consequences resulting from bombardments'. Ermacora relied on witness statements and reports from organisations, including Helsinki Watch and Amnesty International.[13] Their staffs had observed that 'just about every conceivable human rights violation is occurring in Afghanistan, and on an enormous scale'.[14] In addition to civilian deaths, animals were being killed, villages were being destroyed and houses were being burned without any regard for the impact of these actions on the social fabric of the country.

Despite a unilateral ceasefire being declared by the Kabul government in February 1987, the Afghan Information Centre *Monthly Bulletin* claimed that in October–November that year, 'the Russian forces carried out daily operations of mass killings and destruction in many areas in Logar, resulting in the killing of 206 children, women and old men, and the destruction of 1043 houses'.[15] The use of force was allegedly indiscriminate and disproportionate. Once the withdrawal of Soviet troops was announced in February 1986 and the Soviets lost their uncontested control of Afghan airspace with the supply of American anti-aircraft weapons to the mujahideen, the destruction of entire villages and the massacre of the inhabitants occurred much less frequently.

Most external observers were convinced that Soviet soldiers had almost no knowledge of the Law of Armed Conflict. They had little acquaintance with ROE and were subject to illegal orders they felt unable to resist. A Soviet conscript described his preparation for Afghanistan in the following terms:

> Before I went into the army it was Dostoyevsky and Tolstoy who taught me how I ought to live my life. In the army it was the sergeants. Sergeants have unlimited power. There are three to a platoon. 'Now hear this! Repeat after me! What is a [paratrooper]? Answer: a bloody-minded brute with an iron fist and no conscience! Repeat after me: conscience is a luxury we can't afford'. The message of the twice weekly political seminar given to some of the Soviet army in Afghanistan was: 'the army must keep healthy and we must banish pity from our minds'.[16]

A Soviet private in the intelligence corps recalled:

> Only once something snapped inside me and I was struck by the horror of what we were doing. We were combing through a village. You fling open the door and throw in a grenade in case there's a machine-gun waiting for you. Why take a risk if a grenade can sort it out for you? I threw the grenade, went in and saw women, two little boys and a baby in some kind of box making do for a cot. You have to find some kind of justification to stop yourself going mad. Suppose it's true that the souls of the dead look down on us from above?[17]

The consequences of this behaviour were apparent even to the newest member of the 40th Army. A junior Soviet soldier was in no doubt as to why he and his colleagues were hated so intensely by the Afghans:

> To them you're just a Russky, not a human being. Our artillery wipes his village off the face of the earth so thoroughly that when he goes back he literally can't find a trace of his mother, wife or children. Modern weaponry makes our crime even greater. I can kill one man with a knife, two with a mine ... dozens with a missile.[18]

Those who tried to deflect criticism of the 40th Army's misconduct pointed out that:

> the whole of Afghanistan had become a battlefield. Our soldiers had seen and experienced all the horrors of such a war ... the whole atmosphere, the situation, resulted in perfectly normal, decent Soviet lads becoming xenophobes, killers, and sadists. Such is the price of internationalism – it can't be helped.[19]

It was not only the Soviets and the Afghan secret police who engaged in misconduct. The mujahideen were also motivated by revenge.

Until 1987, when an attitude of restraint was adopted, they killed most Soviet soldiers, including those who were wounded or tried to surrender, on sight. The dismembering of Soviet soldiers was reported as early as February 1980. Writing in the *Far Eastern Economic Review*, John Fullerton reported:

> Early on the fate of captured Soviets was often gruesome. One group was killed, skinned and hung up in a butcher's shop. One captive found himself the centre of attraction in a game of *buzkashi*, that rough and tumble form of Afghan polo in which a headless goat is usually the ball. The captive was used instead. Alive. He was literally torn to pieces. Russians who display no interest in or knowledge of religion are regarded as infidels, unbelievers [atheists, technically]. According to the custom of *badal* or revenge, their deaths may properly be demanded by the locals, many of whom will be involved in feuds with the Soviets through the loss of relatives in the war.[20]

The mujahideen also executed Afghan Army soldiers. After a battle at Jawar in Paktia province in March 1986, 45 officers 'confessed' to being Communists and were shot by members of the Hezbe-e Islami political party. Their bodies were not buried in Muslim soil as they were deemed 'infidels'. Members of the National Islamic Front of Afghanistan allegedly claimed to have executed between 6000 and 7000 prisoners over the preceding six years.[21]

There were few instances of Soviet troops being held to account for their actions in Afghanistan. Those facing disciplinary proceedings were charged with 'freelance' crimes, meaning those not sanctioned by commanders in the conduct of a formal operation. A rare instance of a disciplinary action prompted by an authorised operation was revealed in the weekly journal, *Literaturnaya Gazeta*, by the experienced war correspondent Gennady Bocharov.[22] It reported that Soviet soldiers had murdered a group of innocent Afghan civilians at the direction of a senior officer who remarked that he did not 'need captives'. The date and place were not disclosed but the circumstances resembled an incident known to have occurred during operations in Laghman province in 1985. In brief, a detachment of soldiers stationed at a checkpoint was ordered to prevent weapons being smuggled to the mujahideen from Pakistan. The driver of a car that was directed to stop appeared to accelerate before being fired upon. A woman was killed. A man and a teenager were also injured. Another four passengers, including two children, were unharmed. No weapons were found in the car, although it was later claimed they were in possession of Chinese-made weapons. The checkpoint commander requested a helicopter to evacuate the civilians. His superior, a lieutenant colonel, replied twice for effect: 'I don't need them.' The civilians were to be dealt with 'quietly' and there was to be no trace of them. They were shot by Private Alexei Markov.

Reports that innocent civilians had been executed apparently reached higher authority, as a trial was subsequently held at Tashkent in Uzbekistan. The officer ordering the executions and the soldier who shot the civilians were found guilty and sentenced to imprisonment for five years. The officer's sentence was immediately commuted but he was later convicted of killing an unarmed Afghan in a fight and sentenced to six years' imprisonment. The checkpoint commander was subsequently injured in the field and avoided prosecution. Public sentiment in Tashkent was firmly in favour of the convicted men. The lieutenant colonel claimed: 'the men under my command disposed of 850 spooks [mujahideen], with minimal losses to our side. And now I am in a prison cell just because I happened to kill one! Where's the justice to that? I believed him to be the enemy.'[23] Markov's comrades demanded a review of his sentence because 'a commanding officer's order is law to his subordinates'.

In the same article, Bocharov recounted another story of soldiers who stole flammable liquid to burn the bodies of the mujahideen they had killed. They also shot the camels the men had been riding and had a sniper kill an injured man who had attempted to escape. Bocharov's story implied that Soviet soldiers despised all Afghans principally because they could not distinguish friends from foes or allies from spies. But it is not clear why this particular incident had attracted disciplinary proceedings when so many others went unreported and unpunished.

On 28 November 1989, the Supreme Soviet, the principal legislative body in Moscow, which was disbanded less than two years later when the Soviet Union was dissolved, granted to soldiers deployed to Afghanistan an amnesty that excluded future prosecution for deliberate or indiscriminate attacks on Afghan civilians.[24] No-one would be held to account as the Soviet Union closed the book on a shameful war that was fought without honour. The 40th Army was disbanded shortly after its withdrawal from Afghanistan. It was re-formed in June 1991 but, following the dissolution of the Soviet Union, was absorbed into the Kazakhstan military and renamed the First Army Corp.

There were three broad reasons for the atrocities committed by the 40th Army in Afghanistan. The first reason was dysfunction and ill-discipline. The Soviet high command sent an ill-equipped and poorly provisioned force on an operation requiring personnel, training and tactics that the 40th Army lacked. In supporting a mission that required military flexibility and diplomatic nuance, they were the wrong army in the wrong place at the wrong time. The 40th Army was structured for major battles in Eastern Europe. There was an over-confident belief that 'where Soviet military power trod, political domination would inexorably follow'.[25] It was incapable of the subtleties required to prosecute an effective counterinsurgency campaign. The tactics the Soviets had used in Czechoslovakia in 1968 were ill-suited to Afghanistan a decade later.

Because its deployment was meant to be brief, the infrastructure sustaining the 40th Army was deficient and operational oversight was defective. Moscow's attitude to the mission was miserly. Although the operational budget was tight, results were expected immediately. The 40th Army was required to succeed without delays but without adequate provisions and with too few men. Although Moscow committed 100 000 men, there were too few to control the cities, towns and rural areas. At least three and perhaps four times that number were needed but never committed. Atrocities were considered a short-cut to quick victory when fighting war on a strict budget. Rather than carefully selecting targets and avoiding collateral damage, which would have required an investment in intelligence gathering and assessment beyond available resources, it was easier to kill anyone and destroy everything. The Soviets hoped their ruthlessness would deter the mujahideen and dissuade the civilian population from supporting them. The use of indiscriminate and disproportionate force only served to harden insurgent resolve and increase the likelihood that captured Soviet soldiers would be tortured and executed – which they were. Ironically, the Soviet Army accused the mujahideen of employing 'terror and ideological conditioning on a peaceful populace as well as on local government representatives'.[26]

The second reason for misconduct was the 40th Army's attitude to the local population and the problems faced by the Afghan people. The Soviet high command was angry that the foolhardy actions of the PDPA had precipitated an untimely invasion. They were infuriated that the regime's political weakness and administrative inadequacy had necessitated an occupation in a place of marginal strategic significance to the Soviet Union. The 40th Army did not consider the mujahideen to be either accomplished foes or even worthy adversaries. According to the Soviets, the mujahideen were not professional soldiers; they lacked training and supervision; did not wear uniforms; failed to acknowledge rank; preyed on vulnerable people; exploited human weakness; and were duplicitous and deceitful. It was, 40th Army commanders claimed, impossible to distinguish between civilians and combatants as everyone beyond Kabul was suspected of assisting the insurgents – willingly or otherwise. Soviet officers and soldiers did not have confidence in the loyalty of their Afghan allies, nor did they have faith in their ability to fight. Collective professional disdain for Afghan insurgents, the so-called 'bandits', became the basis of individual personal disregard for the dignity of all Afghans. As pre-deployment training was intended to desensitise them and dehumanise the Afghans, Soviet soldiers had few inhibitions about killing Afghan combatants and civilians. In Afghanistan, human life had been devalued on all sides. With combatants and civilians being killed on an industrial scale, a few more unnecessary deaths and illegal killings made little difference. Most went largely unnoticed.

The third reason for the prevalence of so many atrocities was the belief among 40th Army soldiers that they could act with complete impunity. Official policy supported this belief and rarely did politicians or commanders challenge the confidence of those holding it. Crimes at the unit and formation level were committed because, in the absence of news media and independent observers, there would be no consequences – other than for those who refused to participate. For the soldiers, the war was not about revolution and internationalism. There were no worthy causes or lofty ideals to pursue. They were there to do battle: 'to destroy those they were told to destroy'.[27] The soldiers created their own stories to justify the war and to rationalise their part in its conduct.

When reports of atrocities emerged from Afghanistan, *Los Angeles Times* journalist Ernest Conine observed that in contrast to universal condemnation of Nazi atrocities during the Second World War, 'the world seems hardly to notice (or care) that the Soviets and their supporters are committing the same kind of deliberate atrocities in Afghanistan'.[28] After asking why those sensitive to the injustices of apartheid in South Africa were silent on Soviet crimes in Afghanistan, he suggested a few answers:

> Out of sight, out of mind. A reluctance to believe that the atrocities are really occurring because, once the reality was

accepted, there would be an implicit responsibility among civilised people to do something about it ... 'Never again' obviously doesn't apply to Afghanistan. It turns out to be more convenient to hurl thunderbolts at the perpetrators of atrocities that occurred more than 40 years ago than to be beastly to those who are committing such crimes in the here and now.

The 40th Army was entirely unconcerned with public opinion either in Afghanistan or in the Soviet Union. When rumours and then reports of systematic misconduct began to circulate, the response was to deny the rumours, denounce 'inaccurate' reports as no more than insurgent propaganda, and increase physical efforts to prevent external agencies gaining access to the area of operations. The 40th Army's leadership was neither chided nor constrained by allegations levelled against its personnel by human rights groups or international organisations, including the United Nations. Military imperatives and strategic priorities always prevailed over moral norms and ethical standards. Fears about the consequences of wrongdoing were never allowed to dictate the content of military plans or the conduct of tactical operations. Colonel Yuri Starov explained that 'it's senseless to make up rules in war. Especially in this war, where there's no front or rear'.[29]

In the absence of smartphones with cameras and drones flying overhead, individual war crimes could be easily concealed from scrutiny and were readily overlooked by loyal comrades. Other than deserters whose motivations were mixed – few Soviet soldiers absconded because they refused to participate in criminal acts – there were no reported instances of a morally outraged comrade or commander in the 40th Army drawing attention to human rights abuses and demanding justice for the victims. There was no Hugh Thompson, the American military helicopter pilot who intervened to stop the My Lai massacre in 1968, within the 40th Army. Most Western militaries do not tolerate operational misconduct. It detracts from the mission focus, erodes respect for commanders, weakens unit morale and dissolves individual discipline. In sum, atrocities are always indicative of organisational decline. Soviet soldiers thought they would never be punished for war crimes in Afghanistan. Put simply: few officers seemed to care about the atrocities they had not actually ordered; fewer expressed any interest in preventing atrocities in any general sense.

In the context of a highly permissive culture in which there was so much killing, the Soviets were aware that the Afghan Government was killing its own people and that the mujahideen were killing their rivals. There is no evidence that this behaviour was more prevalent or tolerated in particular units or among specific corps. The motorised infantry battalions were probably no better or worse than the Spetsnaz reconnaissance teams. It was a general malaise that existed across the Soviet forces deployed to Afghanistan. One soldier, Alexander Kirillov, reflected that nothing in Afghanistan:

> remains of your previous aims and ideas. After your first outing in the combat zone, trying to unite these ideas is unreal, as impossible as collecting together a head, a leg, and a body torn apart by a shell. When I was saying goodbye to my wife back in the Soviet Union, I understood right away that I was saying goodbye not only to her but to myself – the myself I can never be again.[30]

Others were embittered by political interference which gave the impression that soldiers were expendable:

> If the military had been allowed to conduct the war as it saw fit, we would have eliminated all this so-called opposition long ago ... They should have listened to the military and positioned garrisons on the Pakistan border. If we'd closed all the roads and the caravan routes, we would have squashed the [rebels] without

any military action. Naturally, however, we would have had to increase the limited number of troops so that politicians could claim credit for an invasion. Gibberish![31]

Middle-ranking officers believed operational reporting was intended to assure Moscow that all was well rather than inform it of what was really happening. Sensible proposals to create autonomous districts were overlooked and requests to negotiate with mujahideen leaders were rejected.

In his overall assessment of Soviet military performance in Afghanistan, United States Army officer and military historian Scott McMichael believed it no exaggeration to think 'every Soviet soldier assigned to Afghanistan witnessed or participated in atrocities … at some time in their service'. McMichael concluded that the frequency of atrocities was 'perhaps the best indicator of the failure of Soviet leadership and the evidence of an Army without a soul'.[32] The 40th Army's misconduct left another lasting legacy:

> The Afghan people will long remember the thousands of times they endured the plunder of their homes, the stripping of their belongings at search points, the rape of their women, mutilation of bodies, the torture of their men, and the callous, indiscriminate slaughter of villagers.[33]

The Afghan people had become intimately acquainted with unrestrained violence. It was normalised behaviour for the Afghan Government and its backers – the Soviet Union and the 40th Army – and became so for the mujahideen. Atrocities were routinely perpetrated by all sides. They proliferated and were not punished. They escalated in the form of revenge, reprisal and recrimination as the central pillars of human civilisation dissolved. Respect for human life and regard for human dignity were diminished as ethical dilemmas and moral challenges were deemed too difficult or disruptive to address.

There was an especially bleak dimension about fighting in Afghanistan that demanded superior leadership and stronger discipline if human dignity was to have any role in mediating the use of lethal force. This was the way of things in Afghanistan and a consideration that any future foreign military force entering the country would need to bear in mind.

With the political culture poisoned and in the absence of a unifying national vision, Afghans turned on each other with enormous ferocity after the Soviet withdrawal in February 1989. There would be no reconciliation, only revenge. The prospect of peace and prosperity would remain the faintest of hopes unless there were genuine attempts to confront the past and heal its wounds. It was difficult to believe things could become worse, but the people of Afghanistan were to have their beliefs tested even further.

5

IMPLOSION OF A SOCIETY: TALIBAN EXTREMISM

1992–2001

Most nations try to influence the affairs of other nations in ways that serve their interests. At times, they directly intervene. When the Cold War between the United States and the Soviet Union ended in 1989, a number of simmering intra-state tensions erupted into open warfare as the conflicting parties could no longer rely on eliciting superpower support. When some of these tensions led to mass deportations, ethnic cleansing and genocide, groups of nations felt the need to intervene in the affairs of sovereign states as never before.

Over the past 30 years there have been Western-led interventions in the former Yugoslavia, Cambodia, Rwanda, Somalia, Sierra Leone, Liberia and, nearer to Australia, Bougainville, East Timor and Solomon Islands. Although an element of self-interest resides beneath the humanitarian veneer, these interventions were prompted by crises that could not be ignored by those with the capacity to end violence and restore order. In each instance, attempts were also made to heal nations, rebuild states and revive civility. Even in places where there was negligible trust or goodwill between the conflicting parties, the remnants of the pre-crisis nation-state provided sufficient resources for the revival of political processes (other than, perhaps, in Somalia).

The decade-long Soviet occupation devastated the Afghan nation and state. By the early 1990s, Afghan society was gradually imploding; cities and towns were reduced to rubble as crime and corruption attacked the foundations of trust and goodwill. Fifteen years after Daoud Khan deposed the Afghan king, Zahir Shah, Afghanistan was starting to resemble a wasteland. Few Western nations had any desire to intervene in Afghan affairs. The problems were profound and would not be resolved readily. Lots of time and money would be needed. To make the situation even more dire, those with power in Afghanistan neither wanted nor would allow foreign intervention. Lacking the diplomatic will and the military means to intervene, the West left Afghanistan to whatever fate its strongmen were prepared to inflict upon it.

There was, then, an inevitability about the civil war between rival mujahideen factions that began in mid-1992 as the country inched towards virtual disintegration. Throughout the decade-long Soviet occupation the principal militia leaders were united in their opposition to foreign intruders. They quarrelled between themselves and jostled for resources from international donors but the focus remained on pressuring Soviet forces to withdraw. Beyond their common foe, the factions reflected different ethnicities, regional loyalties, religious outlooks, foreign allegiances and leadership personalities. With the demise of Najibullah's government in April 1992, it was clearly apparent they had different visions of the Afghan state and how their country ought to be governed, and by whom. There were debates about the location of authority and disagreements over the distribution of power. Alongside genuine concern for what best served Afghanistan was personal striving for position and prestige. The absence of a formalised opposition during the Soviet occupation meant the political landscape remained fractured and unyielding to compromise in a country which had never experienced stable democratic rule.

The United Nations, lacking the financial resources to overcome the chronic underfunding of public programs initiated as part of Operation Salam (the office established in 1988 to coordinate international economic and humanitarian programs in mujahideen-controlled areas),[1] was not well placed to play an effective role. The two peacekeeping missions mandated by the 1988 Geneva Agreement had failed. Neither mission was sufficiently large nor adequately resourced to succeed. The prospect of Afghanistan hosting free and fair elections, ratifying a constitution to undergird democratic rule and forging a broad-based democratic government was minimal. The country lacked the institutions and officials to facilitate and supervise such a process while political power, to quote political scientist Barnett Rubin, was now 'broken into very small pieces'. Political disintegration made coalition-building an extraordinarily difficult undertaking, even presuming the existence of considerable goodwill.[2]

While there was widespread interest in an integrated political order, few of the diverse factions and parties seemed willing to imperil their individual status and standing to achieve it. In any event, the struggle between the militia leaders soon led to the destruction of Kabul's southern suburbs, much of its critical infrastructure and thousands of civilian deaths. The memoir of a young Afghan woman known as 'Zoya' highlighted the chaos and carnage of these years:

> Far from rejoicing that the Russians had been defeated, Grandmother told me that a new worse Devil had come to my country. There was a popular saying around this time: 'Rid us of these seven donkeys and give us back our cow. The donkeys were the seven factions of the Mujahideen, and the cow was the puppet regime' [of Najibullah].[3]

The interim government headed briefly by Sibghatullah Mojeddedi (as acting president for two months) and then by Burhanuddin Rabbani lacked authority and power. Rabbani, an ethnic Tajik and respected Islamic scholar, was the president of Afghanistan in name only. He was unable to end the chaos engulfing the country. Consistent with events of the previous decade, atrocities abounded as none of the belligerents honoured the principle of non-combatant immunity or abided by any rule of law. Intimidation, theft, rape and murder were everyday occurrences. Civilian populations were deliberately targeted to achieve tactical gains and propaganda victories. One of the worst incidents was at Afshar, a densely populated district on the western side of Kabul.[4]

On 11 February 1993, forces led by Ahmad Shah Massoud (who was also the Defence Minister), Abdul Rasul Sayyaf (the only Pashtun leader within Massoud's Northern Alliance) and Rabbani turned on those loyal to Gulbuddin Hekmatyar (the Prime Minister) and Abdul Ali Mazari (the Hazari leader of the Hezb-e Wahdat party). Around 1000 Shia Muslims, mostly Hazaras, were murdered. Sikhs and Hindus were accused of sympathy for Najibullah (whose government had been supported diplomatically by India), who had tried to leave Afghanistan before taking refuge in the United Nations compound in Kabul. Alliances between the militia leaders were formed and just as quickly abandoned. Accusations of duplicity were followed by allegations of wrongdoing. In the absence of any real consensus on the way ahead, there was little trust between the factions, who represented a range of constituencies and interests.

The challenge was settling on a set of acceptable political arrangements in which decisions could be made that would not be forcibly or unilaterally contested by one or more militia leaders. There was a need for institutions and structures, processes and people to support a democratic government with the political authority to administer the country. These arrangements needed to be clear in defining the source of authority but flexible in dealing with Afghanistan's diverse citizenry. Should the emphasis be on provincial or national government? If authority were decentralised and power dispersed within a federal system of government, how would revenue raising be managed and projects of national significance be funded? Nation-building of this magnitude was a major undertaking. It would not be completed in weeks or months. After the Soviet occupation it would take even longer to rebuild trust in state institutions and revive confidence in individuals holding public office.

Before much of substance could be achieved, public order needed to be restored alongside respect for the rule of law. The difficulty was the paucity of building blocks for a new society. There were few remnants of either the Daoud or Karmal–Najibullah regimes that could be retrieved or salvaged. Furthermore, all of those pursuing political office in the new government had a sullied past. None was without factional enemies or ethnic rivals. The tensions between them were bitter and unrelenting. Each faction had enjoyed some form of foreign patronage although their backers' real intentions were often veiled. While a political settlement was being attempted, 1.4 million refugees were gradually returning from Iran and Pakistan. They returned to a country that was neither safe nor secure. It was dangerous to walk the streets in many parts of Afghanistan.

As the factional leaders struggled for supremacy in a country that was sliding into chaos and anarchy, a new group was gaining momentum and followers. They were called the *Taliban*. (The Persianised plural of the Arabic word for 'student' is usually translated *talib*.) The movement originated in madrassas at Kandahar, the second largest city in Afghanistan, as a conservative Sunni Pashtun minority that attracted extremists from Libya, Egypt, Sudan and the Gulf states. The Taliban's leader, Mullah Mohammad Omar, had been trained by the Pakistani Inter-Services Intelligence (ISI) Directorate during the Soviet occupation. He was dismayed that Islamic law had not been embraced by the post-Najibullah government, which was dominated, he contended, by criminal warlords who lacked spiritual fervour. A tall and physically imposing man who had lost the sight of his right eye fighting as a mujahideen, Omar gathered around himself a group of angry and dispossessed young Sunni Pashtun men whose religious and political passions were inflamed by veterans of the anti-Soviet struggle. Beginning with fewer than 50 followers, Omar insisted that Afghanistan's internal divisions would be overcome by strict adherence to what he believed was the purest expression of Islamic moral teaching – a tradition known as 'Deobandism' – which took its name from Deoband, the Islamic seminary in India where this distinct set of beliefs originated in 1867.[5]

The original aim of the seminary was to offer moral leadership to Muslims in India (which then included the provinces that now constitute Pakistan) after they were implicated in the 1857 mutiny against British colonial rule.[6] The leaders of this tradition, the 'Deobandi', demanded strict and literal scriptural authority for their doctrines and beliefs, and had strong views on the legitimacy and necessity of particular Islamic observances. This approach to the authoritative texts of Islam imparted to adherents certain attitudes towards civil authority, individual freedoms including the status of women, the standing of other religions, and Muslim social organisation. Although Deobandist thinking was nuanced and subtle, its customs and conventions required standards of behaviour and devotion that exceeded the disciplines and observances of most pious Muslims. To many non-Muslim observers and Muslim scholars, the Deobandi mindset seemed extreme and, to use a loaded and often misunderstood term, 'fundamentalist'. Deobandi religious schools, many of them located inside the Pakistani border with Afghanistan, had become centres for indoctrination rather than learning. Reciting Qur'anic scripture was deemed more important than learning to read.

A similar spirit animated both the PDPA Khalq and Parcham factions during the 1970s and 1980s, with each claiming to be Communists committed to the same cause. There was much more uniting than dividing them ideologically. But they turned on each other without restraint or remorse. Their long-running dispute was, in part, a struggle for socialist doctrinal purity. With each side believing their view was 'correct', any concession involved the embrace of 'error'. It was much easier dealing with opponents than colleagues. Opponents obviously had mistaken views, whereas the motives of colleagues were more likely to be malevolent – driven by ambition and self-interest. Afghanistan had become a society unable to grapple with nuance or subtlety in either its ethnic or religious relations.

It was not surprising that many Afghans were drawn to the Taliban in the mid-1990s. There seemed few alternatives given the long-running failure of conventional politics. A pristine society needed a pure religion. Taliban thinking was not sullied by Western liberalism nor tainted by the worldliness of the militia organisations. It was unimpressed with the least strict and most tolerant of the four schools of jurisprudence within Sunni Islam, the *Hanafi* (named after its 8th-century founder, Abu Hanifa), with which most Afghan Muslims identified. The Taliban were rigorous in their own observance of religion and unrelenting in their desire to impose it on others. They were able to attribute Afghanistan's plight to both Western secularism and Muslim moral laxity derived from Hanafi thinking.[7]

The Afghan people, the Taliban announced, were partly responsible for their sufferings. Only those who refused to compromise with error – whether temporal or spiritual – would be able to restore the nation's dignity. The movement insisted that Omar was a divinely appointed leader. He was not only right; he was incapable of being wrong. A society led by someone who knows the mind of God and lives entirely according to divine precepts would be obliged to follow his instructions because they would illuminate the path to holiness. This sense of Omar's infallibility in religious and civil matters permeated the Taliban movement. The French essayist and terrorism expert Roland Jacquard considered the Taliban to be the most ardent form of politicised Islam the world had seen. It was 'bolstered by a simple ideology, an iron discipline, and the rigorous moral values imposed by its leader'.[8]

Within a year of the movement being launched, the Taliban secured control of Kandahar with the passive approval of the people, who simply wanted relief from the chaos and corruption of the previous few years. In fact, most Afghans welcomed an end to the lawlessness and degeneracy associated with the militias. The cure would prove worse than the disease. The Taliban imposed strict Islamic law to end both the in-fighting and crime that followed the cessation of PDPA rule. In terms of nation-building, however, the Taliban were more concerned with theological purity than economic recovery. They were not interested in a better future when the aim was to more accurately replicate an exalted past. The next world was more important than the present one, and fashioning a society that conformed to modern norms was of no consequence to those pursuing a religious utopia. It was better to die poor in a shabby country than to risk a rich inheritance of heavenly splendour.

Within months and enjoying substantial material support from its theological sympathisers in Pakistan, who finally realised the scheming Hekmatyar was unable to form the stable and sympathetic Afghan Government they wanted, the Taliban movement was preeminent in the southern and central provinces of Afghanistan. The Taliban stamped out official misconduct, condemned paedophilia and declared the growing of opium poppies un-Islamic (although it would later rely on the drug trade to finance its military operations). Although the Taliban made no effort to export its theocratic vision to Pakistan or Iran, the Talibs inspired extreme movements across Central Asia and served as a role model for change elsewhere.

With the full support of Pakistan and having fashioned itself into an effective military force, the Taliban finally conquered Kabul on 27 September 1996. Massoud's forces withdrew to avoid a siege they would probably lose. In addition to military victories which were made possible by aid and assistance from Pakistan, the Taliban bribed its adversaries and coerced its enemies with promises of patronage to change sides. President Rabbani fled to territory controlled by the Northern Alliance, now styled the 'National Islamic Front for the Salvation of Afghanistan', from where he led a 'government in exile'. Overnight, the United Nations compound was breached. Najibullah, who had taken refuge rather than flee the country, was captured, beaten, castrated, tortured, shot and his body hung from a light pole on a Kabul street.⁹ It was a grisly public spectacle announcing a new era in Afghan history. The regime was neither modern nor liberal. Omar was then declared the 'Emir of Afghanistan'.

Notwithstanding its name, the movement was not led by younger students but by older veterans of the anti-Soviet struggle. They had the experience and the credibility to harvest the emotional anger and religious fervour of the rising generation shaped by the madrassas. There were also plenty of opportunists who thought it wise to embrace the winning side, and there were moderates who hoped the realities of government might temper the radicalism often associated with opposition.

Taliban Afghanistan, or 'Talibanistan' as some referred to it, soon became the world's most oppressive regime. Its edicts intruded into all facets of everyday living, as no part of life was deemed 'private'. Music and games were prohibited. The popular pastime of kite-flying was banned. Women were effectively imprisoned within their own homes, although many female Afghan scholars have argued the plight of women was little better before the Taliban seized power. They have pointed to the longstanding patriarchal nature of gender and social relations that were deeply embedded in traditional communities.

Afghans were exhorted to embrace a medieval lifestyle and to resist every modern advance and innovation. Those who defied the Taliban's narrow interpretation of Islamic texts or who were accused of crimes against people and property suffered corporal punishment, possible removal of limbs or public execution. The Taliban limited personal freedoms, restricted human rights and restrained political liberties.

The Pashtuns, mostly from Kandahar, soon dominated the Tajiks, Uzbeks and Hazaras in the country's affairs. Public officials were chosen on the basis of their religious beliefs rather than administrative expertise or their ability to speak languages other than Pashto. There were no political parties, no parliament and no elections. Omar possessed complete authority and wielded absolute power, aided by a subservient oligarchy that included his friend, the similarly tall and imposing Osama bin Laden.

The Taliban recognised no external authority and were utterly indifferent to international opinion. They continued to mount military operations against Massoud's United Front, concentrated in the Panjshir Valley, and Uzbek and Turkmen forces loyal to Abdul Rashid Dostum in the north of the country, who fashioned a secular micro-state centred on Mazar-i-Sharif and the surrounding provinces. Crops were destroyed. Whole villages were forced to relocate to neighbouring valleys, where their presence was unwelcome. Unsympathetic populations were subjected to economic blockade. The Taliban's adversaries were slaughtered in combat or killed in prisons with corpses left for domestic dogs to dismember and devour. Afghanistan's cultural heritage, which reflected the ability of tribes and religious groups to co-exist peacefully across centuries, was destroyed or discarded. Diversity – whether religious or tribal – was considered the swiftest route to apostasy.

The ultimate aim was a monochrome Pashtun Sunni Islamic society. There was constant turmoil and seemingly endless violence. For a traumatised generation of Afghans, most especially women and children, fear and suspicion were constant companions. This was a deliberate policy designed to eliminate the need for individual discretion and, therefore, the possibility of falling into religious error. Compassion, charity and generosity were not among the spiritual virtues animating the Taliban's social outlook.

The international community overlooked the conflict because it was largely preoccupied with crises elsewhere. In contrast to the 1980s, Afghanistan rarely attracted much international attention despite its pressing needs. A rare visitor was Canadian writer-turned-politician, Michael Ignatieff, who travelled to Kabul in 1996. He compared the Afghan capital with what he had seen in the former Yugoslavia and Angola where war had become endemic:

Kabul is in a class of desolation all of its own. It is the Dresden of post-Cold War conflict: mile upon mile of rubble and dust, abandoned and windswept, populated here and there by ragged families eking out their survival inside abandoned truck containers that had been sawn in half. Ranging up the hillsides were thousands of roofless and windowless houses, deserted by their former inhabitants. The warring militias had spared nothing: the blue-domed mosques, the minarets, the hospitals, the schools.[10]

Ignatieff concluded that Kabul in 1996 was 'the graveyard of the Afghan warriors' honor'.[11]

With the United States showing little interest in the people it had helped to liberate from Communist domination, Pakistan continued to meddle in Afghan affairs.[12] As many as 80 000 to 100 000 Pakistanis fought for the Taliban. They received logistical support, weapons and ammunition from across the border at a time when Pakistan was dealing with its own internal religious radicalisation and growing fears of a major conflict with India, its principal adversary. Without the assistance of Pakistani state institutions, particularly its military, the ISI and the Minister for the Interior, Naseerullah Babar, the Taliban would neither have succeeded nor survived in power very long.[13] Pakistani commandos and fighter aircraft directly attacked the combined forces of Massoud and Dostum, while the ISI helped to recruit and equip replacement Taliban fighters. The Pakistanis kept alive the vision of a wider Islamic revolution throughout Central Asia in addition to seeking economic and strategic benefits from a grateful ruling regime in Afghanistan.

The United States and most of its Western friends and allies were largely unmoved by the Taliban's rise to power. They initially believed the Taliban might have had the capacity to create a workable national government. Despite its questionable political legitimacy, the Taliban Sunnis would distract the Iranian Shi'ites, who were so detested by

Washington, and restrain Tehran's regional ambitions. American hopes were short-lived. Within months of the Emirate being proclaimed, the dark heart of the Taliban regime was revealed, ending any expectation of a positive new beginning. While Taliban excesses were contained within Afghanistan's geographical boundaries, there was no basis for an intervention and no plans for 'regime change'. Afghanistan's seat at the United Nations continued to be occupied by 'President' Rabbani, who represented the 'legitimate' government, which was still based in the north-east. Although unable to rule the country, the Rabbani-led organisation was still the government established by the 1992 agreements. The absence of United Nations' recognition meant nothing to Omar despite the Taliban's continuing attempts to secure control of the entire country and crush the resistance groups. Its tactics had not softened with time.

The Taliban's attack on Mazar-i-Sharif, the only major city controlled by the United Front, on 8 August 1998 was among its most brutal offensives.[14] A 15-hour battle was followed by a three-day massacre of more than 8000 surrendered combatants and unarmed civilians. It was likened to a genocide but attracted very little international attention because it occurred in Afghanistan – a country whose travails were troubling fewer and fewer people. There were no news reporters or television cameras to record the carnage as bodies lay in the streets for almost a week. A 150-word snippet appeared in *Newsweek*. The *New York Times* mentioned the massacre within a story about Iran (because the Taliban had entered the Iranian consulate and killed eight diplomats and a journalist) although the Australian scholar William Maley referred to a 'frenzy of killings' which were 'in all probability the worst single massacre in the entire history of modern Afghanistan'.[15] In this and other atrocities, the Hazaras were the principal targets of violence. They were told to become Sunnis – the only 'true Muslims' – or leave Afghanistan.

With the resolution of several high-profile African and East European conflicts by 2000, the United Nations Security Council refocused its attention on Afghanistan, imposing an embargo on all military support to the Taliban, whose rule continued to lack any diplomatic credibility despite the best efforts of its sympathisers in Islamabad. United Nations officials had, in fact, made explicit reference to Pakistan's unhelpful role in continuing civil strife. Pakistan and the ISI were undeterred, although the government in Islamabad was embarrassed by the Taliban's use of violence and the continuing financial drain of supporting its survival. In the absence of stable sources of public revenue, the Taliban was completely reliant on Pakistani aid. The only other nations to recognise the Taliban as the legitimate government of Afghanistan, and only after the capture of Mazar-i-Sharif, were Saudi Arabia and the United Arab Emirates. With the violence still largely contained within Afghan borders, the fighting was likely to continue indefinitely, with the Northern Alliance maintaining its defiance. Resisting the Taliban would only become a regionalised conflict if the neighbouring states were affected. It would become a globalised conflict if the Taliban ever attempted to export its jihadist ideology abroad – including to the Muslim world.

The Howard Government in Canberra shared the United Nations' dismay over Taliban rule but its reaction was limited to diplomatic statements. Few Australian governments had ever shown much interest in either Afghanistan or its people. In the second half of the nineteenth century, Afghan camel herders came to Australia and provided an important form of transport during early inland exploration. A few Afghans became involved in mining and the grocery trade but their collective influence on the Australian colonies was negligible. After Federation, the restrictive 'White Australia' immigration policy precluded Afghans from entering and settling on the continent. The ageing Afghan population was barely discernible in the population statistics. In Victoria during the 1930s, Afghans numbered fewer than 20. As Afghanistan was neutral during the two world wars and Australian attention was focused on Britain and Europe, there was little official contact between the two nations until

March 1969, when Australia decided to make the head of its diplomatic mission in Pakistan its accredited representative in Afghanistan as well. There were four Australian ambassadors to Afghanistan between 1969 and 1979 – all experienced career diplomats who had worked in developing countries before their appointment to Islamabad. Maley described the relationship between the two countries as 'low key'.[16]

Afghanistan's contact with Australia was managed by its embassy in Japan. Half of its ambassadors did not travel to Australia or present their credentials to the Governor-General in Canberra. Nevertheless, in 1975 Governor-General Sir John Kerr became the first official Australian visitor to Afghanistan.[17] He travelled to Kabul from Peshawar through the Khyber Pass and met the Afghan president, Mohammed Daoud Khan, and other government officials as part of an East Asian tour that included India, Pakistan and Iran. Following the Soviet invasion in 1979, Prime Minister Malcolm Fraser joined other Western leaders in condemning Moscow's actions and suspending diplomatic ties with Kabul. Fraser was concerned that the Soviet Union was attempting to gain influence around the Indian Ocean, including over Middle Eastern oil fields. In January 1980, he announced there would be sanctions against the Soviet Union and that the Commonwealth Government would try to prevent Australian athletes from participating in the 1980 Moscow Olympic Games as a protest against the invasion.[18] He was only partially successful, with the Australian Olympic Federation resisting pressure to boycott the games and 120 athletes deciding to compete.[19]

In February 1980, Fraser visited a number of European countries to discuss the Afghanistan invasion and possible responses. During a meeting with President Jimmy Carter in Washington, he offered the United States access to Australia's defence facilities including the Western Australian naval base, HMAS *Stirling*, and staging facilities in Darwin for United States Air Force B-52 bombers. The United States welcomed the offer but wanted to see a greater Australian military presence in the Indian Ocean region. The Minister for Defence, James

Killen, feared supporting the United States might involve Australia in operations that were 'in conflict with national interests'.[20] Fraser did not agree. He insisted that Soviet expansionism was a threat to global stability and praised the 'valiant national resistance campaign that seems to have united significant elements of Afghan society'.[21] He had little interest in Afghanistan itself; its value lay in thwarting Moscow's ambitions.

After the Fraser Government was defeated at the March 1983 election, the Hawke Labor Government confirmed in 1985,[22] and reaffirmed in 1988,[23] that it did not recognise the 'puppet' Karmal and Najibullah regimes. Australia accepted a small number of Afghan asylum seekers and supported the work of the United Nations High Commissioner for Refugees (UNHCR) and the International Committee of the Red Crescent (ICRC) among displaced Afghans in Pakistan. The continuing war in Afghanistan was routinely depicted in the Australian media as yet another superpower struggle with the Soviets supporting the Communists and the United States supporting their opponents. The Labor Government and the Coalition Opposition adhered to this narrative, although never suggesting that its close ally, the United States, had imperialistic aspirations in the region. There were consistent calls from Australian politicians for the Soviets to withdraw their forces and allow the Afghan people to determine their own future.

Australia's response was sometimes slightly more than diplomatic posturing and political rhetoric. In May 1989, less than six months after the Soviets withdrew, Australian Defence Force (ADF) personnel were training Afghans to remove landmines the 40th Army had left behind.[24] In July 1991, Australian military personnel were permitted to enter Afghanistan to monitor local efforts as part of a wider United Nations program. Indeed, Australians were the only foreign military personnel to be allowed into Afghanistan by the Najibullah regime as part of this program. Two years later, Defence Minister Senator Robert Ray decided to end Australia's contribution despite strong recommendations from the ADF, the Department of Foreign Affairs and Australia's senior defence and diplomatic representatives in Pakistan, that it continue.[25] The work was, however, far from finished. Australia's reputation in the region, and within the United Nations, had been substantially enhanced by the expertise and experience that Australian Army personnel had contributed. It was a short-sighted decision. It might have saved a little public revenue but substantial diplomatic influence was lost. The Keating Labor Government was rightly criticised for the decision.

With the end of Najibullah's regime, there was considerable discussion about the level of Australia's official representation in Kabul. The Department of Foreign Affairs settled on a consular presence with the Afghan Government nominating an honorary consul in Australia from September 1994. Australia had no dealings with the Taliban after it captured Kabul.

There was no need for the John Howard–led Coalition to have a policy on Afghanistan when it was elected to office in March 1996. It would sensibly maintain the diplomatic stance taken by the outgoing Keating Government. On its own, Australia could not constructively influence Afghan affairs and did not have a pressing desire to do so. From afar, Afghanistan resembled another failed state with a tragic history of internal discord and external interference. Neither the Najibullah nor the Taliban regimes had been able to impose domestic order, promote economic growth or conduct productive international relations. Civil unrest would continue because the Western world was unwilling to intervene. Any attempt by external parties (other than Pakistan) to assist the population would be interpreted as meddling and forcibly opposed.

After decades of civil strife, Afghanistan could not be 'fixed' by Western nations with good intentions and deep pockets. It needed long-term, carefully devised, collaborative assistance. There were no simple solutions and no obvious shortcuts. In Canberra, parliamentary discussion related to the influx of Afghan refugees by boat, their exploitation by Indonesian people smugglers, and the oppression of Afghan women and girls. The Labor member for Sydney, Tanya Plibersek, told the Parliament on 28 June 1999:

> I believe that we here in Australia and people throughout the international community cannot allow these terrible crimes against women and girls to continue with impunity. We must do everything within our power to stop what is happening to women in Afghanistan.[26]

Despite this heartfelt plea, Australia was powerless to intervene and did nothing influential.

Australia was more concerned about a range of other pressing issues nearer to home. There was a looming missile crisis in the Straits of Taiwan. There were tensions with China over ministerial visits to Taipei. The government had released the nation's first White Paper on Foreign Affairs and Trade. The end of the Suharto regime in Indonesia had the potential to cause internal unrest throughout the archipelago. Australia was monitoring United Nations' efforts to disarm Iraq of weapons of mass destruction. Most interest was concentrated on East Timor, where Australia led an international intervention in September 1999 after a referendum conducted by the United Nations to determine the province's future within the Indonesian Republic prompted widespread militia violence. Australian forces continued to be involved in East Timor, which was preparing for independence in mid-2002, and were active on the island of Bougainville, where a ceasefire had been negotiated to end a long-running civil war. Canberra was also keeping a close watch on Fiji, which had suffered its third coup d'état in 15 years, and noting the deterioration of law and order in Solomon Islands.

Afghanistan was not within Australia's area of immediate strategic interest nor adjacent to its fringes. It had never been an ally nor posed a military threat. It was simply too far away, and most government advisors believed Afghanistan did not have the capacity to make any difference to Australian affairs at home or abroad. There was never any chance the Australian Government would recognise the Taliban regime as the legitimate government of Afghanistan and, consistent with the policy of its friends and allies, it had no formal dealings with the regime. Neither *Australia's Strategic Policy*, which was published in 1997,[27] or the Defence White Paper released in 2000[28] contained a single reference to either Afghanistan or counterinsurgency warfare. (Counterterrorism was mentioned but only in terms of domestic threats and local extremists.) The emphasis was on defending Australia from unlikely attack, contributing to regional stability in the Indian and Pacific Ocean basins, attending to the rise of China as a global power and recalibrating military capability in anticipation of looming future threats. The government would continue to 'support a global security environment' that discouraged interstate aggression, noting that 'our alliance with the United States is our most important strategic relationship' and needed conscientious stewardship.

The only reminder that the Taliban continued to rule much of Afghanistan was community concern and public controversy over the arrival of Afghan asylum seekers by boat. A substantial proportion of the population did not want to see Afghans, or refugees from other Middle Eastern and Eastern Asian countries, enter Australia as 'unauthorised arrivals'. The government's view was that Afghans could come to Australia but only as part of the Commonwealth's annual humanitarian quota of 12 000 approved refugees.

There was little in reality that the Commonwealth Government could or would do about the Taliban. Australia's interests in Afghanistan had always been minor, not because the people and their plight did not matter, but because the two nations were so far apart geographically and diplomatically, and had little in common politically and economically. Other than a few academics and a handful of expatriate commentators, Australians knew little about the complexity of Afghan politics and nothing of the challenges associated with rebuilding a country whose population had been brutalised, traumatised and radicalised.

The only viable option was to wait for the Taliban to either implode as a religious movement or be overthrown by whoever among the strongmen might succeed in uniting the others. Neither scenario looked remotely likely at the turn of the millennium. The majority of the Afghan people would continue to endure a regime they opposed but were unable to resist. Unless, of course, the United States and the NATO nations were compelled to play a more direct role in Afghan affairs. When events within Afghanistan had a direct bearing on people and places beyond Afghanistan, the Taliban risked bringing down foreign military might upon itself. Quite unexpectedly, this was about to happen. The thought that the ADF might be deployed to Afghanistan seemed utterly inconceivable until the morning of 11 September 2001 when the world was about to change.

PART II
THE PLAYERS

6
ADVENT OF AUSTRALIA'S SPECIAL FORCES
1957–2003

Militaries are an important source of national pride. They embody a government's authority and its power to order domestic, regional and sometimes even global affairs. Heads of state are usually the armed forces' commander-in-chief – a position that affords them considerable prestige. At great national occasions when the past is commemorated and the present is celebrated, sailors, soldiers, and airmen and women symbolise the highest expressions of citizenship.

Throughout its short national history, Australia has made much of its military tradition with the oft-repeated claim that it uniquely encapsulates the essence of the Australian character. The Anzacs, the volunteer soldiers who fought in the Great War, were revered for their ordinariness. They did not resemble a martial caste. Most were farmers, tradesmen and labourers. They were amateurs who announced the potential of the newly formed Commonwealth. Their easygoing attitude and laconic outlook made a virtue of eschewing pride and resisting professionalism. Between 1914 and 1918, a hastily assembled citizen army had earned a reputation for being among the world's most resourceful and resilient.

For Australia, the two world wars were fought predominantly by 'hostilities only' men and women who answered the nation's call to arms in a time of emergency. After 1945, and with tensions between the United States, the Soviet Union and China becoming an enduring feature of international relations, Australia decided to maintain a small standing army in peacetime that would be supplemented with conscripts should the nation face a crisis. The *Defence Act* prevented the deployment of conscripts overseas, but the majority were willing to complete their national duty and to be deployed, if only to secure the financial rewards and social recognition that went with being a 'returned' man or woman. Young men (women were excluded) were called up for 'National Service' between 1950 and 1957 as the Korean War and the Malayan Emergency created the need for additional personnel. There was also a growing demand for men with advanced skills and for units with enhanced resourcefulness, such as the 1st Special Air Service (SAS) Company, which was raised in 1957.

The interest other nations had shown in establishing 'Special Forces' for 'irregular warfare' did not gain much ground in Australia until the mid-1950s, when the nation's commitment to the Korean peninsula decreased and the contribution of land forces to repelling a Communist insurgency in Malaya increased. The Army decided to raise two Commando companies within the Citizen Military Forces, exploiting the experience and expertise of those who had served in similar units during the Second World War. Led by full-time Regulars and staffed by part-time Reservists, their operational capacity was limited. Senior Australian officers were aware, however, that British SAS squadrons had been effectively employed against the Malayan Communists and considered the possibility of forming an Australian equivalent.

In 1956, the Army proposed establishing a mobile brigade group that could be deployed to deter and defeat hostile action anywhere in South-East Asia. The brigade would include an SAS company which could be drawn from the 'existing airborne platoon and … other men who have been trained as parachutists'. The SAS company would consist of 'specially trained men' who were competent in 'sabotage, the collection of intelligence, and similar commando-type roles'.

The emphasis was on long-range reconnaissance and destroying vital infrastructure deep within enemy territory. The core operating unit was the 'patrol'. They were small teams, numbering five to seven men, who were usually led by a non-commissioned officer (NCO). The emphasis was on stealth and endurance.

Although details of the proposal were sparse, the Menzies Government accepted the Army's advice: an SAS company would be raised as a 'form of Commando group'. It would consist of volunteers from all Army corps who were parachute-qualified (or willing to undergo parachute training), of an 'appropriate' age, without any known medical conditions, reasonably well educated with a higher level of aptitude than average soldiers, with a consistently good discipline record. Volunteers were to range between 160 and 185 centimetres in height and be no more than 82.5 kilograms in weight to ensure they could manage their way through an aircraft exit door. The emphasis in training was on creativity and initiative, strength and endurance.

From the outset there was debate on which word in the new unit's title needed to be emphasised: was it 'special', 'air' or 'service'? It was much more than an esoteric discussion. The unit would develop *special* capabilities that drew on its *airborne* expertise that would *serve* the mission of the Army. In attempting to settle the issue, the Deputy Chief of the General Staff, Major General Hector Edgar, explained that the SAS company was the 'first component in a new type of infantry regiment'. In time, he thought the new unit 'should have its own identity and build its own traditions' that would distinguish it from conventional battalions. His statement raised as many questions as it answered. As the historian David Horner observes of this period, 'to a large extent the role of the SAS in Australia's defence would depend on the SAS itself'. This observation had enduring significance as an Australian ethos began to evolve.

Over the first few years, the company was obliged to fulfil the high hopes of those who recommended its formation. The Minister for the Army, Jack Cramer, said its members would be 'Australia's most highly trained fighting men'. The brigade commander said it would be 'the cream of the army'. The Australian company would not replicate the British SAS, despite sharing a name and drawing on its experience and expertise. Its operations and organisation would reflect local conditions and customs. The Australian company did not adopt the embellishments or motto of the British SAS and gave its troops and patrols different designations. It adopted the red beret adorned with the Royal Australian Infantry Corps badge.

By 1960, the company had recruited its full complement of officers and soldiers, refined an annual training and exercise program, and secured the resources and basic facilities it needed to ensure a satisfactory level of operational readiness. Its permanent home was Campbell Barracks in the Perth suburb of Swanbourne. The location had advantages and disadvantages. In being separate from the rest of the Army, the unit could concentrate on its needs. It would be free to fashion a culture and generate momentum. The disadvantages were also apparent. Perth is the most remote capital city in the world and many of those who went there on posting wanted to stay permanently. None of the Regular infantry battalions were based in Western Australia, meaning the unit could isolate itself from the rest of the Army and, at least potentially, define its own roles and remit.

The SAS took some time to attract the mystique that would eventually envelop its members. Its training priorities routinely shifted as the tasks it would be required to perform when deployed were constantly changing. The emphasis was sometimes on reconnaissance but also included small-scale offensive operations. At its core, every aspect of SAS training was meant to expose weakness and reveal potential. Company officers and soldiers were to be known for their mental toughness and physical endurance. The most immediate challenge was explaining to the rest of the Army what the Company could do and where it fitted into the overall order of battle. These explanations were also intended to prevent the SAS being merged with the two Commando companies in the eastern states (one was located in Sydney and the other in Melbourne), some of whose members completed selection and served in the SAS.

The press certainly warmed to the SAS and actively promoted its spirit. On the fifth anniversary of the SAS's formation, the *West Australian* observed that 'the Australian Army called on its toughest, fittest, and best trained soldiers to trade their traditional slouch hats for the exclusive red beret'. The notion that SAS members were 'super soldiers' deeply troubled the Company's leadership which usually tried to avoid publicity. They wanted humility and not hubris to be the core premise in the unit's ethos. If members of the SAS were encouraged to think of themselves as 'super', they would be more likely to become self-satisfied and arrogant. The Company's members were about to find out how good they were in the only test that ultimately mattered – armed conflict.

The impending formation of the Federation of Malaysia provoked strong protests from Indonesia's President Sukarno. Malaysia's government, he claimed, would obscure Britain's continuing interference in regional affairs and pose a threat to his country. There was every possibility that an Indonesian-backed armed insurgency – a 'Confrontation' – would gather momentum, first in Brunei and then in Sarawak and Sabah (North Borneo). When clashes between insurgent and government troops became more frequent and intense, the Australian Government acceded to a request from the Malaysian Government to deploy an SAS company and the Third Battalion, Royal Australian Regiment (3 RAR). To allow for the inevitable rotation of soldiers within the SAS element, the Company was redesignated a Regiment to eventually have squadrons as sub-units. The SAS Regiment was about to commence its first operational tour of duty, arriving in Brunei on 16 February 1965.

For the next 17 months, SAS squadrons conducted a range of operations in Borneo, consisting principally of deep reconnaissance and intelligence gathering carried out through jungle patrolling.

Extant military doctrine required the SAS to establish and maintain relations with indigenous communities. Both British and Australian SAS patrols lived in jungle camps, gathering intelligence about Indonesian troop movements and protecting villages from Indonesian attack. It was important but often unappreciated work. The Australian SAS personnel earned a reputation for efficiency and effectiveness, discharging their mission in a disciplined and purposeful manner. There were instances of bravery but there was no bravado. They were still establishing a tradition, and lapses of judgment and failures of character would have been exploited by those who resented the title 'super soldier' being applied to SAS members. In any event, its squadrons and patrols did not operate alongside other Australian units who might have appreciated the breadth of their capacities and the extent of their abilities. This would soon change in another part of Asia.

In 1962, the Australian Army Training Team – Vietnam (AATTV) had been formed in Sydney and sent to different parts of South Vietnam as part of the American-led Military Assistance Advisory Group. The first rotation included officers and soldiers who had served in the SAS.[1] Their role was to mentor the South Vietnamese Army, which was opposing a rapidly escalating Communist insurgency sponsored by North Vietnam. The insurgency's aim was a single and united Vietnamese state ruled from Hanoi. By the end of 1965, and with SAS operations in Borneo likely to end in mid-1966, the decision was made to deploy an SAS squadron to South Vietnam, although some uncertainty remained about its tasking.

Members of 3 Squadron SAS conducted their final pre-deployment training in April–May 1966, presuming they would be involved in reconnaissance undertaken by patrolling. They were not involved in the 'decapitation' raids that tried to destroy the Viet Cong's political leadership. These raids were mainly conducted by American and South Vietnamese forces and a small number of Australians serving with them. From June 1966 until October 1971, the SAS would operate as part of an Australian Task Force (ATF) of two, later three, infantry battalions in addition to combat support units. They were based at Nui Dat in Phuoc Tuy province, east of the South Vietnamese capital, Saigon.

The inclusion of the SAS squadrons would ensure the gradual accumulation of vital knowledge about the enemy's organisation, tactics, weaponry and logistics. They would gain insights into the operational mindset of the Viet Cong insurgents and the North Vietnamese Army and their likely reactions and responses to threats and challenges. At the same time, patrol ambushes aimed to reduce freedom of movement and interrupt resupply. Although there were many markers of progress in terms of reducing enemy activity and enhancing community life throughout Phuoc Tuy, the insurgency increasingly resembled a civil war as the fighting continued year after year.

In 1971, the McMahon Coalition Government announced a gradual draw-down of Australian ground forces. Australian ships and aircraft were finally withdrawn in 1973. It was not until April 1975 that the war formally ended with the capitulation of the Saigon Government and reunification of the entire country as a Communist state. Over six years, close to 600 SAS members deployed to South Vietnam, many completing two rotations of 12 months' duration and a very small number completing three rotations. With the focus on reconnaissance, and harassing and ambushing the enemy in his own base area, the Regiment's members did not fight in any of the major battles involving the ATF and conducted only six bunker system attacks compared to the 240 undertaken by the infantry. The SAS suffered only two fatal casualties.

The Regiment was entitled to be proud of its service in South Vietnam. There were, inevitably, some minor disciplinary breaches, with 80 disciplinary charges laid against SAS members.[2] This represented a relatively low rate of offending when compared with the rest of the Australian Army. It was a reflection of the cohesion and camaraderie that existed within SAS patrols and squadrons. Only one charge, the accidental loss of a weapon, related to the conduct of operations. The remainder were offences ranging from insubordination to assault while off duty in the Australian base at Nui Dat or at the nearby town of Vung Tau. For the greatest part, the conduct of SAS soldiers was exemplary and their performance in the field was well calibrated to the demands of the campaign.

There were no allegations or reports of serious misconduct involving SAS personnel in South Vietnam. They felt empathy for the civilian population and generally respected their adversaries. In common with other Australian units, the SAS adhered consistently to the Law of Armed Conflict and the Rules of Engagement (ROE), which had a greater prominence in Vietnam than in previous conflicts. The latter were concise:

> Persons are not to be engaged unless a) they are positively identified as enemy, or b) they open fire first and are not obviously friendly, or c) they fail to stop when challenged and are not obviously friendly … The most important implication is 'IF IN DOUBT, DO NOT FIRE'.[3]

There were no instances of civilians being deliberately targeted or killed by SAS patrols in South Vietnam or any evidence of prisoners and wounded insurgents being executed.[4]

Unlike the Americans, the Australians never adopted a 'body count' mentality. There was, however, subtle pressure on Australian infantry battalions to 'get kills' as evidence of effective performance in the field.[5] Some Australian units in Vietnam, including the SAS, erected 'scoreboards' showing friendly and enemy kills.[6] They were uncommon among SAS rotations, given that engaging the enemy was not their main mission, and did not mean that killing civilians was condoned or a common occurrence. The massacre of between 347 and 504 unarmed Vietnamese civilians near the village of My Lai by American forces in March 1968 was universally condemned and considered a major blow to the mission. Twenty-six American soldiers were charged with a range of offences but only one junior officer, Lieutenant William Calley, was ever convicted. He was found guilty of premeditated murder.

Of the approximately 3900 ATF contacts (incidents involving gunfire) during the Vietnam Conflict, only 74 involved Vietnamese whose combatant status was unknown or unconfirmed, resulting in 84 killed and 52 wounded. These incidents were reported and recorded. There were only two such incidents involving SAS patrols. The first occurred in October 1966 when a patrol observed two men chopping a log that was lying across a jungle track. They were shot in the head and killed. A woman then appeared. She too was shot and killed. Although in a 'free fire zone' where they should not have been, the fact they hid whenever an aircraft flew overhead was insufficient justification on its own for them to be engaged. The ROE were not strictly followed in this instance.[7] The Vietnamese could not read maps and did not own watches. They had, at best, a vague sense of where the authorised and unauthorised zones probably began and ended. This incident no doubt retarded Australian efforts to gain the goodwill of the people.

The second incident involved a patrol that sighted a man carrying a bow and arrow. He was accompanied by a child. A member of the patrol thought the bow and arrow was an automatic weapon and opened fire, killing the man and wounding the child. The decision of the patrol member to fire may have been too hasty although, in his defence, the man and child were in an area where contact with the enemy was expected.[8] Although these deaths appear with hindsight to have been avoidable, there was never any suggestion that these or other SAS patrols were using unnecessary and excessive force. They were among the tragic outcomes of a war that made more sense to strategic planners than combat soldiers. None of the SAS patrols went 'rogue'.

Drawing on an enormous amount of operational data from its deployments to Borneo and South Vietnam, the Regiment was able to reform its organisation, review its manning and refine its training. The previous ten years had taken its toll and renewal was needed. The most pressing question was whether the lessons the SAS had learned from the previous decade were instructive for the one to come. Was this capability relevant to national security thinking that was increasingly preoccupied with continental defence? Was the Regiment a remnant of an era that was passing, with the consolidation of South-East Asian nation states, the decline in guerrilla warfare and a desire to avoid conflicts in which Australia did not have an obvious national interest? After decades of turbulence, nations like Australia were entering a period of relative peace and stability that appeared to obviate the need for Special Forces.

After the political protests and cultural conflicts of the 1960s, the 1970s was a time of contemplation and introspection. The Whitlam Labor and Fraser Coalition governments promoted conflicting visions of Australia and its place in the world. In the absence of regional threats, observers asked whether Australia had a defence and security problem. Indeed, was there a continuing need for standing military forces in peacetime? What prevented the nation from disarming gradually or pursuing armed neutrality? Couldn't Australia simply rely on the surrounding oceans as a bulwark against any adversary? The issue dividing the nation's politicians was whether Australia's historically close relationship with the United States was now a blessing or a bane.

Of all the Australian Army's units, the SAS probably had the least certain future. Although service with the SAS offered more opportunities for those interested in developing professional skills and experiencing physical adventure, it was far from an attractive career advancement option for either officers or soldiers. The location of Campbell Barracks also made service with the SAS less appealing to those with family and friends in the eastern states. Less than one-fifth of the Army's new recruits came from Western Australia. The majority of Australians had never even visited the geographically largest state in the Commonwealth. While the officers came and went to postings elsewhere across the country, the soldiers changed positions and were promoted within the unit. Unlike the rest of the Army, which was highly mobile, SAS soldiers spent most of their careers in Perth, where they purchased houses and settled their families. Their wives secured jobs and were frequently better paid than their husbands. The introduction in 1980 of a Special Action Force Allowance provided another imperative for soldiers to remain in the Regiment and resist postings elsewhere. A proposal in the early 1980s to relocate the Regiment to Jervis Bay on the New South Wales south coast where it would have access to an airfield, the Parachute Training School (which would move to nearby Nowra in 1986) and naval facilities was soon overcome by political considerations. The Army could not be seen reducing its already modest presence in Western Australia. The SAS Regiment would stay in the west.

A succession of commanding officers realised they had to confirm the Regiment's future and prove it could make a continuing contribution to Australia's uncertain defence needs in the absence of clear directives from either Army Office or Field Force Command. In this context there was renewed interest in amalgamating the SAS and the Commandos into a single 'Special Action Force group', a proposal first mooted in 1969. Those unaware of the distinctive remits of the two units thought they were essentially complementary functions which could be melded into a single organisation. Shortly after he became the Chief of the General Staff in 1977, Lieutenant General Donald Dunstan asked a series of fundamental questions about the future of the SAS. Why did it not have a Reserve component to make use of former members who were still resident in Western Australia? Why were recruits now drawn only from the infantry? Was a Special Forces directorate needed in Army Headquarters? And, most crucially, were there officially accepted roles and responsibilities for the SAS or was the Regiment determining its own remit to the detriment of the Army and Australia?

At Army Headquarters, a former SAS Regiment commanding officer, Colonel Neville Smethurst, commented on the 'seemingly never-ending discussion' of whether the SAS Regiment and the Commando Companies had competing or conflicting roles. He blamed the confusion and uncertainty on the 'failure to create a proper command and control organisation for special forces by Army Office and Defence'. His next comments were equivocal:

> The failure to achieve this organisation is perhaps based on a strong feeling that Special Forces are unnecessary. They may well be. If they are considered to be necessary, the vital aspects of command and control in peace and war must be considered with their roles and tasks.

By the end of 1978, formal guidance was finally issued. The remit of the SAS would be to:

> conduct long range reconnaissance and surveillance, often by deep penetration; to harass and disrupt the enemy in depth; and as a secondary role, to provide officers and NCOs who have been trained in guerrilla warfare cadre postings.

A year later, a Directorate of Special Action Forces was established at Army Headquarters in Canberra with another former SAS Regiment commanding officer (and later Governor-General), Colonel Michael Jeffery, serving as Director. By this time, officer selection for the Regiment had become more rigorous and was deliberately structured to ensure officers were selected by officers (rather than by senior non-commissioned officers (NCOs)) and assessed on their ability to lead SAS soldiers. Recalcitrant NCOs from the Vietnam era who resisted the need for change were moved on. There was also greater emphasis on SAS personnel having an experience of the wider Army, and those beyond the Regiment having a better appreciation of SAS capabilities and expertise.

Over the next decade, the Regiment's priority shifted towards counterterrorism (CT) duties, with 1 Squadron committed to this task. The need for such a capability had been demonstrated by a series of Palestine Liberation Organization (PLO) and Black September (a breakaway militant faction of the Palestinian political organisation Fatah) operations in Europe. The relevance of a terror threat in Australia was confirmed in February 1978, when Sydney's Hilton Hotel was bombed in an attempt to kill the Indian prime minister, Morarji Desai. The Tactical Assault Group (TAG) was established in 1979 and tasked the following year with developing a maritime assault and recovery capability to protect Australia's offshore gas and oil rigs, which were considered strategic assets vulnerable to terrorist attack. As these threats were unpredictable in terms of time and location, TAG duties required a constant level of operational readiness. In addition to preparing urban assault teams, the Regiment also maintained its commitment to training in long-range surveillance and harassing invaders in northern Australia.

Despite the release of Defence White Papers by the Fraser Coalition Government in 1976[9] and the Hawke Labor Government in 1987,[10] documents which were intended to provide an overview of official policy to guide departmental planning, there was continuing uncertainty about the SAS Regiment's role in time of war. This was not surprising considering the difficulty of discerning the conflicts into which Australia might be drawn and the absence of credible threats to its sovereign territory and international trade. Given the investment that had been made in developing a 'direct action' capacity through foreign exchange programs and specialist training abroad, there was obvious frustration with the 'hands off' approach of Army Headquarters in Canberra. The Regiment's capabilities could have been more closely mapped to the nation's needs to avoid wasted effort.

The SAS also wanted to know more about the Commandos' remit to prevent duplication or the revival of amalgamation plans. More than a decade after the Vietnam Conflict, fundamental questions of principle and policy were still being discussed.

The SAS nonetheless continued to attract energetic and adventurous officers and soldiers who wanted to prove their personal and professional prowess, and pursue a passion for an unconventional approach to warfare. SAS selection had become the Australian Army's most physically and mentally demanding course. An Officer Selection Course was introduced in 1975 to complement the Other Ranks Selection Course. Those who thought about attempting this course would need to prepare rigorously for 12 months and few would succeed on their initial attempt. The course was intended to determine if the officer had the strength of character and leadership attributes to command SAS soldiers. It probed the depths of an individual's character and the extent of their personal resilience. How much discomfort and pain could an officer tolerate? Having endured hunger and sleep deprivation, could they still function and make sound decisions?

The Regiment tended to attract two types of soldiers. The first were the quiet professionals, loyal to their leaders and attentive to the best interests of the team. They were dedicated to honing their tactical and technical skills to broaden the collective capability base and optimise effectiveness. The second were the big personalities, strong-willed men who resisted institutional authority and defied convention. They could inspire others with their charisma and capacity to overcome limitations and constraints. The unit needed both types: thinkers who could fight, and fighters who could think. The first type risked becoming compliant; the second were susceptible to hubris. Extremes of both types were usually excluded unless there were strong compensating factors.

With firm leadership and discipline, however, the Regiment could harvest the complementary abilities and aptitudes of its members while preventing the formation of factions and cliques that could undermine shared commitment to common purposes. The SAS did not want any officer or soldier who seemed too eager to use lethal force or appeared to derive pleasure from killing. The Regiment was not the place for psychopaths or sociopaths. Its ethos did not condone lawlessness or immorality. SAS patrols were constantly reminded to operate within the law and in a manner consistent with Army values. When exercising its 'Aid to the Civil Power Role' as part of its counter-terrorism function, these principles were critical.

War crimes were considered heinous and anathema to its identity. As SAS patrols often operated in isolation and its detachments were not always visible to commanders, a premium was placed on trust. Officers needed to have absolute trust in the discretion of senior NCOs and the discipline of Patrol Commanders to avoid even the possibility of misconduct. Any hint that an officer or soldier in a responsible position might act outside the law or in a manner contrary to the Regiment's values was a basis for removal. The potential strategic ramifications of mistakes and misconduct were so significant that commanding officers tended to act swiftly, and sometimes severely, to prevent malignant attitudes from gaining ground. No-one within the unit could be allowed to 'go rogue'. Hence, the emphasis on character.

Officers and soldiers who passed selection and were judged suitable for SAS service, albeit by those who had gone before them, were sent to the Parachute Training School. Soldiers would then undertake a five-month reinforcement training cycle of foundation courses. Officers completed the Patrol Commander's course and one of the specialist insertion skills courses (free fall, water operations and vehicle mounted) before being posted to a troop in command. Receiving the coveted sandy beret at a formal parade marked the inclusion of both officers and soldiers in the Regiment. (During the 1980s and 1990s, the 'beret parade' usually followed selection or completion of parachute training, which was scheduled immediately after selection for those who had not previously qualified. It was subsequently held after completion of reinforcement cycle training and substantially extended the 'observation' period for aspiring members.)

Long periods spent training together created strong personal bonds, including close friendships, between officers and soldiers, with the potential to distort the exercise of command. Although there were no SAS-specific courses for junior officers, soldiers gained secondary qualifications as medics or communicators. The separate Officer Selection Course was later discontinued when its training serials were incorporated into an all-ranks selection course and a common reinforcement cycle extended to 18 months. Most SAS officers were subject for extended periods to the supervision of their senior NCO trainers, another potential source of friction when junior officers were later required to exert command authority. The collective emphasis was on continuous skills improvement and the relentless pursuit of excellence. When members were not preparing for operational tasks they were training for future challenges or the increased responsibilities that came with promotion. Unsurprisingly, there was a personal dimension to the expectations associated with belonging to such a community.

While the 'officially' preferred demeanour remained the 'quiet professional' whose self-confidence precluded boasting and assured SAS personnel of anonymity, the cult of the Special Forces *warrior* gained ground in American popular culture, principally through films and television. The Regiment needed to guard against its less mature members believing they were elite soldiers who were exempt from the rules and regulations that applied to other members of the Army. The temptation to believe they were exceptional and, therefore, entitled to special treatment was contrary to Regimental values, which included humility.

Hubris was also likely to generate ill-will, if not hostility, from the conventional side of the Army, which ultimately determined priorities for resources and operational deployments. It was not surprising that the Regiment's access to resources and its ability to attract the best soldiers was resented, particularly by some infantry officers. Lacking an awareness of its culture and ready to accept unsubstantiated stories of irregularities, outsiders thought the Regiment did things its way rather than the Army's way, and that it managed to avoid external scrutiny because of its location in Western Australia. While some senior officers were perhaps unreasonably suspicious of the SAS, it was one of very few Army units with an operational remit in peacetime, they did not interfere because the Regiment consistently fulfilled its tasking.

There were few calls for comprehensive organisational reform because the Regiment gave the government options for a measured Australian response to defence and diplomatic crises. This was certainly true after the first military coup in Fiji during 1987, and before the removal of Iraqi forces occupying Kuwait in 1990–91. On neither occasion was an SAS squadron needed but the Regiment's preparedness impressed the government. Over the next decade, SAS-qualified medics and signallers were detached to United Nations missions in Western Sahara, Rwanda and Cambodia, and an SAS personal and force protection team engaged Somali gunmen north of the capital Mogadishu in August 1994, killing two of them. Others separately deployed as peacekeeping observers in Egypt, Lebanon and Kashmir. Driven by the operational readiness required for counter-terrorism, this level of preparedness came at a very substantial cost. The Regiment's worst training accident occurred on 12 June 1996 when two Black Hawk helicopters collided over the High Range Training Area near Townsville. Fifteen SAS personnel and three Army aviators were killed.[11]

By the end of the 1990s, the SAS were keen to deploy as a formed unit. They finally had their chance in 1998 when the Australian Government decided to send a squadron to Kuwait. The SAS would be part of an American-led operation that was designed to prevent Iraq's attacks on United States Air Force surveillance aircraft, and force it to comply with United Nations resolutions on weapons inspections. The Iraqi regime backed down, admitted the inspectors, and the Australians returned home. It had nonetheless been a chance to raise a tactical headquarters and prepare for battle as part of an integrated international operation. The Regiment did not have to wait long for another opportunity to deploy. This time it was much nearer to home.

The majority of East Timorese never accepted the invasion and subsequent occupation of their land by Indonesian forces at the close of Portuguese colonial rule in 1975. They were given a chance to determine their own future in an internationally supervised independence referendum on 30 August 1999. After more than 78 per cent of the population voted for independence from Indonesia, pro-Jakarta militias and elements of the Indonesian security forces plunged the territory into a maelstrom of death and destruction.[12] Pro-independence politicians and their families, Christian organisations and their leaders, and international aid agencies and their staff were targeted for violent reprisals. The SAS assisted with the evacuation of Australian nationals, United Nations officials and Timorese refugees before the Indonesian Government conceded it had lost control of the province and consented to the deployment of the Australian-led International Force East Timor (INTERFET) in mid-September 1999.

Together with personnel from the New Zealand SAS (NZSAS) and the British Special Boat Service (SBS), officers and soldiers from 3 Squadron of the Australian SAS were among the first international forces to arrive in the provincial capital, Dili, where they secured the airport and the harbour. Over the following weeks the SAS operated in the Timorese hinterland mounting vehicle and foot patrols, and conducting surveillance in former militia-dominated areas. The two main engagements were at Suai on 6 October, when two SAS soldiers were wounded after an attempted ambush, and at Aidabasalala on 16 October.[13] SAS personnel also led INTERFET's insertion into the former Portuguese enclave of Oecusse (in West Timor) on 22 October.[14]

East Timor was a critical moment for the SAS. This was the Regiment's best opportunity since 1971 to demonstrate its continuing value to the nation and, just as importantly, its importance to the conventional Army. Within a few weeks, the Regiment had shown that it was mobile, nimble, agile and flexible. The SAS was self-contained and brimming with self-confidence. SAS officers and soldiers were eager to work and never gave any hint of being strained or stressed. Unsurprisingly, their 'can do' attitude made them the force of choice, especially when a commander faced a situation requiring creativity and ingenuity. The deployment was more a test of regimental organisation than the professional skill of individual personnel. The militias comprised poorly trained, ill-disciplined villagers, most of whom were capable of little more than bravado before they slipped across the border into Indonesian West Timor. These groups were reinforced by well-trained but deeply vengeful Indonesian military personnel in civilian clothing, who were more of a challenge. With the militia groups either dissolved or defeated, 1 Squadron replaced 3 Squadron in December 1999, before it was withdrawn in February 2000 to be followed by troop level rotations until the end of the year.[15]

INTERFET handed responsibility for East Timorese affairs to the United Nations Transitional Administration in East Timor (UNTAET) on 25 October 1999, in anticipation of East Timor becoming an independent and sovereign nation on 20 May 2002. The Meritorious Unit Citation (MUC) was awarded to 3 Squadron on 25 March 2000 for its achievements in East Timor. The MUC was awarded despite questions being asked about its conduct. Seventeen allegations involving murder, torture and assault were referred for investigation by the Military Police (MP) at the end of 2000.[16] The Chief of Army and former INTERFET commander, Lieutenant General Peter Cosgrove, told reporters: 'I am hoping that the outcome will show that our soldiers behaved properly. If they haven't behaved properly we will take very resolute action. It is extremely out of character for these sort of events to be alleged against the sort of soldiers who are presently involved in the investigation'.[17]

Public confidence in the SAS was undiminished when the Howard Government sent SAS personnel to board the Norwegian cargo ship MV *Tampa* off Christmas Island in August 2001, and prevent the disembarkation of 439 asylum seekers. Using the SAS to 'subdue' the asylum seekers was considered heavy-handed by the government's critics and an 'over-reaction' by a former squadron commander.[18] By way of contrast, the SAS mission to arrest the Togo-registered MV *South Tomi*, which was caught poaching Patagonian Toothfish from the Australian Antarctic Economic Zone earlier in the year, was widely acclaimed.[19] Goodwill towards the Regiment within the media, however, never seemed to last long.

The findings of an Australian Army Military Police Special Inquiry into the 17 war crimes allegations relating to operations in East Timor were reviewed by the Australian Federal Police (AFP) in April 2002. Although no 'additional material' substantiating the most serious allegations had been uncovered, there were several potential witnesses to the alleged mistreatment of detainees.[20] Early in October 2002, ABC News reported that investigators attached to the United Nations' serious crimes group had exhumed the remains of two militiamen from a mass grave on the outskirts of Dili.[21] The men were killed when they attempted to ambush an SAS vehicle near Suai on 6 October 1999. Nine militiamen were injured and more than 100 were captured. It was alleged that at least one of the dead had been shot at close range with a handgun by a senior SAS member who was angered at the injuries that had been inflicted on his colleagues. In other words, the man was executed. At the end of 2002, the only evidence of misconduct that had been uncovered during an investigation that had been running for two years was the mistreatment of a corpse.

The shadow Defence spokesman, Senator Chris Evans, asked the Minister for Defence, Senator Robert Hill, to explain:

> why has it taken more than two years to conduct an internal investigation into allegations that war crimes were committed by the SAS in East Timor? If there is no substance to those allegations, don't the troops concerned deserve to have their names cleared as soon as possible? Why, then, haven't more resources been allocated to the investigation, and why does the public have to learn about the investigation from media reports?[22]

Hill replied that the investigation was 'complex ... and required interviews not only of Australian personnel but of personnel from other military forces'. More than 350 people would eventually be interviewed in East Timor, Britain, New Zealand and Australia. The minister said those accused of misconduct deserved an objective and thorough investigation of the claims being made against them, and he would not comment further.

The exhumed bodies were subjected to extensive examination by a pathologist while ballistics experts examined bullet fragments and confirmed they were 'portions of 5.56 calibre projectiles made by Australian Defence Industries for the ADF'. Neither militia member had been shot at close range or with a handgun. A preliminary report was presented to the Chief of Army in February 2003. The Inquiry also found that a senior NCO in the SAS intelligence cell who was involved in the interrogation of wounded militia from Suai was falsely accused of assaulting the men to extract information.[23] According to the same NCO, these allegations originated not with witnesses but with the Australian MP. He stated:

> The SAS are hand-picked people of integrity, whereas MPs, in my experience, are volunteers who are not going to get promoted

in their own unit so they go somewhere where straightaway they are somebody. They were saying they were doing it properly (handling detainees) and everyone else was doing it wrong.[24]

The MPs apparently thought prisoner abuse was 'institutionalised' within the SAS and, according to SAS personnel, were employing innuendo and rumour as part of a long-running vendetta that had escalated into the protracted inquiry that had eventually shown most of the allegations were baseless.

There were four instances where the allegations had substance but the conduct was considered not to have been illegal.[25] Although prisoners were bound and deprived of sleep during their interrogation, the allegation that they were tortured, assaulted and held without food or water for 90 hours was not substantiated. Although their treatment was described as 'robust' and consistent with the relevant Geneva Convention, the Army indicated it would amend its interrogation guidelines. The most serious finding was that an SAS member (a senior NCO) had kicked the body of a dead militia member. Although a potentially illegal act, and the man was clearly dead, the accused soldier could have argued he was ensuring the militiaman was not pretending to be dead.

The senior NCO was charged with misconduct. After eight preliminary hearings, the case was finally heard by the Defence Force Magistrate.[26] The prosecution had difficulty producing witnesses although a group of around 50 Special Forces soldiers from Australia, Britain and New Zealand were reported to have been present during the alleged incident. The prosecution case ultimately relied on the evidence of three New Zealanders. In a *Sydney Morning Herald* article published before the trial, journalist Deborah Snow was told by an investigator that 'the legendary team spirit in the regiment – its greatest strength in times of peril – became … a near impenetrable barrier'.[27] There were also suggestions the SAS was concealing other misconduct. One investigator remarked: 'Heard of the Cosa Nostra?

It was that sort of brick wall. The regiment is family. It does not shit on its own. They think they're above the law, beyond the law, can do what they damn well like and they're never going to be held accountable.' The fact of an investigation and the convening of a trial showed the SAS would be held accountable. The counter-claim was that some of its members were relying on their resistance to interrogation training to prevent the detection of misconduct so as to avoid prosecution.

On 8 August 2003, the charges against the senior NCO were dropped when, at the last minute, the New Zealand witnesses reportedly refused to testify.[28] Nearly four years had passed since the alleged offence. Senator Evans was critical of the entire Inquiry process:

> Because the allegations have not been tested and a full report not provided, the slur against our troops will remain … it is completely unacceptable that a member of the Australian Army has had to suffer such prolonged and unnecessary stress associated with a trial that has never got past pre-trial hearings.[29]

A series of investigations had not led to any other charges being laid.

The senior NCO complained about the way his prosecution was handled, focusing on the conduct of the MPs. In February 2004 the Chief of Army, Lieutenant General Peter Leahy, conceded 'there were errors in the process and I have provided an unreserved apology to the soldier concerned'.[30] Lieutenant General Leahy admitted 'there were organisational failures such as the length of the investigation'.

Beyond the personal implications, the 'body kicking' episode left the SAS Regiment with an unwanted reputation for unnecessarily aggressive behaviour and impatience with formal processes. Its reputation had been sullied and its relationship with the MPs soured. SAS members believed the MPs were pursuing a vendetta against their Regiment which had subsumed their close protection work. Notwithstanding the adverse publicity, and suspicions that other incidents of misconduct in East Timor might have been concealed, intimations that any problems resided in the Regiment's isolation from the rest of the Army were partly addressed when Special Operations Command (SOCOMD) was established in 2003.

Work on combining Special Forces assets had begun with the formation of an operational headquarters in 1990. Headquarters Special Forces (HQSF) would bring the SAS Regiment and 1st Commando Regiment (which had started as the 1st Commando Company in 1955; 2nd Command Company was raised in Melbourne the same year) under a unified command that understood their capabilities, represented their interests and gave them a profile at the strategic level. The SAS Regiment would undertake a range of small-scale operations at the strategic level while the Commandos would undertake large-scale raids and tactical offensives. By 2000 there were compelling arguments for HQSF to be turned into a separate command. The attacks on the Pentagon and World Trade Center provided the impetus for the inauguration of SOCOMD on 5 May 2003.

It was modelled on existing British and American commands and given the motto 'The Cutting Edge'. The aim was to bring together all elements from across the ADF that conducted or supported Special Operations within a unified structure under a major general. It included the SAS Regiment, the 1st Commando Regiment, the 4th Battalion (Commando (Cdo)), the Royal Australian Regiment (4 RAR (Cdo)), special operations engineers, logisticians and trainers. Unintentionally, it looked like an army – albeit an unconventional one – was being created within an army. There was the possibility that SOCOMD might engender an attitude of being apart from, rather than integral to, the Australian Army and its conventional combat units. It would also create a command position with an enormous workload for the incumbent.

Well before SOCOMD was envisaged, 4 RAR had been designated a Regular Army commando unit. The Deputy Chief of the General Staff (DCGS) directed in 1997 that 4 RAR (Cdo) would conduct offensive and recovery operations beyond the range and capability of other ADF Force Elements. The Commander of Special Forces was instructed to 'develop a plan for the transfer of the domestic counter-terrorism responsibility from SASR to 4 RAR (Cdo). A special recovery capability will be developed post 2001 and will be subject to a separate directive.' The transfer was to be complete by the third quarter of 2001 – after the Sydney Olympic Games.

4 RAR (Cdo) would consist of a regimental headquarters, four commando companies, a headquarters company and a signals squadron and was initially raised on the basis of one commando company per year to be completed by 2001. Unlike the SAS which occupied its own barracks, Commandos were based at Holsworthy Barracks in south-west Sydney, which was also home to engineers, aviators and the MP. In September 1999, a small 4 RAR (Cdo) detachment deployed to East Timor as part of INTERFET to provide personal protection and interpreting services. During planning for INTERFET the decision was made not to include a commando company among the deployed forces, despite B Company being certified for operations. This decision may have marked the beginning of escalating tensions between the Commandos and the SAS. The following year Commandos were involved in evacuating civilians from the strife-torn Solomon Islands. By this time the growth path that was set out in the 1997 directive was disrupted by the decision to deploy 4 RAR (Cdo) as a light infantry battalion to UNTAET in 2001. It was only able to deploy two light infantry companies in the battalion group to UNTAET. Two other commando companies were raised on its return.

As expected, there were elements of commonality between the Commando and SAS Regiments. Those who aspired to service in 4 RAR (Cdo) or the 1st Commando Regiment underwent a selection course. Those deemed suitable for Commando service received their initial employment training as part of a 'reinforcement cycle' before being posted to a commando company where they would receive their distinctive Sherwood Green beret and undertake further specialist courses. The emphasis was on complementarity rather than competition. The Commandos were not meant to challenge the SAS for pre-eminence. They would relieve the SAS Regiment of tasks that were deemed to be distractions from its core role of special reconnaissance. There was also the matter of Perth being geographically isolated from the nation's largest population centres and the assets that would be needed in the event of a major terrorist incident.

There would be some tension between strong-willed men but any rivalry needed to be channelled towards increasing efficiency and raising effectiveness in the pursuit of national goals. No-one believed this tension could lead to competitions that would be settled by increasing propensity for misconduct. There were complaints on both sides of the continent that their respective roles were indistinct or blurred despite the clear guidance provided by the DCGS in 1997. The problems could be attributed to the directive's implementation, and the coincidence of terrorist attacks in 2001 (New York and Washington DC) and 2002 (Bali) that hindered the transfer of responsibility. Army doctrine had not added much clarity, merely stating the Commandos were to 'span the gap between conventional infantry operations and unconventional operations'. In its war roles there was an expectation that 4 RAR (Cdo) would conduct large-scale offensive operations, develop a direct action capability and, when necessary, mount recovery operations deep in enemy held or dominated areas.

Within five years of its transition to Special Operations, 4 RAR (Cdo) had established a stable platform from which to continue the unit's expansion; recruit, select and train suitable members; and turn experience into expertise. Customs were being devised and traditions were laid down, not unlike the journey the SAS Company had undertaken between 1957 and 1964. There was now a distinct Commando approach to problems and their solutions. 4 RAR (Cdo) already had the advantage of a strong Commando heritage associated with the 1st Commando Regiment which predated the SAS Company. Special Forces skills training was mainly provided by former SAS personnel posted to the new unit. Also in its favour, there were no entrenched bad practices to eradicate, malignant cultures to transform or a reactionary 'old guard' to remove. The Commandos, as they were known, shared their base at Holsworthy with mainstream Army units (albeit within a fenced perimeter that required swipe card access) and were readily accessible to visiting politicians and commanders based in Sydney and Canberra. They were pioneers breaking new ground but subject to more direction and closer scrutiny than the SAS had been at its creation.

Although the establishment of SOCOMD marked a new beginning for Australian Special Operations, there were organisational flaws and structural weaknesses that would take time to identify and remediate. The first commanders were faced with an array of challenges including the need to manage competing demands for Special Forces capabilities. SOCOMD units were often the government's 'first choice', but not because the nation's politicians were acquainted with operational concepts or familiar with critical capabilities. By a variety of means they had become convinced there were few limits to what Special Forces officers and soldiers could achieve and without casualties. There was another benefit: Special Operations were always shrouded in secrecy and could not be publicly discussed. This appealed to officers and soldiers who possessed 'protected identity status' and further enhanced their 'special' status. It also made it easier for the government to control the political narrative in times of controversy.

The Command's units and members were certainly trusted to comply with the Law of Armed Conflict, to respect non-combatants and be humane in their treatment of prisoners. Special Forces status did not confer on any regiment or individual the right to break the law, instil fear into the hearts of civilian populations or dispose of anyone they detained. Given the sensitive scenarios in which Special Forces personnel found themselves, a premium was placed on compliance, control and restraint. Notwithstanding allegations of misconduct in East Timor, the conduct of inquiries and the dogged pursuit of truth by senior officers could not have led any member of SOCOMD to believe that war crimes were tolerated or that they were anything other than serious offences that deprived the nation and the Command of moral authority and mission success. Some Australian soldiers might have been inclined to break the law but the Australian Army was not lawless. Indeed, its attitude to the Law of Armed Conflict was a corporate strength from which it could draw when confronted by an adversary whose only law was their determination to prevail. Respect for law would fundamentally separate the opposing sides in what would become Australia's longest war.

7
EVOLUTION OF A COMMITMENT: THE TALIBAN REVIVAL
2001–2005

The Liberal Party led by John Howard won office at the March 1996 general election with a domestic policy agenda focusing mainly on budget repair and public debt reduction. Despite the lack of detail in its previous defence and security policy statements, the Howard Government soon demonstrated a readiness to deploy the Australian Defence Force (ADF) in pursuit of Australia's national interests. In the wake of widespread militia violence following an independence referendum in East Timor in 1999, the government authorised the largest overseas deployment of Australian forces since the end of the Vietnam Conflict in 1972. To restore civil order and facilitate United Nations supervision of East Timor's transition to independent nationhood, the International Force East Timor (INTERFET) consisted of military personnel and equipment from 20 nations, including 5500 Australians and units of the Royal Australian Navy, the Australian Army and the Royal Australian Air Force.

The INTERFET deployment was a remarkable diplomatic and military achievement that drew on support from many Asian nations. Most noteworthy was the absence of American ground forces. Prime Minister Howard revealed:

> I had thought the Americans would provide ground forces. During a long telephone conversation with President Bill

Clinton, he indicated that putting 'American boots on the ground' was not possible. I learnt something during that conversation that I had not appreciated earlier. The Americans had extracted a substantial peace dividend from the end of the Cold War.[1]

Washington was left in no doubt that Canberra was disappointed that Australian solidarity with the United States had not been reciprocated. The Americans did, however, provide airlift, logistics and intelligence while a backup Marine force were deployable from an assault ship anchored off the coast of Dili. It was now clear that Australia's reliance on the United States for security required a continuing commitment for the trans-Pacific alliance to remain relevant and responsive.

In early September 2001, Prime Minister Howard departed Australia for an official visit to the United States as the guest of President George W Bush. He would be in Washington DC to mark the 50th anniversary of the Australia – New Zealand – United States (ANZUS) Security Treaty. On the morning of 11 September 2001, Howard woke early and was preparing for a series of official appointments and public duties in the American capital when two commercial aircraft were flown deliberately into the World Trade Center in New York City, and a third was flown into the Pentagon in Washington DC. Both towers of the World Trade Center later collapsed. The '9/11' attacks were widely portrayed as 'an act of war' against the American state and, more broadly, represented an assault on Western values. Nearly 3000 people were dead and another 25 000 were injured.

Despite strenuous denials, the Islamic terrorist organisation al-Qaeda was quickly identified, and then reliably confirmed, as the perpetrator. Its leader, the wealthy Saudi-born Islamic militant Osama bin Laden, was deemed the mastermind. The Bush Administration demanded the Afghan Government surrender all al-Qaeda leaders for questioning and then expel its members. The United States was not considering invasion at this point. Having thwarted the Clinton Administration, the Taliban initially attempted to negotiate with its successors in Washington. The regime wanted corroborated evidence of bin Laden's complicity in the attack; once this was provided, it proposed relinquishing him into the custody of another Muslim nation for interviews. After obfuscating for several weeks, the Taliban refused Washington's demands. The United States then decided to initiate the 'global war on terror'.

The ultimate objectives of this 'war' were unclear other than effectively re-ordering power relations across the Middle East and Central Asia. It was apparent, however, that the 'global war on terror' was a different kind of conflict. Its principal objective was preventing terrorists from acquiring and deploying weapons of mass destruction. The first mass attack was '9/11'. It would not be the last if terrorists managed to get their hands on nuclear, biological and chemical weapons. The new adversary was the global terrorist network. The rise of these networks was a consequence of the nation-state era in world history coming to a close.

Groups like al-Qaeda were arguably the products of the de-centralised, privatised, globalised and networked world that was replacing the ordered system of nation-states that had been in existence for 250 years. The 'market state' was oriented around trade and wealth creation rather than the territory and identity that defined the traditional nation-state. Terrorist groups were interested only in promoting (or imposing) their globalised ideology. They would do this by disabling markets, disrupting economies and dividing populations. As inhabitants of a country without international land borders and the largest ice-free maritime zone in the world, Australians continued to see themselves as citizens of a nation-state. As a trading nation and a people accustomed to international travel, the threat to Australian prosperity and freedom of movement was not difficult to imagine. Australia's contribution to this new kind of war would soon become clear.

On returning to Australia, Prime Minister Howard convened a Cabinet meeting for 14 September. At the subsequent press conference, he told journalists that Cabinet believed 'the provisions of the ANZUS Treaty should be invoked in relation to the attack upon the United States'.[2] In answer to a journalist's question about the extent of Australia's military support to the United States, Howard explained that 'we would be willing to participate to the limit of our capability. The Americans haven't at this stage made any request for particular support but we will consider any request that is made.' Afghanistan, a country that had never featured in Australian defence and security planning, was now the centre of attention. A number of options for deploying Australian assets were considered although the foremost contribution would be symbolic. Australia's presence mattered substantially more than its participation.

In agreeing to be part of a joint operation, Australia was dependent on the United States for key mission parameters that were still unknown, such as when the invasion would begin and the force elements needed to defeat the Taliban. Practicalities aside, Australia's willingness to be part of an invasion force was primarily intended to strengthen its alliance with the United States. As journalist Graeme Dobell observed: 'the language of the alliance is of an unbroken covenant, but the hard political reality is always of the need to decide, choose and commit'. Australia's alliance with the United States required constant attention. It was not self-activating, calling instead 'for an act of will – a moment of choice at a particular time'.[3]

Rather than foregrounding the need to strengthen the alliance as the principal reason for Australian involvement in Afghanistan, the government told the Australian people that toppling the Taliban and destroying al-Qaeda would lessen the threat of terrorism at home and abroad. Failing to respond forcefully to al-Qaeda in Afghanistan would embolden like-minded groups around the world, including those harbouring ill-will against Australia, to persist with attacks on civilian populations. The government could not be any more specific about either the nature or the extent of the benefits that would flow to Australia from being part of the invasion force. Afghanistan posed no direct threat to Australia nor, at that stage, did al-Qaeda. If pressed, the Australian Government could point to the importance of American support during a time of global uncertainty.

Before the ground invasion began, and conscious the Americans had no interest in a protracted occupation, the German Government hosted a conference in Bonn to consider the form and structure of post-Taliban government in Afghanistan. Some 30 Afghan delegates, including representatives from the major factions, were joined by the United Nations' Envoy on Afghanistan and the United States' Envoy to the Afghan Opposition to devise an agreement that would give Afghanistan a stable and consultative political future.[4] The 'Bonn Agreement' provided for an interim authority that would operate for six months under the leadership of Hamid Karzai, a former mujahideen leader and anti-Taliban militia commander.[5] A transitional administration would then be established by an emergency *loya jirga* (Pashto for 'grand assembly'). It would govern for two years until a follow-up *loya jirga* settled on a new constitution that would provide for free and fair elections.

By 2004, Afghanistan would ideally have a United Nations–recognised central government relying on a democratic mandate for its legal authority and political legitimacy. The Bonn Agreement also proposed the formation of an International Security Assistance Force (ISAF). It was sanctioned by the United Nations Security Council and led initially by a senior British officer. ISAF would have three main tasks: maintain security in Kabul 'and other urban areas as deemed necessary'; train the national security forces; and supervise the repair of vital infrastructure.[6] The establishment of ISAF would preclude Pakistani interference and ideally prevent any return to warlord violence. The agreement rested on two presumptions. First, the Taliban would be defeated and its leaders killed, captured or exiled. Second, the Taliban's military defeat would secure its organisational demise. The movement would not recover from the invasion nor be revived beyond Afghanistan's borders.

Once the Bush Administration decided to invade Afghanistan, it seemed the fate of the Taliban regime was sealed. Most people believed the United States and its allies would prevail and do so swiftly. Australia knew it was on the winning side. Operation 'Enduring Freedom' began on 7 October 2001. The ground invasion of Afghanistan was preceded by air raids and cruise missile strikes. The United States Air Force and Navy would drop 18 000 bombs, of which 10 000 were precision munitions, during the ensuing air campaign. Ten days later, Prime Minister Howard announced that a 'special forces detachment [would] go to selected locations as decided by the Chief of the Defence Force in conjunction with Coalition force commanders to conduct combined operations'.[7] Some 150 members of the Special Air Service (SAS) Regiment would deploy alongside other ADF personnel and assets. This number was consistent with the Special Forces contributions of Canada and New Zealand. The Australians were sent where they could be most useful. The Americans knew they were mobile and agile, and would use them across the country confident in their ability to complete their assigned tasks.

As expected, Taliban and al-Qaeda resistance to the invasion force was fierce but short-lived. In collaboration with the Northern Alliance, by then without its charismatic leader Ahmad Shah Massoud, who was assassinated in a suicide bombing two days before '9/11', the Taliban was defeated militarily on 7 December when Mullah Omar left his home in Kandahar to hide in neighbouring Zabul province.[8] Estimates of the number of Taliban killed in the initial invasion range from 8000 to 12 000.[9] An accurate number would never be known.

Remnants of Taliban and al-Qaeda leadership fled to the mountainous region around Tora Bora (in the east of Afghanistan), where they were pursued by British, American and Australian Special Forces. Others crossed the border into Pakistan, which had again become a safe haven. Although the principal Coalition target, Osama bin Laden, was not captured, al-Qaeda's ability to commit terrorist acts had been substantially reduced. The Taliban had taken two years to gain the ascendancy across much of Afghanistan; it had been defeated within two months. Australia's role in the invasion might have been minor but it produced more than modest results.

The ADF personnel deployed to Afghanistan quietly departed Australia in November 2001 and were absorbed immediately into American command systems. The SAS detachment was too small and too reliant on its Coalition partners to conduct independent operations because, as ever, it did not deploy with the support assets it needed. All three SAS 'Sabre' Squadrons deployed to Afghanistan in separate rotations: 1 Squadron from November 2001 – April 2002; 3 Squadron from April – August 2002; and 2 Squadron from August – November 2002.

The initial focus of Australian operations was southern Afghanistan around Kandahar and the Helmand Valley adjacent to the border with Iran. The SAS operated initially with United States Marines from Task Force 58 located at Forward Operating Base (FOB) 'Rhino' before shifting to eastern Afghanistan, where the fighting was most intense. In addition to a large number of long-range reconnaissance and direct-action missions, the biggest operation involving Australian SAS personnel was 'Operation Anaconda' in March 2002.[10] Conducted on the Paktia provincial border with Pakistan, this was part of a major international offensive in which more than 500 Taliban fighters were killed. SAS patrols moved clandestinely into the Shah-i-Kot Valley ten days before the first combat operations to provide in-depth intelligence of enemy positions and movements. During the operation, another Australian patrol detected a potential escape route for al-Qaeda's leadership, including a man later identified as bin Laden's deputy, Ayman al-Zawahiri, that was subsequently the target of air strikes.[11] As the operation wound down, SAS operators engaged and killed a number of al-Qaeda and Taliban fighters. By the time 3 Squadron arrived, the Australians were based at Bagram and did most of their work on the eastern border with Pakistan, predominantly from Khost to Jalalabad. By May 2002, the entire country had been subdued. There continued to be isolated rocket and mortar attacks on Coalition forces and occasional targeted bombings but the need for major operations against enemy formations had ended. The new Afghan National Army was being trained and refugees were returning to their homes.

During six months of high-intensity operations, Australian SAS personnel had demonstrated their diverse skills and capacity for hard work. There was one incident, however, that would attract considerable media attention over the next three years. It was not a notable success but an apparent mistake.

On 14 May 2002, two vehicle-inserted patrols (callsigns Redback India 1 and Redback Kilo 3) took overwatch positions at night on two sides of high ground above a mountain track in the Taraka Valley, 130 kilometres south-east of Kabul, not far from the border with Pakistan. The track was thought to be used by Taliban and al-Qaeda fighters. At first light, Kilo 3 realised they were perilously close to a Russian-built heavy machine gun in a well-established firing position. The existence of the weapon and the location of the fortification were later explained as part of a long-running dispute between two neighbouring villages, Bhalkhel and Sabari, over possession of a nearby stand of trees. At dawn, the Australian patrol was observed by armed fighting-aged males from Bhalkhel. A gunfight ensued throughout the day and into the next evening. It did not take long for the Afghans to realise they were firing at Coalition forces. An Apache helicopter conducted a Hellfire missile attack during the day and an American Hercules AC-130 gunship was directed to provide nighttime air support into Sabari, killing at least nine men and injuring another 16. The Australians withdrew under the cover of darkness.

The *Age* newspaper claimed three years later that the 'first details of the real story began to emerge when the *New York Times* reported that a brief battle in which the Australian troops played a key role showed how mistakes, confusion and faulty information from Afghan factions handicapped Coalition operations'.¹² The newspaper

> described a shambolic fight in which five SAS soldiers were caught in the open. With bullets flying around them, they dropped their heavy packs and ran for higher ground. While they fought off the attackers they believed to be al-Qaeda or Taliban fighters, the second SAS team, approaching in its vehicles, was attacked by tribesmen from the second village [Sabari], who believed they were under attack.

This story – of Australians being caught in the middle of a local tribal feud – cast serious doubt on the official version. A *Time* journalist was told by residents of Sabari that Coalition officers offered an apology at the nearby village of Zambar the next day. This claim was not independently verified. That the villagers were reportedly never paid the financial compensation for the death of loved ones or the destruction of their property by the Coalition further undermined the credibility of the claims.¹³ The journalist simply repeated what he had been told without checking the facts.

With the Australian Government adhering to the claim that the SAS patrol had received enemy fire over 12 hours and was extracted by vehicle patrol under fire that night, the matter essentially faded from view until details of unresolved tensions within one SAS patrol were conveyed to the media, reviving assertions of subterfuge. In essence, immediately after the Australians returned to their base on 16 May 2002, the patrol members of Redback Kilo 3 accused their patrol command of poor judgment and wanted him removed. The Patrol Commander pressed for one of his troopers to be disciplined for taking a hat and a rifle from a dead villager as trophies. This was a serious matter because it involved a possible war crime. The squadron commander segregated the patrol and relieved Redback

Kilo 3 of operational duties. Two soldiers were subsequently issued 'notice to show cause' letters, inviting them to explain why they should not be discharged from the Army.[14] They insisted the hat and the 'pocket litter' were taken from the dead Afghan for intelligence analysis. Removing an enemy weapon from the battlefield certainly was a standard practice. The patrol suffered from severe 'internal dysfunction', according to an official report, leading to the Patrol Commander resigning from the Army in protest at what he asserted was an official cover-up of misconduct.[15] There were many lessons to be learned from the causes and consequences of these severely strained relationships, and opinions varied within the Regiment about whether enough time was set aside to learn them. This was not, however, the end of the matter.

A young non Special Forces qualified signaller attached to 152 Signal Squadron SAS Regiment, who was posted to Afghanistan with 3 Squadron in April 2002, told *Time* magazine in May 2005 that he was 'pressured to write a report which reflected badly on the patrol commander'.[16] An official inquiry found no evidence of any such pressure being applied to the signaller although he was asked to limit his comments to the Patrol Commander's leadership rather than the specifics of the Bhalkhel-Sabari incident. The signaller later committed suicide, claiming he had killed a child during the engagement.[17] Including evidence gathered by the *Christian Science Monitor* and *Time*, there was nothing to suggest any children were killed in the engagement. Further, the Patrol Commander was confident the signaller had not personally killed anyone or gone close to doing so. The signaller had earlier spoken of being keen to 'get his first kill' and subsequently appeared to have developed a preoccupation with death, viewing a number of short internet videos depicting beheadings. At most, he fired a few warning shots at Afghans attempting to man the heavy machine-gun.

The detailed inquiry following his suicide led to an SAS Regimental policy change. The inclusion of a non-qualified Special

Forces soldier in any long patrol now had to be personally approved by the commanding officer of the SAS Regiment. The principal finding was that only well-prepared operators should be exposed to close-quarters combat of the kind associated with operations in Afghanistan. (All deploying support staff, although not embedded in patrols, were later required to complete long courses in advanced weapons handling, basic close-quarters battle and heightened personal awareness.) The report on the signaller's suicide noted that in Afghanistan he 'found himself in a crucible of intense danger where the stark realities of war came into sharp and terrifying focus'.

War was, of course, the harsh reality for which all Australian soldiers were meant to be prepared. Taking human life and facing the prospect of being killed has always been integral to the profession of arms. The case for reducing the distinction between 'beret'-qualified soldiers – those who had completed Special Forces selection and the reinforcement cycle – and those who were not 'beret' qualified, such as support staff including signallers, had been powerfully made but the question remained: were Australian soldiers being adequately prepared for combat? Every member of the Australian Army, irrespective of their corps, was expected to be familiar with the tenets of basic soldiering. Although Special Forces personnel were required to display higher levels of tactical proficiency, the stresses of combat and the horrors of war could be explained during training and in exercises but they also had to be experienced. Those experiences had to be internally processed and personally digested. Courage and bravery were not at issue, but rather the capacity of soldiers to deal with death and destruction, and to continue discharging their duties with diligence. This was an issue that went well beyond Special Forces personnel.

The Taraka Valley operation had led journalists to challenge the competence of the SAS and the integrity of the ADF. When asked whether there had been a cover-up, Prime Minister Howard responded in general terms: 'Nothing that I have heard about this alters the fundamental fact that they took proper action consistent with the laws of war to defend themselves in anticipation of physical danger or death.'[18] The Labor Opposition leader, Kim Beazley, took a similarly firm line. He thought the SAS would 'be merciful and absolutely check any contact to make sure that the contact was not inadvertently going to be an innocent'.[19] The executive director of the Australian Defence Association, Neil James, remarked: 'Now, people can't sit here in armchairs, years afterwards, taking an antiseptic look at things. You really have to trust the decisions of the people on the ground when you put them in that type of combat situation.'[20]

The variation between the official accounts and media reporting implied major mistakes had been made and serious misconduct had occurred. Neither was actually true. This incident effectively demonstrated both the complexity of operations in Afghanistan and how easily media reporting could turn confusion into controversy. Although journalists were critical of operational intelligence and assumed the villagers were not associated with either the Taliban or al-Qaeda, despite persisting with attacks on Redback Kilo 3 when they must have known they were engaging Coalition forces, the purpose of the mission was strategic reconnaissance and intelligence gathering. It was not a 'kill-capture mission' intended to destroy the last remnants of Taliban resistance. This region in eastern Afghanistan was largely unknown to Coalition military commanders. The best and, in many respects, the only way to improve the quantity and quality of information was to conduct missions such as that given to Redback Kilo 3. The risk of an unanticipated engagement with Taliban or al-Qaeda fighters – or even warring villagers – could never be entirely removed. It was accepted and mitigated where possible.

The media coverage was inaccurate and misleading. Australia's Fairfax newspapers reported that *Time* claimed it was publishing the Coalition's Rules of Engagement (ROE) for the first time. It reported that the ROE allowed for 'incidental collateral damage', which included killing and injuring civilians, when such action was not 'excessive in relation to direct military advantage anticipated to be gained'.[21] To assert that the ROE were being used to excuse an operational blunder and distract attention from the unnecessary deaths of non-combatants was wholly unjustified. There was no need for the ADF to concede the area was *mistakenly* identified as 'a known al-Qaeda stronghold' or to admit it had led to the unnecessary deaths of 11 men. The operation was an exercise in risk management. It was not a mistake. As the ADF explained in a public statement: 'Each Australian element that opened fire, or called in fire, did so in response to direct threats to their safety.'[22] Neither was there misconduct.

This engagement certainly yielded many insights. Plainly, Coalition intelligence was sparse and its appreciation of the local mood in parts of Afghanistan was marginal. Improving the quantity and quality of relevant information was proving to be a demanding exercise. It also demonstrated the complexities of local community conflict; the near impossibility of completely avoiding civilian casualties; the visceral intensity of combat operations; the challenge of predicting individual reactions to violence; the seriousness of mistaken recollections; and the problematic nature of media reporting. At the tactical level, problems revealed in the cauldron of firefights might not always have received the forensic attention they deserved. The pace of operations limited scope for review and reflection. Untried people and untested patrols exposed to combat for the first time acted and reacted in some unexpected and unanticipated ways, notwithstanding training, discipline and leadership.

Expertise is derived from experience. The SAS's people and patrols were distracted from the important task of reviewing tactics, techniques and procedures by non-operational imperatives, such as dealing with flawed media reporting. This would not be the last such occasion. There was more at stake in the Taraka Valley than claims six Australian soldiers might have been killed by local villagers in a case of mistaken identity. Ensuring Special Forces personnel were prepared, organised and equipped to counter a well-disguised and highly erratic adversary that could not be relied upon to exercise sound judgment, let alone tactical prudence, was a first-order challenge deserving close and continuing attention. As only one life had been lost during the three rotations (Sergeant Andrew Russell),[23] the government and the public were led to believe these kinds of operations could, and perhaps would, be conducted with minimal casualties.[24] There were no public calls for Australian forces to be withdrawn following Sergeant Russell's death.[25]

A year after the invasion and with the Taliban defeated and al-Qaeda dispersed, the Coalition was persuaded the transitional Afghan administration could manage the recovery effort. To prevent the appearance of a Western occupation, most international military forces, including those of Australia, were promptly withdrawn from Afghanistan. The Australian Government had other reasons to bring its Special Forces home. They were likely to be placed on standby in the next few months for a possible American-led invasion of Iraq and needed a rest. In Afghanistan, however, the job was far from finished. Despite belated overtures from Taliban leaders offering a negotiated peace, members of the former regime would have no place in the 'new' Afghanistan. There were no attempts at either reconciliation with the factions or reintegration of the men who had been Taliban but had no interest in seeing the return of al-Qaeda. This was a serious mistake with enduring consequences. Ending Taliban rule was a specific objective that was efficiently accomplished by an effective mission. Preventing a Taliban revival meant the conditions that nourished extremism and fed rebellion could not be allowed to coalesce. This work might have seemed a distraction at the end of 2002 when the Afghan state lay in ruins but it was nonetheless vital if Afghanistan was to be a more stable and, therefore, more inclusive society. Tragically, reconciliation and reintegration never achieved the priority their long-term significance required. None of the country's leaders were untainted by the civil war.

Rebuilding a formalised state and a functioning society from what remained of post-Soviet, post-warlord, post-Taliban Afghanistan was a huge undertaking. The Afghan people would need assistance in the form of economic development, primary education and democratic practice. Lacking resources and facing so many seemingly intractable problems, the country could not remake itself. A commitment to both infrastructure and community was paramount because a country that was more materially prosperous and politically aware would resist any return to medieval governance and pre-modern culture. The final objective would be training a new Afghan National Army with the expectation that it would eventually undergird the nation's internal security, obviate the need for external assistance and preclude foreign interference. As the Soviet Union had learned in the 1980s, invading Afghanistan was much easier than governing it. As the Americans should have learned in the 1990s, without substantial foreign assistance the standing of Afghanistan's national government was never completely assured. Najibullah's Government could not survive the demise of the Soviet Union; the Taliban needed support from Pakistan to survive.

At the very moment the shape of Afghanistan's future was being determined, American focus and, consequently, Australian attention, returned to Iraq. Saddam Hussein's regime was again impeding United Nations weapons inspectors from verifying that Iraq had destroyed any remaining weapons of mass destruction (WMD) after its 1990 invasion of Kuwait. After Saddam and his sons ignored an American ultimatum to leave Iraq, a 'Coalition of the Willing' led by the United States and consisting of British and Australian naval, ground and air forces, launched an offensive operation on 20 March 2003.

After enjoying a brief respite following the end of operations in Afghanistan, 1 Squadron SAS was deployed to Iraq's western desert to prevent Scud missiles being used against its neighbours, principally Israel. The Squadron was then directed to capture the Al Asad military air base on the Euphrates River, west of the capital Baghdad, while preventing the entry of any foreign fighters into

Iraq. The SAS operators were supported by members of the 4th Battalion (Commando), Royal Australian Regiment (4RAR (Cdo)). In a largely one-sided battle, Coalition forces captured and occupied Baghdad on 9 April. On the flight deck of the aircraft carrier USS *Abraham Lincoln* off the coast of San Diego, President Bush declared on 1 May 2003 that 'major combat operations' had ended a mere six weeks after they began. The Coalition death toll in Iraq would, however, increase dramatically over the next five years with unrelenting Iraqi opposition to what had become a prolonged American occupation.

By this time the Taliban's resurgence was gaining momentum. Antonio Giustozzi, an Italian-born political economist attached to King's College London, explained in his detailed study of the period 2001–2018 that the 'polycentric' model adopted by the Taliban was highly complex and difficult to analyse because it lacked a structured organisational centre and featured multiple, disparate chains of command.[26] Indeed, prescribing authority structures and centralising power was a hallmark of the modernisation the original Taliban was committed to resisting. After 2002, the Taliban was a movement rather than a political party or a disciplined militia. Only once it began to regain control of isolated districts across Afghanistan did the Taliban's organisation start to change.

To coordinate activity and distribute resources, a Taliban leadership council (*shura*) was formed in the Pakistani city of Quetta in March 2003. The 'Rahbari Shura', as it is known to the Taliban, is called the 'Quetta Shura' by European observers. Another two leadership shuras would be established in 2007 and 2009, and some Afghan local networks shifted their allegiance and obedience, although neither challenged the primacy of Quetta or the supremacy of Mullah Omar. But with the former Emir in hiding from the Americans, the Quetta Shura was chaired by his deputy, Mullah Abdul Ghani Baradar. It appointed 'shadow' provincial and district governors in the southern and eastern parts of the country by 2005, and established 12 national commissions in Pakistan that mirrored the national government departments in Kabul. There was also a growing network of Taliban informers inside the national government, armed forces and security services, and spies who continued to operate as shopkeepers, drivers and builders who could deliver threatening messages to 'collaborators'.[27]

The Quetta Shura sent leaders and fighters back into southern Afghanistan with clear instructions. Small groups would visit villages and discern the presence of sympathisers. Taliban leaders would then urge their followers to incite local rebellions against district and provincial officials, frightening or murdering those who resisted their overtures. Once a village was 'turned' against the government, Taliban emissaries would convene public meetings and call for *jihad* against the Karzai regime, which the Taliban portrayed as a criminal state backed by foreign infidels. Few Afghans were ready to depend on the state or trust its assurances. In larger settlements, Taliban mullahs would preach sermons that linked personal piety to military action while emphasising the Taliban's imminent return to religious and social authority. The central challenge for the Taliban was balancing strategic control with local autonomy, and providing more advanced training to fighters in the face of enhanced Coalition tactics. Realising they could never succeed in conventional warfare, the Taliban looked for asymmetric options, recognising the disruptive potential of improvised explosive devices (IEDs). These devices would hinder Coalition manoeuvres and cause serious injury to a steadily increasing number of ISAF personnel.

As living conditions showed few signs of improvement and hope languished, extremists were able to inflame rising discontent in the cities and in the rural areas. By early 2005, it was clear that the Taliban had not been vanquished. More parts of the countryside were now falling under Taliban control as greater numbers of people were persuaded to resist the central government based in Kabul and oppose the continuing presence of foreign forces. But was the Taliban's outlook ostensibly religious and social, as it had been in 1994, or had it become essentially political and subversive? Were there continuing links between the Taliban leaders and al-Qaeda? Was Pakistan hoping to find new proxies for its influence?

Although claiming continuity with the ousted regime and remaining subject to the symbolic leadership of Mullah Omar, the Taliban was a very different organisation after 2001. Twelve months after the invasion, most Taliban fighters who had avoided being killed or captured had either returned to their homes in Afghanistan or fled to safe havens in other countries. The end of the regime did not prompt expressions of regret from the bulk of Afghanistan's population. During its ascendancy, the Taliban's religious zeal and moral purity were not enough to persuade the majority of Afghans they offered the best vision for the future of Afghanistan. Compliance could be coerced but personal convictions could not be compelled. The population might have had less chance to be worldly under the Taliban and many people were not well endowed with the things of this earth, but this did not necessarily make them more focused on spiritual ideals. Whatever their beliefs, in Talibanist Afghanistan people kept their dissent private for fear of being denounced, or worse, being deemed apostate.

Support for the Taliban was always strongest in the south among Pashtuns and weakest in the north among Tajiks. Its influence depended on whether support was freely offered or violently coerced, and the ease with which Taliban officials could access supplies from Pakistan. Recalling the threats and intimidation they had endured before 2001, and doubting the Afghan National Army's ability to protect them after 2001, most Afghan villagers complied with Taliban 'requests' for support. Sustained by the proceeds of drug trafficking, Taliban fighters were able to buy loyalty and pay for either information or silence.

By 2003, the resurgent Taliban had become a predominantly anti-Western, anti-Kabul political network, exploiting ethnic tensions and clan rivalries. It had moderates and extremists within the senior leadership group: the moderates disliked al-Qaeda and were prepared to accept a multi-party government; the extremists lauded al-Qaeda and wanted a one-party state. Taliban fighters in the field were variously motivated by the desire for power, prestige and possessions. Many Afghans were lured into insurgent activity with offers of money. They were paid to fight and given bonuses for killing foreigners.

Courage, conviction and corruption would never be enough to overcome international investment in the national government. Ultimately, the Taliban would wait for the resolve of partner nations to weaken. They would leave Afghanistan as the Soviets had done 15 years earlier. Surprisingly, it did not take long for the insurgency to have an effect. In November 2003, the Afghan Research Bureau and Evaluation Unit was reporting that half of Afghanistan's 32 provinces were deemed 'medium to high' risk for the staff of non-government organisations (NGOs) and the United Nations. This meant one-third of the country was off limits to aid organisations, a significant portion given the connection between prosperity and peace in the Coalition's strategy. By mid-2004, the strategy had allowed the Taliban to secure control over 26 rural districts, including six in Kandahar, four in Uruzgan, five in Helmand, four in Zabul and four in Paktika.

The Taliban 'brand' was also becoming a convenient vehicle for opportunists and speculators who were seeking to project their muscle and extend their dominance. In the absence of joining rituals and induction ceremonies, individuals could express their solidarity with the movement and become part of a district network opposing ISAF and the national government while pursuing personal, familial or tribal interests. The 'narco lords' who controlled the considerable drug trade in the already volatile southern provinces were also keen to exploit instability and insecurity in the countryside. By 2004, narcotics represented 40 per cent of the national economy, with Afghanistan producing three-quarters of the world's gross production of opium.[28] Around 1.7 million Afghans were connected to the drug business in some way, including farmers who could supplement their largely subsistence living by growing poppies as a cash crop.[29] There was also widespread use of marijuana, including among troops of the Afghan National Army. As much of the internal funding for the insurgency came from narcotics, considerable effort was expended on preserving production facilities and distribution arrangements. Drugs were one more feature in an already complicated security landscape.

After Hamid Karzai won the October 2004 presidential election, the national government was under pressure to prevent the Taliban from further extending its influence. With a weak economy producing little revenue for public programs, Karzai looked to the international community for support. Australia's contribution was minor. After withdrawing combat forces in November 2002, the Australian Government initially decided against participating in the Provincial Reconstruction Team (PRT) program promoted by the United States in late 2003. The PRTs were drawing on military and civilian expertise to help local authorities govern more effectively and efficiently. The Department of Foreign Affairs had little interest in being involved. Defence was not keen either. Stretched to the limits of its operational capacity, the ADF needed to fulfil its continuing obligations in Bougainville and East Timor, as well as more recent missions in Iraq and Solomon Islands which involved upwards of 2000 personnel. Australia had no spare capacity for Afghanistan although the country was sliding back into armed conflict. On 1 April 2005, the Defence Minister Senator Robert Hill said Australia had no plans to send Australian troops back to Afghanistan and suggested the security situation was improving.[30] Two months later, thinking in Canberra had changed as international expectations increased.

By June 2005, Hill was sufficiently confident that the ADF could provide the personnel and resources for a PRT consisting predominantly of combat engineers. He then took a submission to Cabinet. Notably, the Defence Department did not recommend sending Special Forces personnel despite the strong argument they might have been needed to provide force protection. Prime Minister Howard was concerned that deploying a PRT would lock Australia into a long-term commitment in Afghanistan that would be difficult to relinquish if the circumstances changed or success proved elusive. Both Howard and the Minister for Foreign Affairs, Alexander Downer, thought security ought to precede reconstruction. Neither had much confidence in the 'nation building' strategy. Downer had earlier stated: 'we don't want to get … bogged down in Afghanistan. We don't want Australian troops to be part of managing and running Afghanistan for the next five or six years.'[31] The priority was defeating the insurgency ahead of rebuilding infrastructure. This would involve considerable time and money. There were doubts that Australia had the capacity to do either in any effective way.

These discussions disclosed the real nature of Australia's involvement: the ADF's mission would be shaped by available capabilities rather than what was required based on a detailed analysis of the threat and close assessment of the terrain. The emphasis on the ADF's return to Afghanistan was more about what Australia could do, which was always constrained, than about what Afghanistan needed, which was ever expanding. The national interest that would be served by any deployment was not at the forefront of the government's thinking, other than a generalised commitment to supporting the United States. Although deployed personnel would follow orders, the reasons for sending them were hardly persuasive and far from compelling.

The ADF's leadership did not expect Cabinet's decision. Rather than contributing a PRT as recommended, Cabinet decided to deploy a contingent of Special Forces personnel for 12 months to address the deteriorating security situation. This was little more than a short-term measure that would help curtail the advancing Taliban while giving the Australian Government time to consider other options and to devise a more compelling narrative to justify the ADF's more than fleeting presence in Afghanistan. The government explained that the security situation in Afghanistan had worsened and firm action was needed. The situation had, of course, been worsening for the previous 12 months without any Australian action being contemplated.

Special Operations Command had not been consulted before Cabinet made its decision. The Chief of the Defence Force, General Peter Cosgrove, counselled against thinking this would be a swift 'in and out' operation. He proposed sending a taskforce numbering 45 men. His successor, Air Chief Marshal Angus Houston, thought a critical mass of 170 was needed. The compelling factors had been increasing pressure from the United States for an Australian contribution and the notable absence of Australia among the nations that were represented in ISAF. As both Canada and New Zealand had provided personnel, there was growing international expectation that Australia would do so too. As Senator John Gorton had told Prime Minister Harold Holt in 1966 when Australia was contemplating its contribution to the war in South Vietnam, the size of the force was irrelevant in military terms as long as it was 'not contemptible'.[32] The national interest that was served by the return of Australian personnel could only be expressed in the most general of terms: Australia was being a good global citizen and Australians would eventually benefit from reducing the threat of terrorist violence.

Prime Minister Howard and Defence Minister Hill held a press conference on 13 July 2005. They announced the despatch of:

> a Special Forces Task Group which will comprise some 150 personnel, comprising SAS troops, Commandos and supporting elements. We would expect that group to be in place by September of this year. It will be deployed for a period of twelve months. It will have a security task which is very similar to the task that was undertaken by an SAS taskforce that went in 2001. It will operate in conjunction with forces of the United States. There will be a separate Australian national command, although the SAS Task Group will be under the operational control of United States forces.[33]

The Task Group would conduct long-range patrols and security operations principally in Uruzgan province. The cost would be between A$50 and 100 million. Sending a Special Forces detachment would be less expensive than deploying an infantry battalion and would be more warmly welcomed by the United States.

The announcement prompted a raft of reasonable questions. Why was the security situation allowed to deteriorate to the extent that the Task Group's mandate resembled that given to the invading Coalition forces in 2001–02? What was the impact of the invasion of Iraq on reconstruction efforts in Afghanistan? Why did the Cabinet settle on a Special Forces deployment when Defence had argued for the despatch of a PRT? Why limit the deployment to 12 months? Did the government really think the security situation would be turned around so quickly that Australian forces could return home – permanently? If there was a continuing need for the presence of Special Forces, what plans and preparations were being made for an extended deployment? As they could not remain indefinitely, when would their capacity to contribute eventually be consumed?

The only reason given publicly for limiting the duration of the deployment was to ensure SAS personnel were back home in time to provide security for Asia-Pacific Economic Cooperation (APEC) leaders' meetings to be held in Sydney in September 2007. Keeping his options open, the prime minister also mentioned that Defence had been asked to 'examine the possibility of sending a PRT' that might be ready to depart Australia between April and June 2006. The government apparently saw 'great merit' in sending a PRT but wanted to consult its allies first about where they might be deployed and how they would be commanded. When asked by a journalist about the duration of a possible Australian PRT deployment, the prime minister said it would be 'inappropriate' to comment as many matters were yet to be settled. He privately knew the answer: indefinitely. Five years was probably the soonest the mission might end. Within weeks of the initial announcement, Downer noted that 'mission creep' had started before the first Australian soldier had even arrived in Uruzgan.

Bigger questions remained unanswered: what long-term national interest was advanced by sending the Special Forces Task Group (SFTG) *and* a PRT to Afghanistan? What were the 'key performance indicators' for those who deployed? How would success and failure be determined, and what performance indicators would Australian Special Forces pursue? Given the experience of the Soviet Union in the 1980s, how would the Coalition of Western forces avoid being drawn into a protracted military campaign that was likely to be exacerbated by domestic political turmoil? And given the kind of fighting the SFTG members were about to experience, what measures could be taken to ensure they did not descend into the kind of misconduct that debilitated and ultimately destroyed the Soviet 40th Army? There were moral and ethical, cultural and legal issues that needed close attention. These were not second-order matters. The Australian Special Forces would be placed in harm's way; they were entitled to a mission that was worth the potential loss of human life.

The Australian Government and the ADF already had a sense of the difficulties associated with conducting combat operations in Afghanistan. There were 'people factors' to consider. SAS patrols were usually a mix of assertive personalities. While assertiveness was a necessary requirement for a Special Forces soldier and occasionally led to tensions between some patrol members, the culture and ethos of the Regiment made personal issues subordinate to mission success. Managing egos and resolving disputes were considered routine leadership tasks although the consequences of poor leadership were always greater on the battlefield. Routine leadership also required close adherence to the Law of Armed Conflict and the ROE. There was also the increasingly fractious relationship between SAS personnel and the Commandos to consider. Could the two force elements work collaboratively or was it better for them to operate separately in different parts of the province undertaking dissimilar tasks? Would personal antipathies and professional rivalries hinder the mission or focus instead on the pursuit of excellence?

As the invasion and initial occupation of Afghanistan had demonstrated, the operational environment inevitably challenged virtues and changed outlooks. Most Australians, including the nation's senior uniformed leadership, which contained only a handful of Vietnam veterans, had forgotten that war left an indelible mark on minds and bodies. Peacemaking and peacekeeping deployments, such as Somalia, Cambodia, Rwanda and East Timor, were very different from Afghanistan. This was war. It was intimate and individualised. Australians had not seen this kind of fighting since 1971. What their adversary lacked in training they compensated with tenacity. The resurgent Taliban were armed and aggressive, unrestrained by international codes and conventions prescribing acceptable conduct, unwilling to adhere to any rules but their own, adept at using Western moral principles and ethical standards to curtail Coalition action and ready to exploit any apparent illegality in a relentless information offensive that was intended to turn the population against their own elected government. This kind of fighting would test the ethical standards and moral resilience of those who deployed, especially after prolonged exposure to ethical dilemmas and morally injurious conditions.

Complying with the Law of Armed Conflict was another first-order concern. The enemy did not wear uniforms and there were no front lines. Fighters and civilians were virtually indistinguishable and private homes were used as staging posts. Military victories did not necessarily translate into political advantages and, therefore, mission success. There would be countless provocations, frustrations and humiliations to test their character and affront their conscience. Given the urgency of halting the insurgency, the operational tempo was likely to be intense and the fighting would be close quarters. The Australians would see the people they killed and enter the personal space of those they captured. Detainees would include individuals accused of inflicting unspeakable cruelties on women and children, the elderly and disabled. The Australians would be personally affected by these encounters in ways that were not immediately apparent.

The conditions under which the anti-Taliban insurgency would be fought were the most complicated, and the most constricting, ever faced by Australian uniformed personnel on deployment, including the war in South Vietnam. With one side enveloped by an intricate web of rules and regulations and the other bound by none, the possibility, if not the probability, of the law being violated and ethical principles being ignored had never been greater. As the Task Group was assembled and then despatched with considerable haste, there was not time to address these issues properly and to prepare those deploying adequately. It was assumed that those who were being sent knew what was right and would always act rightly. This was over-confidence, naivety or ignorance of human nature and the realities of combat with Australia, now on the threshold of its longest war.

8
DRAFTING A STORY: SELLING THE AFGHAN WAR
2005–2013

All forms of warfare are complex; some are controversial. My late colleague Jeffrey Grey described insurgency as 'a form of warfare as old as warfare itself, and it has gone by many names in the past: guerrilla warfare, partisan warfare, revolutionary warfare, insurrectionary warfare, irregular warfare, unconventional warfare, peoples' war and terrorism'.[1] Its restraint or defeat is termed 'counter-insurgency'. It is essentially a complex political project more than it is a military problem because it primarily concerns contested state authority. Military power is one component of a multifaceted response to the social, economic, cultural and political conditions that support and sustain armed opposition to state authority.

Counterinsurgencies can be controversial because theorists and practitioners insist on placing counterinsurgency in a distinct category of armed conflict subject to special rules, rather than treating it as another form of war mediated by the usual rules. Like other types of warfare, counterinsurgencies are neither more nor less likely to produce a clear victory. A decisive result in which one side wins and the other loses, such as the outcome of the two world wars, is the exception not the norm. Counterinsurgencies usually lead to negotiated settlements that often fail to satisfy the disputing parties, sowing the seeds for future confrontation.

One element of counterinsurgency has generated a consensus: the importance of gaining and holding the allegiance of the civilian population. Winning 'hearts and minds' is not about persuading the people to wave government flags on national days. It is an attempt to convince the majority with little interest in politics or diplomacy, and by coercive means if necessary, that their immediate practical interests are better served by siding with the government than supporting the insurgency.

In 2003, the Taliban's leadership believed the movement was sufficiently well resourced and adequately organised to challenge the authority of the Afghan National Government in Kabul. Its objective was regaining control of the country which it had lost in late 2001. This political challenge would be pursued partly by military means. To foreign observers, the Taliban insurgency had the potential to destabilise Afghanistan's fragile democracy and turn the country back into the base for violent extremists that it had become before the American-led invasion. The prospect of a resurgent Taliban and a revived al-Qaeda, whose senior leadership was living in northern Pakistan – territory controlled by an ally of the United States – deeply troubled the Bush Administration in Washington. It pressed the Howard Government to send Australian Special Forces back to Afghanistan in 2005.

The Australian Government was reluctant to deploy any troops to Afghanistan, partly because the ADF was already stretched with existing commitments. Canberra was also obliged to consider the considerable costs associated with maintaining hundreds of military personnel and their equipment for operations being conducted halfway around the world. In contrast to 2001, when there was a specific, short-term objective, the new mission would be more diffuse and longer in duration. When it agreed to send a Special Forces Task Group (SFTG) in June 2005, the decision was essentially a show of general support for the United States. Deploying the SFTG did not signify a renewed Australian commitment to Afghanistan or its people. The Australian Government was not concerned with any tactical, operational or strategic objective beyond its principal political goal, which was achieved when Australian personnel arrived in Afghanistan. The Americans wanted to see an Australian flag outside the headquarters of the International Security Assistance Force (ISAF) in Kabul and to have their hard-pressed Special Forces supplemented by professional partner forces they could trust.

The decision produced a varied response from journalists and commentators. The Australian Government had followed the United States into Afghanistan in 2001 and Iraq in 2003. The June 2005 announcement looked like the latest expression of Australian solidarity with the American-led 'global war on terror'. The deployment would certainly strengthen the close relationship between the two nations and ensure American solidarity during any future security crisis involving Australia. For a geographically large country with a small population that felt threatened by its neighbours near and far, it has always made sense for Australia to maintain a military alliance with the United States. Drawing on American goodwill, Australia would have access to advanced war-fighting technology and benefit from intelligence sharing. The cost was participation in American-initiated conflicts with potentially little direct relevance to Australia's immediate interests. Participating in these campaigns was like paying the annual premium on an 'insurance policy' although this phrase, which was often heard during the Vietnam Conflict period, had been replaced in the 2000s with 'alliance management'. It sounded a little more proactive but the intent was the same. If things went badly in Afghanistan, and there was every likelihood they would, it was always possible to blame the United States for military failure. Whatever the outcome, the return on Australian investment in Afghanistan would be a stronger relationship with the United States, which remained the cornerstone of national security.

The SFTG's mission was to disrupt the Taliban's leadership networks and prevent them from using intimidation and coercion to control villages, towns, cities, districts, provinces and eventually the whole country. Counterinsurgency operations would make space for economic growth and community-building to progress in conditions free from interference and sabotage. Mindful that a steadily escalating body count had been an unreliable marker of American progress in subduing the Viet Cong insurgency in South Vietnam, ISAF could not achieve success in Afghanistan by killing every suspected insurgent. The pool of potential fighters was simply too large. Dead and debilitated fighters would be readily replaced by vengeful relatives and like-minded friends. This approach might be effective in combating the insurgency in the short term but would leave the local communities without a positive reason for supporting the national government in Kabul. The overarching objective was to coerce insurgents to abandon armed struggle and to convince civilians that democratic government offered a better future for them, their families, their tribe and their country.

The Australian Government's explanation for the mission drew a mixed political reaction. Critics, such as Greens leader Bob Brown, claimed that Australia remained dependent on the United States and was a tool of its imperialist foreign policy.[2] Hence, he asserted, the emphasis in government messaging on preventing Afghanistan from again becoming a safe haven for terrorists who posed a threat to Australians living and working abroad. As one of the nations that had joined the Coalition invasion of Afghanistan in 2001, the case could be made that Australia was obliged to accept its share of responsibility for rebuilding the conflict-ravaged country. The parliament, press and people were willing to accept the 'keeping Australia safe from terrorism' explanation at a time when there were growing fears of extremist violence. It did not seem to matter that there was little in Afghanistan of immediate importance to Australia or that South-East Asian terrorist organisations posed a much greater threat. Combating terrorism was a sufficiently compelling cause for the public to support the deployment.

The astute foreign affairs commentator Owen Harries noted in relation to Australia's involvement in the invasion of Iraq that offering 'uncritical, loyal support for a bad, failed American policy' was unlikely to enhance Australia's standing as an ally.[3] He also thought having a 'reputation for being dumb but loyal and eager is not one to be sought'. The Howard Government insisted Afghanistan was different to Iraq.

There were obviously altruistic elements in the deployment's rationale that would resonate with the spirit of service animating the outlook of most ADF members: a large group of wealthy nations with a mandate from the United Nations had formed a coalition to protect individual rights in a country blighted by oppression and to promote their material wellbeing through aid and reconstruction programs. These programs were intended to make the deployment more palatable to domestic sentiment. There was, then, nothing that was politically offensive or morally objectionable about the mission.

There were, of course, a few dissenting voices among academics who thought the government's public statements were misleading or disingenuous. They thought the government should have been clear that the principal reason for the deployment was to strengthen the alliance with the United States, although some thought Australia had done enough in recent years to generate lasting goodwill in Washington. Sending Australian forces back to Afghanistan was, the critics argued, unnecessary. It was certainly difficult to contend that those being sent to Afghanistan were defending Australia and protecting Australians. Because the link was essentially about second- and third-order effects, there would always be an element of confusion and perhaps even disagreement about what the Australians were meant to achieve, given it was Australia's presence on Afghan soil rather than its participation in Afghan affairs that mattered.

Some Western nations severely limited what their forces could do once in Afghanistan. Although Australia was part of an international coalition, the United States, the United Nations and NATO could not pressure Australian forces to conduct missions or complete tasks that were not approved by the Australian Government. There was no suggestion that operational orders might unintentionally encourage unlawful behaviour or create intractable ethical dilemmas on the battlefield. On the face of it, deploying to Afghanistan did not present any new or additional challenges to those recently encountered in East Timor, Solomon Islands and Iraq. Australians were being sent to support the elected government of Afghanistan against the actions of armed insurgents who were intent on using violence to subvert the democratic will of the people.

Given the basis of Australia's contribution to the war in Afghanistan and being mindful the outcome would not directly affect Australian security, the Australian Government put a limit on what it was prepared to spend. Not unlike the Politburo's handling of the Soviet occupation, the SFTG deployment was 'war on a budget'. The amount expended would not be determined by the cost of tactical success, given the government's objectives were political not military. It was always doubtful whether anywhere near the requisite investment would be made to defeat the Taliban and rebuild Afghanistan. Australian forces would do as much as they could with the resources they were given. The ADF was expected to be effective and efficient in the conduct of its operations. Whatever they achieved, according to whatever measure of success they devised for themselves (other than demonstrating their capabilities to their American counterparts), was a secondary consideration. Unless there were an unacceptably high number of casualties, whatever they achieved in Afghanistan would not determine the length of their deployment or its ultimate contribution to Australia's national interests.

Conscious of the government's objective in sending ADF personnel back to Afghanistan, the initial suggestion was to base them in Bamyan, a relatively peaceful province in the north of Afghanistan, as part of a traditional Australia–New Zealand (ANZAC) contingent. This was a sensible option and consistent with the desired intent. It would militate against tactical exploration and operational adventurism. It was at this point, however, that the focus of the mission was blurred. The Australian Government was apparently not interested in a 'quiet' corner of Afghanistan. Having decided to send Special Forces, and conscious that ADF units deployed to central Iraq in 2005 had avoided much of the fighting, the government was prepared to unleash Australia's Special Forces on the Taliban. Military pride and lobbying from Special Operations Command (SOCOMD) had begun to assert itself. There were, however, some caveats.

The Australians were not authorised to work closely with some American units, such as the Joint Special Operations Command (a sub-unit command of the American Special Operations Command), which had a wide-ranging irregular warfare remit, and they would not be permitted to operate outside Afghanistan. Prime Minister Howard had a close relationship with President Pervez Musharraf in Islamabad that he did not want imperilled by any covert activity in Pakistan. The Australian Government was aware, of course, of long-running and self-interested Pakistani interference in Afghan affairs. Australian forces would not be sent to a province that bordered Pakistan. As the Americans wanted their forces to be relieved in Uruzgan province, the Australians would go there and be based at the provincial capital, Tarin Kowt.

The insurgency had been gaining momentum in Uruzgan for at least 18 months prior to the arrival of the Australians. There was sympathy for the Taliban across the province. The movement's supreme leader, Mullah Mohammad Omar, was born at Deh Rawood, a district capital west of Tarin Kowt. With longstanding links to the Taliban, Uruzgan managed to avoid the worst excesses of Taliban rule between 1994 and 2000. In many districts the prospect of a resurgent Taliban did not create panic or cause civilians to flee their homes, villages or towns. As their interactions with the national and provincial governments were minimal, they were less concerned about whoever claimed to be in power. The new provincial leadership was also considered pro-Western, pro-Karzai and indifferent to some local customs. When tribal rivals were marginalised and political opponents were targeted, the disempowered and oppressed turned to the Taliban for patronage and protection. For many Afghans, the struggle was not between the Taliban and the national government but between the oppressors and the oppressed. The majority simply wanted to live without interference and thought the Taliban more likely to leave them alone.

The geographic location of the province made it possible for the insurgency to be supported from Pakistan. The Pakistan Army was facilitating the deployment cycle of Taliban forces from their training in Pakistan to their deployment in Afghanistan to their return to Pakistan for rest and recuperation. Pakistan Army and Frontier Corps troops stationed along the border were even shooting at Coalition border posts to provide covering fire for Taliban infiltrating Afghanistan through neighbouring Kandahar, Zabul and Paktika provinces. Uruzgan was becoming a dangerous and violent place. The Australians had no previous experience operating there. They would begin from a standing start and without any prior knowledge of what they would face. Uruzgan was less peaceful than distant Bamyan but not as turbulent as neighbouring Kandahar to the south. Their presence in Uruzgan would, however, involve them in activities that further blurred the focus of their mission.

As Special Forces personnel prepared to depart Australia, two fundamental questions remained to be answered. Could the political problems posed by the insurgency be resolved with military solutions? Were the ISAF partner nations willing to invest the necessary resources to achieve that goal? In 2005, the Americans certainly believed the Taliban could be overcome although they had not quite settled on how to address the underlying political issues. The Bush Administration was strongly opposed to negotiating with the Taliban. It was convinced that any Afghan government that included members of the Taliban would eventually harbour terrorists. It was unwilling, however, to apply direct diplomatic pressure on Pakistan, where the Taliban's senior leadership had taken refuge and from where much of the insurgency's material support had originated. As for the cost, the United States Government was apparently willing to accept a substantial financial burden. But for how long?

Although less strident than the United States in wanting to curtail the spread of extremist violence but conscious of its seriousness after the devastating bombing of two Bali nightclubs by terrorists in October 2002, which killed 203 people including 88 Australians, the Australian Government and like-minded partner nations believed the Coalition task in Afghanistan had two parts. First, a concerted attempt had to be made to prevent Afghanistan from becoming a rogue state or a criminal regime. Second, a substantial investment of funds and forces would delay or prevent this from happening. But any action taken in Afghanistan needed to comply with the Law of Armed Conflict and be conducted in accordance with ISAF and Australian Rules of Engagement (ROE). Would complying with the law limit the scope of counterinsurgency operations? Certainly. Would adhering to rules complicate operations against the Taliban? Definitely. These were, however, limitations and complications the Australian Government was prepared to accept, and would insist its deployed personnel observe. Excessive confidence in the utility of military force after the effective intervention in the 1999 East Timor crisis (which was largely resolved by political negotiation before the ADF arrived) had already given the Australian people the impression that the mission had more than a reasonable chance of success. Sceptical observers thought rescuing Afghanistan from the Taliban might be yet another demonstration of the kind of Western hubris that presumed a six-week international relief mission would end the long-running Somali famine or that a United Nations force of 400 soldiers could prevent the Rwandan genocide.

The Australian Government was still wary about the duration

of the commitment and whether counterinsurgency in Afghanistan could succeed without the enormous investments it was not prepared to make. Cabinet had not come to a firm decision about being part of nation-building in Afghanistan when the SFTG arrived at Uruzgan in September 2005. Until the security situation improved appreciably, the government would reserve its decision on future contributions. In the meantime, the SFTG would gain an overall appreciation of operating in Uruzgan, including an understanding of the human terrain; prevent the Taliban shadow government from returning while countering its propaganda efforts; deny insurgents a safe haven and disrupt bomb-making networks; and accompany and assist local partner and Coalition conventional forces in previously unsafe areas of the province.

In Uruzgan, the insurgency had achieved considerable potency despite being little more than an unruly network of local commanders directed from Kandahar and coordinated from Quetta. Across the province the Taliban's organisation was sparse and cooperation between networks was minimal.[4] Commanders would collaborate for an attack on pro-government and Coalition forces and then resume their private disputes and personal feuds. A few local commanders were paid; the majority of local fighters were not. Financial incentives were not always necessary when there were religious imperatives to inspire action. Ad hoc local assistance could be secured by offering money to poor farmers who could supply information or provide material support. Active resistance could be overcome with intimidation and reprisals although the Taliban realised that coercion could also drive local sympathies towards the government. The main effort was attracting former mujahideen fighters who were angry with the national government and recruiting new fighters incensed by Kabul's reliance on the West.

The provincial government in Uruzgan was beset by 30 different political parties and militia organisations jostling for power and influence in what resembled a political marketplace, where loyalties were secured, traded and abandoned, weaknesses were manipulated and division was exploited. The privileged place traditionally afforded to the landed elite and tribal elders had been diminished over the previous few years by those who had achieved prominence through militia networks, weapons acquisitions and foreign contracts. The foreigners, with their vast resources, were quickly enveloped by the main players when they entered the political and economic marketplace. The Western desire for quick results led to local deals that detracted from the standing of the national government and obscured the distribution of influence within the province in direct opposition to Coalition objectives. In addition to the power wielded by the provincial governor, Jan Muhammad Khan (JMK), who held office from January 2002 to March 2006, and whose suppression of suspected Taliban within the province served mainly to advance his political interests, his ambitious and wealthy nephew, Matiullah Khan (known as 'MK'), had quickly become the dominant figure in Uruzgan.[5]

When the Taliban were defeated in 2001, MK was a poor taxi driver. By 2005, he had secured substantial personal wealth through contracts to provide construction, transport and security. He was literally able to buy influence across the province. He was also commander of the Uruzgan highway patrol, an essentially private organisation numbering several thousand men, who were contracted to provide security for road transport users between Tarin Kowt and Kandahar. As a local strongman, he was a threat to Taliban dominance, and they tried to assassinate him on several occasions. The deadliest attempt was in 2005, when he was targeted by a suicide bomber while attending a dogfight. MK survived but at least 39 spectators at the event were killed.

MK was 'Australia's man in Uruzgan', according to Major General John Cantwell, the task force commander.[6] While one Special Operations Task Group (SOTG) commander referred to him as the 'Robin Hood of Uruzgan', others were more circumspect, seeing him as little more than a necessary evil. With no other viable alternatives, as the Americans had already selected the best forces and partnered with them, his personal army would be Australia's local partner force. In Afghanistan, few middle-aged men in provincial towns and rural areas had clean hands but MK's were more dirty than most. Partnering with him was tactically expedient but potentially strategic folly. Would MK and his men have a corrupting influence on the Australians? Potentially yes, although Australian commanders presumably thought individual discipline and personal restraint would prevail, and corporate values and professional standards would be preserved. This much was sure: MK would make no contribution to promoting respect for human life or strengthening commitment to individual rights. He would need to be restrained more than encouraged in the war against the Taliban. While the Australians were prepared to work with him, other ISAF partner forces were not.

Clearly, the operational, legal and ethical challenges facing the Australians were immense. There was little prospect the security situation in Uruzgan would be stabilised within the 12-month window of the initial Australian commitment. The province was well behind in the reconstruction journey and the insurgency was spreading. The United Nations and most non-government organisations (NGOs) had withdrawn from Uruzgan by early 2006 with only two of the provincial districts considered safe for civilian aid workers. But did this matter beyond Uruzgan? Would stabilising government in Tarin Kowt or in Kabul prevent the spread of global terrorism? The answers did not matter to the Australians who were there to support the United States. Such was the fear of a resurgent al-Qaeda and the proliferation of like-minded groups, such as the Islamist organisation Jemaah Islamiyah, which had masterminded the 2002 Bali nightclub bombings, that few Western governments were willing to be accused of complacency – hence the Australian presence in Afghanistan. They were aware that over the previous decade, 'stateless' terrorists across the world had sought to destroy political systems, damage business confidence and undermine civil order, believing that instability, insecurity and disorder were the necessary pre-conditions for establishing alternative societies in which they and their ideals would become pre-eminent.

Many Western nations responded to fears of cascading political chaos, economic failure and social upheaval within vulnerable countries, such as Afghanistan, with permanent, holistic programs rather than temporary, minimalist solutions. Military-assisted civil reconstruction programs were the most common. A society that had endured intra-state conflict needed time to recover from its injuries. Healing would not happen overnight. The process might take decades if the initial causes of the conflict remained unaddressed or disruptive influences persisted.

These kinds of missions, focused on 'winning hearts and minds' with security sector reform, were closely linked to restoring political authority and reinstating the power of national agencies, including the security forces. There was clear presumption that these activities required adherence to the Law of Armed Conflict and compliance with the ROE. Ill-discipline and misconduct were antithetical to the essence of such missions and a leading cause of their failure. The foremost requirements were restraint and discretion. The use of force was to be avoided when and where possible. This mindset required a recalibration of thinking among those trained to deliver death and destruction. Being able to fight large-scale land battles did not necessarily confer a capacity to succeed in a nuanced counterinsurgency struggle. The requisite 'skill sets' were overlapping. Some areas of expertise needed to be acquired or honed. The conduct of every individual was integral to success. A lapse of discipline or error of judgment by a junior soldier had the potential to imperil ISAF's standing and enhance the Taliban's profile. Hence the emphasis placed on a thorough understanding of the Law of Armed Conflict and the ROE during pre-deployment preparation.

Contributing to civil reconstruction in Afghanistan made practical sense although the Department of Foreign Affairs continued to be ambivalent about its effective contribution to Australia's national interests. Australia had not even appointed a resident ambassador in Kabul because the department was not persuaded Afghanistan warranted a permanent diplomatic presence. Whether Afghanistan, its political system and beleaguered people were best served by military-assisted civil reconstruction that was managed on a regional basis was yet another question. The Provincial Reconstruction Team (PRT) model pioneered by the United States Government seemed the best option and appeared to be working elsewhere in Afghanistan.[7] In addition to preventing the expansion of ISAF beyond Kabul and camouflaging the continuing presence of American troops in Afghanistan, the PRT would bring together military and civilian staffs from a range of government departments to work in places that were too dangerous for aid and charitable organisations to work alone. They suited nations that were not keen on having a combat role in Afghanistan but wanted to be seen supporting the United States and contributing to ISAF.

In Canberra, however, Prime Minister Howard remained hesitant about heading down this path. It was expensive and, to some degree, experimental as every counterinsurgency involved a different mix of emphases and efforts that were largely unrelated to the point of the Australian mission and added to the human costs of being in Afghanistan. Agreeing to a PRT would entrench Australia in Afghanistan indefinitely, a situation he expressly wanted to avoid in mid-2005 when he opted to send Special Forces as a show of international solidarity. By 2006, the general momentum of thinking about Afghanistan within the Australian Government had shifted in favour of a PRT contribution. This was more than mission creep. It was a whole new direction involving a substantially increased Australian presence in Uruzgan. There was no public debate. Nor was there much evidence that government departments grappled with the arguments for and against such a commitment expressed in terms of advancing the national interest. The only caveat on Australia's contribution was its unwillingness to accept overall responsibility for the province. The Howard Government was susceptible to 'mission creep' and this was another such instance as the national objective had already been achieved. Even then, the government's commitment was half-hearted. The British Chief of the Defence Staff, General Sir Michael Walker, suggested that Australia might partner with the Dutch given the two nations had worked together in Iraq. It was a sound idea although yet another expansion of Australia's secondary objectives in Afghanistan.

After considerable diplomatic negotiation and detailed operational planning, Prime Minister Howard announced on 21 February 2006 that Australia would contribute to provincial reconstruction in Uruzgan. In commending the deployment to the domestic political audience, the prime minister said this was 'evidence of Australia's commitment to supporting the Government and people of Afghanistan as they build their new democracy'.[8] On 8 May 2006 he explained that a reconstruction taskforce consisting of 240 uniformed personnel, mostly engineers, would be deployed to 'assist Afghanistan to achieve a stable and secure future'.[9] 'Task Force Uruzgan' would be Dutch-led and include force elements from France, Norway, Singapore, Slovakia, Britain and the United States as well as the Australians and local partner forces. The Australian contingent would be drawn primarily from 1 Combat Engineer Regiment (1 CER). Although a multinational coalition, there was little social bonding between the national force elements. Australian personnel, other than those mentoring Afghan soldiers and sharing distant patrol bases, did not mix with the local Afghan population. They maintained their distance in a secure compound away from assassins and suicide bombers.

The first rotation of the Australian Reconstruction Task Force (RTF) arrived in August 2006. With the SFTG mission scheduled to end in September 2006 and Uruzgan remaining unstable, the deployment of an additional 30 force protection personnel was announced on 9 August 2006 – yet another mission add-on. Australia would also send:

> an infantry company group of about 120 personnel to provide enhanced force protection. The additional deployments will bring the total Reconstruction Task Force strength to approximately 400 ... The force will be equipped with a number of Bushmaster Infantry Mobility Vehicles and a number of Australian Light Armoured Vehicles (ASLAVs).[10]

Eight months after deploying the RTF, the prime minister had announced yet another increase in the Australian commitment without conceding that the withdrawal of the SAS had been premature, if not ill-conceived. Neither the Minister for Defence, Brendan Nelson, nor the Australian Special Operations Commander, Major General Mike Hindmarsh, had supported the SOTG withdrawal. Although Dutch Special Forces in Uruzgan would be asked to 'step up' and preserve the momentum the Australians had generated, there were signs the insurgency had gained ground. If Australian Special Forces returned, it was very likely they would remain until the insurgency was defeated or the RTF was withdrawn.

As expected, and despite earlier assurances from Defence they would not be needed, Prime Minister Howard soon announced the resumption of Special Forces rotations. It looked from the window dressing needed to broaden political support for the deployment that the government was unclear about what it wanted to achieve and why. In fact, the government knew what it wanted to achieve – to be seen supporting the Americans – but did not have a campaign plan because it was not thinking beyond that general objective. Most of the officers exercising command in Uruzgan developed their own plans, although few of these plans survived longer than a single rotation.

What Australians did once they were in Afghanistan still mattered less than the symbolic importance of simply being there. This meant the government trusted the ADF with strategic and tactical decision-making and was prepared to endorse ideas and initiatives originating with the deployed forces at the operational level. The Australians would make themselves useful while building good professional relationships with ISAF partners.

Without explaining why Special Forces rather than conventional infantry were needed, other than to say that 'advice received by the Government points to an elevated threat environment', the prime minister told journalists on 10 April 2007 that:

> a Special Operations Task Group [SOTG] of about 300 personnel will shortly deploy to Uruzgan province for at least two years. It will operate in direct support of ISAF elements in Uruzgan. Its role will be to enhance provincial security by disrupting Taliban extremists' command and control and supply routes. These forces will operate under an Australian commander working within the ISAF framework. The Task Group's activities will directly support the Australian Reconstruction Task Force, support the development of the Afghan national security forces and help reinforce the legitimacy of the Afghan Government with the local population. The existing RTF Protection Company Group (about 120 personnel) will be extended and will continue to provide close protection to RTF personnel until August 2008.[11]

By the end of 2007, the ADF commitment to Afghanistan was continuing to expand. There was no parliamentary debate and no apparent disquiet among the press or the people about the expansion. Although the nation was 'at war', Afghanistan did not feature in the October–November 2007 election campaign or hasten the Howard Government's defeat at the polls. The change of government made little difference to anything the ADF was doing in Afghanistan. There were 950 Australians in Uruzgan with the number increasing to 1550 within the next two years as the SOTG and RTF rotations settled into an established pattern of deployments that were between four and six months in length.

Analysts thought the likely duration of the Australian commitment would be five years. It was difficult for the government to predict a withdrawal date when there was a range of volatile factors that made detailed forward planning problematic. Principal among these factors was the sliding scale of fear felt by ordinary Afghans. They needed to have confidence in the national government to supervise development, and faith that the security forces could prevent chaos before the foreign forces would depart. In 2007, they had neither. The local security forces needed more training and better equipment – things the cash-strapped national government in Kabul could not provide. They were still ill-disciplined, unreliable and corruptible. Coincidentally, substantial investments were separately required in civil policing and the justice system, to avoid military forces being drawn into domestic affairs for which they were ill-suited. The challenges confronting ISAF were escalating as the cost of rebuilding Afghanistan grew exponentially. Foreign aid already constituted 90 per cent of the national government's annual budget.

Not surprisingly, the Australian people were beginning to have doubts about the value and wisdom of these rolling deployments, and whether Australia ought to be in Afghanistan for the long haul. The political narrative was no longer convincing. The Minister for Defence in the new Rudd Labor Government, Joel Fitzgibbon, attended a meeting of ISAF partner nations at Edinburgh in December 2007. He thought ISAF 'was dysfunctional. The planning was hopeless, some countries were not pulling their weight, we lacked coordination and a clearly defined mission statement.' As a partner nation, Australia should be involved in decision-making, Fitzgibbon thought, as the emphasis shifted to training and mentoring Afghan forces who were widely considered to lack motivation and basic technical skills.[12] Battles were being fought but the war was not being won. Fitzgibbon wanted Australian Special Forces to concentrate on Uruzgan and refused permission for their deployment beyond the province. The Australian people needed an assurance that ISAF had a roadmap for its success given the Australian Government exerted little influence in overall Coalition planning. Towards the end of 2008, the majority of Australians surveyed in an opinion poll conducted by the Lowy Institute said they were opposed to Australia's continuing presence in Afghanistan.[13] This opposition was evidently not causing much personal angst as there were no protest marches or public demonstrations, either then or later, calling for the ADF's withdrawal from Uruzgan. The government nevertheless realised it needed to work on selling the story of the Afghan war.

In Uruzgan, local reactions to the Australian presence were mixed. Because of their physical appearance, the Australians were sometimes confused with Americans and occasionally with the Russians who had departed two decades earlier. Any mistakes or hints of misconduct among ISAF forces were exploited for their propaganda value. While the Taliban might have seemed technologically and tactically unsophisticated, they became adept at employing 'lawfare', using international law and NATO ROE to hamstring the counterinsurgency and to preoccupy ISAF with endless inquiries about alleged mistakes or misconduct. The Taliban had time on its side. ISAF did not. It had to win quickly or it would lose through depleted political commitment. The longer the war lasted the more likely was eventual Taliban success. The insurgents did not need to win; they simply needed to avoid losing.

The Australians were the subject of political criticism and negative publicity when civilians were mistakenly killed. One of Uruzgan's three representatives in the national parliament in Kabul, Hajii Abdul Khaliq, told the SBS *Dateline* program: 'The Australian troops don't have a good reputation in Afghanistan. People hate the Australian troops.'[14] These statements were prompted entirely by emotion and anguish at the spiralling loss of life on all sides. The Australians were initially well regarded and were not known for indifference to human life. Nonetheless, the Taliban seized on any adverse commentary as part of an information war that drew on aspirations, perceptions and experiences – good and bad.

By 2009, the overall emphasis of the Australian mission had shifted again. To smooth the path to an honourable withdrawal, the focus moved from reconstruction to training, with a number of Australian-led Operational Mentoring and Liaison Teams being embedded in Afghan National Army battalions. The reaction of the local partner forces to the Australians was consistently positive. A succession of indigenous forces including the Afghan National Army, the Afghan special forces (Wakunish), the Provincial Police Reserve Company (PPRC), the Afghan Local Police and the *Kandak Amniante Uruzgan* (MK's Uruzgan highway police) were mentored by Australian personnel after 2006. The partner forces were taken on missions to ensure they constituted approximately half of the Coalition force, sometimes before the Afghans were adequately prepared for such operations. The emphasis was getting local forces ready for ISAF's eventual withdrawal and, from time to time, ensuring they did not engage in activities that would damage the moral integrity and legal standing of ISAF's mission or personnel.

The capability and integrity of the Afghan police had, however, been a problem for some time and improvement was modest. The police forces were known for stealing from villagers and protecting the narcotics trade. The International Crisis Group noted that many senior police executives secured their positions through corrupt payments which they recovered by extracting bribes and collaborating with 'criminal and insurgent networks in smuggling and other activities, including kidnapping for ransom'.[15] Heroin and marijuana addicts were attracted to joining the police as an easier means of gaining access to cheap or confiscated drugs. Any hope of moving the emphasis from military action to law enforcement depended on the police reaching and maintaining an acceptable standard of competence and probity. The challenges continued to multiply.

The RTF was appropriately renamed the 'Mentoring and Reconstruction Task Force' (MRTF) before the reconstruction element in its mandate was eventually dropped. The new 'Mentoring Task Force' (MTF) was based on a combined arms battle group consisting of four combat teams and five mentoring teams together with communications, logistics and support units comprising motorised infantry and cavalry, combat engineers, aviation and artillery. This was not the primary line of effort envisaged by Robert Hill when he first pitched provincial reconstruction to Cabinet in 2005. The mission drift persisted into the fifth year of Australia's presence in Afghanistan. Neither the parliament nor the people were given a progress report on the state of Australian–American relations, which remained the fundamental premise of the mission.

The media noted that a study of counterinsurgency in Uruzgan produced by Colonel Peter Connolly (a former MTF commander) was critical of the lack of a coherent strategy:[16]

> It would be very useful to have a strategy from Canberra to synchronise and prioritise whole-of-government efforts in delivering nation building effects, but no such strategy is apparent at this stage. Australia has the capacity to marshal resources on an appropriate scale to achieve results in [U]ruzgan, but there needs to be sufficient appetite in government, a matured whole-of-government apparatus, and cohesive national direction to realise a meaningful outcome.[17]

Connolly had put his finger on the problem. There was no coherent strategy because there were no strategic objectives. It was impossible to build a bridge that linked counterinsurgency operations to political outcomes when there were none beyond the Australians being there. Reconstruction and training were worthwhile activities but they were not national objectives.

While the Australians were reconfiguring the form of their contribution, the newly elected Obama Administration in Washington announced a reassessment of America's continuing presence in Afghanistan. President Barack Obama did not have his predecessor's commitment to the war. He was troubled by the mission's lack of clarity. President Obama was also disturbed by the military's attitude to legal principles (largely derived from the policies of the previous administration) and unconvinced that strategic success was being measured accurately. The president observed: 'many people in the United States – and many in partner countries that have sacrificed so much – have a simple question: what is our purpose in Afghanistan? ... And they deserve a straightforward answer.'[18] Obama was recognising the shift in domestic support for the war. The American public's enthusiasm for the global war on terror had waned considerably since 2001. That the president could not give the American people a straightforward answer revealed the extent to which the United States and ISAF had either lost their way or were struggling to achieve genuine progress. Obama ordered a wide-ranging 60-day review of United States policy. He removed General David McKiernan, the Commander of ISAF forces, less than one year into his posting partly because of the growing number of civilian casualties in Afghanistan and because the new administration in Washington wanted a fresh approach to the war.

The new commander of ISAF and American forces in Afghanistan, General Stanley McChrystal, recommended that Washington approve a surge in troop numbers. He thought another 30 000 to 40 000 personnel would 'degrade' the Taliban but not destroy it. The surge, which was ultimately ineffective, would give the Americans more space in which to achieve their honourable withdrawal. The belief that the Taliban could be 'defeated' had certainly been abandoned by mid-2009. Obama accepted the recommendation but announced that a gradual withdrawal of American forces from Afghanistan would commence in July 2011, claiming the 'the tide of war is receding' and al-Qaeda was in decline.[19] The confident predictions of 2005 for what could be achieved had given way to more cautious judgments four years later. McChrystal was also conscious of mounting allegations of misconduct, focusing on the use of force and detention, and expressing his intention to align the legal and moral 'circles' within which Coalition forces operated.[20]

A former Special Forces commander, he called for 'courageous restraint' and extended the prohibition on Coalition night raids – which ISAF forces preferred and Afghan civilians detested – other than in exceptional circumstances. McChrystal also issued a fresh 'Embedded Partnering Directive' on 29 August 2009 'to form a more coherent relationship: we will live, train, plan, control, and execute operations together at all command echelons'.[21] The intention was for Afghan leaders to 'adopt our planning methodologies, administrative procedures and multi-spectral approach to warfare. Meanwhile, ISAF leaders will learn Afghan cultures, norms and values.'[22] The overarching objective was building trust and enduring relationships because 'only the Afghans can win this conflict ... partnering creates a synergy that amplifies our strengths and reduces our individual weaknesses'. Given the war had been underway for more than five years, it seemed odd for an ISAF commander to be emphasising attention to local culture and stressing the need for collaboration. This should have been a priority from the start.

McChrystal's influence was short-lived. After private remarks that were disparaging of Vice President Joe Biden were published in *Rolling Stone* magazine in 2010, McChrystal resigned and was replaced by General David Petraeus, who echoed his predecessor's pronouncements about the need to avoid civilian casualties.[23] He emphasised that 'the centre of gravity in this struggle is the Afghan people; it is they who will ultimately determine the future of Afghanistan'.[24] Whenever firepower was being considered, 'the commander approving the strike must determine that no civilians are present'. This was a basic tenet of counterinsurgency and nothing new.

Petraeus did not concede the perennial difficulty of differentiating civilians from insurgents, another basic feature of counterinsurgency, especially when many Afghan men were farmers by day and fighters by night.

As Afghanistan's political leadership became frustrated with some of ISAF's policies and the rising civilian death toll, ISAF was becoming impatient with Karzai and the poor quality of Afghan state institutions. Some countries felt NATO was arming undisciplined militias lacking any sense of Afghan national interest. If ISAF were to depart, they predicted, these militias would be co-opted by district and provincial strongmen to advance their positions – not unlike the armed factions that led Afghanistan into civil war during the 1990s. Others believed that al-Qaeda had become an international 'franchise' that could recruit effectively using the internet. It no longer required a physical safe haven like 'Talibanistan'. Put simply: al-Qaeda would never be defeated, it could only be dissipated while the reasons for its existence appealed to potential recruits and supporters. The more it was fought, the greater its legitimacy and appeal to potential recruits. The Coalition could not counter its propaganda or dent its resilience. Al-Qaeda had been a minor organisation before 2001. Its denunciation by the United States began the influx of new members and the inflow of fresh funding from around the world. Al-Qaeda had wounded the Americans and become the centre of attention. Global news media had given the organisation what it most wanted: the publicity that terrorism relies upon to succeed.

The Afghan war was increasingly irrelevant as a conflict with international consequences. The war that Australia had joined in 2005 was not the war being fought at the end of 2009. The political narrative justifying the mission to the Australian people, and providing the context for ADF tasking, had not kept pace with changes on the ground in Afghanistan. The war had gained a momentum and a direction of its own.

It was time for Australia to consider its position. In Canberra, the

Labor Party, now led by Julia Gillard, failed to secure a parliamentary majority at the August 2010 federal election. The Greens made a full parliamentary debate on Afghanistan one of their demands for supporting a minority Labor Government. The debate was held in late September and October 2010 and featured more than 100 speeches. It yielded few creative insights or compelling conclusions. Prime Minister Gillard did not mention the prospect of victory in Afghanistan, only that 'progress was being made'. She hinted that another decade of transition was likely.[25]

The Greens' sole member of the House of Representatives, Adam Bandt, claimed 'the war in Afghanistan cannot be won, however you measure victory'.[26] He assumed, of course, that winning militarily was Australia's objective. There was strong bipartisan support for continuing Australia's commitment alongside increasing doubt about the benefits of persisting. Former Defence Minister Robert Hill appeared resigned to an unpalatable outcome: 'one thing that struck me ... is how little we knew about the country and the influences in the country. Sometimes I think we still don't.' By 'we' he meant nations like the United States, the United Kingdom, Canada and Australia. On the dynamics of tribal influences, he mused: 'how ignorant could we have been? And I think with the benefit of hindsight we would've been a little more reserved about what was achievable; and perhaps the missions might've been structured to achieve slightly different outcomes to what has been the case.'[27]

Despite the protracted parliamentary debate and sombre reflection on the lives that had been sacrificed, the ADF's mission in Afghanistan continued towards an unspecified destination as the United States looked for fresh options and a way out. Gillard was correct in explaining that progress had been made according to a number of practical markers but there was no description of an acceptable end state. Australian Special Forces were capturing and killing Taliban leaders and fighters. The MTF was improving the skills and strengthening the resolve of local forces. Under Dutch leadership, provincial reconstruction had achieved favourable results in education, health and sanitation. After extending their mission twice and following a change of government in the Netherlands, the Dutch announced their forces would be withdrawn by the end of 2010. Even with ample warning, Australia remained unwilling to accept overall responsibility for the province. Canberra did not want to be dragged deeper into the conflict, although taking charge would have led to better coordination of all Australian activities in Uruzgan.

The Australians were placed under American leadership as part of 'Combined Team Uruzgan'. The refusal to accept command was perceived by some as embarrassing, given the Australians provided the bulk of ISAF's personnel assets in Uruzgan and an Australian civilian was directing provincial reconstruction efforts. Canberra would not relent. Colonel Jim Creighton of the United States Army was appointed in overall command before the Americans had even settled on their contribution in lieu of the departing Dutch. The new arrangements were not only more complicated (if that were possible), they further distorted the focus of an already disjointed mission. There was little effective interaction between the Special Forces, those mentoring Afghan partner forces and coordinating provincial reconstruction. Those to whom they reported were rarely in the same town. In the absence of clear strategic objectives and a carefully devised campaign plan, no Australian officer seemed to have sufficient visibility of what their colleagues and subordinates were doing to ensure efficiency and prevent mistakes or, worse, misconduct.

Although the insurgency appeared to lose substantial momentum in 2011, ISAF partner nations and the Taliban realised the war was winding down as the conflict entered something of a hiatus. In April 2012, the United States and NATO agreed to a three-phase withdrawal that involved relinquishing combat leadership to Afghan forces, financially supporting the training and equipping of local forces, and providing a residual international contingent to assist and advise the Afghans. Australia played a very marginal role in developing what the Americans insisted was not an 'exit strategy'. Plainly, it was. As the Australians continued to be in Afghanistan to support the Americans, the United States' draw-down prompted parallel Australian planning. When Australia finally accepted overall command of Uruzgan in 2012, in the clear and certain knowledge that the mission would end at the close of the following year, the Defence Minister (and the fifth politician to hold the portfolio in five years), Stephen Smith, claimed that things had changed since June 2010. He said: 'taking on leadership now in Uruzgan puts us in a better position to manage the transition process'.[28] It was all too late.

The Gillard Government and its predecessors had no independent policy on Afghanistan. Canberra never had a plan that did not involve the United States taking the lead and Australia following. In line with other partner forces, the ADF prepared for the return of its personnel and the dismantling (and likely destruction) of its physical assets at Tarin Kowt. Smith announced in March 2013 that the 20th SOTG rotation arriving at Tarin Kowt in June 2013 would be the last. The base would close at the end of the year.[29] In Uruzgan, at least, the Australian Government had effectively announced the Taliban had succeeded. The remaining few months were a chance for each rotation to create the best possible conditions for the Afghan Government and military forces to assume local control ahead of the Australian departure.

As the last soldiers left Uruzgan in December 2013, the newly elected Coalition Prime Minister, Tony Abbott, persisted with increasingly contrived explanations of Australia's presence in Afghanistan to placate the Australian people: 'Uruzgan today is a very significantly different and better place than it was a decade ago … the infrastructure is better, the Government functions much better; girls go to school, medical facilities are in place.'[30] He noted that al-Qaeda had been driven from their safe havens in Afghanistan, Pakistan had become a more stable place and international security had reaped a broad reward. The prime minister did not mention that the Taliban remained undefeated.

In weighing up the 'heavy question' as to whether the war had been justified, his reply excluded any reference to the United States alliance: 'if you look at the benefits for our country, for Afghanistan, and for the wider world then my conclusion is yes, it has been worth it'.[31] This succinct cost-benefit analysis revealed the substantial drift in the narrative explaining the deployment of Special Forces since mid-2005. Forty-one Australians had died and close to $10 billion had been expended over the previous seven years but the aim had never been to make Uruzgan a better place to live.[32] The Australian withdrawal quietly coincided with the substantial draw-down of American forces. Politicians were still reluctant to disclose the essential reason for deploying the ADF to Afghanistan and discuss the actual benefits of a closer alliance relationship with the United States.

With Australia's combat forces returning home, attention could be turned to the legacy of the war. The cost in terms of human life and financial expenditure was known. The emotional and psychological cost of the war was already apparent. There was no hint of a legal leftover or a moral legacy. In the eight years that Australian Special Forces operated in Uruzgan, there was never any suggestion that the mission would, *by its nature*, lead to misconduct. No observer within or beyond the Australian Government had publicly drawn comparisons between Afghanistan and similar campaigns to warn there was a greater likelihood that the Law of Armed Conflict would be breached nor counselled more rigorous attention to the ROE because there was increased possibility of violations. In other words, no special vigilance had been required in Afghanistan despite most counterinsurgencies over the previous half-century producing allegations, at least, of human rights violations. The complexity of the operating environment might have led to mistakes but these were very different from the causes of misconduct.

In the absence of credible information about wrongdoing, the Australian Government was entitled to believe its uniformed personnel had brought credit to the nation, the ADF and themselves. Australia and its military had left Afghanistan in 2014 with an enhanced reputation. The next chapter gives an overview of Australian Special Operations in Afghanistan between 2005 and 2013, and why misconduct really was an ever-present possibility.

9

SEARCHING FOR SOLUTIONS: AUSTRALIA'S LONGEST WAR

2005–2013

The initial decision to deploy Australian Special Forces to Afghanistan was echoed in the eventual decision to withdraw them. The Australians were sent to Uruzgan to support American efforts to prevent a Taliban resurgence. With the draw-down of American forces set for 2014, the Australians were also leaving, although the insurgency was far from defeated. There were hopes the international Coalition of forces had done enough to stabilise Afghan security and fortify Afghan institutions, principally Afghanistan's Army (parts of which were capable of conducting independent operations). Measuring the effectiveness of Australia's contributions in terms of enhanced Afghan peace and prosperity (albeit second-order concerns) had never been easy. Was it worth 41 Australian lives and the future wellbeing of everyone who deployed? Possibly. Those who were there – soldiers and civilians – were guided by the simple principle of doing their best with whatever they had. But there was no shortage of hurdles and hindrances alongside an array of dilemmas and conundrums that tested their discipline and integrity.

The previous chapter dealt with the political management of Australia's strategic objectives in Afghanistan. This chapter describes the mission that was handed to the Australian Defence Force (ADF) and the challenge of translating the government's objective of 'being there' into activities that would demonstrate Australian willingness to be an effective civil-military partner to the United States and NATO. The Special Operations and Reconstruction/Mentoring Task Forces (RTF/MTF) were given considerable latitude to do the things they believed they ought to be doing, consistent with American and Coalition plans and priorities. Being useful and doing things well served to mask the absence of a national strategy and a campaign plan. This masking was difficult to express in a set of orders that could be communicated to ADF members and shared with the Australian public. If there was a lack of oversight it was because the activities that might have required closer supervision did not ultimately matter.

There is one consistent theme linking both the previous chapter and this one – trust. Although Canberra is 11 500 kilometres from Kabul, the government believed it could trust those it sent to Afghanistan to conduct themselves in a dignified and disciplined manner. It did not matter whether the policy objectives were compelling or the practical outcomes were worthwhile, the politicians were confident that Australian officers and soldiers would be effective ambassadors for their country. They would need to be calm and controlled to win the battle of hearts and minds. In 2005, they were less embarking on a new venture and more resuming an unfinished journey. But when and where would the journey end? And how would they recognise the destination when they got there?

Much was unknown and perhaps unknowable about Afghanistan's future. Little attention was paid to the influence of its tumultuous past and turbulent present on incoming Australian military personnel. They would support the Afghan National Government in Kabul and its efforts to defeat the Taliban insurgency. On some level, their mission would enhance Australian security by preventing global terrorism of the kind promoted by al-Qaeda from proliferating. The professional challenges would prove less pressing than the personal dilemmas that would confront many soldiers. The possibility of mistakes and the potential for misconduct was largely overlooked. After all, the Australians were well led and vocationally motivated.

Their thorough preparation would preclude mistakes and their values would prevent misconduct.

Two months after Prime Minister Howard's announcement that Australia was committing its forces to the anti-Taliban campaign in June 2005, the first rotation of the Australian Special Forces Task Group (SFTG) arrived in Afghanistan. The Australians were based in the province of Uruzgan and would occupy a portion of the former American base on the edge of the provincial capital, Tarin Kowt. Over the next few years, they shared the facilities with an assortment of civilian and military personnel from the Czech Republic, Slovakia, the United Arab Emirates, the United States and the Netherlands. The Dutch contributed the largest contingent and exercised overall command.

The SFTG established Camp Russell (named in memory of Sergeant Andrew Russell, who was killed in 2002) as their secure area. It was not accessible to anyone but their own personnel. Around them was a vast array of demountable buildings, shipping containers and makeshift awnings which were contained within a security barrier made of large earth-filled bags interrupted by the occasional gate and observation post. Most living quarters were initially poorly fabricated plywood huts that were eventually air-conditioned and connected to subscription television services. From 2008, rocket-proof concrete accommodation and German-made pre-fabricated rocket-proof work buildings were erected.

Running the length of the base was an airstrip and associated flight lines. It was functional and temporary. Everything built by the Coalition forces would be dismantled when they departed. The military base was a world apart from the nearby town and the local population of 70 000 people.

The SFTG was an ad hoc unit created for service with the International Security Assistance Force (ISAF) in Afghanistan.[1] The first rotation consisted of 214 personnel: 95 from the SAS (Special Air Service) Regiment, 56 Commandos and six engineers together with support staff.² The SFTG's personnel did not train or travel as a combined unit. Although their mission was collaborative, they rarely worked together and lived as separate communities in their own clearly segregated areas of Camp Russell.

The headquarters was a composite group drawn from Special Operations Command (SOCOMD) units, the SOCOMD Headquarters in Canberra, other Special Operations–qualified personnel and support staff drawn from the wider ADF.³ In 2005–06, the headquarters was located at the Bagram Air Base, 64 kilometres north of Kabul and 550 kilometres from Tarin Kowt. The headquarters then shifted to Kandahar before being co-located with most other SFTG personnel in Tarin Kowt. The SFTG operated as part of Combined Joint Special Operations Task Force – Afghanistan (CJSOTF-A), a multinational force that was usually commanded by a senior American officer.⁴ The SFTG reported to the Australian Joint Task Force Commander (initially located in Iraq and later in the United Arab Emirates), the commander of ISAF Special Operations Forces in Afghanistan and the commander of ISAF's Southern Region, as well as the Australian Chief of Joint Operations in Canberra. The Special Operations Commander – Australia (SOCAUST) also maintained technical control of the Task Group during this time.⁵

The fighting components were Force Element-Alpha (FE-A), comprising SAS personnel, and Force Element-Bravo (FE-B), consisting of Commandos from the 4th Battalion, Royal Australian Regiment (4 RAR), (Commando), which was renamed the 2nd Commando Regiment in January 2009. They were supported by Force Element-Echo (FE-E), based on a troop from the Incident Response Regiment (IRR) later renamed Special Operations Engineer Regiment (SOER), which would deal principally with high-risk searches for bombs, mines and improvised explosive devices (IEDs). From November 2008, Force Element-Charlie (FE-C), drawn from the 1st Commando Regiment (which remained a Reserve unit), was deployed during the usually quieter winter rotations to give their Regular Army colleagues some respite. Prior to the formal establishment of FE-C, 1st Commando Regiment members had deployed with the Special Operations Task Group (SOTG), the name of the SFTG from 2007, to provide base security. Some members were also used as patrol reinforcements. The deployment of the two fighting elements did not neatly align and there were often periods when the bulk of one element was absent from Tarin Kowt.[6]

For the initial rotations, the Special Forces commanders were either the commanding officers of the SAS or the 2nd Commando Regiments. In later rotations, Special Operations–qualified lieutenant colonels were appointed who had commanded other Army units, or who were deemed to have appropriate expertise. Most SFTG and SOTG commanders ranged from 35 to 45 years of age and had at least a decade of Special Forces service with extensive unit, company, squadron, troop or platoon leadership experience behind them. Some of the commanders had served in both the SAS and Commando Regiments. The Regimental Sergeant Major (RSM), was a highly experienced senior non-commissioned officer (NCO) in the rank of Warrant Officer Class I and, like the commander, was either drawn from one of the SOCOMD units or from elsewhere within SOCOMD. Most commanders had been responsible for selecting, training and preparing some of the SFTG and SOTG members but none had been responsible for assembling the whole group.

FE-A consisted of an SAS 'Sabre' Squadron. The size and composition varied but FE-A was never at its full strength of three troops, each made up of four patrols. More often FE-A usually consisted of a Squadron Headquarters and initially two troops but sometimes only one. There were additional support personnel including members of 152 Signal Squadron to provide specialist communications capabilities, and intelligence and additional staff for operations and logistics. The Squadron Officer Commanding (OC) was a major who had previous experience as a Troop Commander. He worked closely with the Squadron Sergeant Major (SSM) who held the rank of Warrant Officer Class II. The Troop Commanders were captains. This was usually their first SAS appointment after being deemed fully Special Forces qualified. Most were in their late 20s to mid-30s. Some had seen operational service in regular Army units, predominantly East Timor, and some had been commissioned from the ranks. They worked alongside a Troop Sergeant who was able to draw on his previous experience as a Patrol Commander. Troop Commanders and sergeants were in the field for most operations (other than those involving a single patrol), usually in overwatch positions and in contact with the Special Forces command centre at Tarin Kowt that directed and supported missions. Squadron Commanders relied heavily on their Troop Commanders and junior non-commissioned officers (NCOs), who were best placed to gain a sense of the mood within individual patrols, to keep them informed of any personnel problems or operational issues that might require their attention and occasional intervention.

Each patrol was commanded by a Patrol Commander who usually held the rank of sergeant. (Several experienced corporals who had completed the SAS Patrol Commanders' course, but not been promoted to sergeant because they could not be freed to complete the standard promotion courses, served as Patrol Commanders in Afghanistan.) Patrols consisted of five or six men, each with specific functions, and additional specialist personnel, usually signallers or intelligence operators. The levels of responsibility shouldered by SAS Patrol Commanders were without parallel in the Australian Army. They were given considerable discretion and latitude in the planning and execution of missions at the tactical level and the requisite authority to employ resources and make decisions which may have had enduring strategic consequences.

FE-B consisted of a Commando Company Group. The size and composition of the force element varied year by year. In 2005 and 2006, it consisted of a Company Headquarters (whose members were largely used in the SFTG Headquarters in Bagram or to support operations in Tarin Kowt) and a single Commando Platoon (divided into a number of teams) with support elements including snipers, reconnaissance operators, mortars, signallers from 126 Signal Squadron, intelligence operators and logisticians. As SFTG operations were directed by the SAS Squadron Headquarters, the Commando Company was initially used in supporting roles, such as base security and low-level patrolling. By the third rotation, the Commando platoon with its support staff outnumbered the SAS Squadron and was allocated more diverse tasks.

The command structure of FE-B was similar to FE-A. The Company Officer Commanding (OC) was a major with previous experience as a Platoon Commander. It was common for the SAS Squadron OC and the Commando Company OC to have known each other since their initial entry officer training and to have completed courses together. The Company OC worked closely with the Company Sergeant Major (CSM), who held the rank of Warrant Officer Class II. The Platoon Commanders were captains. This was usually their first Special Forces appointment after being deemed fully qualified. Most were also in their late 20s to mid-30s and had served with their SAS Troop Commander peers in previous postings in conventional units. They worked alongside a Platoon Sergeant (although sometimes a Warrant Officer filled the role). The platoon was supported by a number of officers (generally captains), NCOs and specialists including an Artillery Forward Observer Team and Joint Terminal Attack Controllers (JTACs) who were certified by the United States to request American air support and other Coalition air assets. Commando sections of 12–20 men were led by a Section Commander who would hold the rank of senior corporal or sergeant. A team, similar to an SAS patrol, was led by a sergeant (occasionally by a corporal) and consisted of 6–10 men, each with specific functions.

Unlike many of their SAS counterparts, Commando officers almost always directed and supported FE-B tactical missions in the field. Commandos were predominantly drawn from other parts of the

Army where they had acquired operational experience and technical expertise. A smaller cohort of soldiers were sourced from the Special Forces Direct Recruiting Scheme (SFDRS).[7] These recruits were usually younger (aged in their early to mid-20s) but they also included pilots, medical practitioners and tradesmen who expanded the overall capacity of the Special Forces community.

Although briefed on the politics and culture of the country, the province and the district, none of the Australians had previous experience in Uruzgan, and it was unrealistic to expect them to grasp the subtleties and complexities of the networked relationships that made Afghanistan appear so enigmatic to outsiders. In fact, little could have prepared them for the morally compromising landscape they encountered where double-dealing and back-stabbing, deception and betrayal were normalised behaviours among Afghan politicians, administrators and commanders. It would take several years for a cohort of contracted academics from complementary social science disciplines to produce a reliable map of provincial affiliations and allegiances, and to prepare a composite picture of the motivations and means that were driving the insurgency.

The self-interested allegiance of the Afghan people was always critical to mission success. The Australians organised hundreds of community engagements – known as *shuras* – to explain the ISAF mission, generate local goodwill, promote the national government, and deal with any fears about the way combined ISAF and Afghan partner force operations would be conducted. The contours of Afghanistan's civil strife were more difficult to navigate than those of the previous decade in war-torn Cambodia and famine-ravaged Somalia. While insurgent incursions were more intense in other parts of the country, the situation in Uruzgan was among the most difficult to decipher given the province's intricate web of obligations and dependencies. Even with the most altruistic of intentions, every ADF member needed to be aware and alert to avoid being drawn into intrigues and schemes that might compromise their adherence to Australian standards and Army values. They also needed to resist being provoked by the Taliban into seeking revenge or over-reacting in ways that would fuel its information warfare campaign. Cheaper than rifles and more enduring than tactical military success, the insurgency's principal weapon was propaganda and the Australians were seen as a potential source of ammunition. The SFTG members needed to be sufficiently ready for the moral challenges they would face when trying to avoid the unnecessary and excessive use of force in conducting operations.

Although Uruzgan was not a geographically large province – it was only five times the area of the Australian Capital Territory – Coalition forces were often stretched in a war that was without a front line or concentration of enemy forces. There was no point in the Australians roaming the province looking for insurgents. As SFTG force elements could not be everywhere, informed decisions had to be made about the districts and villages that needed a stronger Coalition presence, the villages and compounds that were more likely to be sheltering insurgents and bomb-makers, and the roads and 'ratlines' that the insurgents preferred for transporting supplies and munitions. During their initial 12 months in Uruzgan (comprising three rotations each of four months), the Australians were highly active and made their presence felt throughout the province. They were on patrol for 306 days and in contact with insurgents on 139 occasions. They quickly realised that Taliban fighters made up for their lack of technical equipment and tactical skill with courage, ingenuity and local knowledge.

In line with the government's original announcement, the SFTG was withdrawn in September 2006. It had collaborated with American and Coalition Special Forces and, along the way, prevented the insurgency from gaining further momentum in Uruzgan. No-one thought the counterinsurgency task had been completed or that the province was now benign. SFTG personnel had nonetheless shown their proficiency and the ease with which they could be absorbed into

United States and ISAF mission planning and joint operations. For a number of SAS operators and Commandos, these rotations were the first time they had seen combat. For those who had deployed to East Timor in 1999 and Iraq in 2003, the Taliban insurgents were much more aggressive than the pro-Indonesian militias and fleeing soldiers of the Iraqi Western Desert Force. Tactical success was hard to measure and, at times, the mission was unrelenting. The insurgency resembled a hydra: whenever experienced fighters were killed or captured it was not long before their replacements appeared. The Americans would not be overly worried about this until 2009, when it became apparent the Coalition could not rely on the attrition of Taliban forces to achieve its political objectives.

By mid-2006 the Howard Government had decided to deploy a Reconstruction Task Force (RTF). This was a major undertaking, essentially committing Australia to a substantial presence in Afghanistan for at least the next five years. There were many factors involved in the deliberations that preceded the decision, including the cost. As Australia was enjoying a record run of budget surpluses and accumulated public debt had nearly been eliminated, the substantial financial burden associated with deploying an RTF was not the government's foremost concern. In pledging to support the United States and fearing the consequences of reneging on a commitment, the main worry was being bogged down in a protracted war with marginal bearing on Australian security that was bound to become unpopular if progress proved elusive. Such was the pressure being exerted by Australia's friends and allies to increase its commitment to Afghanistan that the government relented. The first RTF members began arriving in Uruzgan during August 2006.[8] Their home base would be Tarin Kowt with forward operating bases (FOBs) spread across the province. The combined Australian–Dutch Provincial Reconstruction Team (PRT) was reinforced by a Dutch battle group that consisted of infantry, armoured vehicles, artillery and fixed-wing and rotary aircraft from the Royal Netherlands Air Force.

Neither the expansion of Coalition combat forces nor the practical progress achieved by the PRT over the first 12 months was expected to end the insurgency. The ravaged country was still being rebuilt and the insurgents were yet to be deprived of resources and resolve. The Taliban seemed emboldened by the ISAF build-up and amended its tactics to exploit new vulnerabilities. The PRT became the focus for insurgent bomb-makers who were determined to make it unsafe for aid and assistance projects to be completed. The engineers needed to be protected while they concentrated on infrastructure development. Although the RTF had its own force protection element, the Australian Government announced that Special Forces rotations would resume in May 2007 for an initial two-year period. The interregnum between rotations was barely six months. Their withdrawal in September 2006, against SFTG and SOCOMD advice, had been an operational miscalculation – the first of several.

The mission assigned to Australia's Special Forces was very similar to the work being done in other provinces where ground forces had been deployed. In this sense they were not unique or even different. Elsewhere in the country comparable missions were being undertaken by non–Special Forces units. In Helmand, the British had deployed Royal Marine Commandos and battalions from the Parachute Regiment (which, by comparison, were better trained than Australian conventional forces) although operations were conducted on a much larger scale against bigger enemy formations.[9] Rather than concentrating on its traditional tasks of long-range patrolling and strategic reconnaissance, the main SAS effort gravitated towards individual targeting and direct action.

FE-A concentrated on disrupting the Taliban's leadership – which, in Uruzgan, usually involved low- or medium-value leaders – by focusing on those recruiting new fighters and directing the insurgency. Target packages were carefully developed from an array of intelligence sources. After securing multiple official approvals, the

Australians would launch missions to kill or capture insurgent leaders and fighters. Like their operating partners, the Australians preferred night operations to exploit the substantial tactical advantage their superior equipment conveyed. Once the 'objective' was secured, identities were confirmed, photographs were taken, physical evidence was collected, villagers were questioned, suspects interrogated and reports prepared highlighting lessons learned and intelligence acquired. Although these military missions originated with the SFTG, they resembled civilian policing in a number of ways. Any firefight with insurgents was treated like a crime scene. The aim was to collect sufficient evidence to have Taliban fighters charged and convicted of offences that usually attracted lengthy prison sentences.

During the three SFTG rotations (and during the earlier deployment to Iraq), the Commandos were given mundane tasks that reflected the SAS's lack of confidence in the abilities and capacities of their operationally untried colleagues. The Commandos were openly denigrated by their SAS counterparts, leading to resentment and bitterness. The result was that both force elements engaged in petty rivalries that detracted from the effective and efficient execution of their mission. It was not long, however, before the Commandos' extensive store of technical skills and infantry experience equipped them for more challenging tasks than sentry duty and goodwill patrols. During a nine-day operation in the Chora Valley, 25 kilometres north-east of Tarin Kowt, in June 2006, the Commandos demonstrated their fighting prowess and left no-one in any doubt about their readiness to fight and determination to succeed. Equally impressive was resistance to the apprehension of a Taliban commander, codenamed Objective Nile, several days later not far from Tarin Kowt. A combined operation with Canadian Special Forces, an intense firefight followed the killing of Objective Nile and led to the death of an Afghan soldier and several Coalition injuries. It was perceived by some as a 'coming of age' for FE-B and an engagement that deeply impressed some of their FE-A colleagues.[10]

After 2007, FE-B was usually deployed on larger-scale operations, sweeping through valleys, cordoning and searching villages, preventing the insurgents from developing strongholds, driving them into the open or pushing them towards SAS ambushes. Demonstrating their versatility, the Commandos were part of Operation Eagle's Summit, an operation to transport a 220-tonne turbine from Kandahar through Taliban-controlled territory to the Kajaki dam and hydroelectric powerplant in Helmand province in August 2008. Over the next 18 months, they were involved in a number of major engagements in Helmand (March – April 2009), Gizab (April 2010) and Shah Wali Kot (June 2010).

Enjoying an enormous tactical advantage enabled by superior technology and substantial resources, ISAF's principal challenge was acquiring accurate intelligence about insurgent networks and activities, and discerning who among their Afghan partners was loyal to the national government and could be trusted with confidential information. These were tasks for which the Australians were well trained and more than adequately prepared. The operating environment was, however, always complicated by the difficulty of identifying adversaries and avoiding civilian casualties. The Taliban recruited young men, eager to prove their manhood and old men, wearied by foreign interference, to gather information or spread disinformation. The work was made physically more arduous by climatic conditions – the extremes of summer when the temperatures reached mid-40s Celsius, sapping physical endurance and winter when snow and ice made travel near impossible – and the difficulty of relying on combat support, for which there was always strong competition among rival force elements. There was also the ever-present threat of IEDs littering the countryside and unexploded mines remaining from the Soviet occupation.

Although parts of Uruzgan and some of its people looked medieval, Taliban fighters were hardened by everyday life and determined to defend their land. Despite having foreign fighters in their own ranks, the Taliban were aggrieved by the intrusion of foreigners, whatever their motivations. The Taliban had no reservations about inflicting pain and suffering, injury and death on Coalition forces, their local partners and anyone in the civilian population who dared support them. The most committed fighters were prepared to die in battle with the promise of a martyr's reward. As the insurgents had no interest in discussion and no plans to negotiate, only death would end their contribution to what they considered a holy cause. In contrast to the absence of any constraint on Taliban fighters, the SOTG operated within very strict command and control arrangements that were accompanied by multiple layers of legal and political oversight, the attention of independent human rights organisations and the expectations of their own government. Their operations were subject to several tiers of official approval and guided by intelligence that was thoroughly vetted and reviewed.

As Australian officers and soldiers were now deploying to Uruzgan for their second and third rotations, they were gaining a better sense of emerging threats and imminent dangers and amending their tactics, techniques and procedures (TTPs). Their experience was gradually being translated into expertise as the SOTG collectively gained a deeper knowledge of where the Taliban were operating, when they were likely to engage Coalition forces, how they were able to infiltrate local forces and why they prioritised some objectives over others. The Australians continued to nurture local sources of information and deepened relationships with community leaders. They relied on personal friendships with members of other Coalition forces to leverage greater access to intelligence and assets, and refined their own command and control arrangements. Once they settled into an operational routine, attention shifted to regularising the administrative arrangements for the constant arrival and departure of personnel and the ordering and servicing of equipment. The SOTG's presence was far from temporary or short term. Canberra had told Washington that Australia was 'in for the long haul'. Being seen as a loyal and consistent American ally was the mission's principal objective. To ensure legal compliance and the maintenance of ethical standards, thousands of soldiers had to become thoroughly conversant with the Law of Armed Conflict (which was well established) and familiar with the Rules of Engagement (ROE) (which could evolve over time).

There was nothing to suggest the laws were too difficult for the Australians to understand or that the discipline they demanded was too strenuous. The foremost challenge was interpreting the law and applying the rules when many tactical situations were neither black nor white. The insurgents strove to fight in the 'grey zone', using the civilian population as either surrogates or shields, where they could use ethical dilemmas to morally compromise forces they could not militarily defeat. Soldiers frequently needed to make tactical decisions quickly and with minimal reflection on the factors and forces that could influence any course of action. Laws and rules were not just a series of prohibitions, they offered a range of protections. In addition to protecting civilians and non-combatants, they protected soldiers from committing illegal acts in the heat of battle and protection from accusations of lawlessness and barbarism. Laws and rules defined morality as well as legality, and were especially important during counterinsurgency, when goodwill could be won and lost as a consequence of personal behaviour.

Chaplains contributed to values education and character development, reinforcing the importance of personal commitments and professional obligations to the maintenance of ethical resilience, moral character and spiritual wellbeing. Legal officers were embedded within the SOTG to give advice on all matters relating to the Law of Armed Conflict and ROE, including their interpretation and implementation. They clarified when, where and against whom lethal force could be used, and offered guidance on responding to accusations and allegations of unnecessary and excessive uses of force. There was the potential for weak or risk-averse commanders to defer to legal officers, seeking their review of 'command decisions'. Officers and soldiers received briefings on their legal responsibilities before they departed Australia and after they arrived in Uruzgan. Handy pocket cards and aide memoires were produced to guide soldiers on what they could and could not do, when they could open fire and who they could engage. This was one of the most rigorous areas of pre-deployment preparation and the subject of discussion before and after each operation. As so much would happen in the 'grey zone', reducing ambiguity was critical.

Apart from the complexities and controversies of the Afghan war, the ADF released its revised doctrine, *Law of Armed Conflict*, in April 2006. It contained an exhortation that it be read closely by those deploying.[11] The publication outlined key principles and offered a commentary on their application. A number of practical examples were drawn from recent experience in Afghanistan. It began by explaining that

> while it is the military objective of all commanders to win in battle, there must be limits to the means and methods that may be used. Commanders must be aware of their legal obligation to prevent unnecessary injury and suffering and to alleviate as much as possible the calamities of war.[12]

This was a point of principle and pragmatism. Provoking opposition to the national government by unnecessary and excessive uses of force violated a vital counterinsurgency principle.

The publication went on to stress that the main purposes of the Law of Armed Conflict are to:

> protect combatants and non-combatants from unnecessary suffering; to safeguard certain fundamental rights of persons who fall into the hands of an enemy, such as prisoners of war (PW), the sick and civilians; to maintain the distinction between

combatants and non-combatants; and to facilitate the restoration of peace.[13]

Every Australian officer and soldier deployed to Afghanistan knew that some conduct was prohibited and illegal. Most important was observing the principle of 'non-combatant immunity'. Civilians were not legitimate targets and could not be attacked under any circumstances. This unequivocal prohibition included direct attacks on civilians and attacks that might indirectly lead to civilian harm, such as indiscriminate use of artillery or air-launched weapons. The Australians were entitled to engage combatants, including members of insurgent groups, even if they were not in uniform. They could also fire at anyone else who was armed and participating directly in hostilities. ADF members were left in no doubt that they could not engage someone who was *hors de combat* – that is, out of the fight. Rule 47 of Customary International Humanitarian Law defines someone *hors de combat* as:

> (a) anyone who is in the power of an adverse party; (b) anyone who is defenceless because of unconsciousness, shipwreck, wounds or sickness; or (c) anyone who clearly expresses an intention to surrender; provided he or she abstains from any hostile act and does not attempt to escape.[14]

The Law of Armed Conflict was supplemented by ROE which were intended to provide authoritative guidance on when, and against whom, force could legitimately be used. Within ADF doctrine, 'ROE outline and emphasise the critical aspects of the laws of war relevant to a specific mission or operation rather than a restatement of the law generally.' While the Law of Armed Conflict 'determines which actions are lawful and are therefore permissible' the Australian Government could use ROE to place 'further limitations upon the ADF (for operational, political, diplomatic and legal reasons)'.

Notably, 'ROE do not override the inherent right of individual or collective self-defence'. When 'multinational forces [are] operating in the same theatre', it is crucial that coalition partners reach agreement 'on the interpretation to be given to the terms of the ROE to ensure they comply with the domestic law of each state and to avoid confusion and inconsistent application of the ROE during the operation'. The Chief of the Defence Force (CDF) had authority to issue ROE for all ADF operations.

The ROE should have been sufficiently clear that the circumstances in which soldiers could fire their weapons were not in doubt and certainly not in dispute. Officers were expected to monitor compliance with ROE and, when required, to clarify any confusion about their interpretation or application when the prevailing situation appeared to be grey. If a soldier was in doubt about whether they were entitled to fire their weapon, they were not to shoot. If the adversary changed tactics or attempted deception, officers could seek ROE extensions or amendments to cover new and evolving situations. As Special Forces soldiers were often pursuing known individuals, they were usually able to decide whether or not they would engage – other than when they were personally threatened and exercised their right of self-defence. For security reasons, ROE were not published or discussed in open forums to prevent the Taliban from gaining an advantage by knowing what the Australians would and would not do.[15]

The ROE drafted for Afghanistan reflected the Law of Armed Conflict and Australian domestic law. They could not authorise assassinations, which were defined in ADF doctrine as the unlawful 'sudden or secret killing by treacherous means of an individual who is not a combatant, by premeditated assault, for political or religious reasons'.[16] The most challenging dimension of interpreting and then applying the ROE related to the engagement of individuals referred to as 'spotters' and 'squirters', and establishing 'hostile intent'.[17]

A 'spotter' was someone who assisted the insurgency by alerting

Taliban fighters to approaching Coalition forces and provided information on their location, number and weaponry. Their role was to ensure the insurgents were best placed for either attack or withdrawal, helping Taliban leaders to escape and evade capture, and luring Coalition forces towards an ambush or IED site. Some spotters were stationary and communicated whatever they observed within their field of view; others moved on foot towards Coalition forces in ambush or overwatch positions. Men and boys served as spotters. As it was usual for women and children to leave the area before any anticipated engagement with Coalition forces, lone individuals in unexpected places attracted suspicion. Although spotters were not usually armed and rarely engaged enemy forces, they often carried mobile phones or ICOM (a brand of commercial communication device) ultra high frequency (UHF) short-range, handheld, two-way radios, which could be evidence of participation in the insurgency. Under the Law of Armed Conflict, spotters could not be engaged if they were unarmed and were not carrying a communications device. It would, however, be permissible to engage a spotter if there was reason to believe they were using an ICOM radio to convey tactical information to Taliban fighters ahead of an imminent attack and were, therefore, directly participating in hostilities. The deaths of unarmed spotters were readily exploited by the Taliban, who would usually claim the spotter was an innocent civilian.

A 'squirter' was someone who ran from Coalition forces in a manner that suggested involvement in insurgent activity and direct participation in hostilities. Squirters could have been Taliban fighters fleeing approaching Coalition soldiers, moving towards concealed weapons or gaining a superior tactical position. In the absence of any differences in their appearance, someone observed running could just as easily have been a frightened civilian non-combatant fleeing an approaching helicopter or vehicle convoy.

Conversely, Coalition soldiers were not entitled under the Law of Armed Conflict to open fire simply because an individual was seen running. The person needed to be doing more than running; the critical consideration was displaying 'hostile intent'. As most Afghan compounds in rural areas had a firearm for self-defence, the Australians needed to avoid shooting civilian non-combatants who may have possessed a firearm for self-defence or the protection of their families. Admittedly, it was difficult to determine hostile intent quickly and among fearful people known for erratic behaviour.

SOTG commanders were convinced that the leadership and discipline to which Special Forces soldiers were subject, when coupled with the experience and expertise they acquired, entitled them to feel confident that their soldiers would adhere completely to the ROE and would not employ unnecessary or excessive uses of force. They were also guided by the Joint Prioritised Effects List (JPEL), revealed by Wikileaks in 2010, which required its own compliance regime. Only Taliban leaders of note made it to the JPEL and only after considerable time and effort were expended justifying their inclusion. The JPEL was mistakenly referred to by media commentators as an 'assassination list'. Its foremost purpose was helping ISAF disrupt and, if possible, destroy insurgent networks by removing key leaders and major organisers. It was essentially a prioritised inventory of people, referred to as 'objectives', that the Coalition needed to pursue. They could be killed or, preferably, captured. The JPEL contained details of the individual's appearance, activities, affiliations and their position within the Taliban hierarchy. Most of the JPEL objectives in Uruzgan were either low- or middle-ranking leaders or technicians with specialist skills, such as bomb-making and communications. As hunting JPEL targets was an important element of ISAF operational planning, 'time sensitive targeting' became the norm. The targeting cycle was known as 'F3EA' – find, fix, finish, exploit and analyse – and was supported by a Fusion and Targeting Cell. The 'finish' element meant capturing or killing the insurgent leader.

When reliable information on the location of a JPEL objective was received, the Australians needed to be 'out the door' without delay to ensure the insurgent could neither flee nor hide. If the suspect had been located and positively identified, and apprehending them was not possible, he (it was almost always a male) could be targeted. If a suspect was co-located with civilians, air strikes with the potential to cause collateral damage were not an option. Force remained the option of last resort because Afghan civilian deaths produced antipathy that the Taliban could exploit to discredit the government and attract support.

The most frustrating aspect of these particular missions was the ISAF detainee policy, which became known unofficially as 'catch and release'. Suspected insurgents could only be detained by ISAF forces for a maximum of 96 hours. If there was not sufficient evidence to bring charges against an individual, they would be released. In other instances, suspected insurgents bribed judges and prison officials to secure their freedom. On occasions, the system seemed farcical. Fighters were removed from the battlefield only to reappear a week later with better insights into how ISAF operated and more effective strategies for defeating the legal system. There was obvious temptation to kill rather than capture known or suspected insurgents, although nothing of intelligence value could be gained from a dead man.

Following any engagement in which individuals were detained and questioned, captured and charged, and wounded or killed, a designated SOTG member was required to undertake Site Sensitive Exploitation (SSE). It served a number of purposes including evidence collection for criminal proceedings, intelligence gathering for future operations and as a record justifying the use of lethal force. Any 'pocket litter' was removed from the clothing of insurgents; weapons (including ammunition, magazines and chest rigs) were rendered safe; any communication devices were retained; the dead and wounded (those without life-threatening injuries) were fingerprinted and photographed; and extensive information was collected on the site of the engagement, including its topography and built environment.

On returning to Tarin Kowt there would usually be an After

Action Review (AAR), also known as a 'hot wash up', to capture recollections while they remained fresh and reliable. The AAR would inform an operational summary (OPSUM) and an intelligence summary (INTSUM) which were prepared for distribution to senior commanders within and beyond Afghanistan. In the event of civilian casualties or when an engagement had been the subject of comments or complaints from the Afghan Government or agencies such as the International Committee of the Red Cross (ICRC), a number of command and administrative authorities could order an inquiry which would determine whether further investigation was warranted or information existed to commence legal or disciplinary proceedings against an individual.

Most of the time-sensitive targeting work fell to SAS operators who had acquired advanced and well-rehearsed direct action skills. The work undertaken by the Commandos reflected their special skills and different organisation. While the Taliban's leadership networks had been disrupted, an attempt was made to target another of their critical vulnerabilities – finance. As they operated in large formations, the Commandos were ideally placed to debilitate the narcotics trade upon which the Taliban depended to acquire weapons and pay fighters. Like most insurgent groups – the IRA, the Kosovo Liberation Army, the Tamil Tigers and Hezbollah – the Taliban relied on drug trafficking to fund their attacks. But destroying drug crops did not guarantee success. The World Bank noted there were 'pluses and minuses' associated with the opium economy. The production and sale of opium substantially 'boosted rural incomes' but created opium-related debt 'which may precipitate drastic measures like mortgaging and losing land, or giving up daughters in marriage to pay off opium debt … and drug addiction'.[18]

This risk of losing local support was considered to balance the benefit of de-funding the insurgency in Afghanistan. It was a complicated equation involving a number of variables including market forces. When supplies dwindled, prices went up. The destruction of marijuana and opium crops, albeit temporarily, also appealed to domestic sentiment among ISAF nations. Drugs produced in Afghanistan were usually sold in Europe. Assertions that Afghan drugs would not be available on Australian streets overlooked the preponderance of Asian production and supply networks. Nevertheless, suppressing the manufacture and distribution of narcotics appealed to community sentiment wherever it was mentioned. The Commando element of the SOTG partnered with the United States Drug Enforcement Agency to conduct anti-narcotics and counter-nexus operations.[19] These operations targeted individuals whose involvement in the drug trade assisted the insurgency. This work had the added benefit of separating the Commandos from the SAS, easing intra-unit tensions and lessening competition for scarce resources.

There were many turning points throughout the war in Afghanistan. Within a few years of the Australian arrival, the Taliban's leadership was being depleted and the narcotics trade had been disrupted. The local community had benefited from infrastructure development and the exponentially expanding ability of Australian combat engineers to clear mines from roads and villages and render safe a variety of explosive devices. Although there was modest progress, it had taken considerable time to achieve, and time was what the counterinsurgency forces did not have. Several ISAF partner nations indicated their intention to withdraw before the insurgency was defeated. The Dutch went home at the close of 2010, the Canadians would depart the following year and the French would leave in 2012. The governments of most ISAF partner nations had wearied of the war. They were troubled by corruption in the Afghan Government, the weakness of Afghan forces and the persistence of the Taliban. They were also struggling to find sufficient military personnel to fulfil their ISAF commitments. Every member of the 'Five Eyes' intelligence-sharing alliance – the United States, the United Kingdom, Canada, New Zealand and Australia – sent the same soldiers back to Afghanistan multiple times. It was becoming clear that the entire

NATO Special Forces community were showing signs of fatigue. The same was true for Australia as some soldiers contemplated their fifth and sixth SOTG rotations without an end to the conflict in sight.

Given SOCOMD personnel were a finite resource, planners asked whether well-prepared Australian infantry soldiers could have replaced SAS operators and Commandos? The answer would become significant when commentators later argued the conduct of Special Forces soldiers gradually deteriorated because they were over-used. The question itself created a deep divide within the Army. An audacious infantry officer, Jim Hammett, published a provocative article headed 'We were soldiers once'.[20] Hammett spoke for many of his colleagues when he argued the Royal Australian Infantry Corps was in decline, largely because it was 'rated as a distant second choice for combat operations behind the special operations forces'.[21] He pointed to a 'Special Forces-generated mission creep that usurps the role of the Infantry' which, he felt, was 'over-trained and under experienced'. He observed that the infantry 'are trained to fight, equipped to fight, and being indoctrinated to expect to fight – they are doing many other things but they are not fighting' because, he fears, the Army 'does not consider the infantry capable of the job, and trusts only the ability of Special Forces'.

It was not that the Army lacked trust in the infantry. There was a perception that Special Forces personnel were more highly trained, operated in smaller contingents, were unsuited to major battles and were less likely to be killed and in significant numbers. Casualties threatened public support and depleted political will. The ADF knew deaths in action had to be avoided. The problem for the SAS and the Commando Regiments was ensuring a steady supply of suitable personnel were available for deployment. SAS sergeant and Patrol Commander Harry Moffitt thought the Regiment's personnel were being overused and their skills poorly applied. His misgivings were revealing in other respects:

> It was understood the SAS would never be used to do conventional operations ... but during the Afghanistan campaign, year by year this was changing. We were in some ways a victim of our reputation: because we were good, we were seen as capable of doing anything and everything, and were therefore in danger of believing this. Where we had been trained for unconventional work, now we were increasingly being sent in as an elite commando force to sledgehammer an enemy with high risk and high casualties, relatively conventional operations that over time were conducted in full daylight, robbing us of our advantages to dominate the enemy. From then, we were no longer playing to our strengths.[22]

He referred to this thinking as 'creeping conventionalism' – the SAS being used to do work usually allocated to conventional forces – and acknowledged that it created tension between Special Forces and conventional infantry units who 'appeared to resent us, which led to communication issues'.

Believing that Special Forces soldiers were less likely to be killed in battle and desperate to minimise casualties to avoid depleting public support for the war, the Australian Government decided to persist with SOTG operations as the 'tip of the spear' in Afghanistan. This persistence played well with the Americans too. The most pressing problem was not the composition of the Australian contribution to ISAF but the standard of the local partner forces to whom the Australians would eventually transfer responsibility for provincial security. Notwithstanding the training provided by exemplary Australian officers and soldiers, the Afghan forces were still considered ill-disciplined and unreliable. Absenteeism and desertion were common. Tribal loyalties worked against command authority and drug abuse was widespread. The Afghan National Army needed to be capable of sustained independent operations if ISAF were to withdraw and the insurgency was not to prevail.

By 2011 the ISAF and Australian emphasis shifted to

mentorship and partnering. The RTF had become the Mentoring and Reconstruction Task Force (MRTF) before the reconstruction component of its mandate was dropped altogether and it became the MTF. The SOTG were directed to work more closely with Afghan personnel. The force assigned to every major mission would include Afghan forces, comprising half when possible. As it was their country, they needed to be fully committed to the fight. While the Australians were not willing to disclose details of an impending mission in advance for fear the Afghan uniformed personnel would warn the insurgents of their intentions and tactics, they were also not prepared to rely on the Afghans in battle. Afghan forces either lacked commitment and determination, or their close combat proficiency was less than it needed to be in a gunfight.

The relationship between the Australians and their local counterparts was further strained by the threat of 'insider attacks' from 'rogue' Afghan soldiers and local police who had decided to fight for the Taliban. 'Green-on-blue' (Afghan on ISAF) attacks were contrary to Afghan national law. These attacks would result in the deaths of over 150 NATO personnel and nearly 600 Afghans between 2005 and 2015,[23] including seven Australians in three such attacks.

Lance Corporal Andrew Jones was shot dead by an Afghan soldier, Shafied Ullah, on 30 May 2011 at a patrol base in the Chora Valley. Ullah was located by American forces two weeks later and killed after resisting arrest. On 29 October 2011, Captain Bryce Duffy, Corporal Ashley Birt and Lance Corporal Luke Gavin were shot dead by an Afghan junior officer, Darwish Khan, at a patrol base in Shah Wali Kot. Khan was later shot dead. The third insider attack occurred on 29 August 2012 when an Afghan sergeant, Hekmatullah, shot and killed Sapper James Martin, Private Robert Poate and Lance Corporal Stjepan Milosevic at patrol base Wahab in Uruzgan province.[24] Another three Australians were wounded when an Afghan soldier opened fire on them in November 2011. Insider attacks on ISAF forces would escalate from one or two each year before 2008 to

44 in 2012 and became the Taliban's preferred tactic for advancing the insurgency and depleting Coalition morale, constituting 15 per cent of all ISAF combat deaths in 2012.[25]

The highest number of ISAF combat deaths was in 2010, when 711 soldiers were killed. This was two years before deaths caused by insider attacks reached a peak. The 'insider attack' strategy might not have prevented the ISAF death toll from falling substantially in 2011 to 566 killed, but it was an effective tactic that hardened the resolve of some NATO nations to leave Afghanistan without delay.[26] By the time the 'insider attack' strategy had gained momentum in 2012, the withdrawal of Coalition forces had already been announced. Notwithstanding the increasing number of ISAF personnel killed in such incidents, these attacks inevitably led to distrust and resentment of Afghan soldiers among the Australians and may have influenced their attitudes to the civilian population as well.

A decade after the 2001 invasion, peace in Afghanistan remained a distant prospect. The Coalition had made progress in many parts of the country, including the traditional Taliban heartland of Kandahar, but the insurgency's leaders were showing little interest in negotiating and no intention of capitulating. Despite the demonstrable success of night raids, and concessions from Taliban leaders that they had been effective, President Karzai told a *loya jirga* of 2000 specially chosen tribal leaders and political figures in November 2011 that he was willing to grant an extension to America's mission beyond President Obama's 2014 withdrawal date on the condition they cease the night missions that had effectively muted the insurgency.[27] The Australians remained deeply frustrated at having to operate in daylight against an adversary who was unconcerned by the prospect of an endless war. It was another marker of the insurgents being handed tactical success.

Most Taliban fighters had known nothing other than perpetual armed conflict throughout their adult lives. The struggle against the Coalition was anything but an aberration. It gave them purpose, prestige and, ultimately, position. The only person who might have called an end to the insurgency was Mullah Mohammad Omar and he had been a virtual ghost since 2001. Indeed, there were doubts he was still alive. (He died in April 2013 from natural causes.) It seemed the movement could continue without him. A memorandum circulated by senior Taliban leaders in October 2011 urged closer attention to domestic policy issues. The Americans were scheduled to withdraw from 2014 and the insurgents started to sense ultimate victory.

The only existential threat to the insurgency was Pakistan, which was showing no signs of ending its support to the Taliban. Indeed, there was evidence that higher grade explosives from Pakistani sources were made available to the insurgency from mid-2011. Despite Pakistan's consistent public denials that it was offering the insurgency any support and American insistence it had irrefutable evidence, the relationship between the United States and Pakistan was at a low ebb following the killing of Osama bin Laden by United States Navy SEALs at Abbottabad on 2 May 2011. It was a bold action on Washington's part that defied international conventions and national law. In essence, it was an armed attack on a foreign national within a sovereign state conducted without its knowledge or permission. The Australians were aware their adversaries were sheltering across the Pakistani border where they were untouchable. It gave the war a surreal feel. At every point, law or diplomacy prevented or precluded firm and decisive action, although no well-informed Australian soldier believed the Coalition could kill its way to victory. They realised that fresh Taliban fighters were being recruited every day and that replacements for those they took off the battlefield would arrive sooner or later. There would always be someone to fight while a political solution remained elusive.

Australian combat losses had not been large when compared to the world wars, Korea and Vietnam.[28] Three soldiers were killed in late 2007: one from the RTF, one from the SAS and one from the Commandos. Another three were killed in 2008; two Commandos and one from the SAS. There were four soldiers killed in 2009:

one from the Commandos, two from the MRTF and one from the Incident Response Regiment (IRR) during the defusing of an IED. In 2010, 10 soldiers lost their lives: six from the MTF, three from the Commandos, and one from the SAS. In 2011, it was seven from the MTF, two Commandos and one from the IRR. Seven soldiers died in 2012: three from the 3 RAR Task Group, two Commandos, one from the IRR and one from the SAS. One soldier died in 2013 and another in 2014, both from the Commandos. In total, there were 41 deaths in Afghanistan including 15 Commandos and four SAS operators.

There was growing domestic unease about the number of soldiers killed in 'unacceptable' ways. It was inevitable that Australians would be killed in action as a result of enemy small arms fire, bombs and explosive devices. Less acceptable were helicopter accidents and completely unacceptable were 'insider attacks'. The Australian public were outraged by the murder of Australian soldiers by their Afghan allies. Alongside the deaths and posthumous awards, dozens of living officers and soldiers received honours and awards. Public opinion had had little influence on government decision-making or the conduct of the war.

When the SOTG was withdrawn at the end of 2013, Australia had proved to the United States that it was both a loyal ally and an effective military partner. Unlike Australia, which had achieved its main objective, the Coalition simply ran out of time to achieve its objective – defeating the insurgency. Could Australia have made much of a difference to the way the war was conducted? Not really. Its contribution was small and intended to complement American efforts. Lessons were being learned but incremental changes of policy could not overcome the fragility of Afghan democracy, the frailty of its institutions and the failings of its National Army. Afghanistan belonged to the Afghans, who struggled to make much progress fashioning the kind of nation-state the foreigners hoped it would become.

In Canberra, the principal activity was coordinating effort rather than defining strategy. The war lacked a sponsor and an advocate. This was partly a consequence of two changes of government (in 2007 and 2013 – excluding the replacement of Kevin Rudd by Julia Gillard as prime minister in June 2010, which had no bearing on the war in Afghanistan), the appointment of five different Defence ministers (Robert Hill, Brendan Nelson, Joel Fitzgibbon, Stephen Smith and John Faulkner – excluding David Johnson, whose tenure started after the withdrawal had been announced) and the usual turnover of service chiefs, senior commanders and unit commanding officers. Afghanistan was someone else's problem and everyone else's war.

There were political priorities and diplomatic aspirations but these were never translated into a coherent military strategy or a consistent campaign plan. Afghanistan was foremost a failure at the strategic level, due to the inability to link real political objectives with sound operational planning. It resulted in command chain dysfunction that was more about activities than achievements. In the absence of a consolidated plan, those deployed to Afghanistan did the best they could with the resources that were available. They rarely complained about problems not of their own making. They sought 'work-arounds' when they lacked people or assets; they accepted partial victories rather than seeking lasting success. Few commanders were temperamentally disposed to complaining about the factors and forces that prevented them from executing their mission. They were characteristically 'can do' people who realised that no-one rises to the top by identifying difficulties and embarrassing superiors, especially when the most serious problems could be attributed to the military–political nexus. The 'can do' people within the SOTG looked for ways to break the insurgency when the hurdles and obstacles imposed by ISAF and ADF officialdom appeared increasingly insurmountable.

Nonetheless, the SAS and the Commando Regiments emerged from the Afghan war with enhanced reputations. Australian Special Forces personnel appeared to have adhered to professional standards and maintained their ethical moorings. There were suspicions that some soldiers might have gone too far in their personal determination to defeat the insurgency but these suspicions had not caught the attention of Australia's political or military leaders as the last soldier departed Tarin Kowt and the base was closed. The post-mortems had begun. The lessons to be learned were soon to be overshadowed by the legacies that needed to be managed.

PART III
THE DRAMA

10

RUMOUR AND REFORM: THE CROMPVOETS AND IRVINE REPORTS

2014–2018

In 1987, 15 years after the last Australian servicemen and women departed South Vietnam at the close of a war that had led to reunification of the Vietnamese people under the Communist regime in Hanoi, there was a belated welcome home parade for all personnel who deployed there between 1962 and 1972. The Hawke Labor Government was persuaded of the need for a highly symbolic occasion, acknowledging the bitterness and resentment that many veterans harboured at the reception they had received on returning home to a country divided over the merits and morals of a controversial war. By way of contrast, in 2015, just 15 months after the last combat troops departed Afghanistan, welcome home parades for Australian Defence Force (ADF) members, police, defence and diplomatic officials were held in all capital cities and in Townsville. Noting that many Vietnam veterans had felt 'unloved and unappreciated' for decades, Prime Minister Tony Abbott urged everyone who went to Afghanistan to participate in one of the parades.[1]

In an address delivered at the Australian War Memorial in March 2015, the prime minister observed the war in Afghanistan had 'ended not with victory, and not with defeat, but with hope for a better Afghanistan, and for a safer world'.[2] It echoed a comment he had first made at Tarin Kowt in October 2013. He told those who deployed: 'we are grateful to have you home, we acknowledge your achievements, and we thank you for your service'. The Labor Opposition Leader, Bill Shorten, 'saluted those who had served in Afghanistan and brought new honour to the Anzac tradition'.[3] The Chief of the Defence Force, Air Chief Marshal Mark Binskin, claimed the Australians had given Afghans 'new hope' while the nation could 'never repay the debt of those who served'. Former Special Air Service (SAS) Regiment commanding officer and veteran of the 2001 Afghan invasion, Major General 'Gus' Gilmore, remarked that 'every soldier, officer, sailor, every air man and woman who went across there did their job magnificently'.[4]

The prime minister's admission that the Australian contribution had 'ended' in neither victory nor defeat involved considerable sleight of hand on two counts. First, Australia sent its forces to Afghanistan in support of the United States. Other nations withdrew but the Australians remained. Irrespective of the outcome, Australia's objective of strengthening its relationship with the United States had been fulfilled. Second, as the conflict in Afghanistan had not ended, the prime minister could not forsee the Taliban victory in August 2021. His declaration about raising hope in Afghanistan was essentially an expression of Australian optimism. At least, he could reasonably contend, those who represented Australia had striven to uphold the nation's values. ADF personnel had brought credit to themselves, their families and their country.

Although 2015 was far too early to offer any comprehensive appraisal of the ADF's performance in Afghanistan, many lessons had been learned at the strategic, operational and tactical levels. Some of these insights had been gleaned from analysing the effectiveness of policies and procedures, and from investigations and inquiries into accidents and incidents where people had made mistakes or equipment had malfunctioned. Dozens of 'quick assessments' had been made of Special Operations Task Group (SOTG) engagements in which the force used *might* have been unnecessary or excessive or when the deaths of non-combatants, sometimes children, *might* have been avoided. The only public pursuit of an alleged breach of the Law of Armed Conflict was the discontinued prosecution of three members of the 1st Commando Regiment after a 2009 raid in which a family had been killed (one adult and five children).

There were, however, claims that Australian operations led to unintended civilian casualties. Members of both the SAS and the Commando Regiments were the subject of these claims in roughly equal measure. The first such claim was made within 12 months of the Australians arriving in Uruzgan in September 2005.[5] A member of the Afghan parliament complained that his family had been unnecessarily fired upon by SAS soldiers as they were fleeing the town of Chora in a private motor vehicle in July 2006, inflicting one death and other serious injuries. The ADF initially claimed there was no evidence of an SAS patrol being in that area when the firing occurred. Later advice confirmed the SAS had fired on the vehicle (although in another location) because they believed its occupants were insurgents. The ADF was accused of a cover-up when relevant information held in Afghanistan was not conveyed to Canberra ahead of a Senate Committee hearing on 14 February 2007.[6] In November 2007, a compound clearance led to the accidental deaths of an infant and a teenage girl, and complaints that detainees were mistreated. The Afghan deaths were attributed to unintentional collateral damage and the physical abuse claims were later withdrawn. An Australian Commando was also killed in the operation.[7] In 2008, there were allegations that ADF personnel had treated Afghans with disrespect; fired mortar rounds that killed a youth and some livestock; and needlessly shot an off-duty Afghan soldier at a checkpoint.

Subsequent inquiries made no formal findings of wrongdoing. Similar incidents were reported in subsequent years with consistent complaints that Australians were applying lethal force without adequate oversight; resorting to airstrikes against poorly or misidentified targets leading to civilian casualties; citing 'hostile intent' as the standard explanation for non-insurgent deaths; blaming flawed intelligence for preventable civilian deaths during cordon and search operations; mistreating detainees and assaulting individuals under interrogation; and destroying private property without justification.[8]

The first detailed allegation of serious misconduct was featured in an ABC Television *Four Corners* program entitled 'In their sights' which was broadcast on 5 September 2011.[9] The program examined three raids conducted in 2008, 2009 and 2011. In two of the raids, the 'wrong' people were killed. The most egregious raid was the third because it constituted misconduct rather than a mistake. Based on interviews with local Afghans, *Four Corners* reported that a group of Australian soldiers entered a warehouse and asked for the owner, the well-known Tarin Kowt businessman Hayat Ustad. When Ustad raised his hands and identified himself, an SAS operator was alleged to have led him away and killed him. The provincial governor, Muhammad Omar Shirzad, claimed the Coalition did not have any reliable intelligence implicating Ustad. Others told *Four Corners* that the raids were based on false intelligence from Matiullah Khan (MK), who was seeking to eliminate his political rivals, such as the Chora District police chief, Rozi Khan, later killed in September 2008. (MK later replaced the provincial chief of police, Fazi Ahmad Shirzad (no relation to Provincial Governor Shirzad), in August 2011.) In sum, *Four Corners* alleged that the actions of Australian Special Forces personnel were alienating the civilian community in Uruzgan from the national government in Kabul and involved, in at least one instance, the commission of a war crime.

Given the difficulties of accessing and gathering reliable information it was not surprising that *Four Corners*' presentation of the killing of both Khan and Ustad contained inaccuracies and deliberate fabrications.[10] Rozi Khan was killed after he and members of his militia mistakenly ambushed an FE-A patrol. The incident occurred at night and was deemed a 'friendly fire' incident, one of many during the Afghan war, and not a raid conducted on the basis of false intelligence. Khan's son later admitted that his father's men thought they were engaging the Taliban and not the Australians.

Concerning the Ustad case, journalist Chris Masters reported that the International Security Assistance Force (ISAF) had firm evidence of his Taliban connections and the ADF confirmed the SOTG had obtained a signed warrant authorising his arrest.[11] Ustad drew a pistol when evading capture and was shot by an Australian soldier in self-defence, as permitted under the Rules of Engagement (ROE).[12] Had the Australians been manipulated into killing one of MK's business associates? Defence explained that as part of:

> ISAF efforts to help stabilise Afghanistan, Australian forces regularly engage with a wide range of tribal and community leaders in Uruzgan in an inclusive and impartial way. In this setting, Matiullah Khan is one of many influential figures that Australians have engaged. Australia works with such individuals in a way to ensure that their influence is used positively, in support of governance and security in Uruzgan.[13]

Defence explained that it was constrained by security considerations from revealing all that was known about Ustad and his links with the insurgency.[14]

Further, Defence claimed, 'the ADF has built a very good understanding of the tribal dynamics, familial associations and insurgent propaganda in Uruzgan. Allegations against prominent individuals are commonplace.' Whether its understanding was 'good' or merely adequate, the ADF was at least alert to the issues and the prospect that Australian forces could be 'played' by politically astute, media-savvy Afghans. Conversely, the Australians did not disclose what the Coalition knew about Taliban affinities or how its intelligence was derived. In this instance, however, they did share enough to convince the provincial governor and MK of Ustad's links to the insurgency as the mission had government approval. As much of the activity reported in the *Four Corners* program involved issues of operational security which prevented the release of information to confirm the legality of the SOTG's actions, the seriousness of the allegations and the conviction with which they were reported meant public confidence in the leadership and discipline of Australia's Special Forces was inevitably diminished. The *Four Corners* program placed excessive reliance on one-sided Afghan testimony. Its account was distorted without a detailed response from Defence, which it was unable to provide because of operational security.

The published reports of some ADF inquiries into civilian casualties suggested that the SOTG was generally afforded the benefit of the doubt when Australian soldiers shot unarmed youths and men who were judged to have 'hostile intent', or to have been 'manoeuvring tactically' or considered to be 'directly participating in hostilities'. As explained in the previous chapter, 'squirters' and 'spotters' could be lawfully engaged under specific conditions. The legality of an action turned in a split second on what a soldier claimed to have heard or seen, and relied on their personal judgment that a particular individual indeed posed a threat to them and their colleagues. The spirit of the Law of Armed Conflict and the ROE could, of course, have been disregarded by those too eager to take down potential insurgents. For instance, an unarmed 'fighting age male' observed running near a target compound may have been complicit in hostile action, justifying lethal engagement, or simply afraid of being shot. It was possible for two soldiers to have interpreted the situation differently and then to have reacted differently. Both were accountable for the decision they made.

In most inquiries into apparent mistakes and alleged misconduct, the explanations provided by Australian soldiers were accepted by investigators who presumed SOTG members were honest witnesses who spoke truthfully about their actions and those of their colleagues.

Conversely, information provided by Afghans was considered unreliable and untruthful, exaggerated and self-serving and, in some instances, concocted purely for propaganda purposes or financial gain. This was sometimes but not always true. According to successive Defence ministers and senior commanders, the Australians had been aggressive and unrelenting in the conduct of their counterterrorism and counterinsurgency tasks but had always operated within the law. The parliament and people were assured they respected legal limits on what they could do.

During a number of in-theatre inquiries into insurgent or civilian deaths, senior SOTG officers sometimes gave less than their full support to these time-consuming inquiries, while some SOTG members exercised their right not to speak with the ADF Investigative Service. By way of contrast to the explanation of battlefield deaths which were readily accepted without serious challenge, *injuries* to detainees were closely scrutinised. Detainees displaying any signs of physical duress often triggered investigations launched from Australia.

The impression created during some of these proceedings was that some members of the SOTG, principally SAS soldiers, were either hiding things from official investigations or they did not trust 'outsiders' to interpret correctly what they might find. In other words, mistakes might have been deemed misconduct. After the SOTG was withdrawn late in 2013, unnamed ADF members claimed that several SAS patrols resembled cliques, fuelling speculation about their behaviour 'outside the wire'.[15] They spoke of occasions when patrol members were heard boasting of acts that were contrary to the ROE, only to assert later when challenged that the stories had been made up, misheard, misunderstood or manufactured by colleagues. It was said that particular officers felt the need to observe certain soldiers closely and to reaffirm constantly the importance of complying with the Law of Armed Conflict and abiding by ROE. Both were, of course, integral to the overall success of ISAF's mission. With time, it was suggested, suspicions were compounded by rumours of wrongdoing that were second-hand or even third-hand.

Stories of alleged misconduct, usually involving SAS patrols rather than Commando platoons, circulated more widely once Australian forces were no longer in harm's way. Some of those who served in Afghanistan decided to pursue civilian careers, including as private security contractors, once they returned home. These officers and soldiers felt less constrained by operational secrecy and less bound by regimental loyalties when it came to speaking about what they had seen and heard. But it was difficult to differentiate fact from fiction or accuracy from exaggeration in the absence of first-hand accounts and verifiable information. It appeared that stories spread by a variety of means. By way of illustration, one officer heard a colleague expressing reservations about the official account of an insurgent's death; one soldier knew two mates who no longer spoke to each other because of an incident in Afghanistan that neither would talk about. By such means, a number of stories about alleged wrongdoing began to spread as rumours. There were no formal statements to substantiate any rumour and no official complaints to authenticate the hearsay that was gaining momentum and acquiring gravity. In this environment, soldiers harbouring resentments could easily find ways to discredit those they despised either because they had been promoted more quickly or recognised too generously with honours. There was no shortage of personal enmities within the deeply divided SAS community in particular.

With hearsay spreading, no former or serving officer or soldier apparently availed themselves of whistleblower protections to make a formal report of what they had heard or seen – even if what they heard was hearsay. This was understandable, not simply because of their unwillingness to 'dob in' mates but also because whistleblowers in Australia sometimes end up suffering personally and professionally. Nothing incriminating was leaked to the media, neither videos nor photographs, although there was reportedly plenty of such material.

The ABC journalist Mark Willacy mentioned in one news story there were 'hundreds of images and more than 10 hours of [film] footage', in private hands that might have either aroused distrust or averted suspicion.[16] Cryptic comments were made during training courses, gossip circulated on social media and journalists became aware of angst over the bestowing of decorations and citations to some and not to others within each rotation. The SAS was the usual focus of these stories. Either the Commandos had always acted within the law or there were fewer personal enmities to set one against another.

Not everyone added to the now-swirling stories. There was no record of any SAS member, other than Ben Roberts-Smith, identifying himself as a veteran of the Afghanistan war and commenting publicly on any aspect of the material that was being cited to implicate Special Forces soldiers. Those who had deployed refused to confirm or deny rumours and counselled their colleagues to leave the past behind and say nothing. The conventional wisdom was that whatever had happened in Afghanistan should remain there. The units within SOCOMD needed to prepare for the next conflict and the adversary was unlikely to resemble the Taliban insurgent. Others felt differently about the past and the future. There were lingering legacies of the Afghan conflict, other than alleged misconduct, that needed to be addressed candidly and conscientiously.

On becoming the Australian Special Operations Commander (SOCAUST) in December 2014, Major General Jeff Sengelman was directed to 'identify and remediate what was then, disturbing evidence of governance and behavioural lapses' in his command (SOCOMD).[17] Sengelman was well acquainted with SOCOMD units. He commanded an SAS Squadron in the early 1990s and 4 RAR (Cdo) in 2000 when it deployed to East Timor. As SOCAUST he detected 'double standards, compromised leaders, unconscious bias, the assumed adequacy of norms, a reluctance to fault correct outcomes below Army standard, defensive to critique [and] an instinct to cover shortcomings rather than to declare them'.

Focusing specifically on the SAS Regiment, he noted that in the financial year 2014–15, a senior NCO was charged with removing explosive ordnance and other Army property from Campbell Barracks; a member of SAS support staff was arrested by the civilian police over his involvement in an armed robbery; and a beret-qualified SAS member reported that private firearms stored in a personal locker at the barracks were missing.[18] The implication was that discipline at Campbell Barracks was poor and that members of the SAS Regiment were among the worst offenders. In reality, the level of offending was no greater than elsewhere in the Army and SAS members did not feature among the worst offenders.

Sengelman discerned that mateship was prioritised over leadership, 'resulting in an undermining of the chain of command and a confused notion of what was acceptable'. There were 'systemic failings' that included 'a normalised deviance from process, tribalism, trust deficits, responsibilities disproportionately matched to accountabilities and a bias that favoured responses to symptoms, rather than causes'. Sengelman did not infer, however, that any of these matters were implicated in misconduct as he was not then aware of any specific allegations of criminal behaviour.

Just as he was gaining a sense of SOCOMD's challenges, the urgent need for reform and the extent of rumoured misconduct, SOTG rotations IV–XX were awarded the Meritorious Unit Citation (MUC) on Australia Day 2015. Defence initiated the nomination and drafted the wording, which was approved by the Minister for Defence, who forwarded a recommendation to the Governor-General for the citation to be awarded. Those who served in these rotations received a small insignia to be worn on their uniforms above the right pocket. It would prove to be a fateful decision. The citation bulged with superlatives; 'outstanding' appeared three times. Notably, every member of the 17 SOTG rotations was commended:

For sustained and *outstanding* warlike operational service in Afghanistan from 30 April 2007 to 31 December 2013, through the conduct of counter insurgency operations in support of the International Security Assistance Force. Over a six-year period, Task Force 66 rendered *outstanding* service on operations in Afghanistan where it conducted highly successful counter insurgency operations within Uruzgan and surrounding provinces in support of the International Security Assistance Force. The Task Force's *outstanding* performance against an unrelenting, cunning and ruthless enemy, in an unforgiving environment, was achieved through the collective efforts of every member of the contingent over the duration of the commitment. The superior combat operations results of Task Group 66 further emphasised the Group's exceptional courage and commitment [emphasis added].

Six months after the MUC was awarded, the Army command that had provided the main constituent forces for Task Group 66 over eight years was deemed 'not fit for purpose'. In November 2015, Sengelman advised the Chief of Army that SOCOMD's problems were beyond its capacity to resolve. It was a startling admission. Sengelman had come to this view after receiving reports about the Command's structure, organisation and culture that had confirmed 'substantial evidence of governance, accountability, leadership and behavioural shortcomings'. Sengelman remarked that his response to these systematic failings, which were principally associated with 'leadership and oversight at all levels', would unsettle 'those who feel threatened at the prospect of transparency, personal accountability and the evidence of inadequate standards'.

The picture painted by these reviews of SOCOMD 'starkly contradicts the public image and reputation many unconditionally hold'. He was most concerned that the Command had 'allowed a culture to emerge that conceals reportable incidents, masks unacceptable behaviour, encourages arrogance and fosters favouritism'. He noted that a 'growing body of actual and anecdotal evidence from the past decade suggests that the personal and professional ethics of some have been deeply compromised'. Things looked different from the inside among those then serving within the SAS Regiment, who thought that poor practices and professional lapses were being addressed and corrected in a more consistent and conscientious way by a series of internal reform measures initiated after 2011.

In preparing the Command for reform, Sengelman commissioned Samantha Crompvoets, a consultant sociologist, who had previously conducted research into the wellbeing of uniformed personnel, to examine SOCOMD's corporate culture. She was not employed to gather evidence of misconduct nor tasked with cultivating the confidence of 'whistleblowers' to elicit information that was unavailable or inaccessible to the Command. The first report, entitled *Special Operations Command (SOCOMD): Culture and Interactions: Insights and Reflections*, was completed in January 2016 and ran to seven pages.[19] The second report, entitled *Special Operations Command (SOCOMD): Culture and Interactions: Perceptions, Reputation and Risk*, was completed in February 2016 and was 37 pages in length.[20]

The media mistakenly referred to her first report as an 'Annex' to her second report. They were, however, two separate documents with the first relating specifically to alleged misconduct about which she had heard when preparing the second report – which was the principal 'deliverable' in her contract. Sengelman gave me a copy of the second report in April 2016 when he was proposing the establishment of a small SOCOMD Ethics Advisory Group and invited me to be a member. He made no mention of the first report other than to say he was pursuing rumours of misconduct.[21] A copy of the first report was apparently leaked to the journalist Nick McKenzie in June 2018 with some of its contents published in October–November 2020.

As part of the research for these reports, Crompvoets said she conducted 'formal interviews and informal discussions with current and ex-serving Army, and [Special Forces] in particular, soldiers and officers'. She also spoke with external stakeholders, including the Department of the Prime Minister & Cabinet, the Department of Foreign Affairs and Trade, the Australian Federal Police (AFP) and the Australian Security Intelligence Organisation, about their interactions with SOCOMD.[22] Notably, she did not visit the SAS Regiment nor interview a representative sample of those posted to Campbell Barracks. While her initial brief did not include canvassing allegations or collating evidence of misconduct, she heard 'unverifiable accounts of extremely serious breaches of accountability and trust' that included 'unsanctioned and illegal application of violence on operations, disregard for human life and dignity, and the perception of a complete lack of accountability'.[23]

Crompvoets noted that since 2000 (when an SAS Squadron deployed to East Timor) there had been allegations, most originating with the SAS, of 'at one end, unacceptable behaviour' and 'skylarking' and at the other, a lack of respect for human life, 'death squads', war crimes, cover-ups and botched investigations.[24] When these 'weak signals' were aggregated, they pointed to 'a consistent pattern of unacceptable behaviour and dysfunctional culture'. One external stakeholder thought the Special Forces were 'like bikie gangs, defining themselves by their outsiders; by exclusion and exclusivity … it's seen like a black art – mission focussed, obscure all ills; very disciplined in the combat environment yet rules are ambiguous, bent and broken'.[25] She observed that Special Forces had been depicted by the media 'as heroes and as hooligans' whose elite standing and exclusive status had led them to forget they were part of the Army.[26]

Although not linked to any specific allegation of misconduct or a particular unit or ADF member, several stakeholders observed that the Special Forces 'can't be trusted as they have afforded themselves low levels of corporate and personal accountability' and that 'most if not all of their transgressions and "sins" are generally well hidden from view and are forgiven and buried swiftly when surfaced'.[27] She documented the sometimes intense animosity that existed at all rank levels between the SAS and the Commandos, implying that it was mutual and occasionally a serious impediment to operational effectiveness. There was, she noted, the perception that marketing and protecting 'Brand SAS' had given some members the impression they could act with near impunity. This was not how those in Perth saw things at all but it was the impression given to her by outsiders willing to pour scorn on the Regiment.

One unnamed SOCOMD staff officer thought the problem began with the Regiment's name:

> it all comes down to one word, it comes down to *special*, and that is actually the root of many of the cultural issues – we're special in what we do, we're different, we're better, therefore the rules don't apply to us and we can basically do what we like.[28]

Others thought SAS members only complied with directions they deemed to be important. This explained, for example, disregard of the official policy on alcohol consumption in Afghanistan. Crompvoets also commented on the highly elevated status of the SAS Patrol Commander who 'seems to have far more power, influence and agency on the behaviour of an SAS team and subsequently the formation of a bottom-up culture'.[29] The emphasis on operational experience and expertise meant that senior non-commissioned officers (NCOs), some of whom had received the nation's highest awards for bravery and gallantry, exercised a disproportionately large influence on the overall ethos of the SAS, more so than senior officers within the Regiment or in SOCOMD.

Significantly, half of Crompvoets' first report was a highly personalised explanation of her approach to gathering data and why she thought accounts of alleged misconduct were accurate and reliable. In addition to those identified by SOCOMD as useful interviewees, she was approached by 'a current junior member of SASR, someone from AHQ [Army Headquarters] and someone who worked for a support organisation outside of the ADO [Australian Defence Organisation]' who, she says, 'referred to some of the same events and triangulated the authenticity of the stories'. Alternatively, she might have conceded, they could have heard the same rumours but from different sources.

Despite her background, Crompvoets felt herself 'ill equipped to offer a sophisticated analysis' of misbehaviour with 'disturbing regularity and normalization', believing herself to be a 'naïve observer'. Having heard that some SOTG rotations were led by 'exceptional soldiers and officers', she asked: 'why did they not intervene?' The interviewees apparently supplied a series of answers:

> they were too high up the chain to see it; the tempo was so high the priority was to just try to keep everything ticking over; they did try to do something about it but were dismissed/ marginalized/moved on; they only saw one incident in isolation not the pattern over time.

It was, of course, entirely possible that these soldiers and officers simply did not know of midconduct. SAS missions were often disaggregated with only one or two patrols 'on target' at a time. Those with knowledge of what occurred during a mission were always small in number. Importantly, there was no mention of misconduct in post-action reports.

Having painted a 'bleak picture', Crompvoets then explained that she was given 'one, maybe two, names at most' although, she was also told 'repeatedly, "everyone" knows who the culprits are'. There was no mention of whether any of the 'culprits' were Commandos. She later remarked that 'details of events were scant (ie no names)'. Revealing one name would inevitably have a domino effect as the number of people complicit in the misconduct was apparently substantial: 'if they didn't do it, they saw it. If they didn't see it, they knew about it. If they knew about it, they probably were involved in covering it up and not letting it get back to Canberra.' There were no personal admissions and only one eyewitness account.

Her interviewees, who were not electronically recorded when referring to alleged misconduct, essentially relayed what they had heard or been told about a series of 'scenarios' rather than incidents. They included the Joint Prioritised Effects List (JPEL) being 'reverse engineered' so that it became a 'sanctioned kill list'; the 'direct participation in hostilities' interpretation being used to commit 'just about any atrocity that took their fancy' including 'sanctioned massacres'; the extended detention of whole villages for days without 'food, water and medicines'; and the failure of legal officers embedded within the SOTG to prevent bad behaviour. Reflecting on what she heard, Crompvoets did not think 'everyone' within the SOTG was 'behaving the same way. It seemed that for those whose "tolerance framework" it challenged, they would invariably leave the unit.' The impression she conveyed was that the majority of those serving in the SAS knew there were problems and more than a few miscreants but did nothing to address the issues or restrain the misconduct.

She thought those describing these scenarios were reliable because the stories were 'told with little emotion and so matter of fact that I was left feeling quite disturbed'. She did not believe what she was told could be exaggerated, embellished or embroidered hearsay although those with whom she conferred knew they would not be identified in her report to SOCAUST. For example, one alleged incident relayed to her involved a group of unnamed 'SASR soldiers' on patrol who observed two teenage boys they suspected were Taliban sympathisers. The boys' throats were allegedly slit and their bodies bagged and dumped in a river. This was not, according to Crompvoets' sources, an isolated incident but reflective of a pattern of behaviour. She later remarked of this particular allegation:

> I was confident the person was telling me the truth. I don't see how they could tell me a range of accounts that have been substantiated and then throw in something like 'Here is one I made up'. It makes no sense at all … I didn't want to exaggerate, I didn't want to overstate things, I didn't want to report things that were perhaps unlikely. I only wrote things where I had no doubt.[30]

There was every possibility that these accounts of alleged misconduct could have been built on little more than individual boasting and the apparent desire of immature SOTG members to 'shock' their mates in the Mentoring and Reconstruction Taskforces with colourful 'war stories'. It seemed from her report that many of these stories had gained a life of their own, uncoupled from whatever grain of truth might have originally animated them. The most dramatic part of her first report, the story of the two murdered teenage boys, was not reported to SOCAUST with any mention of a date, a place or a patrol.[31]

Crompvoets ended her first report with a despairing reflection:

> Can anything be done with a whole lot of vague, nameless scenarios? Is the calculus that weighs up these behaviours against the national security imperative valid or faulty? Is it a pandoras [sic] box too complex and with too much organizational risk to prize [sic] open? I don't know the answers. My hunch though is that reputation risk does not stop at SOF [Special Operations Forces], and is far greater than even Army.

This reflection was most notable for its understatement. She had stirred up a hornet's nest.

Subsequent descriptions of her as a 'whistleblower' were mistaken. She was never under any pressure to withhold information nor to conceal any rumours. Crompvoets simply conveyed a synopsis of what she had been told by people whose connection with alleged misconduct was, at best, marginal. Her sources were unidentified. There was no evidence presented to corroborate anything she had heard. No-one then serving within the SAS Regiment – which was clearly the focus of her report – was asked to comment on the allegations nor to present a contrary view on what had happened in the past or was happening in the present. With complete anonymity, those damning the SAS Regiment were not held to account for repeating what were only rumours nor asked to substantiate any of their claims. There was no commentary from Crompvoets on her interviewees' capacity to comment accurately and reliably, and no concession in her conclusions for the possibility of hyperbole or malevolence among those she interviewed.

There were some clear answers to what she thought were merely rhetorical questions about what was to be done. Having received allegations of systematic misconduct and serious war crimes, Sengelman was obliged to act even without the alleged perpetrators being identified. Before Crompvoets reported, Sengelman had already become concerned about hearsay. He had earlier invited members of the SAS Regiment to write to him about issues and problems as part of a 'Redemption Program'. He promised confidentiality to those who responded candidly. In Perth, SAS officers and soldiers were advised to confine themselves to procedural irregularities and organisational matters. This was not, they were told, an appropriate forum for airing allegations of misconduct. There were other mechanisms for reporting wrongdoing. Sengelman later returned the majority of the 209 letters he had received in response to his invitation, stating 'no evidence of criminal behaviour was presented'.

After receiving Crompvoets' first report, Sengelman referred his concerns about possible misconduct to the Chief of Army, Lieutenant General Angus Campbell, on 9 March 2016.[32] The 'scenarios' outlined in the report, which included allegations of torture, murder and conspiracy to conceal serious crimes, obliged Campbell to act.

Either the rumours were true, and crimes had been committed, or they were false, and reputations had been unfairly tarnished. There was no alternative but to take the rumours seriously.

Campbell wrote to the Acting Inspector-General of the Australian Defence Force (IGADF), James Gaynor, on 30 March 2016 suggesting, in the absence of a specific allegation which could be used to commence a criminal or disciplinary investigation, a 'scoping inquiry' into 'unsubstantiated stories' of serious misconduct in Afghanistan.[33] Such an inquiry might be more effective, he thought, in penetrating the SOCOMD 'code of silence' and would avoid the inquiry being terminated if and when it was presented with *prima facie* evidence of criminal conduct. Handing the matter to the IGADF was essentially the only option on offer, other than doing nothing.

The office of the IGADF was established in January 2003 after the Burchett Inquiry into military justice suggested that a 'Military Inspector General independent of the normal chain of command and answering directly to the CDF would provide greater assurance of independence for those cases where complaints do need to be brought forward'.[34] The Inspector-General is 'a statutory office holder appointed by the Minister for Defence and is independent of the ADF chain-of-command'.[35] Among its functions, the IGADF provides 'an avenue for the Minister or CDF to conduct inquiries into or investigate any matter concerning the ADF'. An IGADF inquiry rather than, for example, an AFP investigation, was considered the most effective and efficient way to assess the rumours. The public still knew nothing of the reviews commissioned by Sengelman.

On 16 April 2016, Campbell surprised the parliament, the press and the people when he announced there would be an independent inquiry into the conduct of Australia's Special Forces personnel in Afghanistan. He told Fairfax Media that a 'range of unsubstantiated, third-person, hearsay stories' warranted 'deeper consideration'.[36] Campbell wanted the IGADF to 'consider the range and nature of those stories and to understand the basis of those stories' but did not elaborate on either the circumstances or the conduct prompting the investigation. Subsequent media speculation suggested that 'some within Defence have become concerned that the high-tempo, souped-up intensity of deployments have meant Special Forces regiments have developed their own, closed-off culture forged in the heat of operations'. This superficial speculation relied entirely on tired clichés. The media had been taken completely by surprise. Journalists had no idea of what was happening nor why.

The significance of the announcement required no elaboration. The Army's leadership wanted an objective investigation of the conduct of its own people. The possibility of misconduct among uniformed personnel on overseas operations was sufficiently serious to warrant such action, given Australia was a signatory to the Rome Statute, which established the International Criminal Court and obliged ratifying states to investigate allegations of war crimes.[37] The standing of the Australian Army and its capacity to operate overseas with moral authority was at stake. Had the highly trained members of the SAS and the Commando Regiments violated the ethical standards that are a mark of the professional excellence and exemplary conduct expected of uniformed personnel by the Army and the nation? Could Australia continue to claim that, despite ethical breaches by the deployed forces of other Western nations, its personnel had consistently acted in line with the ADF's corporate values and within the Law of Armed Conflict? Concerns about the organisational culture of the Special Forces were especially troubling because it implied misconduct was not individualised but part of a wider pattern of behaviour that was unethical at best and illegal at worst. If nothing else, the investigation would need to consider the ethical standards to which the Special Forces had been trained and to which they were held accountable.

As the IGADF Afghanistan Inquiry was being established and key personnel were appointed, Sengelman continued to pursue his reform agenda within SOCOMD. The problems he detected transcended rumours of misconduct. They were the consequences rather than the causes of the institutional failings and shortcomings he was determined to rectify. The foremost concern was making SOCOMD 'fit for purpose' through organisational and cultural renewal. There were changes to governance structures and accountability regimes, reassertion of Army values and ethics, and review of force element 'raise-train-sustain' mechanisms. The Command would be re-integrated more effectively into the Army and its overall objectives.

Two years after Sengelman started reconfiguring SOCOMD's headquarters (rather than its constituent units), the Deputy Chief of Army (and soon to become Chief of Army), Major General Rick Burr, approached David Irvine, former Director-General of the Australian Security Intelligence Organisation (ASIO) and the Australian Secret Intelligence Service (ASIS), to undertake an organisational review of the Command. This review was conducted during March and April 2018, and would run parallel with the IGADF Afghanistan Inquiry.[38] Irvine visited the SAS and the Commando Regiments and spoke with a number of former and serving Special Forces officers and soldiers. Fairfax Media journalist Nick McKenzie reported in June 2018 that Irvine was 'investigating the defence force's handling' of war crimes allegations, 'the third investigation into the special forces to be launched in two years'.[39] McKenzie's 'senior Defence sources' were mistaken. Irvine later made a point of stating that he did not 're-investigate the rumours and allegations of past behaviour'. Defence had complete confidence in the IGADF Afghanistan Inquiry to find facts and make recommendations on misconduct. It did not need a second opinion or a supplementary investigation.

As Irvine was a respected diplomat and civil servant, his views held great weight. After deliberating on all he had observed, Irvine submitted a 60-page report in August 2018. It was marked 'Secret' and remained so until declassified on 16 April 2020.[40] Irvine made 14 recommendations that presumed there had been 'significant discipline issues' across the Command in Afghanistan but did not mention misconduct or war crimes. Nor did he single out the SAS Regiment for particular attention. He thought the problems that had been reported to him could be prevented in future by better governance, stronger accountability, clearer values, improved education and more attentive supervision. The solutions focused on both individual and institutional factors involving compliance and leadership.

For Irvine, particular problems were part of a general malaise. SOCOMD had become 'ragged and rundown' towards the end of combat operations in Afghanistan in 2013, although the existence of issues affecting the Command's overall performance were first noticed in 2011. By 2014, the Command was not 'broken' but was in 'serious danger of becoming so'. With the conclusion of combat operations, the principal impediment to initiating extensive change was gone although the problems predated the first SFTG rotation in 2005. They originated with the formation of the Command in 2003. Irvine thought SOCOMD was essentially a 'federation of independent units' that sometimes acted as warring tribes. Each unit had embraced a form of 'bottom up' entrepreneurial management that was largely indifferent to other parts of SOCOMD. Elements within the Command had gradually deviated from Army values and eventually become organisationally isolated. This was unhealthy for the units and deleterious to the Command's overall effectiveness. For its part, the Army's attitude to SOCOMD was one of 'unconscious neglect'. The demands of the heightened operational tempo meant that fixing the problems would wait until the war in Afghanistan was over.

There had also been an attitudinal shift within the Command's units. Whereas previous generations of Special Forces personnel were marked by restless creativity and obsession with professional excellence, Irvine thought the war in Afghanistan had warped the outlook of both officers and soldiers. 'Arrogance began to replace confidence' and 'can do' thinking had become an 'only we can do' mentality. A sense of elitism brought with it a feeling of entitlement. 'Special' no longer meant different; it meant 'superior' and applied to individuals and not their missions. Alcohol abuse was inadequately addressed; ill-discipline was left unpunished. Secrecy was used to avoid accountability, aided and abetted by a 'warrior culture' that deprecated all activity but close-quarter combat. Experience usually spoke more loudly than expertise, allowing some NCOs to 'run a parallel line of command filled with rumour-mongering'.[41] Irvine concluded that SOCOMD's culture 'under the influence of multiple factors both within and outside the organisation, became unanchored. In hindsight, it is not surprising that elements of the Command's culture began to drift in adverse directions.'[42]

Disciplinary problems were an inevitable product of this drift. Some soldiers began to believe they were 'above the law' or that *ordinary* laws did not apply to *special* soldiers. Over-familiarity between ranks had trivialised the responsibility of officers to enforce compliance and allowed mateship to gain priority over leadership, undermining the capacity of leaders to make hard decisions. The 'protected identity' status of Special Forces soldiers was used to hinder investigations while outsiders were shunned because they might draw attention to 'departures from accepted Army standards of behaviour and conduct'. After 2015, and sensing the recent origins of ill-discipline, a number of 'adverse influencers' – those whose personal presence was deemed to be malignant – were removed from SOCOMD units or forced out of the Army. Irvine observed that insubordination was again taken seriously and minor misdemeanours were being 'corrected instantly'. He concluded: 'I believe that SOCOMD is getting the message on accountability.'[43]

Irvine thought the introduction of a SOCOMD 'Code of Conduct' was a welcome innovation but remained 'concerned the Command does not yet have a comprehensive pan-Command approach to infusing ethical-decision-making into military decision-making'.[44] Irvine noted that future wars would be more complex.

There would not always be 'clarity as to which rules apply'. Although attitudes to accountability had changed, he explained that 'high levels of secrecy militate against effective normal methods of oversight – and increase the risk of inappropriate behaviour and errors of judgement, poor governance or simple mismanagement going undetected and uncorrected'.[45] He believed even closer independent oversight was needed to ensure Special Forces 'act lawfully and with propriety, and comply with military orders and defence policy'.[46] Irvine ended his report with encouragement to persist with positive change to avoid the possibility of 'back-sliding and misdirection'.[47]

To its credit, the Army had not waited for the IGADF Afghanistan Inquiry to report before implementing change. Some problems were obvious and could be addressed without delay. The nature and causes of serious misconduct remained unknown but the exercise of professional intuition among senior uniformed leaders about the likely causes of what they imagined had occurred in Afghanistan had already led to interim improvements. According to Irvine, SOCOMD was heading in the right direction. With determination and resolve, the future would be different.

Irvine completed a second report in June 2020. He examined the progress of reforms initiated within SOCOMD after 2015, the implementation of recommendations he made in 2018, and continuing work to prepare the Command for future challenges. He concluded that SOCOMD had started to deal effectively with leadership and cultural issues and was on track to meet the directives issued by senior ADF and Army commanders. He thought the Command 'now has a very different and more positive feel by comparison with the low point of 2014–15. It has a clear purpose and mission. Its governance is sound and its operating culture is developing in the right directions.'[48] He stressed that SOCOMD's leaders would need to manage the fallout from the IGADF Afghanistan Inquiry report. It would influence morale and shake commitment although, he pointed out, fewer than 20 per cent of those serving in the Command had been part of an SFTG/SOTG rotation. Nevertheless, 'the issues raised cannot be swept under the carpet, but must be confronted transparently within the Command'. He explained:

> There are no excuses for proven criminal behaviour but there was understandable disappointment in the focus groups to whom I spoke that the hard-won operational successes on the battlefield were now being overshadowed by those allegations about behaviour on the part of some Special Forces personnel. This was not to excuse such alleged behaviour; they saw it as unconscionable and totally repugnant to the values of Army.[49]

Although Irvine made no comment on media stories and offered no opinion on the nature of any wrongdoing or the extent of any misconduct, he assumed with most observers that the Inquiry's findings would be serious and the recommendations substantial. Without knowing what the Inquiry would find and, therefore, having no clear sense of the forces and factors that might have attributed to the alleged commission of war crimes, there was little more the ADF could do but wait for the report to be released.

There were likely to be recommendations of disciplinary and possibly criminal proceedings. In all probability, there would be criticisms of the ADF's organisation, policies and procedures. Plainly, character development and ethics training packages would need to be addressed. Future reforms would depend on analysis of past problems. There would definitely be some comment on leadership, command and management, and the critical importance of trust between members of the Regiment and throughout its chain of command, extending to the Army's senior leadership and the national government. Repairing the ADF's reputation would depend on the seriousness of the allegations and the strength of the criticisms contained in the report, and the willingness of the media to accept there might have been some mitigating factors.

11

REVELATIONS AND ALLEGATIONS: MEDIA REPORTING 2016–2020

In a seminal article published in 1948 entitled 'The structure and function of communication in society', the American scholar Harold Lasswell identified what he felt were the three key functions of the mass media in a democratic society.[1] The first function, *surveillance*, involves the responsible transmission of accurate and reliable information about people and places, conditions and conflicts, to assist enlightened discussion and educated decision-making. Individuals need to be informed. The second function, *correlation*, points to the development of editorial content, including the presentation of interpretations and perspectives that are intended to enforce norms, generate consensus, challenge stereotypes and promote opposition. The community needs to think. The third function, *transmission*, refers to the communication of ideas and aspirations from one generation to the next with the aim of increasing social cohesion by widening the base of shared experience. The society needs to reflect. The elements of each function were evident in Australian media reporting of military operations and alleged war crimes in Afghanistan.

The nuances of tactics and technology, and the preservation of operational security, work to complicate and obfuscate the exercise of the media's 'surveillance' function when it comes to reporting

Australian Defence Force (ADF) activities. This observation partly explains the paucity of public debate over things like capital equipment acquisitions and threat assessments. Disinterest in military affairs also reflects widespread community complacency about the costs of national security and the intentions of potential adversaries. 'Good news' stories that focus on individual courage and collective dedication appeal more readily to television audiences and newspaper readers, who like to think that uniformed people embody elevated ideals that are usually beyond the ordinary reach of the civilian population. Australians want to believe the ADF consists of high-minded people dedicated to altruistic service in the national interest. This desire can have a warping influence on the content of media reporting, bringing only some kinds of stories to public prominence.

As the Commonwealth Government is the biggest generator of information about military affairs, the media often attempts to fulfil its 'correlation' function by seeking contrary views from opposition political parties and dissenting opinions from rival interest groups. In the absence of its own inhouse expertise, the media relies on expert commentators and former ADF members (including disgruntled veterans) to explain decisions and developments to a general audience which has little awareness of context or complexity. At times the media is unable to distinguish between insightful analysis and special pleading but gives currency to uninformed perspectives on the pretext of providing editorial balance. As the flow of official information is constrained by operational security and the need to protect classified material, there tends to be more comment and complaint in media reporting than evaluation and analysis of military affairs. In sum, more opinions than facts are presented to the public.

When exercising its 'transmission' function, the media commonly attempts to convey respect for uniformed personnel and esteem for their deployed service, albeit through the lens of fading Australian egalitarianism and the abiding myth of the omnipotent 'digger'. This is true of commercial news outlets and publicly funded broadcasters.

Recognising that most ADF members are well meaning and are precluded from speaking directly to the media, other than with permission and only then in highly controlled circumstances, the media customarily gives uniformed men and women the benefit of any doubt. Mistakes and misconduct are of interest to the populist media not because they show that ADF members are human but because they embarrass the elite – the ministers and the generals – who are often portrayed as being unworthy of those they lead. The Australian media of all political complexions willingly promote veneration of the nation's military history and celebration of its martial heritage while condemning conduct that is considered contrary to the 'Anzac spirit' or beneath the standards expected of those afforded iconic status.

Since 2001, the Australian media have contributed energetically to elevating the standing of Australia's Special Forces. Although their 'protected identity' status obliged Special Forces soldiers to shun publicity, those who came out of the shadows to receive bravery and gallantry awards were invariably feted. It was obvious from the reporting that the nation still had need of heroes. The media wanted to profile Special Forces training facilities to learn the 'secrets' of their success. There were hopes of turning Special Air Service (SAS) and Commando candidate selection processes into reality television for commercial television networks. Mention of the Special Forces was always prefaced with the word 'elite'.[2] They were set apart from other soldiers by their character and competence: the 'best of the best'. Australians were told they could sleep soundly at night because the Special Forces stood ready to protect them. In moments of dire national need, the media was quick to report that the government had turned to the Special Forces. There seemed no limit to what they could achieve. These soldiers could board ships, free hostages and neutralise terrorists. Hyped by a succession of Hollywood films beginning with *Rambo* (which was so successful that it spawned another four movies), Australia had its own military supermen. News Corporation journalist Ian McPhedran published *The Amazing SAS* in 2007.³ Former Fairfax newspapers journalist, Robert Macklin, published *Warrior Elite: Australia's Special Forces – Z Force to the SAS Intelligence Operations to Cyber Warfare* in 2015.⁴

There was never a unitary media view of SAS operators and Commandos but they had evidently generated a considerable store of goodwill with most media people. Until, that is, there were allegations of serious wrongdoing. It did not take long for the aura of Australia's Special Forces to dissipate. The headlines were dramatic and the commentary was merciless. Some of the journalists reporting misconduct allegations gave the impression they had been personally betrayed by those they once professionally revered. It was almost as if the media felt the need to unmask the fraud and expose the fakes. The expectation that reporting be balanced produced little more than ambivalence: the Special Forces included both good men and bad men; the good substantially outnumbered the bad; the integrity of the good outweighed the depravity of the bad; and the good secured notable successes and the bad undermined their achievements. In the interests of even-handedness, journalists were forced to concede that the allegedly bad men were also capable of demonstrably good deeds or that the war in Afghanistan had turned once good men into now bad men. It was difficult for the public to get a sense of what they were being told as veterans both denounced and defended those caught up in the growing controversy.

Both the reputedly good men and the allegedly bad men were interviewed during the Inspector-General of the Australian Defence Force (IGADF) Afghanistan Inquiry. They were required to attend interviews and compelled to disclose what they had heard and seen. Those interviewed were not permitted to reveal what they had been asked or how they had answered. Strict confidentiality was to be preserved. Some SAS operators and Commandos also spoke with journalists. Lacking trust in the rigour of previous ADF inquiries and fearing the official response might dismiss their evidence and deny their claims, they felt that media stories would ensure their allegations became widely known and were not easily disregarded. Media stories also served as a vehicle for like-minded men with knowledge of alleged misconduct to know they were not alone and should contact the Inquiry staff. No serving member of the SAS or the Commando Regiments ever sought official approval to speak with a journalist concerning war crimes allegations. Although journalists knew the identities of the accused and their accusers, they chose initially to preserve their anonymity.

The first media story to allege serious misconduct appeared on 13 October 2016. A former Commando sergeant claimed he had helped a Commando colleague to conceal the execution of a wounded and detained Afghan insurgent in 2007. The former Commando, who suffered from post-traumatic stress and drug addiction, told the ABC's Andrew Greene:

> I can't remember if he cut the cuffs off first, or if he cut the cuffs off after he shot him. That's the one point I can't remember there 'cause I wasn't looking. I didn't want to look. I turned around and the guy was dead. He'd been shot through the forehead.[5]

The ABC report noted it had 'been unable to independently verify his battlefield claims'. The man was clearly motivated by intense personal remorse: 'I believe I should be punished with the full weight of the law, justly. I do not believe this should be brushed under the carpet.'

After a lull of several months, a 'Special Forces veteran' who could 'no longer remain silent' supplied ABC News with a personal statement on 9 July 2017. He claimed to have witnessed the emergence of 'an insidious, infectious and influential minority that indulges in self-glorification at the expense of the greater reputation of special operations'.[6] This behaviour was threatening core values, leading to 'an increasingly dangerous battle space for our troops'. This minority bent the Rules of Engagement (ROE) and lied about the killing of non-combatants. Although the ABC's source had not personally witnessed any murders, the desire of this minority to surpass others led to 'the deaths of large numbers of innocent civilians ... deaths which are unjustifiable and serve no strategic or practical value'. He conceded that the 'IGADF Inquiry has merit, but it's not the best method to implement change. This must come from within Special Operations Command', which needed 'to be mature enough and honest enough to admit things haven't gone as well as they could'. The ABC's source did not seem to understand the purpose of the IGADF Afghanistan Inquiry. Its primary objective was uncovering evidence of misconduct; promoting cultural change came a very distant second.

The next day, the ABC's Dan Oakes and Sam Clark published the first instalment in a seven-part series. It was based on hundreds of classified documents, dubbed 'the Afghan files', which had been leaked to three senior ABC journalists by David McBride, a former Army lawyer.[7] McBride claimed he was acting on a duty to disclose potentially illegal conduct and had only given the documents to the ABC because both Defence and the Australian Federal Police (AFP) wanted the matters 'swept under the carpet'. McBride's original intentions were very different, as *Sydney Morning Herald* journalist David Wroe explained:

> He was convinced the much bigger story was that Australia's special forces had been hung out to dry by politicians and Defence brass obsessed with their own careers and popularity, and that this was just one element in a corrupt and degraded system that has left Australia's national security dangerously exposed.[8]

In essence, McBride claimed that amending the ROE as a consequence of political aversion to Afghan civilian casualties was increasing the risk that Australian personnel would be indicted for war crimes.[9] It also raised the possibility of uniformed deaths which, McBride claimed, served the interests of politicians who attended military funerals and looked good on television. The latter claim was overlooked, even by McBride's sympathisers, as being an unworthy imputation against the nation's leaders.

The leaked documents detailed 10 incidents that occurred between 2009 and 2013 that included the alleged killing of unarmed men and children. The ABC provided a summary of each incident, why the engagement had prompted an inquiry, and what a Defence investigation had concluded. One of these summaries related to an incident on 2 April 2009:

> Australians hunting for a 'medium value' target arrived at the village of Jalbay [Uruzgan Province] in helicopters after dark. The Taliban target was not there, but the Australians killed three men, including one who was hiding in a haystack, one hiding in a chaff pile, and another trying to take cover in a line of trees nearby. The Australians later said that the men who were hiding in the chaff pile and haystack were in a 'firing position', but no weapons were found afterwards.[10]

A subsequent inquiry found the Australian soldiers had:

> acted within the rules of engagement, yet admitted no weapons were found, and that a number of intelligence sources said the men were civilians, not insurgents. The inquiry officer also claimed that an alleged lack of protest by locals over the killings, and the fact the dead men supposedly did not behave like 'uninvolved' Afghan civilians when the soldiers arrived, meant they were likely to have been 'associates' of the Taliban member being targeted.[11]

Another document mentioned systemic cultural and organisational problems in Special Operations Command and the apparent readiness of the SAS Regiment to overlook disciplinary breaches. Another referred to SAS soldiers being 'desensitised' and departing from the Regiment's values. It mentioned the fraught relationship between the SAS and Commando Regiments. The relationship between the SAS and the ADF Investigative Service (ADFIS) was also severely strained; the SAS alleging the ADFIS was trying to conceal its failings in the conduct of one inquiry and the ADFIS accusing the SAS of being uncooperative with its efforts to ascertain facts.

The ABC report included information about an alleged incident in December 2013 between an SAS operator and a female member of the Australian Secret Intelligence Service (ASIS) in Kabul.[12] The soldier was part of a detachment directed to guard a contingent of ASIS officers. After a heated argument, which was fuelled by excessive (and unauthorised) alcohol consumption during an evening barbeque, the soldier pointed his personal firearm, a loaded 9mm Glock pistol, at the ASIS officer. He later placed the muzzle under her chin in a threatening manner. Both individuals denied alcohol had played a part in the incident but later changed their stories. They were sent home within days.[13] ABC News initially reported the incident in October 2014 although there were few details of what had occurred.[14] The incident was reportedly investigated by the Inspector-General of Intelligence and Security, Dr Vivienne Thom, and there was undisclosed administrative action against those involved.[15] The public were naturally entitled to have doubts about the professionalism of some members of the SAS Regiment and ASIS, and about the quality of leadership being exercised within both organisations.

Other documents suggested that Afghan authorities, including President Harmid Karzai, who spoke personally about unacceptable civilian casualties in Uruzgan with senior Australian officers in Kabul, were troubled by the number of Afghans that Australian forces were killing in allegedly questionable circumstances. There were internal debates about the meaning of ROE and whether they needed clarification. When taken together, the 'Afghan files' planted a seed of doubt about the consistency of Australian actions and the credibility of many explanations given for the deaths of innocent civilians and unarmed men. At this stage, media attention was focused primarily on the alleged commission of war crimes. There was insufficient detail to determine the existence of patterns or whether the behaviour was systemic or isolated. Other suggestions of cultural 'drift' were reflected, media reports suggested, in a particular kind of violent bellicosity.

On 18 April 2018, the Chief of Army, Lieutenant General Angus Campbell, banned the use of clothing and equipment emblazoned with 'death-style' imagery.[16] Much of this imagery was derived from American popular culture. The prohibition included 'Sparta', 'grim reaper' and 'skull-and-crossbones' symbology as well as depictions of the fictional vigilantes Phantom and Punisher.[17] Campbell said such imagery was 'always ill-considered and implicitly encourages the inculcation of an arrogant hubris and general disregard for the most serious responsibility of our profession: the legitimate and discriminate taking of life'.[18] He was widely criticised for succumbing to 'political correctness' and continuing the controversial 'diversity and inclusion' program initiated by his predecessor, David Morrison. He was accused of failing to consult with senior soldiers and chided for waiting until the day after he had been named as the new Chief of the Defence Force to issue the ban. This was incorrect. The minute headed 'Use of Symbols in Army' was actually dated 10 April 2018 – eight days before his new appointment was announced.[19] Surely, the critics asked, Campbell had personally encountered this imagery throughout his three decades of Army service. Why ban them now?

A former infantry sergeant and Medal for Gallantry recipient, Justin Huggett, condemned the ban because:

> the Army, in particular the Infantry, are a fighting force designed to kill! We are not and never should be a reflection of society, we are trained and programmed that way. Although it seems every effort is being made at the top levels to denigrate combat effectiveness.[20]

August Elliott was one of few former soldiers who supported the ban:

> In the end, the difference between an Army that marches into battle beneath a symbol like the Rising Sun and an Army that marches into battle beneath symbols of vigilantism, lawlessness, extreme militarism and death is the difference between a force that values professionalism and obedience to the law and a force that defines itself by its own violence. The difference between an army and a 'death cult', if you will. It's not difficult to guess which fighting force the Australian public would prefer to have represent them on operations abroad.[21]

Fears that parts of the Army had embraced ultra right-wing ideology were further fuelled on 14 June 2018 when ABC News published an image of an Australian Army patrol vehicle in Afghanistan flying a Nazi swastika flag.[22] The photograph was taken in August 2007. It reported that 'two separate Defence sources have identified a particular soldier as the individual who took the flag to Afghanistan'.[23] Defence issued a statement:

> The flag was briefly raised above an Australian Army vehicle in Afghanistan in 2007. The commander took immediate action to have the offensive flag taken down. It is totally inappropriate for any ADF vehicle or company to have a flag of this nature. The personnel involved were immediately cautioned at the time and subsequently received further counselling. Additionally, steps were taken to reinforce education and training for all personnel who witnessed the flag.[24]

Defence did not disclose the force element that was operating the vehicle at the time. An unnamed Defence source described the image as a 'twisted joke' rather than evidence or expression of neo-Nazi sentiment. The Vice Chief of the Defence Force condemned the action and advised that 'when the patrol returned to its base, the flag was destroyed'.[25] Prime Minister Malcolm Turnbull told journalists that flying the flag was 'completely and utterly unacceptable'.[26] The chairman of the Jewish Anti-Defamation Commission thought 'this vile display of bigotry is a reminder of the ever-present need for people of good to speak out against such abhorrence, and that racism is still rampant in parts of our society'.

Stories of misconduct continued to appear regularly in news outlets. They detailed additional incidents of misconduct and named one of the accused: former SAS Corporal, Ben Roberts-Smith, who was also the nation's most highly decorated soldier. Roberts-Smith denied any wrongdoing during his deployments to Afghanistan. He insisted the allegations, which related to a series of incidents between 2006 and 2012, were motivated by professional jealousies and longstanding vendettas that were intended to damage his reputation. He would remain the only SAS operator accused of misconduct to be publicly identified. The other accused were usually identified by rank and an initial, such as 'Sergeant B'.

Roberts-Smith later commenced defamation proceedings against the *Sydney Morning Herald* and the *Age* (owned by Fairfax Media before becoming Nine Newspapers)[27] after the publication of a series of articles by Chris Masters, David Wroe and Nick McKenzie in August 2018.[28] The opening front-page article carried the headline, 'Cracks in a war hero's façade', and was accompanied by a caricature of Roberts-Smith, suggesting a tarnished image. The newspaper announced the action would be defended on the grounds of truth. An online petition[29] was started to 'Stop the witch hunt' against the Victoria Cross and Medal for Gallantry recipient, whose public supporters included a number of high-profile Australians, including his employer at Seven West Media, Kerry Stokes, and broadcaster Alan Jones, who later remarked: 'they will never, ever find anything against him'.[30]

In October 2018, former Defence Minister and War Memorial

Director Brendan Nelson was publicly critical of Fairfax Media for publishing war crimes allegations and asked how the national interest was served by 'tearing down our heroes'. He believed allegations of misconduct should be dealt with by the IGADF Afghanistan Inquiry but was unhappy with its apparent slow progress: 'I say to the people doing the Inquiry: can you damn well get on with it.'[31] Nelson had earlier suggested that war was a 'messy business' and unless there was clear evidence of the 'most egregious breaches of the laws of armed conflict, we should leave it all alone'.[32] These remarks were considered an attack on Justice Paul Brereton, who had been commissioned to conduct the inquiry on behalf of the IGADF.

In reply, former New South Wales Court of Appeal judge Anthony Whealy said it was 'inappropriate to attack Justice Brereton or to push him to speed up an inquiry that needs to be painstaking and thorough'.[33] The president of the Victorian Bar Association, Matt Collins QC, added: 'it is vital for the integrity of the Inquiry that the judge feel unconstrained from pressure from any party. Justice Brereton is hugely respected and known for his fairness.' There was no doubting the depth of feeling that was aroused by both the Inquiry and the matters it was considering. Much of the commentary was ill-informed and offered without context. The alleged misconduct was viewed in virtual isolation from Afghan affairs, Taliban tactics and how the International Security Assistance Force (ISAF) was prosecuting the war.

Stories of misconduct continued to appear in the Australian media. It was well over two years since the 'Afghan files' stories appeared. The trickle of stories was now a torrent. On 16 October 2019, Newscorp journalist Rory Callinan and ABC reporter Mark Willacy published an article about an SAS raid on the village of Sarkhum, 18 kilometres south-west of Tarin Kowt, in mid-March 2012. The target was a suspected Taliban bomb-maker. They alleged that an unarmed Afghan man, Haji Sardar, was unnecessarily shot in the thigh by Australian SAS operators and was taken to a nearby mosque, where he later died in suspicious circumstances. His distraught son recalled: 'we were not allowed inside but we heard shouts and cries for an hour ... when they left the mosque we got inside and they had martyred him. He had bruises all over his neck. Before that he was wounded, but not critically'. His family also claimed there were 'boot marks over his heart'. In an adjacent field, the unarmed Mirza Khan was confronted by military dogs before being shot dead without warning. Investigations into complaints from the villagers concluded the raid was justified and the two men were armed combatants. This conclusion was rejected by Afghanistan's Independent Human Rights Commission (AIHRC), which insisted they were unarmed civilians. The Commission had found evidence of other violations of human rights by Australian forces operating in Afghanistan between 2010 and 2013.

By the end of 2019, the duration of the Inquiry was again the subject of critical comment after the former Commando, who claimed in 2016 to have concealed a war crime in 2007, was found dead. His lawyer, Glenn Kolomeitz, accepted the Inquiry was complex and that the 'allegations arise in an operational setting overseas which is still a war zone. But three years is a long time in anyone's books.' The reason for the Inquiry taking so long was revealed in February 2020. The IGADF's annual report stated the Afghanistan Inquiry was examining 55 separate incidents, 'predominantly unlawful killings of persons who were non-combatants or were no longer combatants, but also cruel treatment of such persons'. The number of incidents exceeded the assumptions of journalists and commentators who thought they were much fewer in number, and created a very substantial investigative workload.

Notwithstanding the steady flow of allegations from former soldiers and leaks from official documents, there appeared to be a segment of the population that remained unpersuaded, refusing to accept that Australian soldiers were even capable of serious crimes. The strong presumption was that Australian soldiers would never kill unarmed or disarmed people and it was difficult to imagine the circumstances in which they would do so. Within the ADF, the collective opinion was that a few soldiers had probed the limits of acceptable conduct but that the media stories were probably driven by individual feuds and personal jealousies.

The turning point was the ABC Television *4 Corners* program, 'Killing Field', which screened on 16 March 2020.[34] It presented what reporter Mark Willacy described as graphic visual evidence of serious misconduct by Australian Special Forces personnel in Afghanistan: 'the execution of a bound prisoner, the killing of another Afghan who'd had his hands in the air, a wounded farmer taken away by an SAS soldier and later found beaten to death'. He noted that 'the men of the SAS and commandos have been held up as heroes and role models by our political leaders, and some have been showered with awards and decorations. Yet, here were some of them ... being accused of the most heinous of crimes, including the murder of innocents.'[35]

Much of the program's commentary was provided by a former Australian Army signaller who claimed that SAS operators had routinely engaged in murder, torture and reprisals. On arriving in Afghanistan, a senior SAS soldier allegedly told him: 'I hope you're ready and prepared for this deployment because you have to make sure that you're OK with me putting a gun at someone's head and pulling the trigger.' He thought to himself: 'OK, we're executing people now.' Significantly, he did not report what he had heard to anyone. Through this signaller and others, Willacy managed to gain access to hundreds of images and 10 hours of film. Why these images and videos were ever created and stored by Special Operations Task Group (SOTG) personnel was not canvassed. The material was essentially an unauthorised unofficial archive that could be used for the end-of-rotation video that would be made for private screening.

Much of the imagery in the *4 Corners* program was, according to Willacy, drawn from a database of photos and videos that was generated by SOTG Rotation XVII between February and July 2012.

The material was stored in a shared drive on a computer located in the patrol common room that could be accessed by most SAS operators at Tarin Kowt. Helmet camera footage of four particular incidents was confronting and, from all appearances, highly damning of those involved. A week after the program went to air, there was confirmation the AFP were already conducting two criminal investigations into incidents that occurred in Afghanistan.

This was the first time that evidence rather than just allegations of misconduct had been shared with the Australian people. As expected, the response was immediate and insistent. Journalists Chris Masters and Nick McKenzie commented in the *Age* newspaper: 'No Australian could now credibly deny that a small number of our special forces soldiers committed executions of Afghans.'[36] An unnamed former SAS soldier responded: 'I've seen plenty in Afghanistan but nothing so rotten. That behaviour shames us all. That leadership was abysmal. We lost our respect for human life and that means we lost our self-respect.' The director of the advocacy group Human Rights Watch, Elaine Pearson, contended that:

> Justice and accountability for alleged war crimes by Australian special forces members in Afghanistan is long overdue ... Investigations into alleged war crimes should focus on the people responsible, not those who exposed the atrocities ... Australia's reputation as a rights-respecting nation both during peacetime and at war will hinge on how the government addresses the most egregious cases of alleged abuse.[37]

Even those who usually sprang to the defence of Australia's Special Forces were silent. Further allegations of SAS misconduct during 2012 appeared in Nine Newspapers on 7 May. These allegations were more detailed and included references to dates and places, perpetrators and victims. Masters and McKenzie were clearly relying on well-placed sources with first-hand knowledge of Special Operations.

Confirmation that letters had been sent to 'potentially affected persons' (PAP) by Justice Brereton signalled to the media that the window was closing for the publication of any new allegations. There were also hints the IGADF Afghanistan Inquiry would conclude in July 2020. Once the report was released, whatever stories the media had been holding in reserve would be stale and unnewsworthy. Those accused of wrongdoing were now aware of the specific accusations being made against them and the identity of their accusers. Most of the incidents of alleged misconduct that were later included in Mark Willacy's *Rogue Forces* could only have been observed by two, or perhaps three, soldiers other than the Afghan witnesses whose recollections had featured in media coverage.[38] When these stories are viewed as a collected body of journalistic work, there was no apparent strategy and no obvious objective among media outlets – other than informing the public that bad things had happened in Afghanistan and individuals and institutions needed to be held accountable. It looked like the media were publishing whatever came their way with little fact checking. Much of this material was highly damaging to the SAS Regiment in particular. Given the source of the stories appeared to be former soldiers, they plainly had little regard for the standing of their former units. In fact, it looked like the SAS Regiment was at war with itself.

On 27 June 2020, the *Age*, the *Herald* and *60 Minutes* featured the story of an Army medic, 'Dusty' Miller, who deployed with the SAS to Afghanistan.[39] Miller claimed that during the Sarkhum operation on 14 March 2012 (an operation that had already been the subject of a report by Mark Willacy), a wounded Afghan, father-of-seven Haji Sardar, was taken away and killed by an SAS operator. The Australian people were now hearing from a second accuser. Two of Miller's medical corps colleagues spoke of him as a courageous and dedicated medic who 'risked reprisals' for drawing attention to the death of Haji Sardar.[40]

On 14 July, the ABC's Mark Willacy and Alexandra Blucher

drew on 'Afghan witnesses and Australian sources' to claim that a December 2012 Special Forces operation at Sara Aw in Kandahar province left 10 unarmed civilians and at least five Taliban dead. It was 'believed to be the worst one-day death toll uncovered to date of alleged unlawful killings by Australian soldiers in Afghanistan'. A local farmer told the ABC:

> It was 11am, three [helicopters] landed. There were three Taliban in nomad houses [near the village]. They resisted and were killed. But then they killed other people – civilians. Civilians were terrified when the shooting started, because they were mass shooting people.[41]

The next day the ABC reported on yet another raid and revealed the use of 'throwdowns'.[42] During an operation in the village of Shina in May 2012, the same AK-47 rifle was photographed alongside two bodies in separate locations. The rifle 'with teal-coloured tape wrapped around the stock' was used to justify the killing of two men whose families insisted they were civilians. A soldier who was part of the same SOTG rotation explained the use of 'throwdowns' to the ABC: 'often people who had been killed had weapons placed on them and [they were] photographed with these weapons … that happened on numerous occasions'. Of the three civilians allegedly killed, one was driving a tractor with a load of onions bound for market. Another chased a cow when it was frightened by the incoming helicopter. None of those killed, which included a man in his 80s and a man with an intellectual disability (referred to by an SAS operator as 'the village idiot') aged 20, was found to have been armed. The story was accompanied by photographs of the principal witnesses and the burial site of those who died. The son of the old man killed in the raid was naturally deeply distressed:

He was on his own land. He never stole or did anything bad to anyone. He was an elderly person. This is impossible to forgive and I won't forgive it ... I want [the Australians] to be tried ... If the government cares about us, if they care about our widows and orphans, then they must summon them and try them in the court.⁴³

If true, not only was such conduct illegal, it defied the essence of the ISAF mission: protecting the people and building community trust. Unnecessary killings would give the population the impression that the Afghan National Government and its supporters were no better than either the old warlords or the re-formed Taliban.

A week later (21 July), the ABC reported on a raid in the village of Nawjoy on 7 January 2013.⁴⁴ The Australian soldiers were after one man: Mawlawi Sher Mohammad. Willacy and Callinan claimed the Australians apprehended a man and then took him into the stables adjacent to his home, where he was shot twice in the chest at close range. In an alleged case of mistaken identity, the dead man's neighbour said the man the Australians killed 'was an innocent man, he was the imam of our mosque. He had no links at all with the Taliban.' The villagers also explained that 'his corpse was in a very disrespectful situation, he was dragged in the stable. This is a place for animals. His head was in the stable and his feet were sticking outside.'⁴⁵ They also claimed that 16 villagers were unnecessarily detained and the Australians 'burned people's motorbikes and one car ... They burned them because they thought the vehicles belonged to the Taliban. But they were the property of villagers.'

The following day, the ABC published a photograph of 'two SAS soldiers smiling and holding' what appeared to be an American Confederate flag bearing the words 'Southern Pride'.⁴⁶ The ABC report included commentary from a former serving American lieutenant colonel who had worked with Australian forces in Uruzgan in 2012. He remarked: 'this flag ... is a symbol that should not have been displayed by any unit. It's been displayed by the Ku Klux Klan, by racist organisations, American Nazis have used it.' The American officer was 'stunned' that the Australians had displayed the flag (which looked more like a bedspread) and added: 'ignorance is not an excuse'. A government spokesman said 'the ADF does not condone behaviours, gestures, flags or symbology that are unprofessional or found to be supporting extremist ideologies'. Although the incident would be reviewed, including the source of the offending item, the story fed claims the SAS Regiment was racist and redneck.

As speculation continued that the IGADF Afghanistan Inquiry report would soon be released, deep feelings were aroused by news that Hekmatullah, a sergeant in the Afghan National Army who turned his rifle on three Australian soldiers, Private Robert Poate, Lance Corporal Stjepan Milosevic and Sapper James Martin, and killed them at Patrol Base Wahab in August 2012, might be released from prison.[47] In late August, Hekmatullah and five other prisoners were relocated to Doha in Qatar ahead of peace talks with the Taliban that were being brokered by the United States. Prime Minister Scott Morrison wrote to President Trump in Washington and President Ghani in Kabul stating: 'our position is that he should never be released'.[48] The Afghan authorities assured the Australian Government that he would not be freed without Canberra's consent. If Australians insisted Hekmatullah remain in gaol it could hardly downplay or dismiss allegations of murder against its own personnel.

To further swing what remained of sympathetic public opinion against the ADF, ABC News reported on 3 September that a group of former and current Special Forces soldiers were operating an Instagram account with the title 'State Sanctioned Violence'.[49] The account, which attracted thousands of followers, ridiculed war crimes allegations and offered merchandise that included stickers featuring the slogans 'Make Diggers Violent Again' and 'Taliban Tears', and t-shirts with 'High Velocity Atrocities' printed across the front. The website carried biographies of deceased and serving Special Forces soldiers.

There were also videos of air attacks destroying Afghan compounds, with the mock advisory warning: 'Concern has been raised by the ADF leadership as to the appropriateness of some of the content shared in some of our write ups.' Text alongside one video read: 'The content is about as genuine as the current commander pretending to care about his best warriors as he prepares to throw dozens of them under the bus "to save the reputation of the command".' Two pointed messages were being conveyed by a small group of Special Forces soldiers and their sympathisers: they were unwilling to condemn their colleagues for killing Afghans, whatever the circumstances, and they expected any accountability to extend to officers in command positions who ought to lose their decorations and be reduced in rank.

The Army condemned the actions and attitudes of those maintaining the site, stressing these views did not align with the Army's values and were, of course, unacceptable. It was worrying that this kind of thinking plainly existed within the ranks and had either survived military indoctrination or been prompted by an experience of military service, in this instance, combat operations in Afghanistan. The real fear ought to have been the existence of this mindset among soldiers rather than its juvenile expression on the internet. Some soldiers plainly loathed Afghans even though the Afghans were their operating partners and improving their welfare was the point of the ISAF mission. Contempt for those who took the allegations of war crimes seriously was an indictment of either their education or Australian culture as a whole, given the ADF recruits from the general population and reflects its collective outlook. There was little the ADF's media and communications advisors could do. Nearly all of the reputational damage was self-inflicted. The nation's armed forces were beginning to resemble an obnoxious rabble.

The first former SAS officer to make a public comment was Mark Wales. He, too, attempted to broaden the circle of responsibility for alleged misconduct to include senior politicians and military planners in an article he published in the *Australian* on 7 September. Under the heading, 'Unfocussed, not fully committed, disjointed – our Afghanistan mission was always doomed to fail', Wales claimed it 'was politically expedient to overuse special forces in combat, to the point of systemic and moral failure. Now we are looking at punishing some of those who returned from the failed expedition'. He also linked the decision to withdraw Coalition forces gradually from 2010 to the loss of '20 more soldiers' and noted that 'a majority of the alleged war crimes have been committed during this period'. Wales must have spoken with former colleagues in receipt of PAP letters to conclude that the majority of misconduct incidents had occurred after 2010, or he accepted the reliability of media reporting. He blamed Coalition and Labor governments for strategic and operational failures, implying these deficiencies had contributed to alleged war crimes although he did not say how or why.[50]

Former *Canberra Times* editor Jack Waterford asserted that the

> politicians who decided to send Australian men and women into this debacle placed such a premium on standing by America that they cared little about the military or social cost of going. Nor did they weigh the long-term impact on Australian honour and morale, or the reputation and integrity of our military forces.

Waterford assumed the Inquiry would find 'a significant number of Australians committed war crimes in Afghanistan' but demanded Defence's leadership in Canberra accept some of the blame given many officers 'were looking the other way' and 'denying there was a problem'. He assumed the existence of drones and satellites meant commanders were aware of every move made by SAS operators. Claiming ignorance was not, therefore, an option. Harder to detect and deter was 'a developing unhealthy culture, resistant to obedience to Australian military doctrine'. Waterford thought Special Forces' 'professionalism is not much good in conventional battles' before declaring 'some of our military elite were murderers'.[51] These sweeping statements and generalisations were without qualification or clarification. His moralising admitted no mitigation. According to Waterford, there were no clean hands. Every reputation – those of commanders and combatants – was blackened by what had occurred.

The reporting of misconduct throughout this period was made more complicated and certainly more controversial by the defamation action launched by Ben Roberts-Smith, the alleged compromise of concurrent police investigations by former AFP commissioner Mick Keelty,[52] the personal support offered to SAS members accused of misconduct by the chair of the Council of the Australian War Memorial, Kerry Stokes, claims the ADF was insufficiently attentive to the emotional distress caused to serving and former serving uniformed personnel by the IGADF Afghanistan Inquiry and media reporting of alleged crimes. Defence gave up attempting to influence the media narrative or to shape public perceptions. When invited to offer an alternative interpretation on any incident or to correct any reporting errors, there was rigid adherence to the standard response: 'It is not appropriate for Defence to comment on matters that may or may not be the subject of the Afghanistan Inquiry.'

John Bale, a former Army signals officer and founder of the support organisation Soldier On, was especially critical of ministerial restraints on what he considered would be constructive public comment:

> The lack of Australian stories from Afghanistan now haunts our ability to show the overwhelmingly good job done and the professionalism and care in which it was carried out … In failing to let the ADF tell its story in Afghanistan as it happened, we robbed ourselves of the opportunity to easily show the nation that these alleged war crimes were but the actions of a few … Afghanistan veterans cannot let those who forgot our country's values write our narrative.[53]

The reputation of the SAS and the Commando Regiments was, however, already in free fall.

By the end of September 2020, there were more rumours the IGADF Afghanistan Inquiry would soon be completed. Every interested party was planning for its release and preparing for the fallout. Senior uniformed officers emphasised the independence of the Inquiry from the ADF chain of command to prevent those accused of misconduct from contending that its proceedings were biased against soldiers of junior rank. The *Australian* claimed the Inquiry was focused 'on eight to ten of the most serious alleged crimes' and had eyewitness accounts of misconduct.[54] Masters and McKenzie revealed that 'some insiders have received general briefings' about the IGADF's findings. They believed the Inquiry report would find that:

> a rogue group of SAS soldiers, variously consisting of four to five men, executed multiple bound or defenceless prisoners to boost 'kill counts' – a personal tally of Afghans shot dead – with no regard for the laws of armed conflict; a small number of commandos and SAS soldiers executed prisoners believing more senior soldiers had given tacit support for unlawful killings, and; poor leadership and oversight, with some officers blind to warnings signs that pointed to a collapse in basic morality among small soldier cliques.[55]

The 'rogue group' was soon mentioned by other media outlets and quickly became a 'rogue SAS squadron', not unlike a criminal gang, that resorted to intimidation, torture and murder. These accounts were consistent with the 'few bad apples' theory. There were no 'rotten barrels' or signs of a diseased orchard. The problems were individualised not systemic. It appeared that senior officers were not to blame.

Former Newscorp journalist Brendan Nicholson interviewed the Chief of Army, Lieutenant General Rick Burr, in early October, publishing an article that implicated a 'distorted warrior ethos' and an 'entrenched culture of impunity' as the principal causes of misconduct.[56] Ahead of the Inquiry report's release, the Army evidently felt sufficiently aware of the crimes that had been committed and confident of the factors contributing to their commission to initiate the substantial reform program outlined in the previous chapter. The Army's senior leadership readily accepted that there were structural problems within SOCOMD, that soldiers were not reporting misconduct for fear of recriminations, and that the culture within some units exuded exceptionalism, hubris and arrogance. The implication was that parts of the Army felt themselves at liberty to accept or reject directions according to whether or not they liked them. That such serious deficiencies existed within the command, and had taken some time to manifest, implied the existence of long-term inattentiveness to the fundamental elements associated with maintaining an effective and disciplined fighting force. The key message from the reform program was that any departures from Army-wide principles and procedures would be detected more efficiently and effectively. The conditions that managed to coalesce with such malignance in Afghanistan would not be repeated because they could not re-occur. But the media's attention remained on the past and not the present nor the future.

Enough had been reported, leaked and alleged over the previous 12 months for most commentators to believe that Australian forces had indeed committed murder and torture, and then conspired to conceal their crimes. These commentators had sufficient material from which to identify some of the likely causes. Australian human rights activist and lawyer Kellie Tranter evoked the psychologist Philip Zimbardo (of Stanford University prison experiment fame) who claimed, 'all evil begins with a big ideology'. Tranter believed that Australian evils in Afghanistan began with the notion of 'righteous' warfare to 'protect Australia's national security, national interest and beloved lifestyle'. This ideology obscured the reality:

that some soldiers have substituted their own judgement for the laws of war, that it's difficult to distinguish innocent civilians from enemy combatants which blurs the rules of engagement lines, that some perceive the kill count to be a criterion of success, that drop weapons ['throwdowns'] are being used to avoid accountability [and] the development of a culture of 'protectionism'.[57]

She argued the cause of misconduct was the 'dehumanisation of others, de-individuation of self, diffusion of personal responsibility, blind obedience to authority, uncritical conformity to group norms'. As the war had 'long been strategically lost', it became more 'morally groundless' as it dragged on to an uncertain end. That every nation seeks to preserve the lifestyle, interests and security of its people was entirely overlooked, as was the fate of those Afghans who feared the Taliban's return to power.

Canberra academic Michael McKinley thought the problems were a confluence of joining a bad war and deploying the wrong force rather than it being a just war in the wake of the '9/11' terrorist attacks in 2001 that morphed into an unjust conflict after 2005. He failed to mention there were two Afghan wars, fought for different ends and by different means: 2001–02 and 2005–13. After drawing attention to the experience of the British Army in Yemen during the 1960s and in Northern Ireland after 1968, the United States in South Vietnam (1962–75), the Canadians in Somalia in 1993 and the war in Afghanistan after 2010, he argued that 'context is extremely important for explanatory if not excusatory reasons':

> The wars in question were, from the start, wars of choice reflecting imperial power politics rather than principle – hence usually illegal, unethical and unwise. Exacerbating this, they were in theatres of operation that were culturally and politically alien, against enemies difficult, if not impossible to distinguish from the

general population, and in which strategic objectives were either fundamentally unclear, unrealistic or ridiculous.[58]

Victory was elusive and the mission was exhausting. The Taliban's strategy, 'which included a suite of atrocities masked as tactics for which they did not have to apologise, haemorrhaged what remained of the moral fibre of the intervening force'. The predictable outcome, he contended, was that some in elite units took 'refuge in blood-crazed, self-delighting violence'. McKinley's denunciation was based entirely on media reporting; the allegations had yet to be independently verified. He had no personal acquaintance with Australia's Special Forces but implied that he, like Waterford and Tranter, knew the content of their hearts and the evil of which they were capable.

The media 'pile on' continued. King's College London doctoral researcher Christopher Elliott claimed the SAS selection process was a fundamental part of the problem because it was designed to 'elevate and separate an anointed few from the rest of the military' and had 'many of the classic features of cult initiation'.[59] He pointed to the persistence of a 'denialist viewpoint' that either refused to accept there were serious problems or delayed judgment in the hope the Inquiry would find the allegations were unsubstantiated. Given the readiness of the Chief of Army to defend the need for close camaraderie in small Special Forces units despite the existence of 'an unaccountable brotherhood and a general culture of impunity', Elliott thought there was a 'compelling argument to be made that [SOCOMD] be disbanded' because it had 'lost its credibility'.

There was support for Elliott's views among commentators who wondered whether the 'rogue squadron' explanation, apparently preferred by Defence as an explanatory narrative, was intended to be a distraction from 'larger matters'. Vietnam veteran and historian Greg Lockhart contended that 'regardless of the individual culpability of soldiers in the Special Forces, such a squad could not possibly have taken shape if the oversight of proper training and cultural regimes and, crucially, strong command and control procedures were in place'.⁶⁰ He also wondered whether 'the defendants of any charges arising from the Inquiry will get a fair trial after so much official PR spin in the media has blackened their prospective names' and diverted attention from the 'moral leadership and strategic accountability' that resided at 'the highest levels of political decision-making and military command'. These, too, were strong conclusions to draw when the IGADF Afghanistan Inquiry report had not been released and the extent of the problems had yet to be revealed.

As the completion of the Inquiry appeared to be imminent, Defence directed that no documents relating to the war in Afghanistan were to be destroyed. When asked by the ABC why it had taken so long to issue such a direction, a departmental official explained that the invasion of Afghanistan had occurred nearly 20 years earlier and documents more than two decades old were now eligible for destruction. That the direction was greeted with 'concern' by think tanks and university research centres was a sign of deep distrust towards Defence. Some observers thought this distrust had its origins in the controversial 'children overboard' affair in 2001. Defence, some argued, was usually too subservient to its minister. That the initial invasion had occurred 20 years earlier was a reminder that the conflict was more than protracted; it was generational. Most young men and women joining the ADF in 2020 were born after the war began and had only known Afghanistan as a place of continuing bitter conflict.

Defence was also being chastised for its failure to manage the conflict's more personal legacies. On 20 October, the *Canberra Times* reported the proceedings of a coronial inquiry into the suicide of a former sergeant from the 2nd Commando Regiment.⁶¹ Before taking his own life in July 2017, the soldier told a psychologist: 'I've killed so many people, I cannot live with myself, I have killed innocents.' From 2009, the man had become violent and controlling within his family and 'self-medicated' with drugs and alcohol before killing himself. In a note he left before his death, the former Commando wrote:

'Nobody can help me, I'm too far gone, please just let me go, I've suffered enough'. His widow was critical of the Army's management of his mental health and willingness to grant waivers to permit his redeployment. In publicly released statements the man did not admit any specific wrongdoing nor implicate others from the Commando Regiments but obviously felt acute guilt over the lives that had been lost in Afghanistan. In fact, only one of the allegations of misconduct over the previous few years had directly implicated the Commandos until late October 2020.

ABC News reported that a United States Marines helicopter crew chief claimed members of the 2nd Commando Regiment's November Platoon murdered an Afghan man who was taken prisoner in northern Helmand Province in mid-2012 during an operation to disrupt local drug production and distribution networks.[62] The Commandos had seven prisoners who needed to be transported by helicopter to an interrogation centre when they were told by the American crew that the aircraft only had room for six. The American crew chief then heard a pop and an Australian say, 'OK, we have six prisoners.' He recalled: 'this was the first time we saw something we couldn't morally justify, because we knew somebody was already cuffed up, ready to go, taken prisoner and we just witnessed them kill a prisoner'.[63] After initially being keen to work with Australians 'because they wanted to shoot', the Marines and the United States Drug Enforcement Agency (DEA) allegedly later refused to collaborate with November Platoon 'due to their behaviour in the field'. A member of October Platoon told the ABC that November Platoon had a 'bad reputation among the Americans'. Whereas the British forces 'step on the lines' of what was acceptable, the 'Aussies would see the line and just hop right over it'.

The officer commanding November Platoon during the DEA operation was featured on the front page of Sydney's *Daily Telegraph* a week later vehemently denying that any prisoners were killed and lamenting the poor support he and other anxious veterans had received from Defence.⁶⁴ Defence made no comment and the ABC stood by the veracity of the story.⁶⁵ Members of November Platoon called on the ABC for a written apology, a published correction and an independent review of its drafting.⁶⁶ A 10-page letter to the ABC later challenged every allegation or refuted every assertion of wrongdoing. The story had obviously aroused considerable feeling among former and serving Commandos who insisted any misconduct originated within the SAS and not with them. This story was the last major 'revelation' before the release of the IGADF Afghanistan Inquiry report.

The media hurriedly published whatever remaining stories they had been researching before their work would become largely irrelevant. There were a series of indications in October 2020 that the report was complete and that some of its contents would be made public. The media played no part in the establishment of the Inquiry but had been active participants in its conduct, and perhaps in its conclusions as well. In addition to gaining access to material that had not been previously provided to the Inquiry, the publication of hints, rumours and allegations of misconduct gave the impression to some former SOTG members that there was no longer any point withholding information about wrongdoing. The code of silence had been broken. Disloyalty had prevailed.

Much of the media reporting over the previous three years had originated with fewer than 10 journalists. Their work was either recycled or re-reported by other media outlets. They evidently had a number of sources within the Special Operations community who they believed were well placed, reliable and trustworthy. These sources were offered anonymity and received it. Their names were kept out of the public spotlight. In the unfolding drama, their names had not appeared as either the source of information or the subject of allegations.

The ADF was the biggest loser on three grounds. It neither helped nor hindered any journalist but was criticised for failing initially to prevent the misconduct and neglecting to care for those unsettled by the IGADF Afghanistan Inquiry. In refusing to confirm or deny whether the circumstantial details of any allegation were accurate, the ADF was accused of concealing its own organisational deficiencies. As the alleged perpetrators of misconduct were not named (with the one notable exception), the ADF became the target of complaints and censure that might, and perhaps should, have been directed at those who breached the Law of Armed Conflict and violated ROE.

While there was no suggestion that the ADF had condoned such action, it had obviously failed to prevent and punish misconduct. These were sufficient grounds for the media to distribute blame, diversify responsibility and dispense accountability for what had occurred on the far side of the world in the hills and valleys of a remote Afghan province. The release of the IGADF Afghanistan Inquiry report would disclose what had happened and, just as importantly, those who were complicit and those who contributed to what had evolved into a national controversy and an international scandal. In terms of Lasswell's three functions outlined at the start of this chapter, the reporting of allegations fulfilled the *surveillance* function and the refusal to overlook wrongdoing was an exercise of the *transmission* function. The *correlation* function was missing because the information was sensitive and subject to continuing security provisions and because the reporting was tightly focused on specific individuals and particular incidents. The public would have been better served by the media paying closer attention to context and to the experience of Australia's international partner forces in Afghanistan, such as the British, Canadians, French and New Zealanders. The absence of interpretative reporting – the correlative function – did not prepare the parliament or the people for what they needed to conclude about what the IGADF Afghanistan Inquiry had found.

PART IV
COMPARATIVE EXPERIENCES

12

MEDIA AND MISINFORMATION: THE NEW ZEALAND EXPERIENCE

There are many shared experiences and common themes in the military histories of Australia and New Zealand. Initially as a British colony and later as a dominion whose status as an independent sovereign nation evolved gradually, New Zealand provided volunteers for service with British forces in the Second Anglo-Boer War (1899–1902) and, in much greater numbers, the Great War (1914–18). Forty-two per cent of males eligible for military service joined the New Zealand Expeditionary Force after 1914 and there was a 58 per cent casualty rate. Australia and New Zealand were part of a single formation at Gallipoli whose members became known as the 'ANZACs'. New Zealanders also rendered service with the Royal Navy and the Royal Flying Corps. In the Second World War (1939–45), New Zealand military personnel served in the Middle East, across Europe and in the Pacific, while the ships of the newly established Royal New Zealand Navy (RNZN) were made available to the Admiralty in London for deployment around the world. The Royal New Zealand Air Force provided trained personnel for the Royal Air Force and made important contributions to the island-hopping campaign that led to the defeat of Japan in August 1945.

The relationship between Australian and New Zealand forces remained close after the world wars as combat and support troops were deployed under Australian and New Zealand national command as part of international coalitions in Korea (1950–53), Malaya (1948–60), the Indonesian–Malaysian 'Confrontation' (1963–66) and South Vietnam (1964–72). More recently, the two nations have sent contingents to United Nations missions and peace-monitoring efforts in the Middle East, Africa and Asia, the Australian-led multinational intervention force in East Timor (INTERFET), and stabilisation missions in Bougainville and Solomon Islands.

Australia and New Zealand both consider the United States to be an important ally although Australia has been much more committed to the Australia, New Zealand and United States Security Treaty (ANZUS) since the 1980s, when the United States 'suspended' its alliance obligations after the New Zealand Government, led by Labour Prime Minister David Lange, refused entry to American nuclear-powered warships and other warships that refused to 'confirm or deny' they were carrying nuclear weapons. By contrast, the Clark Government immediately supported the American-led invasion of Afghanistan after the '9/11' terrorist attacks. In December 2001, a detachment from the New Zealand Special Air Service (NZSAS) deployed to Afghanistan and participated in Operation Anaconda in March 2002 – the largest joint operation since the Battle of Tora Bora.

As with many similar special forces units, the NZSAS was withdrawn at the end of 2002 but returned to Afghanistan in February 2004 ahead of the scheduled presidential elections. In June 2004 during a firefight with Taliban insurgents in Uruzgan province, Lance Corporal Willie Apiata rescued a wounded colleague and was later awarded the Victoria Cross for New Zealand.[1] The NZSAS returned to New Zealand three months later before being sent back in June 2005, when it again conducted long-range patrols and direct action missions. After four dramatic months that included firefights, improvised explosive device (IED) attacks and vehicle accidents, the NZSAS returned home in November 2005 without suffering any fatalities. The Labour Government told the public that the NZSAS needed to 'regroup'.[2] The truth was quite different.

The Clark Government had been aware of human rights abuses by other nations in detainee management since early 2002. The mistreatment of detainees by American personnel at Kandahar airfield (where the New Zealanders were based) had been the subject of complaints from Danish Special Forces personnel and was featured in stories published by reputable newspapers.[3] Some of these detainees were captured by the NZSAS during a raid on the village of Hazar Qadam in Uruzgan province on 23 January 2002. Following operations near the village of Band-e-Timur, a Taliban stronghold adjacent to a key communication route, New Zealand personnel called a meeting of their Danish, Norwegian, German and Canadian counterparts because they were deeply concerned about the conduct of American forces. The New Zealanders contemplated going public but decided to manage the issue to avoid a scandal.[4]

The Minister for Defence, Phil Goff, later explained that the government had recalled the NZSAS in 2005 'not as a reflection on their integrity or professionalism but because they could be compromised by those they were working with'. The Americans and the Afghans were the principal source of the concern. The Clark Government could no longer ignore human rights abuses associated with America's conduct of the war in Afghanistan. United States policy was compromising New Zealand's commitment to international law and having a corrosive effect on New Zealand servicemen and women. The NZSAS did not return to Afghanistan during Labour's term of office.

After winning the November 2008 general election, the National Party formed government with John Key as prime minister. His Cabinet agreed to send an NZSAS detachment back to Afghanistan in September 2009 as part of Task Force 81.[5] Its role was conducting counterinsurgency operations in and around Kabul in collaboration with the Crisis Response Unit of the Afghan Interior Ministry, which was designated Task Force 24. Although the New Zealanders were meant to mentor the Afghans, they acted as partner forces to prevent bombings and assaults on hotels and offices. Within the first 18 months, the NZSAS had arrested 60 suspected insurgents or Taliban leaders, prevented four terrorist attacks and captured 20 weapons caches. The overwhelming majority of its operations had been conducted without a shot being fired until two NZSAS members were killed in August and September 2011. After an extension to the deployment was approved, the unit was finally withdrawn on 31 March 2012. The recent deaths of New Zealand personnel were among the factors prompting the decision.

Elsewhere in Afghanistan, New Zealand deployed a tri-service Provincial Reconstruction Team (PRT) to Bamyan province in the central highlands to the west of Kabul. It was believed to be one of the safest provinces in the country and an ideal setting for effective civil development. The first rotation, consisting of 122 members, arrived in August 2003. By this time Bamyan was a pilot centre for the Afghan New Beginnings program, which would focus on disarmament and demobilisation of militias and the reintegration of former Taliban fighters.[6] The New Zealand Government made much of the non-warlike nature of the work the PRT was undertaking, giving the impression that its personnel were not under threat of armed attack and were supporting Afghanistan's transition to democracy. Although provincial affairs were initially benign, the security situation in Bamyan started to deteriorate in the second half of 2008. The PRT was withdrawn in April 2013 – a decade after its arrival – with a small detachment of New Zealand soldiers remaining at three locations: International Security Assistance Force (ISAF) headquarters in Kabul to assist with planning and logistics; NATO headquarters managing women, peace and security programs; and as trainers at the Afghan National Army Officer Academy.

The New Zealand people generally endorsed their nation's military contribution to Afghanistan between 2001 and 2010. The national mood turned early in August 2010 when New Zealand suffered the first of eight combat casualties. The death of Lieutenant Tim O'Donnell in a roadside bomb attack near Karimak village in Bamyan affected the entire New Zealand contingent.[7] Not unlike a death in the family, it was also a reminder that all operations involve a degree of risk and military personnel are sometimes killed. The New Zealanders naturally wanted the perpetrators apprehended. Two weeks later, a combined NZSAS–Afghan force mounted Operation Burnham with the purpose of capturing three insurgents. (A follow-up raid was named Operation Nova.) The night raids on the villages of Naik and Khak Khuday Dad were conventional in both their planning and execution. Six Afghan villagers were killed, including a young girl. Another 15 people were wounded. Twelve houses were destroyed. One NZSAS operator was slightly wounded by the collapse of a stone wall.

The initial ISAF press release claimed that 12 insurgents were killed and a substantial cache of weapons was captured. Competing press coverage compelled ISAF joint command to launch an investigation, which produced a vague and inaccurate published report. After the Defence Minister, Dr Wayne Mapp, was asked a series of questions eight months later about the raid, a press release issued by the New Zealand Defence Force (NZDF) claimed nine insurgents had been killed and allegations of civilian casualties were unfounded.[8]

Mapp's role was especially significant. On assuming responsibility for the portfolio, Mapp was briefed on the conduct of operations in Afghanistan and thought that ISAF had been drawn into substantial 'mission creep' with the emphasis moving from defeating terrorism to nation-building. He was also concerned that the government, particularly John Key, had not been sufficiently candid with the New Zealand people about the nature of the NZDF's mission in Afghanistan. Giving the impression that NZDF personnel were 'armed civil aid workers' was misleading and likely to cause problems should one of them be killed in action. Notably, he was not aware (or subsequently made aware) of any previous allegations of misconduct made against any NZDF member. Mapp relinquished the Defence portfolio and left parliament in November 2011.

In June 2014, a New Zealand television current affairs story,

'Collateral Damage', contended that Operation Burnham had left 21 civilians dead or injured, and that no insurgents had been killed or captured.[9] Prime Minister John Key quickly dismissed all the principal allegations, which had, he insisted, been thoroughly investigated by the NZDF. Three years later a six-part television documentary series, *The Valley*, focused on two other separate incidents that were unrelated to Operation Burnham involving New Zealanders.[10] The producers claimed a number of suspicious incidents needed 'to be tested in court'. The first involved an NZSAS patrol in June 2004 and included accusations that it detained people without cause, abused innocent villagers and mistreated human remains. Although the NZDF declined to assist the production team and frustrated its efforts to confirm information its researchers had received, the program prompted Defence Legal Services to conduct an internal inquiry into claims by two Afghan men that members of the NZSAS 'kicked, slapped and punched' them and used abusive language during a patrol conducted in the village of Khor in June 2004.

The inquiry did not accept these claims, noting that 'members of the patrol left their vehicles and talked quite amicably through an interpreter with locals in the bazaar – local villagers and shop keepers – and patrol members even went on to buy bread from the market'. But this amicable visit was before the attack, not after it. The inquiry did find that an NZSAS operator held an old man naked at knifepoint during a search operation:

> It is the NZDF's view that there were aspects of the behaviour of the NZSAS member that fell below the standards of a professional soldier and which, if not precluded by the limitation of time provisions set out in the *Armed Forces Discipline Act*, would have likely resulted in disciplinary charges being preferred. Consequently, the NZSAS trooper received administrative action in 2018 which noted in his file his 'poor judgment' in respect of his actions in 2004. Given that charges were not laid, the NZDF

has determined that the NZSAS trooper should not be named.
The NZSAS trooper left the NZDF in 2018.

The second was the battle of Baghak in August 2012, which led to eight New Zealand, 13 Afghan and two civilian casualties. Two New Zealand soldiers were killed. After disputing details in the official account of the battle, the series looked at how the PRT's role shifted from its original 'hearts and minds' to 'bait and hook' operations after 2009. *The Valley*'s producers argued this shift should have been the subject of a parliamentary debate. The NZDF produced a 34-page response that rejected most of the program's claims and assertions, in several instances arguing that events were open to alternative interpretations.[11]

In March 2017, investigative journalists Nicky Hager and Jon Stephenson published *Hit & Run: The New Zealand SAS in Afghanistan and the meaning of honour*.[12] Hager was known for his political advocacy and generating public controversy. Stephenson was one of few informed commentators on New Zealand's defence and security activities after 2001 and had spent considerable time in Afghanistan and Iraq. He also presented the documentary 'Collateral Damage' for Maori Native Affairs television in 2014. The book drew on interviews with Dr Mapp, former serving personnel and Afghan civilians, claiming that NZSAS personnel were involved in killing civilians, and asserting that senior NZDF officers had colluded to conceal the facts. The authors also claimed that too many former NZSAS personnel were occupying senior positions within the NZDF although Special Operations–trained personnel were often the most able officers and soldiers and their ascendancy was linked to ability. The NZSAS 'takeover' meant these officers had excessive influence over the entire defence force although the allegedly detrimental consequences of that influence were not made clear.

Hit & Run aroused deep concern in New Zealand, with most media outlets expressing suspicion of the NZSAS, its avoidance of accountability and reliance on secrecy. Human rights lobbyists thought government inaction in Wellington could prompt an inquiry by the International Criminal Court, while Amnesty International New Zealand organised an online petition and called for an independent public inquiry. National disquiet was gradually spreading across the political divide. While Hager and Stephenson were accused of having a vendetta against the NZDF – which was certainly untrue of Stephenson, who had recently published stories praising the professionalism of the NZDF – moderate voices also wanted the matter ventilated and the air cleared. The Chief of Defence Force and former commanding officer of the NZSAS Regiment, Lieutenant General Tim Keating, issued a public statement and then held a press conference rebutting criticisms of Operation Burnham, asserting that *Hit & Run* contained major errors of fact, such as where the raid had occurred, and that two separate operations (Burnham and Nova) had been conflated.[13]

Following the September 2017 general election, which brought a Labour–New Zealand First Coalition Government to power, Prime Minister Jacinda Ardern fulfilled an election promise when she announced that a public inquiry would be convened to consider the allegations.[14] In April 2018, the government released the terms of reference for the Burnham Inquiry to be conducted by the former Labour Party prime minister and professor of constitutional law, Sir Geoffrey Palmer, and former Solicitor-General and High Court judge, Sir Terence Arnold. Kristy McDonald QC was appointed counsel assisting the Inquiry. The Inquiry was also assisted by the former Australian Chief of the Defence Force, Sir Angus Houston, and former Australian Special Operations Deputy Commander, Brigadier Vance Khan. Palmer and Arnold were given 12 months to report.

The decision to conduct the Inquiry in secret – a measure deemed necessary to protect national security – was criticised by the lawyer acting for the Afghan villagers whose families had been killed and also by Nicky Hager. During the conduct of the Inquiry, the NZDF was chided for failing to provide thousands of relevant emails in a timely manner and being slow to supply key documents relating to the operation and its aftermath. As evidence was being received, Stephenson qualified some of his earlier claims and the former Chief of Defence Force (and later Governor-General of New Zealand), Sir Jerry Mataparae, admitted that ministerial briefings had been incorrect.[15] With a great deal of material to consider, including access to ISAF documents requiring international approval, a 12-month extension of time was sought and granted. After another short extension, the complete report without redactions was publicly released in July 2020.[16]

A substantial document, the report was thorough and careful, measured and insightful.[17] It was not the dramatic exposé of military brutality that many New Zealanders had either feared or expected. Although neither Palmer nor Arnold had any military experience, they received sound advice and wise counsel that was acknowledged by commentators and critics of their report. The report focused on the key operational and tactical factors and addressed the central cultural and administrative issues.

Palmer and Arnold found that both Operations Burnham and Nova complied with the Law of Armed Conflict and ISAF Rules of Engagement (ROE). Operation Burnham was justified on operational grounds and could not reasonably be described as a 'revenge raid'. Insurgents were active in the area and planning future attacks on both the PRT and Afghan national forces. During the raid, seven men were killed and at least six civilians were injured. A child was killed but not the three-year-old girl mentioned in *Hit & Run*. Only one Afghan was killed by an NZSAS operator although he was later found to be unarmed, possessing only a pocket-knife and a torch. The others were killed by 'air support' provided by an AC-130 gunship and Apache helicopters. The inquirers noted that all NZDF personnel had acted professionally although there were several 'miscalculations' in the planning and execution of the raid. These miscalculations were of the kind that usually beset such operations in Afghanistan. Nonetheless, the civilian deaths were neither intentional nor the result of reckless indifference to human life. NZSAS personnel did not give aid to the wounded (but may not have been obliged to do so in the circumstances confronting them) and, without any return fire, burned civilian houses. Whether the destruction of private property was avoidable and, therefore, deliberate could not be established. Significantly, no shots were fired at either the NZSAS operators or the Afghan and American forces involved in the raid.

The inquiry confirmed the allegation in *Hit & Run* that the treatment of one captured insurgent, Qari Miraj, was 'inappropriate and did not reflect New Zealand's values'. Miraj, who was bound and blindfolded, was punched either in the stomach or ribs by an NZSAS trooper in Kabul immediately after he was arrested. The NZSAS then handed him over to the Afghan National Directorate of Security with the likely knowledge he would be tortured. This was, *prima facie*, a breach of New Zealand's responsibilities under the Geneva Convention. When the NZDF became aware that Miraj had been tortured, an investigation should have been conducted. No action was taken.

The report did not reflect well on the NZDF but the findings could have been much worse. The Defence Minister, Ron Mark, made several public statements following the report's release.[18] Mark said his confidence in 'the men and women on the front line of our Defence Force' during the inquiry had been vindicated but they were 'let down by their senior commanders, whose post operation performance showed serious deficiencies'.

The senior officers questioned during the inquiry appeared to be stunned by its rigour and interest in a matter they evidently did not consider that pressing. The proceedings were not what they expected and the transcript shows they clearly resented their integrity being challenged. Their attitudes to political and public accountability were the most surprising. These officers assumed their professional judgment was not susceptible to public scrutiny by civilians with no knowledge of military affairs, although they held public office and were obliged to act in the public interest. The deficiencies in their performance related entirely to what happened after Operation Burnham:

> [T]he evidence is clear that in the months immediately following the operation, the actions of some senior NZSAS personnel resulted in NZDF advancing what was a false narrative, namely that the Incident Assessment Team had concluded that there were no civilian casualties on Operation Burnham. This false narrative was advanced to the Chief of Defence Force, to the Prime Minister, to relevant ministers and eventually to the public. It was advanced even though some within NZDF either knew or suspected, or had strong reason to suspect, that the narrative was false. There was no proper scrutiny of it by senior NZSAS officers at the outset—contrary evidence was unjustifiably ignored or minimised. Even if there was not a deliberate attempt among a group of senior officers to suppress the truth, the cumulative effect of what they did (or failed to do) was precisely that—to suppress the truth.[19]

Four senior commanders – one general, two brigadiers and a colonel – were named for failing to acknowledge that innocent people had been killed, removing references to civilian casualties in ministerial briefings and public statements, and obscuring their role in the propagation of misinformation. Notably, all four had commanded the NZSAS Regiment at various times after 2001; two had served as the New Zealand Director of Special Operations; and one was serving as the Chief of Defence Force when the inquiry began.

The report variously described some of their evidence as 'implausible', 'misleading' and 'inaccurate' while their leadership failures were deemed 'serious' and 'inexcusable'. The inquirers agreed with *Hit & Run* that 'there were serious deficiencies in the way that NZDF dealt with the allegations', that its 'approach to the book fell below an acceptable standard' and Keating 'erred in giving the prominence he did to the location error in *Hit & Run* and not acknowledging that the book was accurate in important respects'. Keating should have 'focused on the issues of substance rather than on points that were of little real significance'. Although Hager and Stephenson were critical of people and processes, 'criticism, even if it is sometimes unwarranted, is part and parcel of the culture of a liberal democracy such as New Zealand's; organisations such as NZDF have to accept that and be prepared to address criticism constructively, with an open mind'. For his part, Stephenson never claimed there had been a widespread cover-up but he was convinced that a small group of officers had colluded to conceal the truth that there had been civilian casualties. Their collusion rather than the casualties had become the central issue.

Was there evidence of a cover-up? The inquirers were not convinced there had been:

> Standing back and considering the events we have examined overall, we do not believe that there was a widespread conspiracy within the top echelons of NZDF to 'cover up' the possibility of civilian casualties in Operation Burnham, either in 2010 or subsequently. We consider it implausible that there was a coherent strategy of that type extending over a number of years within NZDF. We also consider that, had there been clear evidence of civilian casualties on Operation Burnham at the time, NZDF would have faced up to the consequences of that.[20]

There may not have been an 'orchestrated litany of lies', the controversial phrase Justice Peter Mahon used to describe the cover-up attempted by Air New Zealand after the 1979 crash of a DC-10 aircraft (Flight TE 901) on the slopes of Mount Erebus in Antarctica, but just as damning was the report's imputation that the NZDF did not appear to consider itself answerable to either the parliament or the people. This was 'a failing of culture':

> During our examination of the operations at issue, we have seen evidence of what we regard as failings of culture at the upper echelons of NZDF—confirmation bias, lack of objectivity and rigour in scrutinising 'facts', unnecessary defensiveness coupled with an unwillingness to acknowledge error, failure to follow up inconvenient information, and non-compliance with the disciplines and obligations inherent in the principles of ministerial control of the military and ministerial responsibility to Parliament. While our perspective is a relatively narrow one, so that we cannot say with confidence that these failings are characteristic, we suspect that they go beyond what we have seen.[21]

In sum, the NZDF did not have adequate respect for civilian control of the military, which is a crucial principle in all Western democracies.

The report was critical of former defence minister, Dr Mapp, who failed to correct the public record when he learned there had been civilian casualties. This was considered 'a significant departure from the standards expected of ministers'. Mapp had been an officer in the Army reserve. His successor as defence minister, Jonathan Coleman, was also wrongly briefed, suggesting a 'surprising level of ineptitude and disorganisation within the NZDF', implying the misinformation was inadvertent rather than deliberate.

In receiving the report, the Attorney-General, David Parker, acknowledged that without the sustained efforts of Hager and Stephenson the inquiry would not have been convened and the truth about some matters may never have emerged. He, too, noted the considerable difficulty his predecessors encountered in exercising effective political control of the military: 'the military do not exist for their own purpose'. This was a gratuitous slur on the NZDF but it was in no position to defend itself, at least publicly. Keating's successor as the Chief of Defence Force, Air Marshal Kevin Short, offered an apology on behalf of the NZDF for misleading ministers and the public:

> If we are to maintain the trust and confidence of the people we serve, we must be accountable. We must be better at the way we record, store and retrieve information, and then subsequently present that information to ministers and the public. I will ensure this happens.[22]

The press and the public were largely without sympathy for the NZDF. There was, however, a deep sense of relief that New Zealanders had not committed serious war crimes despite the fact that New Zealand's involvement in the handling of detainees, in common with the other ISAF partner nations who facilitated the transfer of detainees to American custody, was a clear breach of the Geneva Conventions with serious consequences. In its editorial, the *Otago Daily Times* observed:

> These findings will sting the Defence Force, and rightly so. The New Zealand public needs to have confidence its national forces will not only operate in battle zones with the highest levels of integrity and professionalism but will come clean when things go wrong. It is of deep concern that multiple senior commanders at the NZDF let the side down with actions that, to paraphrase Defence Minister Ron Mark, showed serious deficiencies.[23]

Much of the commentary overlooked the principal finding: New Zealand personnel deployed to Afghanistan had acted professionally and had upheld the nation's values. There were behavioural lapses within the NZSAS but they were individual and, when compared to the allegations levelled against American, British and Australian Special Forces operators, they were of a vastly lesser order of magnitude.

But it was clear that the New Zealand Government expected its uniformed personnel to adhere to the highest ethical standards and to be an advocate for exemplary behaviour within ISAF.

The Burnham Inquiry was the first of its kind into the NZDF. The allegations were serious but did not warrant a royal commission. There was plenty of scope under the 2013 *Inquiries Act* to authorise and empower a suitable forum for the allegations to be tested.[24] The handling of classified information added to the complexities but the decision to hold the Inquiry in private resulted in a greater flow of information although Hager and his supporters were unfairly critical of the reasons that were given for preserving confidentiality. To the credit of the inquirers and their counsel, the Inquiry proved to be effective and efficient. Those who were criticised made no public statements. While they certainly disagreed with aspects of the report, NZDF officers were not charged with any offences, there was no suggestion their honours be withdrawn and no recommendation of any disciplinary action. Reputations were, however, tarnished and careers were shortened. The matter had been dealt with decisively and, perhaps surprisingly, it slipped from public gaze within a week.

There are three important contrasts between the New Zealand and Australian inquiries and the allegations that prompted them. To put things in perspective, Australia sent 10 times the number of personnel to Afghanistan. First, the allegations that prompted the Palmer–Arnold Inquiry related to one particular operation involving the conduct of a small group of personnel and a set of specific allegations. The Inquiry did not consider NZSAS operations in June 2004 (which led to the discharge of an NZSAS operator in 2018) or the possible unlawful killing of a Taliban insurgent during the battle of Baghak in August 2012.[25] It was not that these other matters were intentionally overlooked by either the Ardern Labour Government or the inquirers but that the first had already been addressed by the NZDF while the second could not be examined on procedural fairness grounds. The most serious findings relate to civil–military relationships and the inadequacy of administrative arrangements in the Ministry of Defence in Wellington. These inadequacies did not contribute to the events in Bamyan. The principal presenting issue in Australia was individual misconduct during combat operations conducted over a decade involving hundreds of Special Forces operators. There was no discussion of inadequacies in the political–military interface in Canberra during the Afghan war nor an inference that it played any part in the commission of war crimes in Afghanistan.

Second, Prime Minister John Key and his cabinet rejected calls for an inquiry into the NZDF notwithstanding the existence of what seemed credible evidence of misconduct and a reasonable probability that the parliament and the public had been misinformed. The Key Government dismissed the allegations because it believed those presenting them were political opponents seeking to inflict electoral damage on his party. It took a change of government for public disquiet to be addressed. In Australia there was no need for the prime minister or the cabinet to deliberate on whether an inquiry was needed given the existence of independent statutory processes within the IGADF Regulations to deal with allegations of misconduct against any ADF member. Neither the Coalition parties nor the Labor Party has politicised the matter. The Opposition did not need to call for an inquiry and has supported a bipartisan approach. The Coalition has not criticised Labor because the alleged misconduct occurred during its term of office as well.

Third, in 2017 the New Zealand Chief of Defence Force, Lieutenant General Tim Keating, dismissed the main allegations in *Hit & Run*, sought to discredit the authors and insisted the conduct of NZSAS personnel had been exemplary at all times. It was a position from which he could not easily retreat or modify if new information came to light. Alternatively, he might have taken the allegations on notice, pledged a rigorous internal inquiry and confirmed the NZDF's commitment to transparency and accountability. The Australian Chief of Army, Lieutenant General Angus Campbell, on being advised in 2016 that there were *rumours* of misconduct (there was no evidence at this point), immediately initiated an independent inquiry and advised the media of its remit. Although affirming the positive contribution made during Special Forces operations in Afghanistan, he did not commit himself or the ADF to mitigating or defending any individual if the rumours of serious misconduct were substantiated.

Notably, one of the principal recommendations from the Burnham Inquiry was the creation of a statutory office modelled on the Australian IGADF to obviate the need for a service chief to make judgments about individual conduct that might conflict with his parallel duty to support all uniformed members.

Why, then, was there some evidence of misconduct among NZSAS personnel? Palmer and Arnold adhered to their terms of reference and declined to speculate on why the single instance of NZSAS individual misconduct contained in their report – the assault of a detainee – had occurred. (There may have been other instances of misconduct but none for which evidence was presented at the Inquiry.) To a fair-minded reader it appeared to be a momentary lapse of otherwise consistently high standards of individual conduct and unit discipline. A number of NZSAS personnel had deployed to Afghanistan on several occasions between 2001 and 2015 but there was no suggestion in the Burnham report that repeated exposure to combat was to blame or that the moral rigours of Special Forces operations in Afghanistan were overwhelming and some latitude ought to be granted the individual implicated in the assault.

Possibly more useful in accounting for the operational mood and the incident of misconduct was an internal draft report of New Zealand's decade-long commitment to Afghanistan. It was produced by the Continuous Improvement Group in Joint Forces Headquarters early in 2014.[26] The report claimed the reasons for New Zealand's involvement in Afghanistan were unclear and 'it was felt that no consolidated New Zealand campaign plan existed. As such, there was a lack of clarity over the end state and the milestones expected to be achieved'. Each rotation acquired a character of its own and was conducted like an individual operation. Further, it was 'also not clear how the New Zealand plan fitted into the wider ISAF' plan.

The underlying problem, according to some critics, was the refusal of the Clark and Key governments to disclose publicly the actual nature of the missions being conducted by both the NZSAS and the PRT. While it was clear that the New Zealand people understood that the NZSAS would be engaged in combat operations in the invasion and initial occupation of Afghanistan, the government was less clear about the role of the NZSAS after 2004 and the evolving mission of the PRTs. The political mood had turned against combat operations whether conducted by the NZSAS, whose deployment in 2004 several political parties actively opposed, or by the PRT, whose continued presence in Afghanistan was depicted as peaceful, non-violent civil aid. In attempting to preserve the government line that the NZDF was not involved in the use of force, critics alleged that uniformed personnel gave misleading accounts of their activities and were essentially politicised. The government's refusal to be open about the NZSAS's mission was subverting the democratic process, imperilling national trust in the NZDF and leading to operations that were conducted in a manner that increased the risk to those deployed.

Another possible reason for misconduct was the virtual absence of the media and the possibility that misconduct could be readily concealed or easily denied. Public reporting of the war in Afghanistan was similar on both sides of the Tasman. It was inconsistent, uneven and dependent on official sources. The New Zealand Government used national security, and an agreement that the identity of NZSAS operators and the nature of the operations would not be disclosed, to 'manage' news organisations and their representatives. The NZDF was assiduous in keeping the public focus on the heroism of New Zealand's soldiers and away from legal issues and political controversies. The population at home were not given any details of where or when the NZSAS deployed. There was no word on operational achievements or tactical challenges, and no disclosure of any practical issues, such as ill-suited equipment, or reputational problems stemming from how the war was being fought. New Zealanders were intentionally left uninformed. The vast majority of people were ignorant of the dangers associated with service in Afghanistan.

Media management also meant that mistakes could be hidden and responsibility for misconduct avoided. Determined journalists encountered many difficulties and confronted numerous restraints in their quest to report candidly on NZDF activities in Afghanistan. Jon Stephenson, for instance, was eventually able to visit villages, inspect battle sites and speak to local civilians and military personnel. He also received 'off the record' briefings from former NZSAS operators and serving NZDF officers who were certainly keen to present their version of events. While the absence of close and continuing media scrutiny was not linked to increasing the possibility of operational misconduct, it was certainly implicated in the failure of senior civilian and uniformed leaders to explain the nature and progress of operations in Afghanistan.

Why downplay the physical risk to New Zealand personnel? Stephenson argues it was largely because the war was becoming increasingly unpopular; the public could not see the point of persisting with a seemingly unwinnable conflict even as the cost in terms of human lives and financial capital, ultimately 10 lives and NZ$300 million, steadily mounted. There was a lack of political courage in reminding the population that militaries exist and are mandated to use lethal force, and a lack of practical realism among the population that soldiers are sometimes killed.

It is not clear why the NZSAS managed to avoid allegations of serious misconduct, assuming the same factors influencing Australian misconduct would have influenced the New Zealanders. The reasons might lie in differences in their respective experiences. The NZSAS did not deploy constantly over an extended period. There were three distinct phases: 12 months in 2001–02, seven months in 2004, five months in 2005, and 31 months from 2009 to 2012. Each of these deployments was different in terms of mission, equipment, location and size. Operators returned to New Zealand, where they had much more time to decompress. Unlike the Australian SAS, preparation for rolling NZSAS deployments did not occur until 2009 although the initial expectation was for a 12-month deployment that was twice extended. While the uncertainty of deployments was admittedly unsettling for those serving in the Regiment, this was a very different experience from the accumulated stresses of eight years of constant rotations for the Australian SAS.

It is also significant that New Zealand did not endure insider attacks from rogue Afghan soldiers and, until the death of Tim O'Donnell in the second half of 2010, were not dealing with the surging emotions associated with losing a colleague. As a highly specialised 'niche' force with a reputation for courage and creativity, the NZSAS were not 'competing' with the Australian SAS (they also operated separately in Afghanistan) nor did its members feel the need to impress the American Special Forces community, with whom they did work closely. While they could be aggressive when the situation demanded, they were not attentive to a wider, possibly corrupting, agenda. Indeed, the NZSAS was very aware that an element of the New Zealand population was uneasy with their remit and opposed their deployment. Attracting poor publicity in Afghanistan would have played into the hands of those calling for the NZSAS to be disbanded. While these groups were located towards the far left of New Zealand politics, their number and the noise they could produce was steadily rising in a country that was much more sympathetic to the ideals of non-violence and pacifism than Australia.

The Burnham Inquiry report brought calm to New Zealanders unsettled by allegations of serious misconduct. But if it could be proved that a New Zealand soldier did illegally kill an Afghan insurgent during the battle of Baghak in 2012, the incident could be reasonably interpreted as a solitary act by a lone individual behaving in a manner that was clearly inconsistent with the well-known rules and regulations of warfare and the values undergirding the NZDF's culture. There is no evidence of a culture that condoned such behaviour and nothing to suggest this was the fullest expression of systemic abuses that had previously gone undetected and unpunished. If this episode of alleged misconduct were to be proved beyond reasonable doubt, the reputation of the NZDF would be momentarily tarnished but quickly restored by the overwhelming majority of uniformed personnel who had done the right thing instinctively, without hesitation and without coercion. Although it engaged in fewer combat operations with fewer people, New Zealand surpassed Australia in its ability to contain and constrain the attitudes and actions that constitute the motivation and means of war crimes. Whether it could have contained and constrained 'war crimes' on the same scale as those allegedly perpetrated by the ADF is unknown.

13
HISTORICAL LEGACIES AND PUBLIC OPINION: THE UNITED KINGDOM EXPERIENCE

British history makes no sense without grasping the impact of war and the influence of its armed forces on the evolution of British society and culture. Its empire once spanned the globe and afforded the profession of arms a prominent profile and permanent place in the life of the nation. When Britain's national wealth financed missions of overseas conquest and colonisation in America, Asia, Africa and the Pacific, the Royal Navy conveyed well-armed regiments across the world to subdue the original inhabitants and impose Britain's political will, setting up imperial outposts and defending settlements from the ambitions of other colonising powers. The officers and sailors of the Royal Navy also prevented the forces of its European continental adversaries from ever successfully crossing the English Channel. The Royal Air Force earned its place in the annals of British history during the Battle of Britain when it prevented the German Luftwaffe from gaining superiority of the skies ahead of a planned Nazi invasion in 1940. Its personnel rose to greater prominence during the Cold War as they led the way in promoting technological innovation to prevent global Communist expansion.

Attitudes towards the members of the British Army are more complex, partly because some of its missions have been opposed for political reasons and denounced on moral grounds. These attitudes are largely based on stereotypes: admiration for ordinary soldiers who can be relied upon to demonstrate individual courage and bravery, and antipathy for commissioned officers, often parodied as bumbling incompetents who owe their position to the hereditary class system. In Britain during the 1960s, soldiering was widely considered second-class employment for those who could not get a 'real' job or gain entry to a 'worthwhile' profession. This was inaccurate and unfair but it gained currency as military service became less popular and was less revered right across the different strata of British society. Curiously, given they had stood side by side so many times in the same wars and facing the same adversaries, the Australian 'digger' stood much taller in his country than the British 'squaddie' stood in his.

By the end of the 1960s, with most of its former colonies seizing or being granted independence and the withdrawal of its forces in countries and territories located east of the Suez Canal, renewed political unrest in Britain's oldest overseas territory, Ireland, created a crisis that would persist for three decades. The British Army was given the task of preventing sectarian violence, which had reached levels beyond the capability and competence of the Royal Ulster Constabulary to contain.

As the breadth of tasks associated with London's military response to violent Irish nationalism expanded, so did the range of units called upon to render service in a conflict that began with counterinsurgency measures but soon shifted to anti-terrorist operations. In addition to general infantry and specialist engineering units, the British could draw on battalions from the Parachute Regiment, which was first formed in 1941 for service in North Africa, and the Special Air Service (SAS), whose history also dated from 1941, when it was raised for clandestine missions behind enemy lines.[1] The Parachute Regiment was considered a highly capable infantry unit with specialist skills; the SAS was a 'Special Forces' unit with particular expertise. The 'Paras' and the SAS believed their status was comparable, if not superior, to the Royal Marines and the Special Boat Service (SBS) within the Royal

Navy, although considering them rivals. They certainly considered themselves better trained and more capable than the regular infantry battalions from which the SAS recruited its members.[2]

The Paras and the SAS were sent to Northern Ireland after British troops were ordered to the province in August 1969. Both were feared by the local paramilitaries, especially the Provisional Irish Republican Army (PIRA), for their aggressive spirit. The Parachute Regiment sent whole battalions (of which there were three Regular battalions and three Reserve battalions) to Northern Ireland at different times whereas the Special Forces contribution consisted of small specialist intelligence-gathering teams until 1976, when a designated SAS squadron was created for service in Ulster. Some observers believed the 'Paras' and the SAS would be ill-suited to an operation requiring considerable diplomacy and restraint. This was not the kind of work for which they were formally designated. Both the Paras and members of 22 SAS were implicated in the controversial deaths of civilians and terrorists throughout the three decades of violence that was eventually ended by the Good Friday Peace Accords in 1997.

The 'Paras' were also associated with persistent rumours of misconduct during the 1982 South Atlantic war. Shortly after Argentinian forces invaded two British dependent territories, the Falkland Islands and South Georgia, claiming they rightly belonged to Argentina, the Thatcher Government launched a campaign to retake the islands. The British received the surrender of Argentinian forces on 14 June.

After marching 145 kilometres with their packs and weapons, the 3rd Battalion of the Parachute Regiment was ordered to secure Mount Longdon, one of the peaks above the administrative centre and major settlement at Port Stanley which was also the Argentine military headquarters. During the advance, members of 5 Platoon allegedly captured a small group of Argentine soldiers who claimed to be Americans. (There is no evidence of any mercenaries taking part in the conflict although a British soldier recalled one of the men, all of whom were young conscripts, producing an American passport.) After the platoon's leaders discussed what they would do with prisoners, one soldier stated:

> [X] comes back over and says, '[Z] says get rid of them'. So me and [X], we lined them up against this rock, and then stood back, and then just started firing ... he put a belt of fifty into them, and I helped finish them off. Then we had to shift the bodies around because it looked a bit suspicious.[3]

After securing Mount Longdon on the night of 11 June but facing artillery bombardment from Port Stanley, a search was made for the wounded and dead on the morning of 12 June. When the possessions of a dead British corporal were collected, one of his colleagues found a collection of severed human ears in an ammunition pouch. There was evidence that at least one of the Argentinians was still alive when his ear was removed. A former member of the battalion later revealed:

> The thing about taking ears is that you've killed your enemy one on one, man on man, and you take your trophy. It was never my thing particularly, but I remember one bloke, we'd overrun a bunker, and he bayoneted this Argy through the throat and as the guy fell back dead he grabbed him and sawed his ear off with the bayonet. 'Right' he said, 'I'll be having that,' and it went into his pouch. It was very much a personal thing, though.[4]

Later in the morning as the dead Argentines were being buried in an open bit, an A Company Corporal encountered a wounded Argentine. He had been shot in the foot or lower leg and was fully conscious and aware of his surroundings. After asking his Company Sergeant Major for instructions on what to do with the wounded man, he received the ambiguous reply: 'Put him with the others.' The wounded man was then dragged to a rocky outcrop by the corporal.

Sensing his fate, the Argentine began to shout and produced a crucifix in the hope of eliciting Christian compassion. He was then shot in the head with an abandoned Argentine officer's pistol the corporal had been given earlier in the operation by his Company OC. Hearing the shouting and gunfire, Captain Tony Mason ran to the open pit and saw the corporal 'was shaking visibly … right on the edge … and I thought he was going to shoot me'. Stunned by what he had seen, he asked the corporal: 'what did you do that for?', to which the agitated corporal answered: 'he was a sniper, he was a sniper.' Another senior NCO pointed his weapon at the corporal and told him to drop the pistol. The corporal was taken away as the Company OC reported the incident to the battalion HQ. The OC and the senior NCO had different perspectives on the gravity of what had occurred.

> Being in the job I've been in for a long time, I was rather unemotional about it but the boss wasn't, he was very angry. I mean, I thought it was a bit out of order but, you know, war's war. I could live with it, but if anyone was to ask me in a court of law, I'd just tell the truth and say, 'Well, that's justice'.

A former Argentine soldier, Santiago Mambrin, who was positioned at the summit of Mount Longdon also claimed to have seen a British soldier murder a prisoner, Corporal Oscar Carrizo.

> I was behind a ridge and from there I could see Corporal Carrizo … two English soldiers took him prisoner. I could see the three of them clearly. They made signs telling him to take off his webbing and hand over his weapons. Then they ordered him to take off his anorak. He was left standing in his vest. The English soldiers began talking to each other. Suddenly, they stared at him and one of them passed his hand across his throat, as if to say they were going to kill him. One of the soldiers fired four shots into his head.[5]

Carrizo survived. The British soldier's account of the incident was, however, substantially different. The Argentine had not been captured and he could have been armed before he grabbed the ankle of one British soldier before being shot by another. It was a legitimate act of war. Carrizo himself later stated:

> As it started to get light I crawled out of my new hiding place in the rocks. I remember standing up. Suddenly I was confronted by two English soldiers. I was shot in the head as I tried to surrender. I passed out, thinking I was dead.[6]

After regaining consciousness and stumbling down the mountain, Carizzo was assisted by two British soldiers: 'Their voices were calm. I felt at ease, almost relieved now it was over.' He was led away to medical care. The possibility of one incident being recalled in three different ways revealed both the fallibility of memory and the need for detailed evidence, especially when serious crimes were alleged.

After a 74-day conflict, 649 Argentinian personnel, 255 British personnel and three Falkland Islanders were dead. The lost war heightened popular opposition to the ruling military junta in Buenos Aires and boosted the electoral fortunes of the Conservative Government in Britain as well as the personal standing of Prime Minister Margaret Thatcher.

Rumours of misconduct circulated until another former member of the Third Battalion, Parachute Regiment (3 PARA), Vincent Bramley, published *Excursion to Hell* in 1991. Bramley claimed a number of Argentinian prisoners and wounded were murdered by junior Paras. His recollections, and they are disputed by officers with no reason to conceal the truth, suggest a pattern of behaviour and not isolated incidents. Days after the book's release and following intense media reporting, the Defence Secretary, Malcolm Rifkind, directed the Royal Military Police (RMP) to investigate the allegations. As their inquiries were inconclusive, Rifkind referred the allegations to the Director of Public Prosecutions (DPP), Barbara Mills, who asked the Serious and International Crimes Section at New Scotland Yard to commence an investigation of the alleged incidents. The media's attitude to the civilian police inquiry was mixed: newspapers on the political left thought that justice and honour were at stake whereas those on the right thought nothing of value would be achieved by an expensive investigation into isolated incidents in such a distant place. The chair of the House of Commons Defence Committee, Sir Nicholas Bonsor, issued a statement: 'I think it is an insult to them to suggest that we committed war crimes. Therefore, unless there is very substantial evidence to suggest that it is true, I do not think this is a useful or proper way to use the resources available to us'.

Over an 18-month period, 470 witness statements were taken by the Metropolitan Police, who also visited Mount Longdon, where the war crimes were alleged to have occurred. They were accompanied by forensic specialists, who tried to find bodies with ears severed within Argentinian mass graves as it was alleged at least one British soldier removed the ears of dead Argentinians as war trophies. The inquiry was broadened to other allegations ranging from murder, incitement to murder, grievous bodily harm, looting, assault, and mistreatment of the dead. After reviewing the evidence, the detectives felt they had sufficient evidence to charge two soldiers with murder or manslaughter. After reviewing the material presented to her, the DPP decided against initiating any proceedings. Her decision was naturally welcomed by a series of high-profile ex-serving military officers, including Field Marshal Lord Bramall, former Chief of Defence Staff, who said the benefit of the doubt should be 'accorded to those who risked their lives in the national interest'.

The death of the wounded Argentinian killed by the 3 PARA Corporal was handled poorly if truth and justice were the priorities. What happened after the corporal was disarmed following the shooting remains unclear. One account includes his immediate arrest, removal from Mount Longdon and detention before being dealt with summarily by his commanding officer. Another suggests no action was taken until the Argentinian surrender and the battalion's arrival in Port Stanley. Contemporaneous records contain no mention of the incident or subsequent proceedings. The Army informed the police that the corporal faced the equivalent of a court martial and the matter was dealt with in accordance with legal procedures although the corporal's commanding officer had no recollection of any disciplinary proceedings. The corporal was separately sent back to Britain, where he continued to serve in the Parachute Regiment.

As authors Christian Jennings and Adrian Weale (a former British Army officer) conclude in their study of the battle of Mount Longdon, 'every effort was made to suppress the story, and that these efforts were, by and large, successful'.[7] The prisoner was unarmed and posing no threat. The Argentinian was not killed during the 'heat of battle' or within the 'fog of war'. In a separate blog post, Weale attempted to give an account of the corporal's action: 'Many of his comrades thought [he] was a strange and unpleasant man; his company commander described him as a "looney" ... it seems likely that it resulted from a breakdown caused by the stress of battle in which [he] had hitherto played a leading role'.[8] Jennings and Weale thought it 'horrifying that a soldier in the army of a humane liberal democracy should shoot a prisoner during a war fought, by the British at least, on a matter of principle'. While they did not think the police inquiry was 'appropriate', those who attempted to conceal 'a serious disciplinary matter ... [had] done the Parachute Regiment a great disservice'.[9] Somewhat ironically, they noted that the principal participants involved in the alleged misconduct had been considered for gallantry and distinguished service honours and awards.

With the legacies of Northern Ireland and the South Atlantic fading into the background, allegations emerged of serious misconduct involving British troops following the invasions of Afghanistan and Iraq. A joint investigation by the BBC and the *Sunday Times* claimed the British Government covered up the results of an inquiry it had ordered into the murder of insurgents, the killing of children and the torture of civilians involving members of 22 SAS and the Black Watch, a widely respected Scottish infantry unit. Drawing on information supplied by frustrated military police investigators, the British Government was accused of doing everything it could to avoid prosecuting any soldier for war crimes after the work of the Iraq Historic Allegations Team (IHAT) and Operation Northmoor (which dealt with Afghanistan) did not lead to any prosecutions. IHAT was terminated in 2017; Operation Northmoor concluded in 2019.

The government ended the IHAT investigations when it discovered that an activist human rights lawyer, Phil Shiner, who had brought 65 per cent of nearly 3300 allegations of misconduct against British forces in Iraq, had paid witnesses for their statements. He was found guilty of dishonesty by the Solicitors Disciplinary Tribunal and banned from practising law. (Similar rumours have circulated about Afghan witnesses being paid to speak about Australian forces in Afghanistan.) But those who spoke to the BBC–*Sunday Times* investigation claimed Shiner's actions were merely an excuse to end an inquiry that had revealed falsification of documents 'serious enough to merit prosecutions of senior officers'. But why launch an inquiry other than to find facts and hold individuals accountable? Was this little more than a stalling tactic to divert attention away from serious allegations?

Operation Northmoor was established in 2014 by the RMP to investigate 675 criminal allegations made by 159 separate complainants relating to the conduct of British uniformed personnel in Afghanistan between 2010 and 2013. (The media mistakenly reported the inquiry only concerned Special Forces.) The focus was on 52 alleged illegal killings. The operation, which involved 120 investigators at its peak, was initially intended to run for five years. There was apparently a view within the Army's senior leadership that the evidence of 'mass executions' was 'credible and extremely serious'. The chair of the House of Commons Defence Committee (HCDC), Julian Lewis, noted that the bulk of Northmoor allegations 'had come from members of our own armed forces, non-government organisations (NGOs) and other bodies working in Afghanistan, rather than claimant lawyers'.

But in 2017, the Defence Secretary, Sir Michael Fallon, decided to reduce the number of Northmoor investigations by 90 per cent. When Fallon was asked by Lewis during November 2017 whether he 'could reassure the public that, in the absence of any mechanism for parliamentary scrutiny, if anything of the nature of a war crime has been committed, it will be properly investigated, and the appropriate action will follow?', he replied:

> I'm afraid, Mr Chairman, that you are making the assumption that there are Special Forces involved in this particular investigation. I cannot comment on whether that is or is not the case, because we simply do not comment on Special Forces' activities. What I can do is to reassure you that this investigation is being conducted independently of the units concerned and independently of ministers. It is not a process that I exercise any control over.

Operation Northmoor investigated a number of individuals. All allegations were considered in detail, with three incidents being expanded into full murder inquiries. The operation ended in 2019 without a single charge being laid despite a six-year inquiry that cost £10 million. By this time Britain had already paid out millions of pounds settling claims of unlawful killings and torture.

The head of the Kabul-based Afghanistan Independent Human Rights Commission, Shaharzad Akbar, was critical of British investigators conducting an investigation into alleged British crimes, insisting it possessed corroborated evidence justifying an independent inquiry. Human Rights Watch (based in New York City) accused the British Government of failing to 'prosecute its own people when they commit war crimes' and warned that 'criminal liability under the principle of "command responsibility" also falls on senior commanders and ultimately Government ministers if they become aware of such crimes and fail to prevent or prosecute them'. Unlike the IGADF Afghanistan Inquiry, those interviewed by Northmoor staff were not compelled to answer questions, provide statements or assist investigators. An RMP detective told the BBC that the inquiry was ended prematurely: 'I wouldn't write off a job until I have spoken to both parties. If you are writing off a job and the only thing you have got is the British account, how is that an investigation? My view is that every one of those deaths deserved to be examined and due process of law to take place.' Another disgruntled investigator said: 'The Ministry of Defence had no intention of prosecuting any soldier of whatever rank he was unless it was absolutely necessary, and they couldn't wriggle their way out of it.'

The Ministry of Defence explained that 'all reasonable and proportionate lines of inquiry have been fully pursued'. The independent Service Prosecuting Authority decided there was 'insufficient evidence to refer any personnel to prosecutors'. The Veterans' Minister Johnny Mercy, a former Army officer who had served in Afghanistan, claimed the outcome was indicative of the British Government's 'war on lawfare' and the 'burden of vexatious claims and a cycle of seemingly endless reinvestigation'.

In August 2020, a BBC Panorama investigative team learned of apparently growing disquiet among British Special Forces commanders in 2011 who suspected their soldiers at Helmand province in Afghanistan were engaged in execution-style killings, reflected in a sharp rise in 'enemies killed in action'. One briefing note conveyed the concerns of a subordinate commander. It contained the chilling observation: 'he felt that this was not necessarily about "degrees of restraint" but possibly a deliberate policy among the current [redacted] Sqn to engage and kill fighting-aged males on target even when they did not pose a threat'. The briefing note counselled 'deeper investigation ... [to] at worst case put a stop to criminal behaviour'. Commanders were concerned about the circumstances relating to 33 deaths over a three-month period. Notably, the alleged deterioration of behaviour among the British SAS coincided with that alleged in Australian media reports, suggesting there may have been common influences or parallel cultural drift.

The only case to proceed after the conclusion of Operation Northmoor was brought by Saifullah Ghareb Yar relating to a night raid conducted by British and Afghan forces on 16 February 2011 at Gawahargin (Helmand province) in which four men from Saifullah's family were shot – in self-defence according to the British forces but without cause according to the Afghan forces participating in the operation. The Afghan commander reported that 'two men were shot trying to run away, and the other two men were "assassinated" on target [that is, at the scene] after they had already been detained and searched'. British operational summaries claimed the men were reaching for grenades and assault rifles when they were shot and killed, although officers with oversight of these operations believed the post-action reports were being falsified using virtually identical cover stories to obscure the truth. Subsequent email traffic revealed that Afghan forces were reluctant to accompany their British counterparts on night raids because they did not believe many of the killings were justified. British Special Forces commanders readily realised, among other things, that such conduct would hamper the conduct of counterinsurgency and put at risk 'the prospects of enduring UK influence' in Afghanistan. There was an echo here of the American experience in South Vietnam, where misconduct was effectively exploited by the insurgency.

Following an investigation, the Ministry of Defence claimed 'there was insufficient evidence to refer the case for prosecution'. But a Special Forces major, who had examined every post-action report between December 2010 and April 2011, noted both similar details and the increasing death toll, concluding 'we are getting some things wrong, right now'. Most of the killings had reportedly occurred when an individual had unexpectedly reached for a previously concealed weapon and was then shot, although curiously the number of people killed was significantly fewer than the number of weapons recovered. In one instance, the RMP investigated a killing and referred charges against a soldier for murder, falsifying documents and perverting the course of justice.

In the Saifullah case, the High Court directed the Defence Secretary to explain why crucial documents dating from 2011 had been withheld. The court also wanted to know why the matter was not investigated on the grounds that no evidence of wrongdoing was presented when there were a series of contemporaneous complaints of which the Ministry of Defence was claiming no knowledge. The former DPP, Lord Ken MacDonald, was driven by incredulity to remark:

> The way a nation wages war tells you all you need to know about its attachment to the rule of law. It is bad enough if British soldiers were systematically murdering civilians in Afghanistan – making themselves liable to criminal proceedings in the UK. But this is compounded if their superior officers and government officials deliberately failed to investigate suspected war crimes, and then tried to conceal evidence that they had occurred from the courts.

A former military intelligence officer who served as a justice advisor in Helmand, Frank Ledwidge, spoke openly and critically about the conduct of his former colleagues:

> Aside from alienating our Afghan allies, the narrative of murderous British forces played into the hands of the insurgents. The actions of some Special Forces actively undermined the overall counterinsurgency mission, which was challenging enough already.

Why did this happen? Ledwidge thought:

> one of the unique characteristics of British Special Forces [is] that they are truly accountable to no-one. Accountability must apply to everyone and particularly to the senior commanders and politicians who have allowed, condoned or ignored these alleged crimes and created the environment for them to happen.

The claim that the Special Forces were unaccountable was emotional rhetoric and entirely false. The commanding officer of 22 SAS was responsible to the Director of Special Forces, who reported to the Commander of Joint Forces, who answered to the Chief of Defence Staff. The lament from Ledwidge was that the practice of accountability was not visible to the public on security grounds. Whether accountability should have been more visible and, therefore, more transparent was another matter.

An entirely contrary view was taken by the historian and journalist, Andrew Roberts, who argued that throughout history 'events have taken place in war that are best ignored or forgotten, or at least left up to historians to opine about, rather than dragged into the limelight while troops are still on the ground fighting, especially when no such self-investigation – such "lawfare" – is being practised by your enemies'. Roberts seemed to accept that from time to time, Special Forces units would use 'terror tactics to punish and try to cow a civilian population'. In fighting a war against an adversary that did not recognise any rules or conventions, Roberts thought that a 99.9 per cent rate of adherence by British forces was good enough and the public should be satisfied lest its ignorance of the realities of modern warfare be allowed to imperil national security. He urged more 'leeway' be given to British soldiers because the Geneva Conventions 'on state-on-state warfare no longer always apply to the realities of modern counter-insurgency'. Occasional breaches of the

Law of Armed Conflict would not, he contended, deprive Britain of moral superiority, which was derived primarily from 'the cause, not the methods of warfare' and from Britain's standing as a liberal democracy. Roberts thought 'the scales have been tipped too far against the British Army as it tries to conduct the sometimes grisly but still necessary business of doing violence on our behalf'.

Two high-profile war crimes prosecutions since 2001 revealed vastly different depictions of the perpetrators and the British public's attitudes towards them.

Corporal Donald Payne of the Queen's Lancashire Regiment pleaded guilty in September 2006 to a charge of inhumane treatment of an Iraqi detainee three years earlier in Basra. After sustained interrogation, one of the detainees, Baha Mousa, died of 93 injuries following 'serious gratuitous violence'. Payne was cleared of manslaughter and perverting the course of justice, with Justice McKinnon noting that those complicit in Payne's behaviour had closed ranks. The corporal was imprisoned for 12 months and dismissed from the Army. He later attributed his conduct to avenging the murder of comrades and conceded that every member of his unit had mistreated prisoners. An inquiry conducted by Sir William Gage, former Lord Justice of Appeal, was critical of inadequate attempts to ban illegal interrogation techniques but did not find a culture of systemic abuse.[10] There was no sympathy for Payne in the popular press. His sadistic conduct was universally condemned, including by Prime Minister David Cameron, who called it 'shocking and appalling' before insisting 'Britain does not cover these things up, we do not sweep them under the carpet. We deal with them.' The national mood had changed. There was public recognition that British forces were at least capable of serious misconduct and were accountable.[11]

A more nuanced 'test case' of British resolve in the face of war crimes allegations involved Sergeant Alexander Blackman of Juliet Company, 42 Commando, Royal Marines. In September 2011, Blackman killed an already seriously wounded Taliban insurgent in

Helmand province. The man was dragged away from the Kestrel overhead surveillance system before being shot in the chest with a 9mm round. Blackman later claimed he thought the insurgent was dead when he shot him. After being shot the man started convulsing, indicating he had been alive. After the man died, Blackman remarked to his colleagues: 'Obviously this doesn't go anywhere, fellas. I just broke the Geneva Convention'. These remarks featured in a video recording from an unofficial helmet camera that was saved on another marine's hard drive. The footage was discovered during an investigation of an unrelated matter.

Blackman was charged with murder and tried by court martial in October 2013. He was found guilty and sentenced to a mandatory life sentence, in this instance determined to be a minimum of 10 years' imprisonment. An appeal heard by the Court Martial Appeal Court in May 2014 instead found Blackman guilty of manslaughter and reduced his minimum sentence to eight years. A second appeal in March 2017 further reduced the sentence on the grounds of diminished responsibility to seven years. The court decided:

> There can be little doubt that on 15 September 2011 the appellant was angry and vengeful and had a considerable degree of hatred for the wounded insurgent. On prior deployments, similar emotions had been controlled by him ... The appellant's decision to kill was probably impulsive and [an] adjustment disorder had led to an abnormality of mental functioning that substantially impaired his ability to exercise self-control.

Blackman had previously deployed to Northern Ireland, Iraq on three occasions and to Afghanistan in 2007. His father died shortly before he deployed to Afghanistan for the last time in 2011. He was sent to a remote command post where he lived in a small mud enclosure. He and his men were patrolling up to 10 hours a day and constantly faced sniper and improvised explosive device (IED) attack. When some of Blackman's comrades were killed in a bomb attack in May 2011, the insurgents hung their dismembered body parts from a tree. The marines were rightly indignant and outraged at the savagery of the insurgents' conduct, which constituted a serious breach of the Law of Armed Conflict and the standards of any civilised society.

Seven men had been killed and another 45 injured during the 42 Commando deployment, which was in its final month. Blackman's troops were overworked (his post had been reduced from 25 to 16 men), under-resourced and stationed in one of the most dangerous districts in Helmand. Those who deployed with Blackman thought it was almost impossible to distinguish between innocents and insurgents as the entire population was dehumanised and ethical principles became relativised. Success was difficult to determine. Blackman felt abandoned by his commanders and a sense of isolation weighed heavily upon him. Clearly, he was ill-equipped to be where he was with too few practical and emotional supports. Blackman developed a deep hatred for the Taliban and a strong craving for revenge. His lawyers claimed he was 'truly the last casualty of a failed war'. These factors were accepted as mitigation when an appeal against his conviction and sentence was heard. With time served, Blackman was freed in April 2017. He had been in prison less than four years.

The initial sentence and its subsequent reduction met with contrasting responses within the uniformed and political communities. Several senior officers described Blackman's conduct as aberrant and his crime as heinous. Those who knew the sergeant believed he was treated harshly. They called for leniency because he had an exemplary record until the moment of his offending. Former Coldstream Guards officer and Conservative parliamentarian, Richard Drax, had campaigned for a review of Blackman's court martial, telling the House of Commons that:

> understandably he feels betrayed – a scapegoat, hung out to dry by the military and political establishments. He was fighting a

war at our behest and on our behalf. He believes that his small patrol was given an impossible mission with little support or command structure. They were undermanned and overstretched, the impossible was demanded and a decent man was pushed beyond endurance. In his words, it was a 'lack of self-control, momentary lapse in … judgement'.

Former Army colonel and Conservative parliamentarian, Bob Stewart, noted that 'Sergeant Blackman has now served longer in prison than many Provisional Irish Republican Army members and Loyalist paramilitaries who were clearly terrorists, deliberately trying to kill people and who were rightly sent to prison for murder.' The former archbishop of Canterbury, Lord Carey, praised Blackman for being 'a magnificent soldier with a long and distinguished record of service to the Queen. I have served myself in the armed forces and know that in the heat and dust of battle, split second decisions must be made and expediency can sometimes overcome strict morality even for the best of men.'

Of course, an illegal killing after a battle remained an illegal killing. Nonetheless, an online petition attracted 100 000 signatures from people who thought Blackman was being unfairly condemned for defending his country. Readers of the *Daily Mail* newspaper, which led the campaign to free Blackman, contributed over £800 000 to his legal fees.

While there was certainly mitigation, Blackman might have self-reported his inner anguish and sought peer support. But in the 'alpha male' culture of the Royal Marines, Blackman considered both courses of action tantamount to weakness. His fitness for deployment and readiness for future promotion were also at stake. By his own actions and admittedly with hindsight, things could have been different for both Blackman and those around him. Conversely, Royal Marine commanders carried some responsibility for creating the conditions that made misconduct on the part of Blackman and his men more likely, and for being inattentive to the warning signs that those deployed with Blackman were being exposed to stresses that would push their self-discipline to the limit.

There was less attention to the willingness of Blackman's men to conceal his actions and their complicity. The video evidence revealed they conspired to place the wounded man beyond aerial surveillance, they collectively declined to provide the man with medical care, were apparently untroubled by their sergeant's conduct in killing the wounded man, knew the Law of Armed Conflict prohibited such action and became active participants in a cover-up without any form of coercion. The moral failure recorded in the helmet camera footage was communal. No-one protested and no-one complained. A dark group mindset had prevailed at the very moment individual moral courage was most needed. This case reflected a deep malaise within Blackman's sub-unit. Its leadership, discipline and ethics were obviously deficient; its culture had plainly become malignant. Curiously, it was acceptable to express sympathy for Blackman with hindsight but less acceptable for Blackman's fellow soldiers to offer support when he was under pressure in the field. Once the support of colleagues was given, it was much harder for them to later report his 'crime'.

A senior Royal Marines officer, Brigadier Ian Huntley, was directed in 2015 to undertake a review of the circumstances contributing to Blackman's actions, the influence of his conviction and the subsequent publicity on the culture, ethos and training of Royal Marines, a 'qualitative assessment of the impact (is this change for the better?)' and whether additional reform was needed to ensure the operational readiness of the corps. He was specifically asked to consider the sufficiency of junior leader selection and training, and the 'adequacy of decompression and post deployment mechanisms intended to manage the traumatising effects of repeated combat deployments'. Huntley was asked to submit an interim report in just six weeks but still managed to produce a very insightful document.

Huntley interviewed 30 individuals from 42 and 45 Commando, using the 'human factors analysis' approach initially developed to investigate aircraft crashes. He looked at four levels of 'active errors and latent failures' that included unsafe acts, pre-conditions for unsafe acts, unsafe supervision and organisational influences. After noting that aggression was always required in conflict, Huntley observed it was easier to encourage aggression than to engender restraint. There were standard operating procedures that ensured individuals adhered to rules and regulations but 'strong leadership and regular oversight' was needed alongside sound training. In 2011, counterinsurgency operations in Helmand province required a measured response given the Taliban wanted to provoke a kinetic reaction as part of their continuing propaganda campaign against ISAF. The battle lines were not 'straight'. But he discovered 'considerable evidence' that the approach taken by 42 Commando was 'overly aggressive' by a commanding officer who was described by one of his own contemporaries as a 'neanderthal'. They would strike so hard against the insurgents that their will to fight would evaporate. It was difficult if not impossible to claim that Blackman was a 'bad apple'.

By way of contrast, the commanding officer of 45 Commando was more attentive to the dynamics of counterinsurgency and the need to rein in those deploying for the first time. The commanding officer devised 10 key principles that placed the Afghans and their needs at the centre of attention. They would kill insurgents when necessary but 'body count will not always indicate success'. He exhorted his men to 'have the courage to use absolute minimum force' because kinetic actions 'result in Afghan funerals which generate brothers and cousins bent on revenge'. Conscious of the war's degrading affects, he stressed: 'we will maintain our discipline always and in every eventuality; there is no place, for example, for feral soldiering because of austere conditions. High standards will win'. Before they departed for Helmand, he told his men:

> We will give those who seek to oppose us an honourable way to become part of the legitimacy of Afghanistan. But if they refuse that and become irreconcilable, we will fight them hard and ruthlessly as 45 Commando always does. And we must look after the people who have known nothing other than war and oppression in their lives to date. It is about Afghans before it is about anybody else, ourselves included. We must and we will, I know, deep in my heart, get this right.

In contrast to 42 Commando, 45 Commando had no firefights with the Taliban during their seven-month deployment in the neighbouring area of operations, reporting an 86 per cent reduction in violent incidents from the previous rotation. The commanding officer of 45 Commando had reported his concerns to the theatre commander about the contrasting approach being taken by 42 Commando. No corrective action was taken.

Huntley also noted that Blackman's company commander (a major) was unfamiliar both with his company and with the sergeant at the time of the incident. Blackman's original company commander was wounded and quickly replaced by another officer, who had been working in the battalion headquarters, and assumed responsibility without any formal preparation. The face-to-face supervision of Blackman and his men was considered inadequate because there were, according to Huntley, 'a number of warning signs that could have indicated that they were showing evidence of moral regression, psychological strain and fatigue'. The foremost contributing factor in Blackman's crime was 'moral disengagement'. He failed to make the necessary shift from trying to kill an insurgent to providing him with life-saving medical care when he was wounded. Killing the man was an extension of his 'moral disengagement'. At that moment, he was not concerned that his conduct was wrong or, indeed, criminal.

Huntley made a number of recommendations for enhancing training and education, improving command cultures and managing internal unit dynamics when one of its members faced an inquiry. He wanted ethics to be the subject of continuing discussion and debate rather than delivered in a 'set and forget' classroom environment. Royal Marines in Helmand were dealing with complex situations that had not been anticipated in their training nor had they been acquainted with how they might respond to ethical challenges when they possessed a certain mindset. An executive summary of his report was released but not the main body. Nevertheless, the Royal Marines used this unfortunate sequence of events to make changes and to improve its management of human factors in warfare. It also had to ensure that Blackman did not become a martyr or a hero. He became the focus of pity and the centre of compassion for all those who endured harsh conditions in Afghanistan. But Blackman had illegally killed a man and brought unwanted attention to Britain's armed forces. A decade after committing a war crime, Blackman remained an ambiguous figure among those who struggled with the admonition to love the sinner but hate the sin.

Blackman's case shows that British public attitudes to misconduct are complex and contradictory – two responses that have permeated the entire uniformed community as well. As soldiers rather than officers are usually indicted for war crimes because of the different duties they perform, there is the almost inevitable objection that individuals are punished for their personal mistakes, rather than institutions and their leaders being held to account for their structural and command failures. Poor leadership, incomplete training, deficient guidance, inadequate resources and unreasonable expectations are not crimes but they contribute to cultures that make misconduct more likely. There is also the somewhat fatalistic view that wars are messy and those who fight them are driven by intolerable conditions and unrelenting provocation to contravene acceptable standards of conduct.

The commanding officer of 45 Commando resigned in 2013 because he disagreed with the attempts of more senior officers to feign surprise at Blackman's conduct and their efforts to isolate the causes of his crime. In his resignation letter he stated:

> I struggle to understand institutionally how we have not taken greater responsibility for Marine A's conduct ... I am convinced we as Royal Marines officers could and should have done more to reduce the likelihood of him behaving as he did.

The commanding officer of 42 Commando was subsequently promoted on three occasions and later served as Deputy Advisor to the Afghan Ministry of Interior Affairs.

There is no doubt that Blackman had been pushed beyond his limits and, by all accounts, a previously good soldier had acted out of character. He did not start the day on 15 September 2011 with the intention of behaving in a manner that would turn his life upside-down. He was already in the midst of a personal crisis although he was not aware of its depth or darkness until he killed the wounded Taliban fighter. Without knowing he was facing an important test of character, Blackman was a danger to himself and to others. Pride and stoicism probably blinded him to the truth of what he had become: someone he could not respect. Before September 2011, Blackman had not believed he was capable of such behaviour; after September 2011 he was ashamed to learn that, in fact, he was. It was an awful insight that could not be ignored. Those sentencing Blackman certainly took his remorse into account.

In addition to posing questions about the moral and spiritual burdens that an individual can carry, the Blackman case prompted a general debate about Britain's involvement in the Afghan war and whether its indeterminate nature had led to misconduct. Was the war justified in terms of the immense human and material cost? Was continuing a morally defensible course of action in itself? With an adversary persisting with conduct intended to exhaust the international community's resolve, when would the war end?

Strategists also wondered whether the kind of war being fought effectively increased the likelihood of ISAF forces being morally compromised and ultimately losing the struggle for hearts and minds.

The British Government could not reasonably assert, given the Blackman and Saifullah cases, that its personnel exhibited the highest standards of ethical conduct in their fight against the Taliban. Plainly, there is sufficient open-source reporting to suggest that in 2011 the British SAS may have engaged in the sort of alleged misconduct detected by the IGADF Afghanistan Inquiry. Whether the alleged British misconduct was on a similar scale and of comparable severity is impossible to determine. The United Kingdom relied heavily on its Special Forces but whether overuse and inadequate supervision may have contributed to misconduct is presently unknown. Clearly different, however, is the attitude of the two governments to dealing with rumours and allegations of misconduct.

Whereas the Australian Government fully supported ADF-initiated inquiries into allegations of misconduct, the British Government and the British Army have been far less cooperative in confronting rumours and circumstantial evidence that the Law of Armed Conflict might have been disregarded in Afghanistan. Publicly stated commitments to transparency and accountability have not translated into overt and rigorous action to pursue and prosecute misconduct. Immediate reputational damage appears to have been accorded greater priority than dealing with conduct and cultures that inevitably lead to wrongdoing and unavoidably damage unit morale. Neither the British forces nor the British people have reason to believe that misconduct really matters to those in Whitehall. The perception is that misconduct only becomes serious when it cannot be denied.

The British Army has been able to deflect external pressure to investigate 22 SAS personnel because of the government's long-standing blanket policy of not commenting publicly on Special Forces operations and reliance on accumulated goodwill towards the Regiment within the parliament and among the people. Australians have been much less sanguine about the prosecution of uniformed personnel when evidence of misconduct is gathered against them. It is not that the Australian parliament and people do not share similar affection for the armed forces and their members. They do. Most Australians, however, appear to have a much less tolerant attitude to misconduct and feel less obliged to defend the nation's military past. It is what it is – a story of success and failure, good and bad. There are, of course, a few notable conservative commentators who prefer a whitewashed version of military history and seem increasingly disposed to dismiss any criticism of the uniformed community as politically motivated. Their influence remains marginal and a more balanced view prevails.

No country has been more influential in Australia's evolution as a nation than Britain. While Australia has become more closely connected to Asia and devised its own customs and conventions, relations between the two countries remain intimate in the military sphere. The Australian and British SAS have continuing bonds that influence doctrine, tactics, training, procedures and personnel. Their cultures remain very similar. At the administrative levels, there are fewer ties and less frequent interactions. The political landscape in Canberra does not much resemble that of London. In contrast to the Coalition parties, there is obvious impatience within the Conservative Party over allegations of war crimes irrespective of whether they relate to recent conflicts or those of the distant past. These allegations either distract government or disrupt the military. Misconduct is rarely considered an indicator of cultural decline.

While avoiding vexatious complaints and combating 'lawfare' is entirely understandable, a more effective policy is raising ethical standards across the uniformed community to make self-serving litigation much less likely and false claims far less persuasive. This was the Australian approach and there was much to commend it.

14

SHAMEFUL SHADOWS AND SUPERIOR STANDARDS: THE CANADIAN EXPERIENCE

Canada's military history is complex and nuanced. It is certainly much longer in duration than that of many nations. During the first century of European settlement, which began in 1608, the British and the French engaged in a series of small wars to extend their possession, and ultimately control, of territory north of the American colonies. Sovereignty was resolved in Britain's favour in 1759 after French forces were defeated on the Plains of Abraham near Quebec City. During the American War of Independence (1775–83) and throughout the early years of the initially expansionist American republic, the Canadians remained loyal to Britain and repelled numerous American attacks, forming a unified Canadian Province in 1841 and then, in 1867, establishing the Canadian Confederation. The Canadian military was used to suppress domestic political unrest, mainly among the Francophone community and First Nations peoples who asserted their territorial autonomy by unilaterally declaring separate homelands.

Paralleling the Australian experience, Canadian troops were made available to the Imperial Government in London for service in the Sudan (1885) and South Africa (1899–1902). Canada created the structures of a standing army in the first decade of the 20th century and established its own Navy the year before the Royal Australian Navy was created by royal decree (1911). The Canadians fought alongside the British in the Great War of 1914–18 and lost 66 000 men, 6000 more dead than Australia. Canada again answered the call to arms in 1939 with land, air and naval forces serving predominantly in Europe and the Atlantic.

After the Second World War, Canada was a founding member of NATO in 1949, and with the United States established the North American Air Defense Command (NORAD) in 1958. Alongside the Australians, the Canadians were part of the First Commonwealth Division of British Commonwealth Forces during the Korean war (1950–53). Canada did not contribute forces to the conflict in South Vietnam although many Canadian volunteers fought in American units. It also decided against establishing an equivalent of the Special Air Service (SAS) units that had appealed to Australia and New Zealand. It did, however, raise and maintain a mechanised infantry brigade in West Germany from the 1950s, and an Air Division consisting of four wings in both France and West Germany. Canada was also an active supporter of United Nations peacekeeping.

With the end of Cold War rivalry in 1989, there was greater scope for the United Nations to intervene in places of dire need without being accused of aiding or abetting either the United States or the Soviet Union. One such place was Somalia. The combined effects of drought, famine and civil unrest following the collapse of the Barre military dictatorship in 1991 had created a humanitarian crisis in the poor East African nation. In December 1992, United Nations Security Council Resolution 794 approved the deployment of peacekeepers to Somalia under United States leadership. The Unified Task Force (UNITAF) was directed to provide sufficient physical security for the civilian population and aid workers to conduct a humanitarian relief mission. Local warlords eager to increase their power resented the United Nations presence and opposed the activity of its personnel, including soldiers from the Canadian Airborne Regiment (CAR, but often referred to simply as the 'Airborne').

The Airborne was closest to a Special Forces unit in the national order of battle. It was a composite formation consisting of personnel from the Royal 22nd Regiment (R22R), the Princess Patricia's Canadian Light Infantry (PPCLI), and the Royal Canadian Regiment (RCR). Each regiment, and they had a different lineage and culture, sent trained officers and men to the Airborne. Overall command was rotated across the parent regiments so that each contributing regiment had a chance to shape its collective culture. Although considered a superior unit, the Airborne reflected the general characteristics and culture of the Canadian Armed Forces (CAF). There were a few important differences. Senior non-commissioned officers (NCOs), who tended to stay longer in the Regiment and were considered the custodians of the corporate memory, sought the compliance of junior officers by stressing the importance of 'how things are done in the Airborne'. Long-serving soldiers set the mood and maintained a disproportionate influence over new arrivals. Their impact eventually led to the evolution of a parallel (and rival) chain of command that was based on customs and conventions demarcating the Airborne 'brotherhood' and normalising deviant behaviour.

The Airborne was not necessarily the best unit to send to Somalia in 1992. It was not mechanised nor was there any need for a parachute capability. It had not been readied or trained for peacekeeping duties. But it was considered 'overdue' for deployment, having prepared for overseas service on previous occasions only to remain in Canada because it was part of the national strategic reserve. Although it was not deemed a Special Forces unit, the CAR was considered an elite force for whom some concessions were made because it was required to fulfil tough assignments. Airborne soldiers also had a reputation for being Canada's most aggressive, with a propensity for indiscipline and insubordination towards those outside the Regiment. Lacking strong leadership, the Regiment had more than its fair share of disciplinary problems. In a difficult and chaotic place like Somalia, a particularly strong hand was needed to keep the soldiers in line.

The 845-man Airborne contingent arrived at Belet Huen in central Somalia in December 1992. Located 330 kilometres west of the Somali capital, Mogadishu, and situated adjacent to the Ethiopian border, Belet Huen had been the scene of sporadic fighting between the United Somali Congress faction and local Darod clansmen only 18 months earlier. It was the last of eight supply staging centres to be occupied in the mission. The initial warm welcome turned to sharp resentment when the Canadians confiscated weapons from marauding gangs and violent individuals who set up illegal road blocks to collect 'tariffs'. When infiltrators began to steal from the Airborne compounds, the Canadian commander, Lieutenant Colonel Carol Mathieu, authorised his men to shoot intruders in the legs if they fled from patrols. It was an unwise direction, given what was about to occur.

On 4 March 1993, two unarmed Somalis suspected of stealing supplies from the Canadian base were shot in the back, one fatally, by members of the Airborne. A subsequent medical examination conducted by an Air Force physician suggested the dead man, Achmed Arush, had probably been shot in the head while lying on the ground. The medical officer reported the death as suspicious and requested an independent investigation. Two weeks later, a Somali teenager, Shidane Abukar Arone, was caught stealing from the Canadian compound and detained by Airborne personnel. By this time the Canadians were deeply frustrated with individual Somalis who showed no respect for either Canadian or United Nations property. Arone was tortured and then beaten to death by two members of 2 Commando, considered by some to be a 'rogue' sub-unit, within the hearing of between 15 and 80 Airborne officers and soldiers who reportedly ignored his screams. Indeed, one sergeant remarked, 'I don't care what you do, just don't kill the guy.'

The Regiment tried to cover up the incident by attributing the teenager's death to injuries he sustained while being apprehended. But the sergeant in charge of the patrol that captured Arone said he was uninjured when first detained. Eventually, two officers and three other ranks were found guilty of offences ranging from murder to torture, issuing illegal orders and professional negligence. Master Corporal Clayton Matchee was charged with second-degree murder and torture but attempted to hang himself after being charged. He was subsequently deemed unfit to stand trial. Private Kyle Brown was convicted of second-degree murder and torture, and was sentenced to five years' imprisonment and dismissal from the Army in disgrace. Sergeant Mark Boland was found guilty of negligent performance of duty but not guilty of torture. On appeal, his sentence was increased to 12 months' imprisonment and dismissal from the Army. Major Anthony Seward was acquitted of intentionally causing bodily harm but convicted of negligent performance of duty and sentenced to three months' imprisonment and dismissal from the Army. Captain Michael Sox was found guilty of the same charges as Seward but was demoted in rank and issued with a severe reprimand. The Airborne's commanding officer was acquitted of negligent performance of duty and, on appeal by the prosecution, was acquitted a second time.

None of those who ignored Arone's mistreatment was charged for their indifference to his plight. Graphic photographs of the teenager's disfigured face and his killers at work shocked and appalled the Canadian people. Little could be offered to mitigate the offences. Matchee and Brown had been cruel and sadistic. Two explanations have been offered to explain their behaviour. The first was the influence of traumatic stress on their behaviour. There was, however, scant evidence that Airborne personnel had been exposed to events so traumatic they might lead to aberrant behaviour such as torture and murder. The second was the influence of Mefloquine, sold under the trade name 'Lariam', which was given to Canadian personnel in Somalia to prevent malaria. It was a problematic explanation.

A 1994 study into the use of Mefloquine identified a range of neuro-psychiatric side effects including sleep disorders, hallucinations and depression, although the incidence of these side effects was approximately 1 in 10 000–13 000 doses. Statistically, it was very unlikely that both Matchee and Brown were experiencing a side effect of Mefloquine when they killed Arone. A Canadian inquiry into the use of Mefloquine in Somalia was unable to reach a conclusion on whether the drug had contributed to violent behaviour.[1] The inquiry, which was conducted in 1997, noted that instances of reported misconduct among CAF personnel were not isolated to the days on which Mefloquine was consumed. Indeed, Arone died on the day before the drug was usually routinely taken (Wednesday). Some soldiers spoke of Mefloquine 'messing with their heads' for 24 hours but none reported feeling that the drug made them violent. Attributing the death of Arone to the influence of Mefloquine on Matchee and Brown was unconvincing.

Media coverage of the Canadian mission to Somalia focused on the tragic deaths of Arush and Arone and overlooked the Airborne's significant operational achievements. The Airborne had demonstrated how an area could be effectively pacified and prepared for the distribution of aid. The Regiment certainly had disciplinary problems but they were specific to elements of units, in this case a small group in 2 Commando, and not the entire formation. Matchee and Brown were considered 'poor soldiers' whom the PPCLI 'dumped' on the Airborne. Unwanted personnel could be sent to the Airborne, which lacked a selection mechanism to vet and reject sub-standard or unsuitable soldiers.

Adding to what was now referred to publicly as the 'Somalia scandal' was the release of several videos depicting appalling hazing rituals in 1 Commando that included racist diatribe. These disclosures destroyed any remaining public support for the CAR and deeply embarrassed the government. As a result, the Minister of National Defence announced in 1995 that the CAR would be disbanded. The Regiment's reputation was apparently beyond repair. Its former members, now shrouded in ignominy, were posted to other units. Four years after the deaths of Arush and Arone, and during a national election campaign, a highly embarrassing public inquiry that had uncovered serious deficiencies in civilian and military leadership was abruptly terminated by the Canadian Government.

Defence funding, which had been cut by the incoming left-of-centre government led by Prime Minister Jean Chretien in 1993, was further reduced. Chretien had also initiated a salary freeze as one of several measures foreshadowed during the previous election campaign to address the substantial budget deficit. Civil–military relations, which were already problematic under a prime minister who had little time for the uniformed community, deteriorated rapidly with the appointing of a Minister's Monitoring Committee to supervise the recommendations contained in the inquiry's final report (although its proceedings had been cut short). The CAF was not trusted to inquire into its own affairs for fear of collusion and cover-ups; its leadership in particular was not trusted to implement reforms owing to doubts about its competence and commitment. This was a low ebb in Canada's peacetime military history and an ugly moment in its national life. The Chief of the Defence Staff, General John de Chastelain, retired under a cloud of suspicion. His successor, General Jean Boyle, resigned less than 12 months later when evidence emerged that he was involved in the cover-up, concealing and then altering documents that were released to the media. Public support for the CAF fell from more than 80 per cent of the population to 48 per cent by 1997. Although other nations had innocent Somali blood on their hands, it was the Canadians who suffered the greatest reputational damage.

Shortly before the Somali deployment, the Canadians had established Joint Task Force (JTF) 2 as a counterterrorism unit that would subsume the existing functions of the Royal Canadian Mounted Police (RCMP) Special Emergency Response Team. Early in 1993, slightly over 100 specially selected soldiers (although critics thought 'JTF' stood for 'just take friends') from the Airborne Regiment and the PPCLI started training for a range of hostage recovery scenarios.

The Task Force later operated small anti-sniper teams during the Bosnian civil war and advised the Haitian Government on how to deal with criminal gangs and insurgency. After the '9/11' terrorist attacks, JTF2 was expanded to over 600 members and began to resemble a special forces unit, although it was tightly controlled for fear it might become a reincarnation of the Airborne Regiment. To forestall any sense of exceptionalism and to prevent any uniformed person thinking they were above the CAF's moral codes and ethical standards, senior leaders made a point of not referring to members of JTF2 or, later, elements of Special Forces Command, as being 'elite'. While acknowledging they had special skills and offered unique capabilities which would become evident in campaign successes, they were bound by Canadian domestic law and constrained by the Law of Armed Conflict and required to observe Rules of Engagement (ROE). Respecting the law and honouring the rules were henceforth to be the hallmarks of Canadian professionalism.

A small JTF2 detachment was secretly sent to Afghanistan in December 2001 without parliamentary debate or the release of any official statement. Working with the American Third Special Operations Group (rather than NATO, which did not want a Canadian presence because of lingering doubts it held after the Bosnian war that the Canadian Government would not allow its personnel to participate in operations), the Canadians engaged in direct action and took prisoners they later handed over to the United States. The first JTF2 rotation in Afghanistan concluded in May 2002 after five months of close protection, reconnaissance and surveillance, intelligence gathering and direct action, with Canadians working closely with partner forces from the United States, Norway, Germany and New Zealand. Their replacements, who were fewer in number, remained in Afghanistan until October 2002 when JTF2 was withdrawn. Canadian troops moved from Kandahar to Kabul in 2003 when they joined ISAF and contributed to civil reconstruction tasks. CAF personnel returned to Kandahar in late 2005, where

2300 personnel were assigned to a battle group with a Canadian officer taking charge of Regional Command South.

The commitment of Canadian troops lasted until 2008 and was extended until the end of 2011 by the Harper Government with the support of the Liberal Opposition. In mid-2011, Canada withdrew its Infantry Battle Group and planned for the remaining combat personnel to return home by the end of the year. After a decade of combat, the CAF and the Canadian people had had enough. Prime Minister Harper explained that his nation no longer had an appetite to remain in Afghanistan. Initial support for the war (a *Washington Post* survey found 74 per cent of Canadians were in favour) had dissipated by 2008 when more than half of those polled by Angus Reid Public Opinion (58 per cent) were opposed to the extension of Canada's contribution. By 2011, only 30 per cent felt the sacrifice of more than 150 Canadian lives was worthwhile. They, too, had either become casualty averse or were oblivious to the human costs associated with armed conflict.

As the Somali affair had cast a long shadow over the Canadian Armed Forces, commanders took every step to ensure subordinates adhered to the high standards of ethical conduct by which the CAF wanted to be known. To ensure adherence to CAF values and to prevent any problems, the JTF2 commander reported directly to the Vice Chief of the Defence Staff in Ottawa and not the Theatre Commander. During a decade of combat operations, JTF2 came to notice in relation to two of four moral–legal issues that attracted international attention and prompted domestic concern.

The first related to the treatment of Afghans detained by the CAF who were turned over to American and then Afghan authorities and, in many instances, were physically abused and mentally harmed during interrogation and incarceration. Some were allegedly tortured. Canada could not 'wash its hands' of responsibility. Like New Zealand, it was a signatory to the Geneva Convention. Under Article 12, detaining countries are responsible for the treatment of those they detain. Prisoners of war are to be treated humanely and their dignity is to be respected. If CAF personnel reasonably suspected that prisoners would be mistreated after their transfer to American and Afghan authorities, and continued with the handover, or did nothing in response to receiving evidence or allegations that these prisoners were abused, those authorising and actioning the transfers could be charged with war crimes. This was a serious matter that transcended administrative discretion. In addition, prisoner transfers involved a large number of individuals, not all of whom were Afghans. There was also the need to make a distinction between recognised combatants and opportunistic criminals and committed terrorists, the latter being dealt with by police, prosecutors and the courts. Citizens of other nations were transferred to Afghan custody as well. Between 2001 and 2011, Canada detained more than 1000 suspected insurgents.

From the initial invasion and occupation of Afghanistan, Canada did not want the responsibility of dealing with prisoners. This was, of course, a failure of political will and another instance of half-hearted commitment to the war. In fact, most countries wanted to avoid detaining people. There were obvious practical reasons for each small ISAF contingent not to have their own detention facilities. Such facilities were usually expensive and attracted extensive external oversight. Dealing with prisoners was generally complicated and often controversial given the uneven character of the local court and prison system. The Canadians would transfer their prisoners to the Americans, who were conducting interrogations and arranging detention.

Two years before evidence emerged of American abuse of detainees at the Abu Ghraib prison in Iraq, Canadian politicians and human rights groups were justifiably concerned about the possibility of abuses given the American stance on detainee status. The Americans were refusing to supply the names of detainees or reveal where they were being detained. As detention facilities were built across Afghanistan during 2002, Afghan authorities gradually assumed responsibility for the administration of prisons and the management of detainees, although the United States maintained its own special sites.

Any remaining Canadian readiness to trust the Americans ended when the Abu Ghraib scandal received worldwide press coverage in April–May 2004. Late in 2005, and ahead of the Canadian combat mission commencing in Kandahar, Canada signed an agreement to surrender prisoners to the local Afghan police and the National Directorate of Security (headquartered in Kabul) which, even then, had a menacing reputation. Early in 2006, the then United Nations High Commissioner for Human Rights, the Canadian lawyer Louise Arbour, revealed that complaints of Afghan officials torturing detainees were 'common', with the Afghanistan Independent Human Rights Commission estimating that 'one in three prisoners handed over by Canadians are beaten or even tortured'. In June 2006, Canadian troops handed over a suspected Taliban insurgent to the local Afghan police. The man was then beaten within sight of the Canadians, who neither encouraged nor condoned the behaviour but seemed to believe it was a regular occurrence and what happened in Afghanistan. They did, however, intervene when the beating continued. The man was taken back into CAF custody. Although the suspected insurgent was not formally deemed a CAF detainee, one Canadian soldier made a formal complaint at the inactivity of his colleagues.

A Board of Inquiry (BOI) was ordered into the allegations. It was headed by Rear Admiral Paul Maddison. The inquiry report noted 'the practice of corporal punishment being meted out on an apparent whim in the street and elsewhere was common and was observed and commented upon by most Canadian Forces members'. There was no need for Maddison's report to make detailed recommendations, as the CAF had already refined its processes for identifying, documenting and detaining alleged insurgents. Several Canadian diplomats claimed to have warned Ottawa after 2005 that abuse and torture were commonplace in Afghan prisons and detention facilities, and that the CAF should halt further prisoner transfers. (Canadian prisoner transfers were halted in November 2007.) There were, in effect, more than two systems of justice operating in the one country, an outcome hardly likely to assist Afghanistan to establish its own effective and widely accepted justice system.

When most Canadian military personnel were withdrawn from ISAF in 2013, activists and academics were calling for Canada's national leaders to acknowledge the 'shameful legacy' of the nation's role in Afghanistan.[2] Stuart Hendin, a civilian academic at the Royal Military College of Canada, claimed that 'Canadian officials, both military and civilian, are exposed to criminal prosecution secondary to the transfer of detainees.'[3] After stressing that he was not suggesting 'any member of the [CAF] during military operations in Afghanistan engaged in torture or any form of mistreatment of any detainee captured', transferring detainees 'to the custody of Afghan authorities and in particular the National Directorate of Security' meant that 'members of the [CAF] are exposed to prosecution as a result of these transferred individuals being subjected to torture or forms of cruel, inhumane or degrading treatment by Afghan authorities'. There was an element of absurdity here: foreign soldiers transferring Afghan prisoners to Afghan authorities on Afghan soil in order to face Afghan justice were being accused of war crimes. The activists could, of course, have pursued the Afghans who actually mistreated their fellow citizens, although they stood little chance of having them prosecuted.

The second moral–legal issue facing the Canadians in Afghanistan related to the sexual abuse of children by Afghan National Security Forces (ANSF) personnel and whether CAF personnel fulfilled their responsibility to prevent and then report such abuse. This was an issue facing personnel from every ISAF partner nation. It was the source of much soul-searching and personal recrimination. In June 2008, the *Toronto Star* published a series of articles on the prevalence and severity of post-traumatic stress disorder (PTSD) among CAF personnel. One of the apparent sources was witnessing the sexual assault of children by ANSF members and, in one case, by an Afghan interpreter employed by the CAF.

A BOI was convened in October 2008. It reported in January 2010 after contacting 800 potential witnesses and receiving sworn statements from 105 people. The BOI found that a series of allegations of child sexual assault with substantial credibility dated from 2006. Such conduct was an offence under international law, Afghan law and Islamic law, and had been publicly condemned by the Afghan Government despite its prevalence in some parts of the country. Owing to 'communication failures within the mid-level chain of command', there was 'no specific and permanent [CAF] action' despite the abuse being widely suspected and, in some instances, broadly interpreted by Canadian personnel as a cultural tradition despite their own abhorrence at the practice. The BOI found that Canadian ROE permitted 'a soldier to use force to stop a serious crime' although the ROE did not create an 'obligation for a CAF member to act'.

This was another legal absurdity. It was illegal to transfer insurgents to government authorities when abuse was *likely* but there was no legal obligation to stop *actual* abuse. The implication is that soldiers are required to know the law – and perhaps also the customs – of the country to which they are deployed. Legal complexities are often easier to grasp than cultural nuances. Soldiers are not police, and cannot be easily re-trained as police. The issues were complex. What actually constitutes abuse? What if the alleged abuser is a parent? What is done with the child? Who looks after an abused child in the absence of alternative forms of care? Does dealing with crimes of this kind take precedence over military tasks? Even well-trained police have difficulty dealing with the sexual abuse of children. It was apparent that some politicians had no idea about what military forces can and cannot do in conflict-ridden, dangerous societies.

In any event, no officer in the chain of command had ever condoned abuse nor ordered any CAF member 'to ignore illegal behaviour on the part of the ANSF'. Although failing to report abuse was not a crime, the BOI recommended mandatory reporting of 'any laws of armed conflict, human rights or serious crime violations to their chain of command', including any 'second-hand or indirect' accounts of abuse. Soldiers were not expected to intervene in an abusive situation or to make difficult judgments about the welfare of an individual but they were required to report what they had observed. The Canadians should have been more forthright in responding to an unambiguous moral evil. Soldiers not only needed to know the law, they were to be acquainted with local customs and cultures, and have confidence in addressing all forms of aberrant behaviour.

The third moral–legal issue concerned the alleged 'mercy killing' of an Afghan insurgent by Captain Robert Semrau, an officer posted to the 3rd Battalion, the Royal Canadian Regiment, who deployed to Helmand and Kandahar provinces in 2008. Mercy killing, also known as 'battlefield euthanasia', is the intentional taking of a person's life for the purpose of ending extreme suffering from physical injuries that, in the absence of medical care, will inevitably lead to death. The person subjected to a mercy killing may be a civilian who was unintentionally injured, or a combatant who was engaged with lethal force. Mercy killing is a war crime because international humanitarian law requires the sick and wounded be respected, protected and treated humanely. This requirement precludes killing the sick and wounded under any circumstances.

Semrau's mentoring unit initiated an ambush while on patrol in Helmand province in October 2008 and an intense firefight with insurgents followed. The commander of the partner Afghan force refused to advance in support of the Canadians when requested. When the situation became desperate for the Canadians, an American Apache helicopter gunship engaged the Taliban forces with devastating effect. One witness later testified seeing a seriously wounded insurgent who was '98 per cent dead'. Another said Afghans were kicking and spitting on him. Semrau was then observed shooting the man twice. He was charged with second-degree murder, attempted murder, conduct unbecoming of an officer, and failure to perform a military duty, becoming the first Canadian officer ever charged with a battlefield murder.

Semrau pleaded not guilty and exercised his right to remain silent at the General Court Martial convened to hear the case. He later wrote: 'I chose to remain silent during my murder trial, and I never gave testimony on the stand, nor did I make a statement to the police. The truth of that moment will always be between me and the insurgent'.[4] In July 2009 Semrau was acquitted of second-degree murder because a jury consisting of military officers was not convinced the Afghan died as a result of being shot by Semrau. The wounds sustained by the man in the gunship attack were deemed to be fatal while the court noted Afghan nationals had refused to provide medical care. Semrau was, however, found guilty of conduct unbecoming of an officer and was sentenced to reduction in rank and dismissal from the CAF.[5] His conduct violated Article 12 of the Geneva Convention, which imposed upon him a duty to protect the wounded: 'Any attempts upon their lives, or violence to their persons, shall be strictly prohibited; in particular, they shall not be murdered or exterminated ... they shall not wilfully be left without medical assistance and care'.[6]

The court accepted that Semrau acted to end the man's suffering but had placed personal convictions ahead of lawful directions. His attitude attracted the strongest condemnation from the Chief Military Judge, Lieutenant Colonel Jean-Guy Perron, who told Semrau:

> You failed in your role as a leader ... how can we expect our
> soldiers to follow the rules of war if their leaders do not?
> Shooting a wounded, unarmed insurgent is so fundamentally
> contrary to our values, doctrine and training that it is shockingly
> unacceptable behaviour ... You made a decision that will cast
> a shadow on you for the rest of your life ... Your actions may

have been motivated by an honest belief that you were doing the right thing, nonetheless, you have committed a serious breach of discipline. Decisions based on personal values cannot prevail over lawful commands.[7]

In sum, Semrau should have allowed the man to die painfully in the absence of timely medical attention. Commentators grappled with the enduring, and not readily resolved, tension between legal obligations and personal convictions.[8] The public reaction to Semrau's conviction was marked by empathy and a growing sense that the Afghan conflict was, at best, morally ambiguous.

While there were certainly other mercy killings in Afghanistan, it was only the strict conformity of all Canadian personnel to the Law of Armed Conflict and ROE that the depiction of Semrau's action as a 'mercy killing' was neither conveniently accepted nor cynically rejected. It was possible to believe Semrau had acted out of compassion because Canadians had re-established their reputation for not killing innocent people or engaging in violent reprisals. Semrau's actions imperilled the ISAF mission but they were not indicative of a malignant culture in either his battalion or within the CAF. That Semrau did not deny shooting the insurgent; that the matter was reported immediately; that his conduct was subjected to rigorous scrutiny; and that he was convicted and chastised, ensured that public confidence in the CAF was not eroded and the international standing of the CAF was not diminished. Although the case had severe consequences for Semrau and difficult implications for the Canadian military, the high standards expected by the Canadian parliament and people were exemplified by the CAF at every level. Canada emerged stronger and not weaker from the Semrau case. It strengthened commitment to due process and provided a case study for future education and training.

The fourth moral–legal issue, and the only incident bearing a similarity to allegations of Australian wrongdoing in Afghanistan, was the subject of an investigation codenamed Project Sand Trap. It was established in 2008 to consider claims that a JTF2 soldier was party to the shooting death of an Afghan who was attempting to surrender in 2006. The allegations were made by another JTF2 soldier who did not see the man raise his hands in the air (as a symbol of surrender) but claimed others did. The complainant also alleged his colleagues recklessly fired rockets into civilian compounds and misbehaved during short-term leave in Dubai. After a thorough investigation lasting several months, no charges were laid. The Canadian Forces National Investigation Service (CFNIS) concluded 'there was no evidence found to support these allegations; moreover, the investigation determined that the [CAF] member acted within the rules of engagement in all instances'.[9]

A second and broader inquiry, Project Sand Trap 2, was launched in February 2009, focusing on claims that a group of JTF2 soldiers witnessed several American Special Forces personnel killing unarmed Afghans during a Canadian-led operation in January 2008. The claims were made by the same JTF2 member who had complained about his own colleagues' behaviour. Thirty months after initially accusing American personnel of misconduct and refusing to trust anyone in the chain of command, the complainant went to the Canadian Forces Ombudsman. A staff member in the ombudsman's office noted the complainant, who was suffering severe PTSD, believed his colleagues were 'being encouraged to commit war crimes by the chain of command, which they may be held accountable for, as their superiors walk away'. He further claimed that more aggressive soldiers whom he thought were complicit in misconduct were being promoted over more cautious soldiers.

After extensive investigation, Project Sand Trap 2 found no evidence of any wrongdoing among Canadian personnel, not even their apparent failure to report 'serious criminal offences allegedly committed by individuals from other nations' in 2007 and 2008. Nevertheless, there was sufficient substance in the allegation for the Canadians to bring the information 'to the attention of the appropriate foreign investigative authorities' – that is, the Americans. The Canadians did not ask the Americans for any confirmation of what they did once the information was received. Project Sand Trap 2 was officially concluded in June 2016. The dates, places, units and names of participants have never been disclosed despite numerous freedom of information requests. Behind the scenes, JTF2 combined operations with the United States were suspended, the Chief of Defence Staff in Ottawa was notified and the American theatre commander was advised. The Americans were told there would be no further combined operations until the Canadians were assured that all Americans in Afghanistan, including civilian contractors, adhered to ISAF standards. Canada would not be party to any misconduct on the part of any partner nation.

A separate BOI, which began in 2009, examined the culture of the Special Operations Forces Command (CANSOF), which was established on 1 February 2006. The inquiry was a consequence of the Project Sand Trap investigations highlighting problems with information flows within the Command and the CAF. After drafting of the BOI report concluded in 2013, its security implications were considered for the next three years before a heavily redacted executive summary was released under freedom of information legislation in September 2018. The BOI took evidence from 124 witnesses and assessed 40 000 documents. The inquiry report included 32 recommendations, focusing primarily on balancing operational security with transparency and openness.

Consistent with the Project Sand Trap investigations, the inquiry did not find evidence of misconduct on the part of JTF2 members but noted the Command's initial investigations were internal, informal and superficial. Information was conveyed along the chain of command but influenced by trusted friendships. The more trusted the friendship, the more information flowed. A judgment about the sensitivity of the information determined whether it was conveyed verbally or in a report. Outsiders were excluded because they were not bound by the same sense of belonging to the Command. The 'need to know' principle was taken to extremes. Senior commanders were either uninformed of incidents or misled by the use of vague and imprecise language. This often made the chain of command, starved of accurate information, ineffective in decision-making. Operational secrecy and organisational confidentiality were often blurred in ways that may have seemed self-serving in addition to being used 'to weaken accountability'.[10] The BOI report noted that 'the mere fact that CANSOF claims something to be a matter of operational security does not necessarily make it so'. There was also the inference that CANSOF was troubled with handling information relating to American misconduct and was concerned that reporting such behaviour might have adversely affected its relationship with kindred American Special Forces commands. That reports of American misconduct were not pursued *could* have given the impression that such behaviour was not being taken seriously or that two rules applied within ISAF: one for Americans and one for other partner nations.

The most senior Canadian Special Forces officer, Major General Peter Dawe, conceded in 2018 that the Command was established quickly with organisational structures and administrative processes that were 'not as sophisticated as they should have been'. The Canadians were learning as they went, including the need for avenues to report abuses of the kind seen in Afghanistan. Although reports were received and were taken seriously, there was clearly collective relief that no evidence of misconduct came to light. CANSOF had been reformed without the need for criminal prosecutions although the fear of prosecution may, of course, have helped.

No member of JTF2 has been indicted for misconduct in Afghanistan, not even for common assault. Nor have any Canadian Special Forces soldiers been accused of misconduct where prosecution was either not pursued or failed for lack of evidence. Allegations were promptly considered and subsequently dismissed. There were no attempts to shield JTF2 members from the consequences of their actions and there is no evidence of any collusion to conceal crime. Unlike the Somalia affair, there were no attempts to deny a crime had been committed before allegations were thoroughly investigated. There was complete transparency at all levels of the CAF. Why, then, was JTF2 able to avoid misconduct among its members, something that was beyond other comparable Special Forces units?

First, Canadians were mindful of the legacy of Somalia in 1993 and the turbulent decade that followed. The CAF's senior leadership during the Afghan war were mid-level unit commanders during the mid-1990s, had witnessed the fallout from the Somalia affair and recognised the need for continuing investment in command, leadership and ethics training, and imposed close scrutiny on those placed in ethically complex operational environments. Drawing on their experiences in the former Yugoslavia, the senior leadership knew the past conveyed a clear warning to the present about the future. There was no room for complacency, even in respect of minor infractions. Misconduct was always possible however unlikely it might seem. A former Airborne junior officer, Ian Hope, who was a battalion commanding officer in Afghanistan, remarked: 'we were determined not to allow transgression of discipline or subversion of sub-cultures' and 'made the foremost loyalty to CAF and Canadian national values'. He told his soldiers on arriving in Afghanistan: 'we need discipline and to keep up our professionalism – that's what distinguishes you from every other guy with a gun in this country'.

Having lost the confidence of the parliament, the press and the people once before, attentiveness to the Law of Armed Conflict, ROE and CAF values (Integrity, Loyalty, Courage, Stewardship, Excellence) were an integral part of Canadian mission design and operating culture in Afghanistan. In the decade after 9/11, the Canadians saw more action in the Middle East than other nations, with the exception of the Americans and the British. The lessons learned from the previous decade were tested in the most demanding of situations.

Second, the deployment of JTF2 to Afghanistan was not something from which either of the major Canadian political parties sought an electoral advantage. As the Canadian political class was not close to the CAF, especially in 2001, there was no electoral appeal in being filmed or photographed with JTF2 members preparing for deployment at home or at a forward operating base in Afghanistan. In this sense, the deployment was not an overtly political act. Until 2009, both the Liberals and then the Conservatives had similar views of deploying Canadian forces to Afghanistan. There was nothing to be gained politically from departing from a broadly bipartisan approach. This may have accounted, in part, for the absence of Canadian politicians at the funerals of CAF members killed in Afghanistan. The distance between the political class and the CAF prevented any member of JTF2 from believing a special relationship existed between the government and the unit, and worked against any presumption that JTF2 members could rely on any residual political goodwill in the handling of allegations. The unit did not operate under a false sense of political security. In the absence of an Anzac tradition and digger myths to afford them the benefit of any doubt, the unit and its members would answer fully for any hint of misconduct. Whether this acted as a deterrent for bad behaviour is difficult to assess, although Canadians had no expectation of a 'free pass' for even minor misdemeanours.

Third, CAF personnel were aware from early 2002 that their parliament and press were attentive to the ethical dimensions of the Afghan war, drawing public attention to issues arising from the transfer of detainees initially to the United States and then to local Afghan authorities. The CAF's senior leadership were always conscious of the ease with which operational practices could become political controversies, and the need to ensure those exercising civilian control of the military were kept informed and made accountable for their decisions. Ethical standards were kept in the foreground by vigorous debates about the treatment of detainees by personnel from other nations, with the obvious implication that all CAF members would be held to the highest standards of conduct if they erred. If Canadians were deeply troubled by the behaviour of those with whom they were cooperating in Afghanistan, they expected their own personnel to uphold international law to the letter and to demonstrate Canada's unequivocal commitment to human rights. Further, the Canadians were the keenest to have journalists embedded in combat units despite the objections of some operating partners. The embedded journalists appreciated this investment of trust, which was repaid by careful and nuanced reporting, especially of 'friendly fire' incidents. As one journalist remarked: 'keeping the thing secret only feeds the sense that there is something to hide'.[11]

Fourth, many of the Western nations contributing military forces to Afghanistan sent well-established units that were familiar with the operating environment. Australia sent SAS squadrons and Commando companies, the British sent 22 SAS squadrons as well as Paratroopers and Royal Marines, the United States sent the Rangers, SEAL teams, Delta Force and the Green Berets. In 2001, Canada's JTF2 was still a young Special Forces unit. It was working to establish a reputation that would not have been served by any instances of misconduct. There was no pressure on JTF2 to prove its worth in terms of the CAF's overall mission and structure as the continuing existence of JTF2 was assured. Nor did it need to demonstrate its supremacy within a Special Forces community with competing stakeholders. The Canadian Government had invested in the overall capacity of JTF2, enlarging its budget and increasing its personnel with the expectation that it would also lead the way in exemplifying Canadian standards and proving Canadian professionalism within NATO, noting initial European reluctance to include Canada in its planning for Afghanistan.

Fifth, the Canadians in Afghanistan did not always take their lead from the Americans. Canadians have never wanted to be Americans and have striven in most aspects of their national life to forge a distinct identity setting them apart from their southern neighbour. Despite a common border and shared history, Canada has been shaped by its English and French heritage, whereas the United States has largely turned away from its colonial past. Although Canada and the United States have operated cooperatively as founding members of NATO, the CAF continued to resemble both the British Army and the United States Army, even in Afghanistan, when they were ISAF partner nations. While Canadians are willing to copy the United States, especially in the conduct of military affairs, they actively promote a distinct national ethos to avoid any confusion. In Afghanistan, Canadians were mindful of the difference between the policies of their respective governments and the attitudes of their senior commanders. The Americans might have been the leading nation but CAF personnel were often wary of following their lead. The Australians were probably more deferential to the Americans than the Canadians and appeared to be keener to secure their general approval, if not approbation.

Sixth, drawing on their collective experience of peacekeeping operations in Somalia and Bosnia, CAF leaders were conscious that the descent into misconduct was gradual and sometimes imperceptible, and that operational service brought out both the best and the worst in people. Those new to combat were confronted with previously unknown anxieties and were required to manage unfamiliar emotions in extreme environments. Canadian leaders did not assume that the training and discipline of their subordinates would be sufficient to avoid aberrant reactions to enemy action in all situations. They were also aware from the demise of the CAR that group cohesion and unit loyalty were important for operational effectiveness but liable to morph into a 'closed brotherhood' in which personal solidarity could lead to professional collusion and the perverted belief that crimes could be committed with impunity. The CAF emphasised the absolute necessity of leadership that demanded high standards, made hard decisions, imposed rigorous compliance and never confused popularity with respect. These changes also made the CAF more ready to investigate rumours and unsubstantiated reports of abuse. The Canadians would not wait until hard evidence was available before taking corrective action. To their credit, they also recognised the ubiquity of 'closed brotherhoods' and the continuing need to prevent their formation.

The CAF had come a very long way since the disbandment of the Airborne Regiment in 1995, when its senior leadership was considered incapable of devising and delivering organisational reforms without close and continuing external oversight. In February 2007, the Chief of the Defence Staff, General Rick Hiller, described the 1990s as the 'decade of darkness'. It was a humiliating time for the entire uniformed community in Canada. The way forward did not start with denial but with acknowledgment. Change was needed and not merely to appease self-interested politicians, an ever-critical media or a fickle civilian population. Plainly, things had gone wrong within the CAF. The causes were internal and external. A lack of strategic guidance created existential crises among senior leaders; deep budget cuts depleted uniformed morale. It was difficult for officers and other ranks to remain motivated and committed to professional excellence. Somalia demonstrated the extent of the CAF's cultural issues. In the shadow of highly publicised disciplinary proceedings, the CAF did not engage in self-recrimination but in positive appraisal of where it needed to be and how it might get there. There was very substantial investment in education and training in leadership and ethics. In many respects, the ADF finds itself organisationally where the CAF found itself in 1997. There is much to commend in Canada's journey from the darkness and much from which Australia might learn.

15

FACING THE FUTURE BY ACKNOWLEDGING THE PAST: THE FRENCH EXPERIENCE

The British historian Niall Ferguson credits France with being the most effective military power in recorded human history. It has played a part in 50 of the 125 major European wars that have been fought since 1495. To go further into history, of the 168 battles that French forces have fought since 387 BCE, they have been victorious in 109, suffered defeat in 49, and another 10 were inconclusive.[1]

The French Army has traditionally protected France's national sovereignty from neighbouring adversaries while the Foreign Legion formed in 1831 extended the boundaries of its global empire in Africa, Asia, South America and the Caribbean. The Army has stabilised and destabilised metropolitan governments. From the heights of the Napoleonic period when the Army was integral to France's imperial dominance in Europe and the Mediterranean, complacency and stagnation saw it defeated in the Franco–Prussian war of 1870 and the subsequent loss of the Alsace–Lorraine region. After halting the Germans in 1914 and inflicting important defeats on the Kaiser's forces in 1918, the French Army entered a period of institutional atrophy following the Great War. A lack of strategic creativity and stale military doctrine left the French Army unable to resist advancing German forces a second time in 1940.[2] Thereafter, the Vichy Government of occupied France collaborated with the

Germans while Charles de Gaulle commanded the 'Free French Army' based in London.

After the Second World War, France deployed military forces to its colonies in Africa and Asia, where it was reasserting its political authority. Encouraged by the success of anti-French forces in Indochina, the Algerian *Front de Libération Nationale* (FLN) launched its insurgency in November 1954. There was a major difference in French thinking about Indochina and Algeria. The French Prime Minister, Pierre Mendès-France, insisted that 'Algeria is France, and not a foreign country under our protection'. The province's population consisted of 9 million Algerian Muslims and one million Europeans, most of whom had emigrated to Algeria after a military invasion and its incorporation into Metropolitan France in 1833. Although many Algerians were satisfied with French rule and were content for Algeria to remain part of France, the left-leaning insurgents secured the willing or coerced support of the majority early in their campaign of 'revolutionary violence' by linking insurgency to both nationalism and socioeconomic progress within an overt Islamic framework. The insurgents were supported by the neighbouring colonies of Morocco and Tunisia, which were about to receive full independence from France.

Among French military officers, there were two competing opinions on the best way to secure the population's loyalty and compliance. The 'warriors' believed that physical intimidation and military conquest were the best approach. The 'pacifiers' were committed to social development and political dialogue. As the American human rights advocate Rita Maran has shown, most French soldiers, especially the large number of younger conscripts, embraced the 'pacify' approach, thinking it was constructive and more consistent with their own social outlook. As representatives of a 'superior culture', they believed their mission was to 'civilise' Algeria by promoting the benefits of French values and denouncing the demands of fanatical extremists. The colonised Algerians were soon defined by the stereotypes applied by their colonial masters. These caricatures played into the hands of the nationalists, who claimed the French overlooked Algerians' political and religious aspirations, assuming the material advantages of living in a more technologically advanced society would have more immediate appeal than the imagined benefits of self-determination offered by the prospect of an Islamic republic.

All of the 'warriors' and some of the 'pacifiers' complained, however, that they were fighting the FLN with one hand figuratively tied behind their backs. These restraints were:

> imposed by Christian ethics that deterred the kind of all-out no-holds-barred assault they believed necessary for winning the war. Their Muslim opponents, they said, were driven by non-Christian teachings – whether Islamic or Communist made little difference to them – and 'that's why it's so hopeless. The struggle between Christian civilisation and communism isn't fair: we'll lose every time'.[3]

Paradoxically, the French thought they could civilise Algeria by uncivilised means. They would destroy villages in order to save them. The murder of Amédé Froger, the Mayor of Boufarik and President of the Federation of Mayors of Algeria, outside his home in broad daylight and the bombing of his funeral procession the next day, was the turning point.

The creation early in 1956 of the 10th Paratroop Division as a 'unit of intervention' for service in Algeria reflected the French metropolitan government's desperation. Thrust into local politics by a government unwilling to align achievable national objectives with a viable military strategy, the paratroopers would take the initiative, believing their elevated public standing gave them immunity from external sanction.

After arriving in Algeria and receiving exceptional powers from the Resident Minister Robert Lacoste, the 4600 men of the

10th Paratroop Division soon became a law unto themselves. The paratroopers' *esprit de corps* had already alienated them from other deployed forces. They openly displayed their scorn for institutional discipline (which made their own officers' jobs more difficult) and lack of interest in collaborating with other units. They were likened to a 'military sect' with their own customs, traditions and rituals. Drawing on their reputation for initiative, the paratroopers would undertake duties the police were ill-equipped to perform and tasks the infantry were ill-prepared to undertake. When they were tasked with containing the Algerian insurrection *by whatever means*, some of their officers assumed they were at liberty to act outside the law, as they increasingly 'resembled less the warriors of antiquity than an especially nasty police force'.[4]

Realising the incompatibility of attempting to crush the uprising while civilising the country, for the paratroopers the war became an anti-Muslim, anti-Communist campaign that soon took on a highly individual dimension. They assumed every Algerian was an insurgent and any Algerian behaving suspiciously was deemed a legitimate target. The divisional commander, General Jacques Massu, authorised highly aggressive, largely repressive missions, principally against the FLN's leadership, to demonstrate the paratroopers' 'credibility'. Exemplars of the 'warrior' approach to the insurgency, they used helicopters to conduct anti-guerrilla operations and kill–capture missions across Algeria. Believing that basic human rights had been 'suspended', torture and summary executions were not, therefore, prohibited in their view. Indeed, Massu believed that without torture and executions, which he later referred to as 'justified war crimes', the French Army could not succeed. The local European population thought the French Army had 'finally acquired some backbone'.[5]

As France retained the death penalty on its statute books and both treason and sedition were deemed capital crimes, attempts to defend summary executions were not entirely without a legal foundation. Torture attracted the loudest protests although it had yet to be codified in French domestic law. Soon after their arrival in Algeria, the paratroopers learned that the local police were already employing torture to extract time-sensitive information relating to the whereabouts of bombs planted in public places. General Paul Aussaresses, then a major in the French Action Service, gave the most candid account of summary executions and torture in his 2004 memoir, *Battle of the Casbah*. He believed 'those policemen were neither monsters nor tormentors, just ordinary men ... swept up in extraordinary circumstances. I quickly became convinced that those circumstances explained and justified their methods ... which became inevitable in a situation that clearly defined every rule'.[6] If the nationalists used terror, the French state was justified in using torture. To defeat insurgent networks, the French needed information they could only acquire, they insisted, by torture. Aussaresses claimed that employing torture was amply justified by the atrocities committed by insurgents:

> Once you have seen with your own eyes as I did, civilians, men, women, and children quartered, disembowelled and nailed to doors [by the insurgents], you are changed for life. What feelings can anyone have towards those who perpetrated such barbaric acts and their accomplices?[7]

As torture was normalised, the morale and discipline of French soldiers started to fray. Only experienced officers and soldiers were required to rely on torture; new recruits were spared, although they knew, or reasonably suspected, that torture was being employed as a weapon of war. Many of the young conscripts who served in Algeria were imbued with patriotic spirit but were horrified by what French liberal-democratic nationalism was able to condone. Most did not speak about what they had heard and seen in Algeria because they were loyal French citizens and did not want to exacerbate existing political instability at home.

In addition to executions and torture, the paratroopers planted bombs in domestic neighbourhoods to kill known and suspected terrorists without regard for the welfare of innocent civilians. Their aggressive tactics sent a strong message. The paratroopers inflamed Algerian resentments, radicalised the population and added exponentially to the insurgency's support. The uprising in the capital, Algiers, was successfully crushed by the end of 1957 although a loose network of FLN fighters continued to operate in the countryside.

Some French officers and soldiers had refused to engage in torture. Others resisted directions to conduct missions that would lead inevitably to unnecessary civilian casualties. The most notable dissenter was Brigadier General Jacques Pâris de Bollardière. He was personally devoted to the pacification program, emphasising the importance of infrastructure development to attracting popular support and achieving political consensus. He was also much more committed to a political solution than Massu, believing that self-determination was critical to Algeria's future, whether as part of France or as an independent nation. He stressed that the manner in which a nation employed force had to be consistent with its national values, which in turn relied on the strength of its national virtues for their promotion. At its core, the Algerian war was a struggle between efficiency and effectiveness. What might have been justified in terms of efficiency came at the cost of effectiveness. A quick solution would not necessarily produce a lasting outcome.

Bollardière resigned his command in Algeria rather than comply with a direction to employ torture. He concluded that the Battle of Algiers was:

> for the government, a dastardly abandonment of its proper responsibility; for the army, the renunciation of its traditions and honour; and, for the country, the most terrible defeat. The defeat of a people with a long-standing humanist and Christian culture who renounce, in indifference and hypocrisy, the sacred principle

of their own civilisation: to see in every other human being a man like himself.⁸

Massu disagreed bitterly with Bollardière, saying he 'despised' his views. Bollardière, who placed a higher priority on living moral values than enforcing legal codes, declared his disbelief that he and Massu had been raised in the same land and imbibed the same culture.⁹ Their disagreement was overtly philosophical and highly personal. By contrast, Aussaresses took a wholly pragmatic line. He rationalised summary execution and torture on the grounds that:

> it was impossible to send them [FLN members] back to the court system, there was too many of them and the machine of justice would have become clogged with cases and stopped working altogether. Furthermore, many of the prisoners would probably have managed to avoid any kind of punishment.¹⁰

There was no clear consensus as to the military means the French and Algerian publics were prepared to accept in pursuit of political ends. Pragmatists conceded it was a dirty war fought by despicable means, including dealing harshly with the accomplices and supporters of terrorism. Whatever an individual's status within the FLN, mere sympathisers were links in a long chain that could be broken by targeting the weakest members.

By 1958, rumours of the extreme measures being used by the paratroopers in Algeria reached Paris. The French Government tried to dismiss this sentiment as 'Communist dissent' even as the paratroopers' military success in Algiers was being celebrated, especially by the European community in Algeria. Sections of the press were willing to overlook the distressing rumours out of deference to the paratroopers' reputation, extolling their effectiveness in preserving order while the country's politicians purportedly dithered. Press coverage tended to simplify the war's social and political issues, 'stripping them of ambiguities. A war in which combat more often resembled a vast police manhunt than it did traditional notions of "warfare" was difficult to convey to the public.'[11]

In a desperate attempt to prevent the 'abandonment of Algeria' and to counter the growing influence of the French Communist Party at home, a group of senior French military officers staged a revolt at Algiers in May 1958. They formed a Public Safety Committee, essentially a military government, chaired by General Massu. The officers called for a government of national union to be headed by a 'national arbiter'. The man they had in mind was wartime hero and former prime minister, General Charles de Gaulle. Paratroopers simultaneously 'invaded' the island of Corsica and prepared for the seizure of Paris and removal of the government. With the country on the brink of civil war, the French president defused the situation by inviting de Gaulle to head a new administration that would rule by decree for six months. A fresh constitution was drafted and approved, with de Gaulle being elected President of the French Fifth Republic in February 1959.

In September 1959, de Gaulle decided to wind down military operations and negotiate 'self-determination' for Algerian Muslims. This was considered a devastating betrayal by many Army personnel and the Algerian Europeans. The first referendum on self-determination was held in January 1961, returning a majority vote in favour. Three months later another group of retired and serving senior officers attempted to establish a military government in Algiers. The putsch was initially supported by members of the 1st Foreign Parachute Regiment of the Foreign Legion but not the rest of the Army. It soon lost momentum and the leaders surrendered. Some of those involved in the putsch had recently formed the *Organisation Armée Secrète* (Secret Armed Organisation – OAS). This far-right paramilitary organisation attempted to thwart Algerian independence through a domestic bombing campaign in France and Algeria. The group also made three attempts to assassinate President de Gaulle.

The Algerian war, not unlike the Indochina war a decade earlier, was yet another national tragedy for France. More than 25 000 French soldiers were killed in an operation to 'maintain order' that eventually dissolved into disorder. In time, Algeria became known as the 'war without a name'. Algerian casualties exceeded 300 000 men, women and children, leading to enduring enmity towards France and its people.

Implicated twice in threats to civilian democratic authority, the paratroopers became the focus of French domestic political antagonism on two grounds. There was anger the province had been lost and outrage at the egregious manner in which it had allegedly been defended. In the context of rapid African decolonisation, Algerian independence was always very likely if not irresistible. As for alleged misconduct, de Gaulle referred only to 'some unfortunate incidents'. The paratroopers were nevertheless portrayed publicly as military delinquents. No longer permitted to wear their distinctive berets and camouflage uniforms, the two parachute divisions (10th and 25th) were amalgamated with an infantry division (11th) to become the new 11th Light Intervention Division in May 1961. Although the paratroopers would not be prosecuted for any crimes allegedly committed in Algeria by virtue of government-proclaimed amnesties, their standing within France tumbled. They were a source of derision until the late 1960s, when the national mood began to change. In their defence, observers argued the paratroopers had not made government policy, only pursued it. The politicians and not the paratroopers were ultimately responsible for France's institutional misconduct although both were consciously complicit. The permissive culture created by the politicians, who decided against prohibiting certain aggressive measures, was one that commanders tolerated because it served their operational goals. It was impossible to restrain the brutality once it was unleashed in 1956.

One insightful French officer, David Galula, who served with a regular infantry battalion to the east of Algiers in 1956–58, attributed the failure of the counterinsurgency mission to distrust of pacification, a refusal to engage with the local population and a belief on both sides that France would ultimately abandon the province.[12] He objected to 'hasty, illegal executions', partly because they depleted the morale of his own troops, and pointed out that these counterproductive killings could have been avoided if an effective and reliable system of justice and detention had existed. Detainees were executed because the soldiers often felt there were few options for dealing with them. The justice system was slow and the prison facilities were inadequate. He thought 'between total action and total inaction there was a wide margin where humanity and common sense can play a part compatible with the spirit of our institutions'.[13] Most soldiers lacked sufficient imagination to grasp possibilities for pacification and usually fell back on the use of force. When a little force did not produce the desired result, the usual recourse was the projection of overwhelming force.

The French knowingly avoided the time and effort needed to pacify hostile segments within the Algerian population. Eventually, killing people was the default solution with its own persuasive logic. It produced an immediate result. As dead insurgents posed no continuing risk, there was more appeal in killing than detaining FLN guerrillas. Galula was not overly critical of his soldiers' behaviour. They carried out the executions but French policy created the conditions that made them more likely, and more frequent. Military misconduct sent a message to the population but not the one France intended. The use of unnecessary and excessive force worked only to harden insurgent resolve and to add revenge to their suite of violent motivations. Galula thought the insurgents ultimately succeeded because they promoted a nationalistic cause that attracted broad support, convinced the population they would eventually succeed and were free 'from any responsibility, and hence [were able to use] any means towards their ends, including terrorism to coerce neutrals and to cow enemies'.[14] Threats of violence made by the FLN were more compelling than promises of safety from the French.

After its fraught experiences in Indochina and Algeria, the French Army was probably the most brutal and the least disciplined military force in Western Europe. Over the next two decades, its strategic role and organisational culture would change substantially as France developed its nuclear weapons capability, distanced itself from the United States, and withdrew from NATO's military command (although it would remain a member nation). It would continue to have a substantial military presence in Germany, play a supporting role in several post-colonial conflicts, such as Western Sahara and the Chad–Libya border conflict, contribute to a series of United Nations peacekeeping missions after 1989, and participate in the international coalition to eject Iraqi forces from Kuwait in 1991. With an end to compulsory military service in 1997, 10 regiments were disbanded and the French Army reduced from 236 000 to 140 000 personnel.

By the turn of the millennium, the French Army was very different from the one that fought in Algeria. It had been totally transformed as an organisation and its culture had been systematically renewed. There was a corporate preoccupation with legitimacy in the drafting of strategic doctrine, in teaching at military academies and in the tenor of professional development.[15] The emphasis was on discerning the limits of an operational mandate and accurately calibrating the use of force to the desired ends. There was collective suspicion of any binary depiction of 'friends' and 'foes' among a local population in a counterinsurgency context. It was important to categorise some groups as 'presumed hostile' without assuming they were intent on causing harm. The French Army was also heavily influenced by NATO and the European Union in a range of legal and operational matters. Legal officers were appointed to all commands at the strategic, operational and tactical levels. It was their task to refine the Rules of Engagement (ROE) at the level of the deployed force.

French forces also supplemented their ROE with 'rules of behaviour' that were gently introduced during the 1980s. These rules were drafted by military commanders and did not require political approval. Their purpose was to regulate interactions with the civilian population in operational zones, promoting a culture of 'being close to and at ease with [local] populations'.[16] There was an expectation that French military personnel would meet local officials and religious leaders, patronise businesses, enhance services and provide medical care when possible. The emphasis was on gaining a total sense of the operating environment. As French forces were generally less constrained than their coalition partners because parliamentary control over deployed operations was minimal, local commanders tended to have more discretion over the targets of offensive action and even the types of munitions to be used. In contrast to the Algerian experience, French officers and soldiers are closely attentive to the legality of their actions, notwithstanding the considerable latitude they are granted to plan and execute missions.

Like many Western nations, France quickly expressed its support for the United States after the '9/11' terrorist attacks. Indeed, the French newspaper *Le Monde* told its readers on 12 September 2001: 'We are all Americans'. Prime Minister Lionel Jospin informed the French National Assembly that 'if France participates in this conflict, it is not against Afghanistan, but instead because the United States have suffered attacks of a rare violence and, as an ally, France has to side with the Americans'. Like many NATO member nations, France's existing strategic priorities had not included Afghanistan. In siding with the Americans, France would, therefore, show maximum solidarity but at minimum cost. The formal mandate given to French forces was to 'secure zones under their responsibility as to allow the Afghan State to rebuild itself, allow development operations, and allow the deployment of the services provided by the Afghan State … [and] allow a rise in power of the Afghan Army'. French air assets were participating in Operation Enduring Freedom by the end of October 2001. A small number of soldiers were deployed to the Kabul region, largely in personal protection and training roles. The initial deployment of French forces did not prompt any public debate because the numbers were small and the French people were preoccupied with domestic economic issues.

Although the French Government was concerned with the cogency of America's strategy in Afghanistan, especially the extent of civilian casualties and collateral damage, President Jacques Chirac agreed to increase France's modest commitment gradually. By 2003, France had contributed 500 personnel to International Security Assistance Force (ISAF) operations in the Kabul region and at Mazar-i-Sharif. They would support anti-narcotic missions but would not take offensive action against those involved in the drug trade nor seek out Taliban insurgents. When French forces detained suspected insurgents, they were transferred immediately to Afghan authorities. It was not until after the G8 summit held at Evian in May 2003 that President Chirac ordered a detachment of French Special Forces soldiers to southern Afghanistan.

From July 2003 to December 2006, the *Commandement des Operations Speciales* (COS) provided 200 men for a four-month detachment to Task Force Ares comprising members of the French Marine Commandos, the 1st Marine Infantry Parachute Regiment, the 13th Parachute Dragoon Regiment and Air Parachute Commando 10. They initially operated at Spin Boldak in the Manif and Arghestan districts of Kandahar province (adjacent to the border with Pakistan) and later Jalalabad in Nangarhar province, patrolling between Kabul and Peshawar (across the border in Pakistan). Their principal objective was preventing groups of Taliban from infiltrating Afghanistan through Pakistani tribal zones.

COS personnel had three main missions: intelligence gathering, patrolling in populated areas and interception of Taliban fighters. Commandant Bruno de Zélicourt, who commanded the taskforce in mid-2006, thought Afghanistan was similar to Algeria in the sense that 'one of the keys for victory resides in the capacity to deliver intelligence, to uncover the networks, to identify and eliminate the leaders, to break the structures'.[17] He lamented the restriction of intelligence sharing to the United States, Britain, Canada and Australia. Although COS personnel were keen to remain in Afghanistan, they were withdrawn after three years when the French Government concluded its Special Forces could be better employed in other overseas missions to which France was more committed. Indeed, Commander de Zélicourt thought their withdrawal could alienate France from its NATO allies and 'lead to losses of know-how and competencies that could jeopardise the future'.[18] There were seven operational deaths among COS personnel in Afghanistan.

France's military commitment remained limited until the election of Nicolas Sarkozy to the presidency in April 2007. To strengthen trans-Atlantic ties, Sarkozy ordered the 'full and entire reintegration' of France into the NATO alliance. He doubled the commitment of French conventional ground forces to 3600 and indicated France would assume responsibility for the districts of Kapisa and Surobi, believing them to be relatively peaceful. These were two small, mountainous areas whose strategic importance was derived from their proximity to both Kabul and the Salang highway. The provinces provided access to the northern part of Afghanistan from Kabul and to Pakistan through Laghman province to the southeast. The French deployed their forces as a brigade formation under ISAF Regional Command-East. In contrast to most other parts of Afghanistan, an American Provincial Reconstruction Team (PRT) would undertake governance and development activities while the French provided force protection. France had earlier decided against being part of the nationwide PRT program because of continuing commitments in the Ivory Coast and Lebanon.

France's population remained largely uninterested in their nation's contribution to the Afghan war until 16 August 2008, when 10 French paratroopers were killed and another 21 were wounded in a Taliban ambush in the Uzbin Valley. The local partner forces fled when fighting started. The bodies of dead French soldiers had been looted and mutilated. The Taliban also claimed they had executed several wounded soldiers and detained a female soldier. After withdrawing with their own dead and wounded to three villages in neighbouring Laghman province, this group of Taliban fighters were subjected to three days of intense NATO bombing that caused 40 civilian deaths, the destruction of 150 houses and the evacuation of 2000 residents. The substantial collateral damage inflicted by the bombing was overlooked by the French Chief of Defence Staff, General Jean-Louis Georgelin, when he defended the attacks which destroyed 'two huge weapons caches helping the logistics of the insurgents'. The deaths of the 10 soldiers drastically reduced public support for the war in France. One poll reported 55 per cent of the population favoured the withdrawal of French forces with only 36 per cent continuing to support the mission.

This firefight resulted in the largest loss of French military personnel since 1983, when a car-bomb attack in Lebanon had killed 58 paratroopers. While the French Government was unable to say when its forces would be withdrawn, and the French people were plainly unwilling to accept more than occasional casualties, the war in Afghanistan quietly transformed the French army.[19] Across a four-year period they were operating as part of a multinational coalition, gaining experience in counterinsurgency warfare, experimenting with new organisational structures involving combined arms, ad hoc battle groups composed of companies and sections drawn from different regiments, developing their tactics and improving their equipment. They were not portrayed as 'super soldiers' by their own commanders or media; the emphasis remained on deploying an organically balanced force and avoiding combat when possible.

When François Hollande ascended to the presidency in May 2012, he fulfilled a campaign pledge to withdraw French 'combat troops' from Afghanistan by the end of that year despite strong criticism from other NATO members. France joined Canada and the Netherlands in ending its combat role in Afghanistan some two years before the formal timetable for withdrawal. Around 1500 French soldiers remained in 2013 to repatriate equipment and prepare the Afghan Army for its assumption of responsibility for security following the planned departure of all NATO combat forces in 2014. At its peak, France provided 3600 troops, making it the fifth-largest ISAF contributor after the United States, Britain, Germany and Italy.

Many of the military personnel withdrawn from Afghanistan soon found themselves involved in a protracted conflict in Saharan Africa following a civil war in Libya that destabilised several adjoining nations. The fighting started in the former French colony of Mali when a separatist movement led by Tuareg ethnic rebels in the north declared their independence in January 2012. A poor country of little interest to France beyond its gold deposits, Mali's strategic importance was its proximity to the uranium mines in Niger that supplied most of France's nuclear energy needs. The conflict proliferated when a multitude of armed groups, several of them jihadist, started vying for control of the central and northern regions of Mali. Dissatisfied with the civilian government's response to the uprising, the Malian military then seized power. The new interim government was accused of political assassinations and targeting members of the Tuareg and Arab communities whom the security forces associated with independence rebels and jihadist groups affiliated with al-Qaeda and Islamic State (ISIS). Deteriorating security led to lawlessness and a humanitarian crisis. At the request of the Malian Government, France intervened in January 2013. The focus of 'Operation Serval' was ending Islamist control over northern Mali. The mission's ROE were considered restrictive but there were no reports of individual misconduct, nor did French or Malian troops complain that they were facing greater risks to their personal safety. The mission was successful and concluded in July 2014.

By this time, however, a larger jihadist movement had gained momentum across the wider semi-arid Sahel region encompassing Burkina Faso and Niger. France launched 'Operation Barkhane' as a counterterrorism mission in August 2014 with French Special Forces conducting night raids and kill–capture missions to remove the leaders of several jihadist groups scattered across Mali and concentrated in Ouagadougou, the capital of neighbouring Burkina Faso. Operations were later expanded to Mauritania and Chad with France eventually deploying 5100 soldiers. Unlike Afghanistan, the French military quickly adapted its tactics in the Sahel. In 2015, General Didier Castres told his forces to 'stop thinking only in terms of attrition, elimination and eradication' – the metrics of success in conventional wars:

> and instead target flows, networks, nodes and centres; look for weaknesses, using a good knowledge of logistics, chains of command and communication systems; think in terms of 'platforms', not 'garrison logic'; be capable of executing a strategy of perpetual movement and adaptation; create surprise in place, time and scale, and use *foudroyance* [a sudden crippling shock].

This strategy was, however, undone by the apparent refusal of both French politicians and the French people to contemplate major casualties. (Fifty French soldiers were killed in Mali between 2013 and 2020.) Consequently, French soldiers 'tend to venture out of their high-security barracks only in armoured vehicles, wearing full protective equipment, which makes them safer, but scares the locals and discourages communication, and makes it hard to conquer hearts and minds, as advocated by counterinsurgency theorists'.[20] While public opinion accepted the need for military action to counter the threat of global jihadism, security fears could be exploited to 'legitimise the establishment of exceptional regimes that breach the rule of law'.[21] Political scientist Marc-Antoine Pérouse de Montclos drew attention to the impunity granted to Malian forces whose atrocities against villagers substantially aided jihadist recruiters, who could present themselves as nationalists fighting a foreign occupation.

Increasingly unpopular in France and later Mali, 'Operation Barkhane' has been dubbed France's 'forever war', an unwinnable and costly military quagmire, comparable to Afghanistan because Paris cannot trust the Malian Army, whose officers and soldiers have been accused of torturing and murdering civilians, stealing and slaughtering livestock, and forcibly removing villagers from their land. French forces have been accused of restricting the movement of journalists to impede their reporting of Malian war crimes, which are usually ethnically motivated. The French Government has acknowledged the 'risks' of operating with government forces in Mali, although a 'Status of Forces' agreement signed on 8 March 2013 committed the Malian Government and armed forces to respecting international humanitarian law, particularly when dealing with prisoners transferred to its custody by French forces. At the time of writing (December 2021), the International Criminal Court is conducting an inquiry into alleged war crimes in Mali committed since January 2012.

In January 2018, the United Nations established its own commission of inquiry into allegations of misconduct between 2012 and 2018. The commission's 340-page report was handed to the Security Council in December 2020. It concluded there were 'reasonable grounds to believe that the Malian defence and security forces committed war crimes, including violence to the life of civilians and persons *hors de combat* suspected of being affiliated or cooperating with extremist armed groups'. Jihadist and other armed groups had committed crimes against humanity, including 'murder, maiming and other cruel treatment, rape and other forms of sexual violence, hostage-taking and attacks against personnel of humanitarian organisations and MINUSMA [the United Nations peacekeeping mission in Mali]'.

The United Nations report also alleged that Malian troops working in combined operations with French forces in 2013–14 engaged in serious crimes, and that it had collected 'credible information' that the Malian contingent in the European Union Training Mission established in 2013 had been involved in 'extortion, ill-treatment and extrajudicial killings'. The report asked whether French officers were aware of this behaviour and why they apparently took no action. These questions were not answered. Further, French forces cooperated with a Malian militia, the Imghad Tuareg Self-Defence Group and Allies, in the conduct of counterterrorism operations in 2017 and 2018, although the group was reported to have committed war crimes and recruited child soldiers. Again, the issue was whether French authorities knew about these illegal activities. The French military told the United Nations that 'this cooperation, which in the past yielded tangible results in the fight against armed terrorist groups, has since ceased'. In each instance, French commanders claimed to have had no knowledge of war crimes.

By the end of 2021 there was still no end in sight to 'Operation Barkhane'. Burkina Faso had become the new centre of jihadist violence. More than 1.14 million people were internally displaced after 2020 in addition to the 20 000 refugees it was hosting from neighbouring Mali.

Despite the savagery of these attacks and their potential to provoke unnecessary and excessive force in reply, there have been no publicly reported incidents of individual French soldiers violating the Law of Armed Conflict or operating outside their ROE in Mali. More controversial was an official inquiry into a French soldier deployed to Niono in central Mali who was photographed in 2012 wearing a death mask resembling a character from the *Call of Duty* video game. Publication of the photograph prompted a press conference at which Colonel Thierry Burkhard explained the wearing of death masks was 'unacceptable behaviour' and an official inquiry had been launched to identify and punish the soldier. Burkhard stressed that such action was 'not representative of the action that brought France to Mali to help'.[22] French soldiers were not, he said, 'messengers of death'. The soldier was subsequently identified and censured.

In the same year, the French Army launched another inquiry into a photograph showing a member of the 8th Marine Infantry Parachute Regiment wearing a uniform sleeve patch bearing a French flag and the motto of the wartime Nazi Waffen-SS, 'my honour is loyalty'. A local parliamentarian where the Regiment was based, Philippe Folliot, claimed the unnamed soldier was a 'young sergeant, who doesn't even know the Nazi reference' despite suggesting it was a 'childish prank … and an isolated incident'. An Army spokesman, Colonel Gilles Jaron, insisted the motto was an 'unacceptable attitude that doesn't reflect the reality of the armed forces'.[23] The patch was never officially sanctioned and was not part of an issued uniform. Colonel Jaron stated: 'the soldier will be immediately suspended as soon as we have identified him'. It is clear the French Army wants to avoid any public impression that its soldiers are undisciplined or unruly. The contrasts between the contemporary French Army and the one that fought in Algeria could not be starker. There is much that Australia could learn from France's experience of war crimes allegations and its efforts to prevent their recurrence.

Since its ignominious withdrawal from Algeria in 1962, the French Army has undergone an internal transformation and shifted from defending serious war crimes to denouncing them. Its forces deployed to Afghanistan in 2001, and the strikingly similar conflict in Mali after 2012, have not been accused of the individual offences reported by the Australian media after 2016, although French soldiers had been deployed for nearly two decades in difficult operations that have featured most of the 'standard' risk factors for war crimes. There were no obvious differences in mission parameters, deployment cycles, personnel policies, ROE nor command and control arrangements to explain the absence of any allegations against individual French soldiers. The single difference was the operational tempo, which was much higher for the Australian Special Forces in Afghanistan, and in the reticence of French forces to engage in combat operations when fighting could be avoided. Although French forces usually outnumbered their Australian counterparts, the statistical probability of war crimes being committed might have been lower for the French if it could be established that the prevalence of war crimes is a function of the opportunities that are available to commit them. This is a reasonable view. Nevertheless, the complete absence of any credible allegations of individual war crimes is a noteworthy aspect of France's recent operational experience and an observation that sets the French Army apart from those of other nations considered in these comparative chapters.

France's main challenges related to official policy and collective responsibility. In common with other ISAF nations, the handling of Afghan and Malian detainees was a continuing French concern. Although Paris wanted to avoid responsibility for managing detainees, it had serious doubts about the commitment of Afghan and Malian authorities to observe international standards of detention. French forces also relied on intelligence whose quality and quantity could not guarantee there would be no civilian casualties. The French did not deliberately target civilians in either Afghanistan or Mali nor act in a manner that revealed reckless indifference to their welfare.

The French were troubled by the indiscipline of their partner forces in the Sahel. They were much less concerned in Afghanistan. In Mali the problems arose because the partner forces were community organisations, not government entities. It was difficult for the French Government to determine that these partner forces were actually engaging in misconduct before they had cause to cease combined operations. The French Government and military command may, in these instances, have failed to perform an adequate due diligence test in advance. The consequence was reputational damage. France was not alone. As described in Chapter 8, Australian forces worked with Matiullah Khan ('MK') and referred to him as 'our man' while the Dutch were deeply troubled by his reputation for corruption and human rights abuses and refused to deal with him. The ADF's international standing may have been imperilled by the decision to work with 'MK', even after acknowledging there were no alternative partner forces in the province at that time. The French and Australian experiences highlight the difficulty of avoiding complicity in war crimes in situations where the integrity and reliability of all local forces cannot be verified before operations commence.

The emphasis in French pre-deployment preparation on political legitimacy and moral authority, a strong sense of collective responsibility to NATO and European Union standards, and the desire to transcend any lingering legacy of lawlessness, is clearly reflected in the conduct of French forces in deployed operations since 2001. To its credit, the French Government recognised that misconduct is a possibility in even the most professional military organisations. Following the release of the IGADF Afghanistan Inquiry report in November 2020, the French Government was critical of a Chinese foreign ministry spokesman for using social media to promote a computer-generated image of an Australian soldier murdering an Afghan child. The French Government stated the 'tweet' was unworthy of a diplomat and was an insult to all countries whose armed forces had been deployed to Afghanistan. The Chinese embassy in Paris responded predictably by claiming that 'France does not condemn the atrocities of war that tore and kill[ed] civilians, but instead accuses those who denounce atrocities'. Politicising the reality of war crimes did nothing to reduce their incidence.

The value of comparing the French and Australian experiences lies in dispelling the notion that war crimes are inevitable in complex insurgencies or that troops operating in extreme circumstances deserve legal latitude or can claim moral mitigation. There is no reason to believe that French forces were inherently more or less likely to commit war crimes in Afghanistan. The Canadians and the French may have been more alert to the possibility of war crimes because they have been acknowledged publicly in their national military histories. Australians continue to avoid the subject of historic war crimes, dismissing them either as a regrettable eventuality in any protracted armed conflict or occasional aberrations that could be explained away with allusions to rough justice. When governments officially recognise instances of military misconduct, and publicly accept the shame that accompanies them, the insistence that a nation's armed forces are incapable of such conduct is impossible to sustain. That being so, there is potentially greater likelihood that action to prevent war crimes will be concerted and consistent. After all, they happen from time to time in even the most professional militaries.

PART V
DISCORDANT NOTES

16

TOWARDS A RECKONING
2016–2020

Most military forces have a range of mechanisms for inquiring into mistakes and investigating misconduct. The Australian Defence Force (ADF) has well-established processes for dealing with accidents, including ship groundings and aircraft crashes, and highly refined procedures for addressing transgressions, such as insubordination and absenteeism. When rumours of misconduct in Afghanistan reached the ADF's senior leadership in early 2016, specific details of what might have happened, as well as the number and identities of the reputed offenders and eyewitnesses, was largely unknown. There had been a succession of media stories between 2006 and 2013 accusing Australian soldiers of mistakes including targeting the wrong people, killing innocent civilians and using excessive force. Few of these stories hinted at deliberate misconduct. The Australian Federal Police (AFP) could have been asked to make inquiries. But rumours were akin to hearsay, and the AFP did not have the power to compel witnesses to answer questions about rumours or perhaps the ability to extract information from soldiers who had been trained to resist interrogation. There was also the 'code of silence' that existed within Special Operations Command (SOCOMD) and its cultural aversion to sharing information with outsiders. An external inquiry was unlikely to be effective.

These were some of the considerations that in March 2016 led the Chief of Army, Lieutenant General Angus Campbell, to request that the Inspector-General of the Australian Defence Force (IGADF) conduct a scoping inquiry to ascertain whether there was any substance to rumours of unlawful conduct by the Special Operations Task Group (SOTG) in Afghanistan. On 12 May 2016, the IGADF appointed Major General the Honourable Paul Brereton, a judge of the New South Wales Supreme Court,[1] an Assistant Inspector-General for the purpose of conducting such an inquiry. It commenced as an IGADF own-initiative inquiry. Following amendments to the *Defence Act*, the Minister for Defence and the Chief of the Defence Force (CDF) were able to direct the IGADF to inquire into or investigate 'a matter concerning the Defence Force'. Such inquiries can compel any person – not just ADF members – to give evidence. In December 2016, the CDF, Air Chief Marshal Mark Binskin gave such a direction. As such, under section 23 of the IGADF Regulations, it had:

> powers similar to those of a Royal Commission to require 'any person' (not limited to present or former members of the ADF) who there is reason to believe has information or a document or thing relevant to the Inquiry, to give evidence and/or produce documents and information to the Inquiry.[2]

On 17 January 2017, the IGADF directed Brereton to determine 'whether there is any substance to persistent rumours of criminal and unlawful conduct by, or concerning, Special Operations Task Group deployments in Afghanistan during the period 2007 to 2016'.[3] Given Brereton's independence as a judge, and as the extent of the rumoured misconduct and the willingness of serving and former SOCOMD members to cooperate was still unknown, the Inquiry's duration was left open-ended. It would take as long as it needed to take, probably several years. By way of comparison, the Bloody Sunday 'Saville' Inquiry into the killing of 14 civil rights marchers by British soldiers in Londonderry on 30 January 1972 ran for over 12 years and cost between £200 and £400 million. That inquiry focused on an incident of less than 30 minutes duration. It was impossible for Brereton to know how many incidents would need to be examined.

As the Inquiry expanded, so did the number of staff who were added to its team. In October 2018, amendments to the IGADF Regulations prescribed a new kind of inquiry.[4] The amended section 28A of the Regulations introduced the concept of an Assistant IGADF who is a judicial officer. Brereton was required by section 28C of the IGADF Regulations to 'conduct the inquiry in such manner as the Assistant IGADF considers appropriate having regard to the subject matter of the inquiry'. On 21 February 2017, the period under review was extended to 2006 and, on 5 April 2017, to 2005 to include all 20 Special Operations deployments to Afghanistan.

Justice Brereton was well equipped to conduct such an inquiry. He was a highly respected judicial officer whose legal practice and experience on the bench precluded any suggestion of bias or partiality. He was known for expansive thought and intellectual diligence. Notably, Brereton's father, Russell, was also a Supreme Court judge who, when a young man and an officer in the Australian 9th Division, was the prosecutor at the first war crimes trial at Labuan in Borneo in December 1945.[5]

Following in his father's footsteps, Paul Brereton joined the Army Reserve in 1975 and was commissioned into the Corps of Infantry in 1979. He held a number of command and staff appointments until he was promoted to major general in 2010 and served as the Head of the ADF's Cadet, Reserve and Employer Support Division. Earlier in his career, Brereton became familiar with conventional infantry tactics, unit cultures, command responsibility and military justice. He would not need to acquaint himself with military titles and ranks, ADF policies and procedures, regimental customs and unit conventions. He had worked with officers and soldiers of all corps and specialisations, and could use his judicial status and his Army standing to both inspire confidence and unsettle complacency among those to be interviewed. Brereton had a firm grasp and a working knowledge of the *Defence Act*, the *Defence Force Discipline Act* (DFDA) and the international laws and conventions relating to armed conflict. He would not be learning 'on the job'.

No-one in legal circles believed for a moment that Brereton would find a way to excuse wrongdoing or strive to preserve the Army's reputation at the expense of justice. That he was a senior Reserve officer would enhance rather than detract from his findings. There was the question of whether Brereton's standing as a senior judge would adversely affect any subsequent proceedings. This possibility was considered at the time of his appointment. While it might seem likely to those outside the legal profession that the findings of one judge might unduly influence the opinion of another, those accused of war crimes would be afforded a trial by jury as required by section 80 of the Australian Constitution:

> The trial on indictment of any offence against any law of the Commonwealth shall be by jury, and every such trial shall be held in the State where the offence was committed, and if the offence was not committed within any State the trial shall be held at such place or places as the Parliament prescribes.[6]

Furthermore, criminal investigations that originated with an inquiry or royal commission conducted by a judge have not been deemed by the Australian courts to be prejudicial to an accused person receiving a fair trial.

Although initially a 'scoping' exercise, the IGADF Afghanistan Inquiry would attempt to find 'substantive accounts or credible information' concerning 'abuse or mistreatment of detainees'; conduct that contravened the DFDA or the Commonwealth Criminal Code, the latter referring to war crimes; 'any systemic, cultural or individual failure (including by commanders and legal officers within SOCOMD) to report or investigate' such behaviour; any instances of inaccurate operational reporting and evidence tampering; and 'any deliberate undermining, isolation, obstruction or removal from SOCOMD units of persons who tried to report or take remedial action concerning such criminal, unlawful or inappropriate conduct'. The IGADF subsequently extended the Inquiry's terms of reference to include 'the cultural normalisation of deviance from the professional standards of SOCOMD' and the existence of a 'culture of silence' within the Command.

To assist with the conduct of the Inquiry, a number of other Assistants IGADF were appointed. They were a 'diverse and dedicated team' who were given a difficult task, 'which would inevitably be unpopular in some circles'. Its members consisted of inquiry, support and witness liaison officers. The Inquiry team recognised that it would have:

> to raise with witnesses events which occurred during their deployments and which may have been traumatic. In that respect, the position is little different from many trials, in which witnesses will have to revisit, and in a sense relive, incidents which have traumatised them.[7]

On 2 September 2017, the IGADF commissioned a series of advertisements encouraging anyone with knowledge of rumours or who had 'heard others talking about' misconduct in Afghanistan to contact the Inquiry team. 'Canvassing complaints', as one conservative media commentator described the advertisements, produced a mixed reaction. In October 2017, former SAS Patrol Commander and Victoria Cross and Medal for Gallantry recipient Ben Roberts-Smith was critical of the IGADF for soliciting 'rumours':

> I don't think these soldiers should be suffering through this ridiculous notion of being investigated for a rumour … When have you heard of a judicial process initiated off the back of

rumours? It's just a joke. We should be looking after our soldiers not persecuting them.[8]

The reference to 'these soldiers' included himself. Over the next three years, Roberts-Smith would be the only former SAS member whose name would be publicly associated with allegations of misconduct. His former colleagues – both detractors and defenders – remained in the shadows alongside members of the Commando Regiments who rarely featured in media stories. It was obvious to casual observers that substantial personal animosities and professional antagonisms existed among Australia's elite soldiers. It certainly looked like a war was underway within the SAS Regiment and its alumni.

Roberts-Smith was correct in pointing to the peculiar origins of the Inquiry. The civilian police usually commence their inquiries with specific accusations of wrongdoing or reports of a crime. Royal commissions are normally established in situations where there are complaints or victims, such as bank malpractice or child abuse. This IGADF Inquiry was indeed different because it began not with tangible evidence or a substantive complaint but with rumours and a concern for the Army's reputation. The Special Operations Commander (SOCAUST), Major General Jeff Sengelman, was taking a personal stand when he made the professional decision to raise his disquiet about the rumoured behaviour of his subordinates with the Chief of Army. As an outsider, sociologist Samantha Crompvoets also had a sense that bad things might have happened in Afghanistan when she conducted her culture review.

Despite a steady stream of objections and protests, Campbell never had a second thought about the need for an Inquiry. Like Sengelman, he was convinced that the persistence of rumours was highly damaging to the ADF, which relied upon the trust of the Australian people. This trust also mitigated against institutional departure from core values. Campbell, too, was taking a risk when he sought an inquiry given he had exercised national command responsibility for operations in Afghanistan during 2011. He could not control the Inquiry nor direct its findings. Campbell explained to journalists that 'what the Inspector-General does, and in what way he chooses to report, and with any form of conclusions or recommendations or finding out, that's all for the Inspector-General to [consider]'.[9] If the rumours were baseless, the Inquiry would be brief. Any discomfort would be short-lived. At least the air would be cleared and the ADF's reputation would be intact.

Perhaps surprisingly, there were never complaints from either the Labor Opposition or the news media that the ADF was conducting an inquiry into itself and could not be trusted to uncover the truth. This may have been because the impetus for the Inquiry had not come from the parliament or the press. There had not been a Senate Committee resolution or a concerted newspaper campaign to force an inquiry. As the IGADF Afghanistan Inquiry originated within Defence, there was a reasonable assumption that the ADF was determined to uncover the truth, however unpalatable, and to deal appropriately with any evidence of misconduct. This was not the first formal inquiry into possible war crimes. Chapter 6 referred to the handling of alleged misconduct by ADF members during INTERFET operations in East Timor during 1999. An inquiry facing similar 'code of silence' challenges was conducted in 2001. Its focus was the command culture within the 3rd Battalion, Royal Australian Regiment (3 RAR). A second inquiry in 2002 considered associated allegations of brutality. Both were conducted with rigour.

Conscious his task was the subject of criticism, Brereton argued that allegations of misconduct in Afghanistan had to be investigated in order to maintain discipline and, further, 'to the extent that there is no substance to the rumours, the undoubted gallantry and sacrifice of SOTG units and their members deserve to remain unsullied and vindicated'. These were persuasive arguments. While Brereton admitted that an inquiry might unsettle veterans and their families, he emphasised that the continued circulation of unaddressed rumours of serious misconduct had the potential to cause deeper and more lasting harm. Welfare support was never going to reduce the Inquiry's deepening emotional toll. Spouses and children were unintended victims. Their pain and anguish were to be endured in the interests of truth and justice. Conscious of the strain the Inquiry was causing, the IGADF's annual report gave some hints of its scope but nothing of its likely findings. Delaying an investigation would only make it more difficult to determine the truth, as the British Government had found when dealing with alleged misconduct in Northern Ireland during the early 1970s.

The Inquiry team members began by familiarising themselves with SOCOMD and its operations in Afghanistan, gathering relevant foundational documents, determining the rumours of misconduct to be pursued, tracking each rumour to its source (or sources), obtaining the physical and testimonial evidence relevant to each rumour, identifying issues and influences shaping the conduct of Special Forces personnel, concluding whether credible evidence existed to substantiate any rumour, and making recommendations about whether a breach of the Law of Armed Conflict occurred and what action should follow. The initial challenge was getting Special Forces personnel to recall distressing matters and to answer questions about the conduct of their colleagues and friends.

The Inquiry team 'socialised' with SOCOMD headquarters staff and units in an attempt to gain trust and demonstrate empathy. 'Sample groups' were asked whether they had any personal knowledge of misconduct or had heard rumours of wrongdoing. There was every likelihood that interviewees, preferring to avoid involvement in an official inquiry that might implicate their former comrades-in-arms, would deny all knowledge of any rumours of war crimes. Despite personal camaraderie and institutional loyalties, former and serving personnel contacted the Inquiry and provided information. The Inquiry went from generalised rumours to specific lines of inquiry about people and places. Recollections and suspicions were cross-matched with written reports and visual imagery to give a clearer picture of what might have happened and who could have witnessed, concealed, assisted or committed war crimes.

Progress was initially slow. Individuals could be required to attend interviews and compelled to give testimony but they needed to be asked insightful questions that elicited useful information. The interviews were confronting, even for men hardened by combat operations. Some officers and soldiers, unfamiliar with serious investigations, were shaken by the forceful interviews and affronted by inferences they were withholding relevant information, refusing to be candid and protecting their mates. Unlike most of the in-theatre inquiries they had experienced in Afghanistan, they were not given the benefit of any doubt and found bluffing was futile. The Inquiry interviewed some officers and soldiers multiple times before receiving information that was nearer to the truth. Some soldiers eventually made personal admissions of wrongdoing.

Section 32 of the IGADF Regulations conferred on witnesses certain immunities from their compelled testimony being used directly or indirectly against them in any subsequent prosecution (known as 'use and derivative use immunity'). It was apparent to the Inquiry team that the availability of these immunities led some witnesses to speak more freely about what they had seen, heard and done. Witnesses were also aware their evidence could be used against others. Although any reprisal against a witness was a crime, many soldiers were still reluctant to give evidence against their former or current colleagues: perhaps from fear of victimisation or a misplaced sense of loyalty. Unlike speaking privately with the media, which was a matter of personal choice (irrespective of whether they had official permission), officers and soldiers were required to attend Inquiry interviews and were compelled to tell the truth. An obligation to be truthful on oath (and refusing to tell lies) surpassed any reasonable expectation of loyalty. The Inquiry would eventually interview over 500 witnesses, all of them privately. There were no public hearings.

Liaison meetings with international Coalition partners would not elicit any evidence of Australian misconduct but gave some insights into similar inquiries. Advertisements were also placed in publications intended for the Australian Afghan community and face-to-face interviews were conducted in Kabul. No source of potentially relevant information was overlooked.

After two years, the Inquiry might have answered the question 'was there substance to the rumours?' with the answer 'probably' rather than a definitive 'yes'. The nature of the alleged misconduct was so serious that the Inquiry was still seeking to corroborate a series of individual accounts. It was concerned with finding substance – evidence – and this meant credible evidence of misconduct. By mid-2019, the flow of information was steadily increasing. Inquiry staff were gradually able to fit together the fragments of a number of stories. The investigation was more targeted and the questions more specific. After three years, the façade of Special Forces impenetrability was crumbling. Snippets of information, some freely offered and others formally coerced, were being assembled into a compelling counter-narrative of some SOTG operations.

On the fourth anniversary of Brereton's appointment as an Assistant IGADF in May 2020, there were rumours that the Inquiry would be completed by the end of June 2020. Although he was not embarking on fresh investigations or pursuing any new incidents, those likely to be named in the Inquiry report had still not been given letters inviting their response to any possible adverse findings. August 2020 was now the more likely completion date. The media continued to suggest the report's release was imminent and commentators were becoming impatient. It was apparent from its longevity that the Inquiry had uncovered more than a handful of incidents. Recriminations had already begun.

On 28 June 2020, journalists Chris Masters and Nick McKenzie reported comments made by Sengelman's successor as SOCAUST, Major General Adam Findlay, during a confidential conversation with

Special Air Service (SAS) personnel at Campbell Barracks.[10] Findlay apparently praised Brereton's knowledge of the Command and the firm 'evidential basis' the Inquiry had established to demonstrate that former and serving members of the Regiment had engaged in misconduct. Findlay implied that serious crimes had been committed by some soldiers while others had enabled these crimes by perjuring themselves during formal in-theatre inquiries. Findlay contended that the 'one common cause' of misconduct was 'poor moral leadership'. Alternatively, he could have said the *cause* was poor moral character whose expression was not prevented by 'poor moral leadership'. Findlay asserted that a small number of 'self-righteous' SAS operators evidently thought the Army's rules did not apply to them. Their arrogance had propelled an internal culture which had 'caused all the problems' besetting the Regiment. More broadly, misconduct had created 'an issue of trust' between Special Forces units, the Army and the Australian people.

Most of those who listened to Findlay had not been to Afghanistan. There was a sense within the Regiment that the majority were being condemned for the actions of a minority. An increasing number of experienced SAS operators with no involvement in the commission or concealment of alleged war crimes were apparently considering leaving the Army. Those who had already left publicly objected to the manner in which the Inquiry had been conducted, and veterans' groups, including the Returned and Services League of Australia and the Australian SAS Association, were concerned by the lack of support the Regiment was receiving from senior officers in Canberra in the face of so much adverse media reporting.[11] It seemed to them that the Army's senior leadership was prepared to let the Regiment bear the blame for everything that had gone wrong in Afghanistan. A decade earlier, politicians and commanders had clamoured to be photographed with SAS members and to be associated with their success. Now they were nowhere to be seen.

Unsurprisingly, relations between parts of the Regiment and

SOCOMD were strained and longstanding tensions between the SAS and the Commando Regiments worsened. SAS members thought it unfair that their unit had suffered reputational damage while the Commandos, whom they believed were just as prone to misconduct, had managed to avoid the opprobrium. Two things were being overlooked. First, most of the allegations had originated within the SAS Regiment. These were largely self-inflicted wounds. Second, whatever the Commandos might have done did not mitigate the seriousness of any misconduct committed by SAS soldiers. They still needed to answer for their actions.

A widely held view beyond Campbell Barracks was that the Regiment's corporate culture was equally to blame for incidents of alleged misconduct and that malignant elements of that culture persisted despite concerted attempts at reform. The individuals complicit in any alleged misconduct would be held to account but the Regiment itself needed to accept responsibility for hosting a culture in which such behaviour was possible, let alone apparently pervasive. Ahead of the report's release, the extent and the seriousness of the misconduct was still not known. It was difficult for commentators to determine whether the cause was a few bad apples, a bad barrel or a diseased orchard. Although there were no leaks from the Inquiry team, media reporting had fuelled speculation that deepened suspicions and led to senseless finger-pointing. The Inquiry report would be the basis for further investigation, potential prosecution, organisational reform and cultural renewal. It would surely prove to be more detailed, accurate and reliable than any of the media stories that had appeared until then.

With the Inquiry report expected by the end of the year, the Chief of Army, Lieutenant General Rick Burr, sent an open letter to all Army personnel on 6 October 2020 warning that the Inquiry report was likely to contain material that was 'extremely serious and deeply troubling'. Accounts of alleged misconduct 'do not reflect who we aspire to be' but, presumably, these accounts embodied what one part of the Army might have become between 2005 and 2013. Burr recognised that the string of untested and unproved allegations had already tainted the Army's reputation and sullied the deployed service of many officers and soldiers. The release of a report containing credible information of misconduct would worsen the reputational damage although it did not (and could not) prove the guilt or complicity of any individual.

Late on Friday 6 November 2020, when most journalists had already filed stories for the weekend editions of their newspapers, General Angus Campbell, who had been promoted to become the Chief of the Defence Force in July 2018, announced that he had received the IGADF Afghanistan Inquiry report. Four and a half years had passed since he had first written as the then Chief of Army to the IGADF requesting a scoping inquiry. In a Defence media release, Campbell indicated he would speak publicly about the 'key findings' after reading and reflecting on the very substantial report, and briefing political leaders and departmental officials. He would also take advice on how much of its contents could be publicly released.

Behind the scenes, teams of Defence and civilian lawyers, IGADF staff and other uniformed and departmental personnel worked on redacting parts of the Inquiry report ahead of its public release. There would be three versions of the report: the first would include the names of those accused of war crimes, witnesses to alleged war crimes, those party to concealing war crimes, and the victims of war crimes and their families (if known); the second would have a code in place of a name; and in the third, identifying information would be redacted along with dates and places of alleged misconduct, matters involving operational security and diplomatic sensitivity, and material that might prejudice any future legal proceedings. As no copies of any version of the report were leaked to the media ahead of the planned public release, speculation abounded about the number of potential charges, accused persons and Afghan victims. As with most media reporting, there was an element of truth in what 'Defence insiders' were quietly telling journalists. The Inquiry report's findings would include incidents of alleged illegal killings involving more than a handful of soldiers.

No-one outside the Office of the IGADF, not even the Chief of the Defence Force, was previously aware of what the Inquiry had found or was likely to recommend. The scale of the alleged offending was still unknown. Sengelman heard rumours and Crompvoets received hearsay. Campbell requested an inquiry and Burr implemented a review. Had the IGADF Afghanistan Inquiry not been initiated in mid-2016, there is little doubt some form of investigation would eventually have occurred. There were too many rumours and too many media stories for the ADF to ignore them. Eventually, the parliament would have found a way to convene some form of inquiry had the ADF resisted, if only to examine the need for the allegations to be examined objectively. There was also the Australian Government's determination to preclude the possibility that the International Criminal Court might conduct its own inquiry into the conduct of ADF members. Eventually, and by a circuitous route, the nation would be obliged to face another version of the Afghan war and how some of its soldiers had apparently fought it.

Even those who had served in Afghanistan and had a personal stake in shaping the public narrative shied away from offering any explanation for whatever they thought might have happened in Uruzgan. Shortly before the Inquiry report was publicly released, an opinion piece appeared in the *Sydney Morning Herald* and the *Age*. An introductory sentence proclaimed: 'For the first time in SASR history, a group of 12 current and former soldiers have stepped out of the shadows to remind the country what they are, and what they are not'. The names of the authors were not disclosed. The newspapers gave it the heading, 'They are not one of us'. It was significant in providing a window into the thinking of some SAS members who had not been accused of misconduct. The authors were unaware of the extent and seriousness of the allegations that had been made against their colleagues but they presumed it was the SAS Regiment, rather than the Commando Regiments, that was the focus of closest attention and most of the adverse findings.

The origins of the article were entirely misreported and, consequently, its intentions were largely misunderstood. One version claimed a draft of an unsolicited contribution was sent to *Army News*, which declined publication. The *Australian* then claimed, somewhat melodramatically, that Defence had tried to 'silence' the signatories while 'it ramps up its own public relations campaign'. There was no attempt in Defence to influence the narrative let alone create a counter-narrative. It had steadfastly declined to comment on media stories over the previous three years, realising nothing was to be gained from contesting public reporting while a confidential inquiry was underway. By October 2020, Defence's attention had shifted to the legal processes that would follow release of the Inquiry report.

The article published by Nine Newspapers actually originated with a request from a journalist working at *Army News* to a former SAS soldier, who was not serving within SOCOMD at the time, to produce an article for publication. It would give an SAS perspective on the misconduct. A draft of the article was circulated to around two dozen SAS operators, who thought its contents fairly represented their general views. The article was then forwarded to *Army News*. As the newspaper's editorial policy did not include publishing correspondence, the Ministerial and Executive Coordination Communication Division would not permit its publication. The principal author accepted this explanation. By this time, however, a copy had been leaked to Nick McKenzie at Nine Newspapers. After contacting the author to ascertain its authenticity, Nine Newspapers published the article without the author's permission and made it look like a Regimental apologia.

Without any knowledge of its origins, the article could be read in several ways. On one reading it was an attempt to influence public opinion ahead of the release of the IGADF Afghanistan Inquiry report by members of the SAS community who were still to grasp the gravity of the situation confronting their Regiment and, indeed, the entire ADF. On another reading, it was a plea by those who had served in Afghanistan to be heard and an attempt to reassure the Australian people that the alleged deeds of a small minority did not reflect the values to which an overwhelming majority resolutely adhered.

The article began by conceding that 'accusations and allegations of war crimes as well as failures of leadership cut to the very core of the SASR'. Those who deployed were 'not indifferent to human suffering. We do not have a callous disregard for human life [and] … we are not out of control'. In fact, they had been selected for SAS service because of their 'unwavering moral compass', which would help them to avoid 'casualties among non-combatants'. After asserting that 'without truth in reporting, we are nothing', the letter explained that SAS operators 'instigated' the IGADF Afghanistan Inquiry because 'we prefer our regimental history to reflect hard truths over comforting fantasy'. While the commitment to truth was heartening, the previous Chief of Army had actually 'instigated' the Inquiry without any prompting from the Regiment although its members had provided much of the information that would be contained in the Inquiry report. The letter might have also conceded that another group of former SAS members thought the Inquiry was unnecessary and condemned it.

Without knowing the extent of the alleged misconduct the Inquiry had found, and rightly asserting that Inquiry findings were not determinations of guilt, there was mitigation for whatever misconduct might have occurred:

> On combat operations, we were forced to sacrifice many of our technological advantages over highly adaptive adversaries who knew no rules or bounds. We accepted continually shifting goal posts and decisions made by governments in the absence of a defined campaign outcome in Afghanistan. We begrudgingly

accepted these strategic decisions while attempting to effectively operate in an environment characterised by uncertainty, danger and our own casualties.

These were highly revealing claims that effectively enlarged the circle of individual culpability, giving the impression that some SAS operators were struggling to adjust to the new operating environment with the Regiment's characteristic creativity and ingenuity.

Presuming most of the allegations related to 'heat of battle' incidents, the article implied that the initiating cause of any misconduct could be attributed to politicians and commanders whose decision-making was inconsistent and whose ignorance of tactical realities was potentially life-threatening. The article invited attention to institutional pressures and organisational tensions, implying misconduct was a function of both dysfunction and desperation. In effect, the article implied, the Regiment's members were more sinned against than sinning.

The article could also be read as suggesting that SAS operators reluctantly operated within the mission parameters and might have declined tasking that, in their judgment, either made no sense or involved excessive risk. The article did not intend to raise the prospect of collective insubordination but it alerted readers to deep disquiet among those who had the most to lose personally from ceding tactical advantages to adversaries. Having moved the focus from individual misconduct to institutional mismanagement, the article nonetheless supported 'removal from the regiment and legal prosecution of anyone found guilty of breaching the laws of armed conflict, the Geneva Convention or the rules of engagement'. Conceding there is 'absolutely no place in the ADF, least of all in the SASR, for any individual who believes they are untouchable or above the law', the article then stated: 'we are committed to accepting the outcomes and consequences of the Brereton Inquiry and to action its recommendations'.

It did seem that those behind the article were oblivious to the enormity of what was happening around them, because what they thought about the Inquiry and the report was irrelevant. The intention of the drafters was to demonstrate acceptance of the need for organisational reform and renewal without argument or animosity. The same spirit animated the letter's next statement: 'Then we will return to the shadows where we belong.' The article highlighted the desire of those then serving in the Regiment to operate beyond the public gaze, because much of its tasking required its members to operate covertly. There was an element of irony here. The Regiment had not operated in 'the shadows' for some time; its personnel and their exploits had attracted the public spotlight and played intentionally to media reporting. Of course, the Minister for Defence and the Chief of Army would decide the Regiment's fate and any changes that would be required in response to the Inquiry report's recommendations. Such was the gravity of the allegations and the seriousness of the likely findings that the Regiment would be subject to highly intrusive oversight with or without the concurrence of its members. This would no doubt cause considerable personal pain and inflict substantial organisational upheaval.

The authors then called for suspension of public judgment, and certainly official condemnation, until the accused had their day in court. This was understandable but unrealistic. Inquiries are used to identify matters in need of urgent attention. They alert senior leaders to pressing problems and possible solutions. Waiting until the outcome of a criminal trial would not help to restore public trust in the ADF. The authors were right to point out that no-one had been found guilty of any offence and that every citizen was entitled to the presumption of innocence and natural justice if accused of wrongdoing. The allegations had disturbed every member of the Regiment. The fact they were apparently being substantiated by members of the Regiment was troubling. There was also the possibility that those accused of misconduct might have made admissions of wrongdoing. Inevitably, the Inquiry report was going to attract criticism of the Regiment and those accused of wrongdoing would invariably be condemned in the court of public opinion.

After so many damning media stories it was reasonable to assume the Inquiry report was very likely to conclude that in Afghanistan some of Australia's most highly trained soldiers departed from the standards of excellence that had previously earned them widespread acclaim. While the courts would ultimately determine guilt and impose punishment, there was no doubt the parliament, the press and the people would respond with alarm to the findings of a legally constituted, taxpayer-funded public inquiry conducted by a senior judicial officer into serious matters that had a direct bearing on national defence. Those accused of misconduct, whose identities would be suppressed in the Inquiry report, would have their day of reckoning but spontaneous expressions of outrage would be impossible to restrain.

Nine Newspapers should have explained the origin of this article to its readers. It started as an individual response to an institutional invitation. On one level it made sense for *Army News* to present a soldier's perspective. That the draft article was considered unsuitable for publication simply because it came in the form of a letter revealed the sensitivity of the political environment and the complexity of public opinion. When it did appear, the article both dampened and inflamed emotions in different parts of the country.

Leaking the article to Nine Newspapers was counterproductive because the text was susceptible to different interpretations without any sense of its origins, principally that the drafter was not acting on his own initiative. My initial reading led me to think the article was a self-interested attempt to downplay the significance of what had occurred and to distance the SAS from the censure that was bound to follow the release of the Inquiry report. After reading the article several more times, I gradually gained a better sense of the drafter's intentions. It was far from an apologia. It was, in fact, an indictment of serious organisational failure and a forthright denunciation of those who had violated the Regiment's values. The article was a virtual expulsion notice. The newspaper sub-editor who imposed the title 'They are not one of us' might not have realised how accurately it portrayed the mood of the signatories. The article nonetheless elicited little sympathy within the political class or the ADF. The Inquiry report would determine the depth of alleged wrongdoing and the breadth of apparent complicity. The public mood was one of uncertainty, caught between residual respect for the SAS and reservations about the recent allegations.

The nearly seven years between the SOTG withdrawal in 2013 and the release of the IGADF Inquiry report in 2020 saw a series of distinct shifts in public opinion. The firm belief that Australian personnel had adhered to the Law of Armed Conflict and observed the Rules of Engagement (ROE) had been replaced with sombre acknowledgment that serious misconduct had probably occurred across a number of rotations involving more than one or two rogue soldiers. There was little in recent media reporting to suggest that the Commando Regiments were implicated in misconduct, other than perhaps in perpetuating the well-publicised inter-unit rivalry, sometimes referred to as the 'beret wars', that blighted many SOTG rotations in Uruzgan. The code of silence that had excluded outsiders from the inner workings of the SAS Regiment had been penetrated to expose apparent lawlessness and alleged brutality. Although damaging to its international reputation, the ADF would formally pursue those who had allegedly violated the fundamental principles regulating the conduct of armed conflict. There was a corporate willingness to face the past and to deal with its legacies: from discerning the reasons for apparent misconduct to prosecuting alleged war crimes.

This dramatic turn of events could not have been predicted in 2013 as Australian forces received the praises of the prime minister as they prepared to leave Tarin Kowt. It was even less predictable in 2015 when the 17 SOTG rotations from 2007 to 2013 were awarded the

Meritorious Unit Citation. Everything changed between 2016 and 2020. The day of reckoning had belatedly come. A heavily redacted version of the IGADF Afghanistan Inquiry report would be made public on Thursday 19 November 2020. It would be one of the most fateful days in Australian military history. The ADF's standing would never be the same. The past could not be erased; its legacy would linger for decades. Public confidence might eventually be restored but the ADF's reputation was tarnished. What happened in Afghanistan had now become part of the nation's story.

17
ASKING QUESTIONS

When Prime Minister John Howard announced in October 2001 that Australia would join a multinational coalition to invade Afghanistan in response to the 9/11 terrorist attacks in the United States, neither he nor his ministers could have imagined the enduring consequences of their decision. They certainly did not think that Australian soldiers would ever be accused of committing war crimes in a country of marginal strategic importance. When Australian forces returned to Afghanistan in 2005, the senior military officers advising the government were confident that every Australian sent overseas would uphold the nation's values in a campaign that might test their physical endurance but not their moral character. There was no need for anyone to determine whether the factors and forces that usually increased the possibility of serious misconduct in operational zones were present to any greater degree than expected in Uruzgan province, where they were sent. They believed that the quality of Australian leadership, discipline and training obviated any such assessment. This judgment was mistaken. Deeper questions about the possibility of war crimes should have been asked. This book has canvassed some of those questions. They begin with the place to which Australian soldiers were sent.

Nearly three decades of political violence had left a terrible legacy for Afghanistan and its people. The tyranny unleashed by the People's Democratic Party devastated Afghanistan as a nation. The oppressive Soviet occupation destroyed the Afghan state. The barbarism of the 40th Army militarised the population. Civil war and repressive

Taliban rule dissolved Afghan society. By 2001, Afghanistan was a broken nation and a failed state with a dreadful past and a doubtful future. It was not the place for foreigners who knew little of the political landscape, and next to nothing about the tattered remains of its social, economic and religious fabric, to attempt to rebuild a nation, revive a state and renew a society. The Afghans encouraging their efforts were conscious of the gulf between what the foreigners wanted and what they could deliver. The Afghans opposing their presence would certainly not fight by Western rules. Indeed, they would turn the international conventions that constrained the actions of International Security Assistance Force (ISAF) personnel to their own military and political advantage. The belief that Western economic power, diplomatic resolve and military might would prevail in Afghanistan was mistaken. Tougher questions ought to have been asked about the challenges a Western-led intervention would face.

These challenges were nevertheless considered well within the capacities of Australian Special Forces. There was nothing in recent military history to suggest members of the Special Air Service (SAS) Regiment or the 1st and 2nd Commando (Cdo) Regiments were disposed to lawlessness or prone to ill-discipline. The commanders of these units were acutely aware of the consequences of such behaviour, not only on mission success, but on Australia's standing and on the Australian Defence Force's (ADF) reputation on the world stage. Neither the Army nor the government thought the celebrated SAS Regiment was hampered by endemic disciplinary problems when an SAS squadron was first deployed to Afghanistan in 2001. The experience of the three SAS squadrons that rotated through Afghanistan during 2001–02 demonstrated the operational complexities, tactical difficulties and ethical dilemmas that all Western forces had confronted, and would continue to encounter, in Afghanistan.

The ADF's capacity to conduct operations simultaneously in East Timor, the Pacific and for an extended period in the Middle East might have attracted more cautious introspection in 2005, when the government sent Australian Special Forces back to Afghanistan for an initial 12-month commitment. The mission eventually ended, eight years later, at the close of 2013. The Australians' very limited knowledge of the enemy, understanding of the human terrain, appreciation of Afghan politics and evaluation of mission priorities, when considered alongside the complexity of measuring progress and managing the mental and physical demands associated with high-intensity operations, should have prompted deeper reflection on the ethical challenges of the operating environment. Difficult questions about human nature and moral resilience might have been asked. They were not.

Although the Taliban insurgency had not been defeated when the Australians were withdrawn, the award of the Meritorious Unit Citation to Special Operations Task Group (SOTG) rotations IV to XX, and well-attended welcome home parades in 2015, gave the impression that the service of every Australian in Afghanistan was above reproach. Some officers had a sense, however, that beneath the surface of operational reporting lay another story. In-theatre inquiries into the deaths of Afghan civilians and unarmed men that might have aroused suspicion among commanders and administrative authorities did not lead to further disciplinary or criminal investigations but to innuendo and hearsay that lingered well after the last Special Forces soldier returned to Australia. Awkward questions were now being asked. They needed to be.

Gossip coalesced into rumours that necessitated a formal inquiry that would determine whether these rumours had any substance. There were procedures for handling specific allegations of misconduct but no roadmap for dealing with rumours of war crimes. The involvement of Special Forces personnel, who were accustomed to secrecy and constrained by loyalty, complicated the inquiry process. Unlike France and the Soviet Union, which had granted its officers and soldiers who served in Algeria (1954–62) and Afghanistan (1979–89) an amnesty against future prosecution, the Australian Government was under an international obligation to investigate all allegations of misconduct, and to pursue prosecutions wherever possible. Intra-unit rivalries, personal animosities, flawed memories, and the need to obtain evidence from Afghans in remote locations, hindered effective progress and made the Inquiry a protracted exercise.

Apart from allegations of individual misconduct, it appeared there had been substantial organisational failures that implicated a number of politicians and commanders. According to media reports, a range of problems from what would have been minor offences under the *Defence Force Discipline Act* to serious breaches of the Law of Armed Conflict had been concealed, denied or tolerated. Despite a vast array of policies, procedures and protocols, conduct that was contrary to Australian values had not been detected, prevented or punished. The trust that had been invested in Australian officers and soldiers appeared to have been comprehensively abused by a cabal of individuals whose antipathies extended to their own colleagues as well as the Taliban.

The public was now being told that the very things that made the prospect of misconduct inconceivable – leadership, discipline and training – had aided and abetted the commission of crimes that had blackened the ADF's reputation. In effect, military leadership was ineffectual, discipline was inconsistent and training was inadequate. Searching questions about leadership, discipline and training that might have been asked in 2005 were belatedly receiving attention. It seemed these institutional strengths had become organisational weaknesses. Trust had been replaced by distrust as men who had operated with expansive discretion were now subject to close supervision. The selection and preparation of officers and soldiers for Special Forces service was being critically examined by 'outsiders' asking unexpected questions. They needed to be asked.

If only a fraction of the allegations being made against SOTG members were ever substantiated, it was nonetheless obvious that the

ADF's customs and traditions had failed to restrain the worst excesses of human behaviour in Afghanistan. If none of the allegations was ever proved to be true, there remained evidence of widespread disregard for the ADF's rules and regulations, the existence of destructive rivalries between units previously praised for their creative collaboration, and the willingness of some soldiers to accuse their former comrades of engaging in either criminal behaviour or criminal defamation. Petty jealousies and personal vendettas were apparently accompanied by bullying and intimidation that extended to reprisals on homes and families. These were hardly the traits expected of elite units.

To inquisitive outsiders it looked like the SAS Regiment, in particular, had been seized by a malevolent spirit that could only be exorcised by disbandment – a fate some observers contended was unavoidable. Others insisted the problems were neither cultural nor unit-wide. They were isolated and related entirely to headstrong, non-compliant individuals. The causes were the attitudes and actions of a small group – the 'not one of us' cohort – who had already left the Army or could be transferred to another unit. Like skin cancers that could be readily excised, removing the people effectively resolved the problems. And yet, so many questions still needed to be answered about how Australia's 'elite' military forces could have descended to these depths of unprofessionalism and, worse, inhumanity. The foremost question was why anyone thought such behaviour was beyond imagination over eight years of counterinsurgency in rural Afghanistan.

Claims that the Australians who deployed to Afghanistan might have engaged in misconduct would have been met with much less shock had the public been aware that every nation contributing forces to ISAF had been obliged to deal with war crimes allegations. The conduct of British, Canadian and New Zealand forces in Afghanistan were the subject of independent inquiries. Although their national commitments, deployment patterns and inquiry regimes differed from those of Australia, they each faced the same challenges: accurately identifying combatants, avoiding civilian casualties, humanely handling detainees, restraining local partner forces and dealing with soldiers whose personal conduct was inconsistent with professional standards.

The French and the New Zealanders had very few incidents of misconduct, partly because their forces were not engaged in close-quarters combat for extended periods. In other words, they had fewer opportunities to be drawn into bad behaviour. The Canadians dealt with more allegations because they had 'raised the ethical bar' much higher than every other nation in Afghanistan. To some degree, they created problems for themselves in wanting to demonstrate they had learned important lessons from their experiences in Somalia during 1993. Notably, both the French and the Canadians remained conscious that their respective military histories were marred by episodes of misconduct and were vigilant in the pursuit of even minor infractions. Alleged incidents of misconduct involving members of the United Kingdom's 22 SAS Regiment (which redeployed from Iraq to Afghanistan in 2009) resembled many of the SOTG stories reported by the Australian media. Despite extensive inquiries into just as many allegations, no charges were laid against British SAS soldiers. If Australia's closest operating partners had faced allegations of misconduct against their soldiers, no-one should have been affronted by serious questioning of Australian soldiers and their adherence to the Law of Armed Conflict. Only hubris would have led Australia to believe its soldiers were less susceptible to misconduct than their New Zealand, British, Canadian and French counterparts.

Seven years after the last SOTG member returned to Australia, the public release of the IGADF Afghanistan Inquiry report was scheduled for 11 am on Thursday 19 November 2020. The Chief of the Defence Force, General Angus Campbell, would stand before the nation as a representative of the ADF and explain what had allegedly been done by men whose uniforms were emblazoned with the national flag and whose values were meant to be those of its people.

The public had been told to brace for distressing news. The Australian Army and Australia's Special Forces had already experienced enormous reputational damage. That the Inquiry had taken four and a half years, was conducted by a major general who was also a senior judge, and involved hundreds of witnesses, conveyed the impression there were numerous allegations and the misconduct was well hidden.

There was a heightened sense of anticipation. For over three years, the Australian public had been drip-fed a series of damning accounts of improper behaviour and criminal conduct. On one level, the actions of these soldiers were mystifying. What they had done seemed completely out of character and served no obvious or useful purpose. Media stories of assault, torture and murder were shorn of any interpretive context and breathlessly reported without explanatory detail. The allegations were almost impossible to believe. The ABC *4 Corners* program, 'Killing Field', had been the turning point in March 2020. Body-camera video of Afghans being killed, and Australians talking nonchalantly about concealing their deaths, precluded any suggestion these stories were a media beat-up.

Stunned former senior officers lined up to condemn what they had seen on television. Although none had known about what had allegedly occurred in Afghanistan, none was prepared to accept responsibility in anticipation of what the Inquiry was likely to reveal. No-one came to the public defence of the SAS Regiment or its now beleaguered members. It had apparently been the sole architect of its dire predicament. The former and serving Special Forces soldiers who broke ranks and spoke with the media were confident the Australian people would not allow their allegations to be brushed aside. Media reporting influenced both the conduct of the IGADF Afghanistan Inquiry and public expectations of what it would uncover.

The Inquiry could only conclude there was no substance to the rumours of misconduct if the rumours were baseless, exaggerated or malicious or if an individual's actions had not actually been observed first hand, crucial elements of the engagement were not visible or an observer had misinterpreted the individual's actions. There was never much chance that the Inquiry would conclude there had been no incidents of misconduct, given the extent of media reporting and the willingness of SAS soldiers to point an accusing finger at their own former colleagues. But would the Inquiry report provide a convincing explanation for alleged misconduct? What had led Australian soldiers to even contemplate committing war crimes? Most media stories had focused on *what* had happened rather than *why* it had happened. Some of the initial explanations were, at best, speculative.

Samantha Crompvoets' work gave the impression that the SAS Regiment was selecting the wrong kinds of people. It may have been that some operators were violent psychopaths when they joined the Regiment and were not screened out while others were drawn into collective 'blood lust' and 'competition killing', hinting at a personal propensity for depravity. Her work suggested that some operators were determined to achieve honours and awards at the cost of innocent lives whereas others simply wanted to be part of an 'in' group and did whatever was necessary to remain there. David Irvine thought the SAS Regiment 'recruited in a mirror' and narrowed the outlook of its members. Crompvoets suggested that hyper-aggression and ultra-violence eventually became 'permissible and equated with being good and effective soldiers'. Both Crompvoets and Irvine identified a creeping culture of exceptionalism which evidently led some soldiers to think laws and rules did not apply to them, and that any breaches or violations would not be pursued or punished. They also mentioned illicit drug-taking and alcohol abuse as being both cause and effect of deteriorating discipline but did not go the next step and implicate drugs and alcohol in the commission of war crimes. (Neither commented on the use of steroids and other performance-enhancing drugs.)

Were there any mitigating factors? In Crompvoets' work there was no mention of any soldier disclosing a philosophical difficulty applying the Law of Armed Conflict nor any reference to practical problems interpreting the Rules of Engagement (ROE). No-one mentioned any conscientious concern about the number of times the same individual was posted to an SOTG rotation nor were there any apparent misgivings about the conduct of Afghan partner forces. None of these things apparently played any part in the incidence or severity of misconduct. In fact, Crompvoets overlooked the challenges associated with the operational context in Uruzgan and the possibility that these challenges might have compromised the personal values or professional standards of any ADF member.

Both Crompvoets and Irvine were critical of leadership at all levels within the SAS Regiment, their remarks drawing on internal dissatisfaction with the strength and integrity of some senior NCOs and officers, but not all. Neither blamed the Regiment's leaders for the alleged misconduct but both concluded that closer and more consistent leadership would have made a substantial difference to collective compliance with the Law of Armed Conflict and the ROE.

There were, of course, bigger issues of context and circumstance. It was impossible to account for misconduct without asking a series of questions about where the fighting occurred, who was involved, how the war was to be won, and what tactics were employed. Each had a bearing on the conduct of individual soldiers. Was there something unusual about the Afghan war – the 'war on terror' – that made war crimes more likely? Did permissive attitudes towards the use of force in Afghanistan contribute to a general climate of impunity? Was Western tolerance of Afghan torture, and support for militias whose human rights violations were equally widespread, play a part in reducing respect for all human life? Did American enemy-centric and kill–capture strategies increase the possibility of war crimes among its Coalition partners? Indeed, was it possible for ISAF forces to achieve anti-terrorist and counterinsurgency success without resorting to extreme measures? Did the Australian Government provide a compelling case and, therefore, a controlling narrative, for Australian Special Operations in Afghanistan? Were sufficient resources and assets provided to preclude the need for legal shortcuts or moral compromises? Had there been sufficient attention to values education and ethics training in pre-deployment preparation? Did ADF policies and SOCOMD procedures unwittingly aid or abet the resort to practices whose fullest expression constituted war crimes? Did the absence of journalists in the area of operations have any bearing on perceptions of individual accountability? There was no suggestion that a lack of strategic success led to aberrations at the tactical level but there must have been something about Australia's approach to the conduct of the war that led some soldiers to break laws, violate rules and ignore values.

The public would want to know whether it was possible to detect patterns or discern themes in the alleged offending. Did the offences occur at the same time of day, the same day of the week, the same week of the month or at the same point in each rotation? Did the alleged offences occur at the same time of year or only when the climatic conditions were severe, such as midsummer or midwinter? Did they happen in the same place among the same people and in the same circumstances? Was there anything linking the alleged victims, such as their age, appearance or ethnicity? Were the alleged victims killed in the same way? What kinds of weapons were used in the alleged offences and were they Australian service issue, sourced from Afghan partner forces or seized from insurgents? Was there any relationship between alleged incidences of assault, torture and murder? Did these offences occur in isolation or was assault the precursor to torture, and torture the prelude to murder? Were particular operations employing specific tactics associated with certain offences?

Just as many questions could be posed of the alleged offenders. Were they similar in terms of age, rank, marital status or religious affiliation? What was their career path in the Army before qualifying for Special Forces? Did they have comparable disciplinary records or similar performance reporting histories? Had they previously been reprimanded for acts of violence? Could they be sorted into categories according to their attributes, abilities or aptitudes? How long had they served in Special Forces and what was their specialisation? When the alleged offences occurred how many times had they deployed overseas, deployed to Afghanistan and deployed to the SOTG? How many days had they spent in Afghanistan before their first alleged offence? How many offences did they allegedly commit, was there any similarity between the alleged offences and did the alleged offending become more serious with time? Were the alleged offenders accompanied by the same soldiers when war crimes were allegedly committed and were those soldiers participants in, or witnesses to, the same alleged offences?

There were questions to be asked of those who concealed serious misconduct, those who discouraged others from making reports, those who witnessed serious conduct but failed to make a report, and those who heard rumours of misconduct or had reasonable suspicion to believe that misconduct might have been committed but did nothing, and remained silent. The public were entitled to answers about why a succession of internal inquiries were unable to uncover the truth; how alleged offenders and their accomplices were able to conceal evidence of misconduct; whether those in command and leadership positions were aware of or suspected misconduct; and if those in positions of responsibility were incompetent or negligent in failing to exercise sufficient control over their subordinates. If officers failed to prevent or punish any criminal acts committed by their subordinates, did this failure constitute a war crime? As the prosecution of war crimes was within the remit of the International Criminal Court (ICC), what action was the Australian Government required to take to prevent the ICC claiming jurisdiction and entitlement to conduct its own investigation? Indeed, did the Australian Government have the legal mechanisms in place to prosecute those accused of war crimes if a *prima facie* case could be established against any ADF member?

The decision to initiate the IGADF Afghanistan Inquiry in March 2016 was the commencement of a process that would possibly take up to a decade to complete. It was a momentous step and one taken without regard to the emotional, financial or reputational consequences – which were substantial. The Inquiry disrupted SOCOMD planning, damaged morale in both the SAS and the Commando Regiments and derailed the careers of many officers and soldiers. While these were unintended and unfortunate outcomes, the distraction and pain associated with conducting a thorough and rigorous inquiry was unavoidable. The tone of the Inquiry interviews might have been less combative, and the questioning could have been less confrontational, but the pursuit of truth in such a situation needed to be remorseless and unrelenting.

The most important question was the least complicated: had Afghans been assaulted and murdered? Their families wanted answers and they were entitled to justice. When Australian commentators were critical of the Inquiry – its commencement, conduct and conclusion – they seemed to overlook those with the greatest stake in its findings and recommendations. For an unknown number of Afghans, a brief encounter with Australian soldiers had led to a loved one being taken from them. In many cases a family had been deprived of its principal provider and protector. In parts of rural Uruzgan, the presence of an able-bodied male was the difference between living and dying. Had the situations been reversed, and Australian commentators found themselves in the shoes of grieving Afghan families, I am sure they would have been indifferent to the havoc caused by the Inquiry and been unmoved by the time needed to produce credible findings. As with the war itself, reactions to the Inquiry revealed that some Australians were often more concerned about themselves than with the fate of the Afghans.

The Inquiry report would be a document of national significance. The reputation of the Aussie 'digger' for valour had been veiled. But much more than the standing of Australian soldiers was involved. At issue was the spirit of the Australian nation, the character of its people and the maturity of its Army. Having received so much testimony and examined so much evidence, the Inquiry team were well placed to say something compelling about the nature of war and the human consequences of employing lethal force. The Inquiry report's release offered a rare moment of self-discovery. The report and reactions to its recommendations had the potential to lay bare the nation's soul and reveal the Australian heart. How would the people respond? It was time to find out.

ACKNOWLEDGMENTS

I am grateful to the hundreds of people who have enhanced this book. They have pointed me to useful sources of information, consented to interviews, refined my arguments, checked my facts and improved my prose. As this book deals with matters that are subject to continuing investigation which may lead to prosecutions, I have decided reluctantly against thanking former and serving Australian Defence Force (ADF) members individually. I would ask them to accept their share of my collective appreciation for their goodwill and generosity. In considering the political dimensions of the war in Afghanistan I was helped by John Howard, John Anderson, Alexander Downer, Brendan Nelson and Joel Fitzgibbon. Among my UNSW academic colleagues I am grateful to Professor Michael Frater (the Rector of UNSW Canberra until January 2021), A/Professor Deane-Peter Baker, Dr Ned Dobos, the late Derrill de Heer, Professor Clinton Fernandes, Dr Bob Hall, Vice Admiral Paul Maddison, Professor James Connor, Mick Cook, Elizabeth Grinston, Dr Andrew Ross, Dr Susanne Schmeidl, Dr Astri Suhrke, Professor Harvi Sidhu, A/Professor Hugh Smith, Professor Peter Stanley and my Howard Library co-workers, Professor David Lovell, Andrew Blyth, Annette Carter and Trish Burgess, who proofread the text and diligently collected and collated media reports. I also thank esteemed colleagues from other academic institutions including Professor William Maley, Professor John Blaxland and Dr Albert Palazzo (Australian National University); Dr Michael Kennedy (University of Western Sydney); Emeritus Professor Murray Goot (Macquarie University); Dr Spencer Jones (University of Wolverhampton); Dr Scott Prasser (Australian Catholic University); Dr Niamatullah Ibrahimi (La Trobe University);

and Professor David Whetham (King's College London). I was also assisted by the official history unit at the Australian War Memorial, including Professor Craig Stockings, Professor Peter Dennis and Dr Rhys Crawley, and by Craig Tibbitts of the Memorial's Historical Research Section. I was able to draw on the expertise of Kearney consultants including Nigel Andrade, Robert Holt, Robert Bustos-McNeil, Alasdair Johnston and Cassandra Cawston. I was generously assisted in Canada by Dr Bernd Horn, Major General Mike Day and Vice Admiral Greg Maddison; in New Zealand by the Hon. Dr Wayne Mapp, Kristy McDonald QC and Jon Stephenson; and in relation to British military affairs by Brigadier Ian Huntley (formerly Royal Marines); Warwick Stacey (formerly 22 SAS), Tony Mason (formerly 3rd Battalion, Parachute Regiment) and Hannah O'Grady (BBC *Panorama*). I am grateful for the encouragement of my friend Chris Masters and to some special companions: David Campbell, Kerrie Rendell, Haydn Swinbourn, Michael Fogarty, Dale Budd, Tony Eggleton, Malcolm Hazell, Stuart Rendell and Tim Sullivan. Marina Loane assisted in collating media stories. As ever, I am grateful for the experience and expertise of my friends at UNSW Press: Kathy Bail, Elspeth Menzies and Paul O'Beirne.

NOTES

INTRODUCTION

1. United Nations (UN), 'War crimes', UN website, no date, <www.un.org/en/genocideprevention/war-crimes.shtml>.
2. Inspector General of the Australian Defence Force, *Afghanistan Inquiry Report*, Australian Government Defence website, November 2020, <afghanistaninquiry.defence.gov.au/sites/default/files/2020-11/IGADF-Afghanistan-Inquiry-Public-Release-Version.pdf>.
3. Samantha Crompvoets, *Special Operations Command (SOCOMD): Culture and Interactions: Insights and Reflection*, Australian Government Defence website, January 2016, <afghanistaninquiry.defence.gov.au/sites/default/files/2020-11/SOCOMD-Culture-and-Interactions-Insights-and-Reflection-Jan-16_0.pdf>.
4. David Irvine, *Review of Special Operations Command: Australian Army*, Australian Government Defence website, 16 April 2020, <afghanistaninquiry.defence.gov.au/sites/default/files/2020-11/Irvine-Report-2018-Review-of-SOCOMD-Australian-Army.pdf>.
5. David Irvine, *Review of Special Operations Command: Australian Army*, Australian Government Defence website, 15 June 2020, <afghanistaninquiry.defence.gov.au/sites/default/files/2020-11/Irvine-Report-2020-Review-of-SOCOMD-Australian-Army.pdf>.
6. Sergeant Robert Bales pleaded guilty to murdering 16 Afghan civilians on 11 March 2012 in Kandahar province. For a discussion of his case see: University of Chicago Law School, 'Robert Bales', University of Chicago Law School website, no date, <www.law.uchicago.edu/clinics/mandel/mental/combat/bales>.
7. Given public criticism of previous works dealing with alleged misconduct in Afghanistan, readers should know I will not be receiving any royalties from the sales of this book.
8. Chris Masters, *No Front Line: Australia's Special Forces at war in Afghanistan*, Allen & Unwin, Sydney, 2017.
9. Mark Wales, *Survivor: Life in the SAS*, Pan Macmillan, Sydney, 2021.
10. Samantha Crompvoets, *Blood Lust, Trust and Blame*, Monash University Publishing, Melbourne, 2021.
11. Mark Willacy, *Rogue Forces*, Simon & Schuster, Sydney, 2021.

1 FROM GALLIPOLI TO URUZGAN 1915–2020

1. Stephen Kuper, 'Every nation has its story, this is ours – Dr Brendan Nelson AO', Defence Connect website, 22 May 2019, <www.defenceconnect.com.au/key-enablers/4094-every-nation-has-its-story-this-is-ours-dr-brendan-nelson-ao>.
2. *Protection of Word 'Anzac' Act 1920*, Commonwealth Consolidated Acts website, <classic.austlii.edu.au/au/legis/cth/consol_act/powa1920261/>.

3   In response to a request from *History Australia*, Kent's personal account of this episode appeared as '"Sack the Bastard!" – David Kent (the now vilest man alive)', *History Australia*, vol. 12, no. 1, 2015, pp. 226–232.
4   CEW Bean, *The Anzac Book*, originally published 1916, third edition, reprint, UNSW Press, Sydney, 2010.
5   See also Sarah Midford, 'Bean's Anzac book shaped how Australians think about Gallipoli', the *Conversation*, 9 April 2015, <theconversation.com/beans-anzac-book-shaped-how-australians-think-about-gallipoli-38203>.
6   Quoted in Alistair Thomson, *Anzac Memories: Living with the legend*, Oxford University Press, Oxford, 1994, p. 60.
7   David Kent, '"Sack the bastard!" – David Kent (the now vilest man alive)', *History Australia*, vol. 12, no. 1, 2015, pp. 226–232.
8   Mervyn F Bendle, *Anzac & Its Enemies: The history war on Australia's national identity*, Quadrant Books, Sydney, 2015.
9   The origins and contours of this debate are dealt with by Peter Cochrane, 'The past is not sacred', *Griffith Review*, no date, <www.griffithreview.com/articles/past-sacred/>.
10 The first three rotations were known as the 'Special Forces Task Group'. After 2007 they were renamed the 'Special Operations Task Group'.
11 Chris Masters, *No Front Line: Australian Special Forces at war in Afghanistan*, Allen & Unwin, Sydney, 2017.
12 Masters, *No Front Line*, p. 503.
13 Masters, *No Front Line*, p. 560.
14 Mark Willacy, 'The inquiry into Australian soldiers in Afghanistan is finally over. The reckoning is about to begin', ABC News, 18 November 2020, <www.abc.net.au/news/2020-11-18/igadf-inquiry-into-special-forces-in-afghanistan-is-over/12816626>.
15 Editorial, 'Australian government "sent soldiers to fight for us, yet now it's attacking them"', Sky News, 13 November 2020, <www.skynews.com.au/details/_6209604029001>.

2   DOWNFALL OF A NATION: AFGHANISTAN'S JOURNEY 1747–1979

1   Shaista Wahab and Barry Youngerman, *A Brief History of Afghanistan*, Infobase, New York, 2007, p. viii.
2   See Nivi Manchanda, *Imagining Afghanistan: The history and politics of imperial knowledge*, Cambridge University Press, London, 2020.
3   Tamim Ansary, *Games Without Rules: The often interrupted history of Afghanistan*, Public Affairs, E-book, 2017, p. 4, <ebookcentral.proquest.com/lib/unsw/reader.action?docID=1044413>.
4   Francois Bernier, *Travels in the Mughal Empire*, Westminster, 1891, quoted by Abraham Eraly, *The Mughal World: India's tainted paradise*, Phoenix, London, 2008, p. 24.
5   Patrick Macrory, *Retreat from Kabul: The catastrophic British defeat in Afghanistan, 1842*, Lyons Press, Connecticut, 2002.
6   Portions of Gleig's diary appeared in *Sale's Brigade in Afghanistan with an account of the seizure and defence of Jellalabad*, John Murray, London, 1846.
7   Ashraf Ghani, 'Production and Domination, Afghanistan, 1747–1901', doctoral dissertation, Columbia University, 1982, pp. 388, 409.
8   Hasan Kawun Kakar, *Government and Society in Afghanistan: The reign of Amir 'Abd al-Rahman Khan*, University of Texas Press, Austin, 1979, p. 169.

9   Churchill minute, War Office, 12 May 1919 quoted in Martin Gilbert (ed.), *Winston S. Churchill, Companion Volume 4, Part 1*, Heinemann, London, 1977, p. 662.
10 Edward M Spiers, *Chemical Weaponry: A Continuing Challenge*, Palgrave Macmillan, London, 1989, p. 83.
11 M Hasan Kakar, *A Political and Diplomatic History of Afghanistan, 1863–1901*, Brill, Boston, 2006, p. 185; and Dorothea Seelye Franck, 'Pakhtunistan: Disputed Disposition of a Tribal Land', *Middle East Journal*, vol. 6, no. 1, 1952, pp. 49–68.
12 Amin Saikal, 'Afghanistan and Pakistan: The Question of Pashtun Nationalism?', <www-tandfonline-com.wwwproxy1.library.unsw.edu.au/doi/pdf/10.1080/13602001003650572?needAccess=true>.
13 Igor Torbakov, 'Russian planners reexamining "Great Games" concepts for clues on future policy', Eurasianet website, 28 November 2001, <eurasianet.org/russian-planners-reexamining-great-games-concepts-for-clues-on-future-policy>.
14 Andrei Snesarev, *Afghanistan: Preparing for the Bolshevik incursion into Afghanistan and attack on India, 1919–20*, translated and edited by Lester W Grau and Michael A Gress, vol. 27, Helion Studies in Military History Series, Helion, London, 2014.
15 Anthony Hyman, *Afghanistan under Soviet Domination, 1963–91*, updated version, Saint Martin's Press, New York, 1992, p. 92.
16 Quoted in William Maley, *The Afghanistan Wars*, third edition, Macmillan Educational, London, 2021, p. 25.
17 Quoted in Vasiliy Mitrokhin, *The KGB in Afghanistan*, working paper #40, Cold War International History Project, July 2009, <www.wilsoncenter.org/sites/default/files/media/documents/publication/WP40-english.pdf>.
18 David B Edwards, *Before Taliban: Genealogies of the Afghan Jihad*, University of California Press, Berkeley, 2002, <publishing.cdlib.org/ucpressebooks/view?docId=ft3p30056w&chunk.id=d0e530&toc.id=d0e530&brand=ucpress>.
19 Quoted in Aleksandr Antonovich Lyakhovskiy, *Inside the Soviet Invasion of Afghanistan and the Seizure of Kabul, December 1979*, working paper #51, Cold War International History Project, January 2007, <www.wilsoncenter.org/sites/default/files/media/documents/publication/WP51_Web_Final.pdf>.
20 Lyakhovskiy, 2007.
21 Lyakhovskiy, 2007.

3   COLLAPSE OF A STATE: THE SOVIET OCCUPATION 1979–1992

1   *Kabul New Times*, 2 January 1980, p. 1. Digital copy available at <content.library.arizona.edu/digital/collection/p16127coll6/id/11040>.
2   See <nsarchive2.gwu.edu/NSAEBB/NSAEBB57/soviet.html> for a series of documents relating to the invasion and subsequent occupation of Afghanistan.
3   For an insightful overview of Azzam's views and influence on Osama bin Laden see: Youssef Aboul-Enein, Radical Theories on Defending Muslim Land Through Jihad, Combating Terrorism Center, United States Military Academy, <ctc.usma.edu/wp-content/uploads/2010/06/Azzam_part_3.pdf>.
4   Leah Farrall, 'Revisiting al-Qaida's Foundation and Early History', *Perspectives on Terrorism*, vol. 11, no. 6, December 2017, pp. 17–37.
5   See Thomas Hegghammer, *The Caravan: Abdallah Azzam and the rise of global jihad*, Cambridge University Press, London, 2020.
6   Steve Galster, *Afghanistan: Lessons from the last war*, The National Security Archive, 9 October 2001, <nsarchive2.gwu.edu/NSAEBB/NSAEBB57/essay.html>.

7   Richar Boucher, 'Designation of Gulbuddin Hekmatyar as a terrorist', press statement, US Department of State Archive, 19 February 2003, <2001-2009.state.gov/r/pa/prs/ps/2003/17799.htm>.
8   Krishnadev Calamur, 'How Jalaluddin Haqqani went from US ally to foe', the *Atlantic*, 5 September 2018, <www.theatlantic.com/international/archive/2018/09/haqqani-death/569275/>.
9   Ken Guest, 'Ram' Seeger and Lucy Morgan Edwards, 'A better path to peace', UK Parliament website, <publications.parliament.uk/pa/cm201213/cmselect/cmdfence/413/413we07.htm>.
10 'Group of Soviet forces in Afghanistan', Global Security website, no date, <www.globalsecurity.org/military/world/russia/gsfa.htm>.
11 Jonathan Gandomi, 'Lessons from the Soviet occupation in Afghanistan for the United States and NATO', Princeton University website, no date, <jpia.princeton.edu/sites/jpia/files/2008-3.pdf>.
12 Olga Oliker, *Building Afghanistan's Security Forces in Wartime: The Soviet experience*, RAND, Santa Monica, California, 2011, chapter 4.
13 'Excerpts from several reports about the situation in the PDPA compiled by the KGB', Wilson Center digital archive, 26 January 1983, <digitalarchive.wilsoncenter.org/document/113129>.
14 David C Isby, 'The Better Hammer: Soviet Special Operations Forces and Tactics in Afghanistan 1979–86', *Strategic Studies*, vol. 10, no. 1, Autumn 1986, pp. 69–103.
15 Staff correspondent, 'Sakharov uses Olympic spotlight to condemn Soviets' Afghan invasion', *Christian Science Monitor*, 30 July 1980, <www.csmonitor.com/1980/0730/073061.html>.
16 Jonathan CR, 'Afghanistan: Moscow's Vietnam?', the *Washington Post*, 10 May 1979, <www.washingtonpost.com/archive/politics/1979/05/10/afghanistan-moscows-vietnam/28d19c3c-43d9-4bb7-a907-2c2724cbfa5d/>.
17 Serge Schmemamm, 'Gorbachev says US arms note is not adequate', *New York Times*, 26 February 1986, <www.nytimes.com/1986/02/26/world/gorbachev-says-us-arms-note-is-not-adequate.html>.
18 For a series of Soviet documents relating to the planned withdrawal see: Svetlana Savranskaya and Thomas Blanton, 'Afghanistan and the Soviet withdrawal 1989, 20 years later', National Security Archive, 15 February 2009, <nsarchive2.gwu.edu/NSAEBB/NSAEBB272/index.htm>.
19 James Rupert, 'Afghan Party Chief Babrak "Ill", is replaced', the *Washington Post*, 5 May 1986, <www.washingtonpost.com/archive/politics/1986/05/05/afghan-party-chief-babrak-ill-is-replaced/bf093035-e616-429a-960a-c5408fbf9bf7/>.
20 Gary Goldberg (translator), GRU Dossier on Najibullah, Wilson Center digital archive, 1986, <digitalarchive.wilsoncenter.org/document/117300.pdf?v=d14c09ed19d0dd1908c11db4300892ac>.
21 Naseem Rizvi, 'Najib's national reconciliation', *Strategic Studies*, vol. 10, no. 3, Spring 1987, pp. 9–11.
22 Jayson Stoinski and Svetlana Savranskaya (translators), 'Politburo on Afghanistan', Wilson Center digital archive, 13 November 1986, <digitalarchive.wilsoncenter.org/document/220088.pdf?v=061e7097dc8d60c53dea49dbcc9e6fcd>.
23 'Politburo on Afghanistan', Wilson Center digital archive.
24 'Politburo on Afghanistan', Wilson Center digital archive.

25　'Politburo on Afghanistan', Wilson Center digital archive.
26　Tad Daley, 'Afghanistan and Gorbachev's Global Foreign Policy', *Asian Studies*, vol. 29, no. 5, May 1989, pp. 496–513.
27　'Record of a conversation of M. S. Gorbachev with the General Secretary of the Central Committee of the People's Democratic Party of Afghanistan CDE. Najib (excerpt)', Wilson Center digital archive, 20 July 1987, <digitalarchive.wilsoncenter.org/document/117237>.
28　Rosanne Klass, 'Afghanistan: The accords', Foreign Affairs, Summer 1988, <www.foreignaffairs.com/articles/asia/1988-06-01/afghanistan-accords>.
29　For the text of the accords and a discussion of their significance see Agha Shahi, 'The Geneva Accords', *Pakistan Horizon*, vol. 41, no. 3, July 1988, pp. 23–49.
30　Shah M Tarzi, 'Politics of the Afghan Resistance Movement: Cleavages, Disunity, and Fragmentation', *Asian Survey*, vol. 31, no. 6, June 1991, pp. 479–495.
31　Mark N Katz, 'Lessons of the Soviet Withdrawal from Afghanistan', Middle East Policy Council website, no date, <mepc.org/commentary/lessons-soviet-withdrawal-afghanistan>.
32　Edward A Gargan, 'Afghan President agrees to step down', *New York Times*, 19 March 1992, <www.nytimes.com/1992/03/19/world/afghan-president-agrees-to-step-down.html>.
33　'The Battle for Kabul: April 1992 – March 1993', Human Rights Watch website, 2005, <www.hrw.org/reports/2005/afghanistan0605/4.htm>.
34　Artyom Boronik, *The Hidden War*, Atlantic Monthly Press, New York, 1990, p. 14.
35　Rafael Reuveny and Aseem Prakash, 'The Afghanistan War and the Breakdown of the Soviet Union', *Review of International Studies*, vol. 25, no. 4, October 1999, pp. 693–708.
36　Borovik, *The Hidden War*, p. 37.
37　Adam Baczko and Gilles Dorronsoro, 'Cross-Border Dynamics and Globalized Salafism: The Islamic State in Afghanistan', *Critique internationale*, 2017/1 (No. 74), pp. 137–152, <www.cairn-int.info/article-E_CRII_074_0137--cross-border-dynamics-and-globalized.htm>.
38　United Nations Development Programme, Human Development Report 1989, Oxford University Press, New York, 1990, <hdr.undp.org/sites/default/files/reports/219/hdr_1990_en_complete_nostats.pdf>.
39　M Siddieq Noorzoy, 'Alternative Economic Systems for Afghanistan', *International Journal of Middle East Studies*, vol. 15, no. 1, February 1983, pp. 25–45; and decade-long figures: <www.indexmundi.com/agriculture/?country=af&commodity=wheat&graph=production>.
40　'Afghanistan', Landmine and Cluster Munition Monitor, Archives 1999–2014, <archives.the-monitor.org/index.php/publications/display?url=lm/1999/afghanistan>.
41　Olivier Roy, 'Islamic radicalism in Afghanistan and Pakistan', UNHCR Emergency and Security Service, January 2002, <www.refworld.org/pdfid/3c6a3f7d2.pdf>.
42　Quoted in Michael Griffin, *Reaping the Whirlwind: The Taliban movement in Afghanistan*, Pluto, London, 2001, p. 5.
43　'Barnett Rubin on the Soviet invasion of Afghanistan and the rise of the Taliban', Asia Society website, no date, <asiasociety.org/barnett-rubin-soviet-invasion-afghanistan-and-rise-taliban>.
44　Pervez Hoodbhoy, 'Afghanistan and the genesis of global jihad', *Peace Research*, vol. 37, no. 1, May 2005, pp. 15–30.

4 DISINTEGRATION OF A MILITARY: THE SOVIET 40TH ARMY 1979–1989

1. Gennady Bochorov, *Russian Roulette: Afghanistan through Russian eyes*, Harper Collins, London, 1990, p. 61.
2. Simon Saradzhyan, '7 lessons Russian strategists inferred from Soviet intervention in Afghanistan', the *Moscow Times*, 10 January 2020, <www.themoscowtimes.com/2019/12/23/seven-lessons-russian-strategists-inferred-from-soviet-intervention-in-afghanistan-a68726>.
3. Simon Saradzhyan, 'Lessons for leaders: What Afghanistan taught Russian and Soviet strategists', Belfer Center for Science and International Affairs website, 28 February 2019, <www.belfercenter.org/publication/lessons-leaders-what-afghanistan-taught-russian-and-soviet-strategists>.
4. Alex Alexiev, 'Inside the Soviet Army in Afghanistan', RAND Army Research Division website, 1988, <www.rand.org/pubs/reports/R3627.html>.
5. Alex Alexiev, 'Inside the Soviet Army in Afghanistan', <apps.dtic.mil/dtic/tr/fulltext/u2/a213733.pdf>, p. 56.
6. Edward Girardet, a correspondent for the *Christian Science Monitor*, was one of few foreigners to visit parts of Afghanistan from 1979 to 1982. Jeri Laber and Barnet Rubin commenced their research in 1984.
7. World Peace Foundation, 'Afghanistan: Soviet invasion and civil war', Mass Atrocity Endings website, 7 August 2015, <sites.tufts.edu/atrocityendings/2015/08/07/afghanistan-soviet-invasion-civil-war/>.
8. Carol Harrington, *Politicisation of Sexual Violence: From abolitionism to peacekeeping*, Routledge, London, 2010, p. 104.
9. Mohammad Hassan Kakar, *Afghanistan: The Soviet invasion and the Afghan response, 1979–82*, University of Southern California Press, 1977, chapters 13 and 14.
10. Jeri Laber and Barnett Rubin, *A Nation Is Dying: Afghanistan under the Soviets, 1979–1987*, Northwestern University, Evanston, Illinois, 1988, p. 18.
11. 'Diplomats report massacre in Afghanistan', UPI Archives website, 14 May 1985, <www.upi.com/Archives/1985/05/14/Diplomats-report-massacre-in-Afghanistan/5791484891200/>.
12. Felix Ermacora, *Report on the Situation of Human Rights in Afghanistan/Prepared by the Special Rapporteur, Felix Ermacora, in Accordance with Commission on Human Rights Resolution 1989/67*, United Nations digital library, <digitallibrary.un.org/record/84296?ln=en>.
13. Amnesty International, *Afghanistan: Unlawful killings and torture*, ASA 11/02/88, London, 1988.
14. Helsinki Watch, 'Tears, Blood, and Cries', 1 December 1984, p. 23.
15. Afghan Information Centre *Monthly Bulletin*, October–November 1987, pp. 3–4.
16. Svetlana Aleksievich, *Zinky Boys: Soviet voices from the Afghanistan war*, Chatto and Windus, London, 1992, pp. 23, 45.
17. Aleksievich, *Zinky Boys*, pp. 171–172.
18. Aleksievich, *Zinky Boys*, pp. 171–172.
19. Bochorov, *Russian Roulette*, p. 80.
20. John Fullerton, 'The Soviet Occupation of Afghanistan', *Far Eastern Economic Review*, Hong Kong, 1983, quoted in Helsinki Watch and Asia Watch, *By All Parties to the Conflict: Violations of the laws of war in Afghanistan*, Helsinki Watch Committee, New York, 1987, p. 69.

21 Helsinki Watch, *By All Parties to the Conflict*, p. 66.
22 Reprinted in the *Washington Post*: James Rupert, 'Red star over Kabul', the *Washington Post*, 7 October 1990, <www.washingtonpost.com/archive/entertainment/books/1990/10/07/red-star-over-kabul/d0c7cb08-2153-4f52-82a9-57ff12527397/>.
23 Bochorov, *Russian Roulette*, p. 82.
24 'Afghanistan: Casting Shadows – War Crimes and Crimes Against Humanity, 1978–2001', Reliefweb website, 18 July 2005, <reliefweb.int/report/afghanistan/afghanistan-casting-shadows-war-crimes-and-crimes-against-humanity-1978-2001>.
25 Lester W Grau (ed.), *The Bear Went Over the Mountain: Soviet combat tactics in Afghanistan*, tenth anniversary edition, Foreign Military Studies Office, Fort Leavenworth, Kansas, 2010, p. 194.
26 Grau, *The Bear Went Over the Mountain*, p. 196.
27 Bochorov, *Russian Roulette*, p. 34.
28 Ernest Conine, 'Why no fury at Soviet atrocities in Afghanistan?', *Los Angeles Times*, 6 May 1985.
29 Quoted in Artyom Borovik, *Hidden War: A Russian journalist's account of the Soviet war in Afghanistan*, Grove Press, London, 2001, p. 51.
30 Quoted in Borovik, *Hidden War*, p. 55.
31 Borovik, *Hidden War*, p. 236.
32 Scott R McMichael, *Stumbling Bear: Soviet military performance in Afghanistan*, Brasseys, London, 1991, p. 125.
33 McMichael, *Stumbling Bear*, p. 125.

5   IMPLOSION OF A SOCIETY: TALIBAN EXTREMISM 1992–2001

1 Office of the United Nations Co-ordinator for Humanitarian and Economic Assistance Programmes relating to Afghanistan, *Operation Salam: 2nd consolidated report*, United Nations digital library, 1989, <digitallibrary.un.org/record/89148?ln=en>.
2 Barnett Rubin, 'The fragmentation of Afghanistan', *Foreign Affairs*, vol. 68, no. 5, 1989–90, p. 166.
3 Zoya with John Follain and Rita Cristofari, *Zoya's Story*, HarperCollins, New York, 2002, p. 63.
4 The massacre is described in detail in Humayun Sarabi, 'Politics and modern history of Hazaras', Masters thesis, Tufts University, 2005, <www.nps.edu/documents/105988371/107571254/Politics_and_Modern_History_of_Hazaras-Humayun_Sarabi.pdf/dcb1063e-ab40-41b2-ae66-547b8c3b6cbc>.
5 For an extensive treatment of the movement see Brannon D Ingram, *Revival from Below: The Deoband movement and global Islam*, University of California Press, San Francisco, 2018.
6 Ziya Us Salam and Mohammad Aslam Parvaiz, 'Madrasas in India', Firstpost, 13 December 2019, <www.firstpost.com/living/madrasas-in-india-how-1857-british-crackdown-on-muslims-led-to-founding-of-pioneering-darul-uloom-deoband-7769651.html>.
7 See MJ Gohari, *The Taliban: Ascent to power*, Oxford University Press, New York, 2000; and Amalendu Misra, 'The Taliban, radical Islam and Afghanistan', *Third World Quarterly*, vol. 23, no. 3, 2002, pp. 577–589, <library.fes.de/libalt/journals/swetsfulltext/13640302.pdf>.

8   Roland Jacquard, *In the Name of Osama Bin Laden: Global terrorism and the Bin Laden brotherhood*, Duke University Press, North Carolina, 2002, p. 41.
9   Phillip Corwin, *Doomed in Afghanistan: A UN officer's memoir of the fall of Kabul and Najibullah's failed escape*, Rutgers University Press, London, 1992, p. 110.
10 Michael Ignatieff, *The Warrior's Honor: Ethnic war and the modern conscience*, Vintage, London, 1999, pp. 141–142.
11 Ignatieff, *The Warrior's Honor*, p. 144.
12 Ijaz Ahmad Khan, 'Understanding Pakistan's Pro-Taliban Afghan Policy', *Pakistan Horizon*, vol. 60, no. 2, April 2007, pp. 141–157.
13 Najib Lafraie, 'Post-Soviet Pakistani interference in Afghanistan: How and why', Middle East Institute website, 18 April 2012, <www.mei.edu/publications/post-soviet-pakistani-interference-afghanistan-how-and-why> and 'Pakistan's support of the Taliban' authorship unattributed, 1 July 2001, <www.hrw.org/reports/2001/afghan2/Afghan0701-02.htm>.
14 Human Rights Watch (HRW), 'Afghanistan: The massacre in Mazar-i Sharif', HRW website, 1998, <www.hrw.org/legacy/reports98/afghan/Afrepor0.htm>.
15 William Maley, *The Afghan Wars*, third edition, Macmillan Educational, London, 2021, p. 193.
16 William Maley, 'Australia–Afghanistan relations: Reflections on a half-century', Australian Strategic Policy Institute, 2019, <s3-ap-southeast-2.amazonaws.com/ad-aspi/2019-09/Australia%20Afghanistan%20relations%20Reflections%20on%20a%20half%20century.pdf?J7zMdXZKTN44j_2wT9wWl9Eov1BZ4vep>.
17 Afghan Embassy, 'The Hon Sir John Kerr Governor-General of Australia Visits Afghanistan in 1975', Embassy of the Islamic Republic of Afghanistan website, 17 April 2019, <www.canberra.mfa.af/news/governor-general-sir-john-kerr-visits-afghanistan-in-1975.html>.
18 PM transcripts, 'Prime Minister interviewed on "Willesee at Seven" on situation in Afghanistan', Department of the Prime Minister and Cabinet website, 23 January 1980, <pmtranscripts.pmc.gov.au/release/transcript-5242>.
19 See Damien Murphy, 'Fraser defied as boycott cuts deep', NAA Cabinet papers release, 1 January 2011, <www.smh.com.au/national/fraser-defied-as-boycott-cuts-deep-20101231-19c1p.html> and Glenda Korporaal, 'Malcolm Fraser: Bitter memories of push to boycott 1980 Olympics', *Australian*, 20 March 2015, <www.theaustralian.com.au/sport/malcolm-fraser-bitter-memories-of-push-to-boycott-1980-olympics/news-story/434a496de9260c104920bb35ecaca218>.
20 Emma Rodgers, 'Documents reveal Australia's Cold War concerns', ABC News, 1 January 2011, <www.abc.net.au/news/2011-01-01/documents-reveal-australias-cold-war-concerns/1891300>.
21 PM transcripts, 'Afghanistan: The challenge and the lessons', Department of the Prime Minister and Cabinet website, 15 June 1980, <pmtranscripts.pmc.gov.au/release/transcript-5379>.
22 PM transcripts, 'Commonwealth Heads of Government Meeting, The Nassau Communique, October 1985, Commonwealth Secretariat, Cable Beach Hotel, Nassau, 22 October 1985', Department of the Prime Minister and Cabinet website, 22 October 1985, <pmtranscripts.pmc.gov.au/release/transcript-6767>.
23 PM transcripts, 'Speech by the Prime Minister of Australia the Hon. RJL Hawke, AC, MP Joint Meeting of the United States Congress Washington – 23 June 1988', Department of the Prime Minister and Cabinet website, 23 June 1988, <pmtranscripts.pmc.gov.au/release/transcript-7343>.

24 For a comprehensive account of this work see Marcus Fielding, *Dealing with a Deadly Legacy*, Echo Books, Canberra, 2020, <www.echobooks.com.au/wp-content/uploads/2020/06/Dealing-with-a-Deadly-Legacy_Sample.pdf> and the official history of peacekeeping, David Horner, 'Australia and the "New World Order"', Cambridge University Press, Melbourne, 2011, <assets.cambridge.org/9780521765879/frontmatter/9780521765879_frontmatter.pdf>.

25 William Maley, *Diplomacy, Communication, and Peace: Selected essays*, Routledge, London, 2020, p. 118.

26 Hansard, Parliament of Australia website, 28 June 1999, <parlinfo.aph.gov.au/parlInfo/search/display/display.w3p;query=Id:%22chamber/hansardr/1999-06-28/0118%22;src1=sm1>.

27 Hansard, Parliament of Australia website, 2 December 1997, <parlinfo.aph.gov.au/parlInfo/search/display/display.w3p;query=Id%3A%22chamber%2Fhansardr%2F1997-12-02%2F0001%22;src1=sm1>.

28 'Defence 2000: Our Future Defence Force (2000 Defence White Paper)', Parliament of Australia website, 2000, <www.aph.gov.au/About_Parliament/Parliamentary_Departments/Parliamentary_Library/pubs/rp/rp1516/DefendAust/2000>.

6 ADVENT OF AUSTRALIA'S SPECIAL FORCE 1957–2003

1 Ian McNeill, *The Team: Australian Army advisers in Vietnam 1962–1972*, Australian War Memorial, Canberra, 1984.

2 I am grateful to my UNSW colleagues Bob Hall and Andrew Ross for their generous assistance with data on 1 ATF disciplinary offences and engagements with Vietnamese civilians. At the time of writing, Andrew Ross was continuing to work on his forthcoming book: *The Forces of Disintegration and Cohesion in 1ATF in Vietnam*.

3 1st Australian Task Force Standing Operating Procedure for Operations in Vietnam, revised January 1971, pp. 2–7 (copy in the author's possession). 1ATF Standard Operating Procedure are also available at Australian Archives A6923, 8/05, Standing Operating Procedure – Vietnam. See the discussion in Robert Hall and Andrew Ross, 'Case Study: Confronting moral dilemmas in combat: Vietnam 1966–1971', Leadership and Ethics Papers (Australian Defence College), no. 1, 2010, p. 10.

4 The only recorded cases of 'mercy killing' in South Vietnam are described in Bob Buick and Gary McKay, *All Guts and No Glory: The story of a Long Tan warrior*, Allen & Unwin, Sydney, 2000, pp. 113–114.

5 Robert Hall, *Combat Battalion: The Eighth Battalion in Vietnam*, Allen & Unwin, Sydney, 2000, pp. 30–31.

6 Hall, *Combat Battalion*, pp. 199–200.

7 AWM95, item 2/6/10. PDF p. 44, Sitrep; Also AWM95, 7/12/5. PDF, 3SAS Squadron, October 1966 p. 64; and AWM95, item 7/6/9, PDF, p. 177. This incident is also discussed in Terry Burstall, *Vietnam: The Australian dilemma*, University of Queensland Press, Brisbane, 1993, p. 102.

8 AWM95, item 1/4/50, PDF, p. 143; AWM279, item 569?R4/62, AWM95, item 7/10/7, PDF 1 SAS, p. 94.

9 1976 Defence White Paper, Department of Defence website, 1976, <www.defence.gov.au/Publications/wpaper1976.pdf>.

10 1987 Defence White Paper, Department of Defence website, 1987, <www.defence.gov.au/Publications/wpaper1987.pdf>.

11 Hansard, *Defence – Outcome of the Board of Inquiry Into the Black Hawk Training Accident of 12 June 1996 – Black Hawk Board of Inquiry – Documents for Public Release*, Parliament of Australia website, 1996, <parlinfo.aph.gov.au/parlInfo/search/display/display.w3p;query=Id%3A%22publications%2Ftabledpapers%2FHS TP06420_1996-98%22;src1=sm1>.
12 See Tom Frame (ed.), *INTERFET: Lessons and legacies from East Timor 20 years on*, Connor Court, Brisbane, 2020.
13 See Keith Richburg, '2 dead, 2 hurt in East Timor ambush', *Washington Post*, 7 October 1999, <www.sun-sentinel.com/news/fl-xpm-1999-10-07-9910060992-story.html>; Keith Fennell, *Warrior Brothers: My life in the Australian SAS*, Bantam, Sydney, 2000; and Tom Frame (ed.), *INTERFET: Lessons and legacies from East Timor 20 years on*, Connor Court, Brisbane, 2000.
14 For a personal account see Keith Fennell, *Warrior Brothers: My life in the Australian SAS*, Bantam, Sydney, 2009.
15 Bob Breen, *Mission Accomplished, East Timor: The Australian Defence Force participation in the International Forces East Timor (INTERFET)*, Allen & Unwin, Sydney, 2000.
16 As reported by BBC News, 'Australia probes "Timor abuse"', 1 November 2000, <news.bbc.co.uk/2/hi/asia-pacific/1001393.stm>.
17 'Oz troops cast as bully boys', *News24*, 1 November 2000, <www.news24.com/News24/Oz-troops-cast-as-bully-boys-20001101>.
18 See Tom Frame, 'A certain political scandal' in Tom Frame (ed.), *Trials and Transformations, 2001–2004, The Howard Government Volume III*, UNSW Press, Sydney, 2019, chapter 8.
19 Rachel Baird, 'Coastal State Fisheries Management: A Review of Australian Enforcement Action in the Heard and McDonald Islands Australian Fishing Zone', *Deakin Law Review* 4; (2004) 9(1), <classic.austlii.edu.au/au/journals/DeakinLawRw/2004/4.html>.
20 A copy of the AFP's Case Note Entry Details can be found at <www.afp.gov.au/sites/default/files/PDF/Disclosure-Log/67-2022.pdf>.
21 Rafael Epstein, 'SAS war crime allegations', ABC Radio, 3 October 2002, <www.abc.net.au/am/stories/s692071.htm>.
22 Hansard, 'East Timor: War crimes investigation', Parliament of Australia website, 12 November 2002, <parlinfo.aph.gov.au/parlInfo/search/display/display.w3p;db=CHAMBER;id=chamber/hansards/2002-11-12/0021;query=Id:%22chamber/hansards/2002-11-12/0000%22>.
23 'SAS clear on charges of torture', the *Age*, 17 April 2003, <www.theage.com.au/national/sas-clear-on-charges-of-torture-20030417-gdvk09.html>.
24 'Officer's reputation at stake after "$2 million witch hunt"', the *Age*, 10 March 2003, <www.theage.com.au/national/officers-reputation-at-stake-after-2-million-witch-hunt-20030310-gdvcne.html>.
25 'SAS clear on charges of torture', the *Age*, 17 April 2003, <www.theage.com.au/national/sas-clear-on-charges-of-torture-20030417-gdvk09.html>.
26 'Former SAS soldier charged over East Timor incident', the *Age*, 22 February 2003, <www.theage.com.au/national/former-sas-soldier-charged-over-east-timor-incident-20030222-gdv9j4.html>.
27 Deborah Snow, 'Rough justice, buried truths', *SMH*, 7 June 2003, <www.smh.com.au/world/asia/rough-justice-buried-truths-20030607-gdgw1q.html>.

28 Deborah Snow, 'Body-booting SAS charge wilts as witnesses back off', *SMH*, 8 August 2003, <www.smh.com.au/world/asia/body-booting-sas-charge-wilts-as-witnesses-back-off-20030808-gdh89h.html>.
29 Hansard, 'SAS inquiry highly unsatisfactory', Senator Chris Evans media release, Parliament of Australia website, 8 August 2003, <parlinfo.aph.gov.au/parlInfo/search/display/display.w3p;query=Id%3A%22media%2Fpressrel%2FK83A6%22>.
30 'Army admits bungling Timor soldier investigation', *SMH*, 17 February 2004, <https://www.smh.com.au/national/army-admits-bungling-timor-soldier-investigation-20040217-gdidhx.html>.

7   EVOLUTION OF A COMMITMENT: THE TALIBAN REVIVAL 2001–2005

1 John Howard, 'A political perspective', in Tom Frame (ed.), *INTERFET: Lessons from East Timor 20 years on*, Connor Court, Brisbane, 2020, p. 17.
2 'Iraq tests no-fly zone', CNN, 4 January 1999, <edition.cnn.com/WORLD/meast/9901/04/iraq.no.fly/>.
3 Graeme Dobell, 'The alliance echoes and portents of Australia's longest war', *Australian Journal of International Affairs*, vol. 68, no. 4, 2014, p. 390.
4 Mark Fields and Ramsha Ahmed, *A Review of the 2001 Bonn Conference and application to the road ahead in Afghanistan*, Institute for National Strategic Studies, NDU Press, 2011, <ndupress.ndu.edu/Portals/68/Documents/stratperspective/inss/Strategic-Perspectives-8.pdf>.
5 The fullest account of Hamid Karzai's life is *A Kingdom of Their Own: The Karzai family and the Afghan disaster*, Alfred A Knopf, New York, 2016.
6 Afghanistan Agreements: A collection of official texts from 2001 to 2011, Civil-Military Fusion Centre, 2012, <reliefweb.int/sites/reliefweb.int/files/resources/CFC_Afghanistan_Agreements_June2012.pdf>.
7 PM Transcripts, 'Transcript of the Prime Minister the Hon John Howard MP press conference, Melbourne', Department of the Prime Minister and Cabinet website, 17 October 2001, <pmtranscripts.pmc.gov.au/release/transcript-11859>.
8 Claims that he lived for a time in Pakistan have been disputed. He died of natural causes in 2011.
9 John Kerry, 'Tora Bora revisited: How we failed to get Bin Laden and why it matters today', US Government Printing Office, 2009, <www.govinfo.gov/content/pkg/CPRT-111SPRT53709/html/CPRT-111SPRT53709.htm>.
10 Paul Hastert, 'Operation Anaconda: Perception meets reality in the hills of Afghanistan', *Studies in Conflict and Terrorism*, vol. 28, issue 1, 2005, pp. 11–20.
11 Lieutenant Commander Youssef H Aboul-Enein, USN, *Ayman Al-Zawahiri: The ideologue of modern Islamic militancy*, US Air Force Counterproliferation Center Future Warfare Series No. 21, March 2004, <media.defense.gov/2019/Apr/11/2002115486/-1/-1/0/21AYMANALZAWAHIRI.PDF>.
12 'In the line of duty', the *Age*, 2 June 2005, <www.theage.com.au/national/in-the-line-of-duty-20050602-ge09zv.html>.
13 'SAS reportedly killed innocent tribesmen', *SMH*, 1 June 2005, <www.smh.com.au/national/sas-reportedly-killed-innocent-tribesmen-20050601-gdlfiz.html>.
14 'In the line of duty', the *Age*, 2 June 2005, <www.theage.com.au/national/in-the-line-of-duty-20050602-ge09zv.html>.
15 Tom Iggulden, 'SAS soldier disciplined over Afghan action', *Lateline*, 1 June 2005, <www.abc.net.au/news/2005-05-31/sas-soldier-disciplined-over-afghan-action/1583190>.

16 Rory Callinan, 'In the valley of death', *Time*, 30 May 2005, <content.time.com/time/subscriber/article/0,33009,1067002,00.html>.
17 See the detailed report available at 'Review of Commonwealth agencies' relationship with the late Signaller Geffrey Gregg', Department of Veterans' Affairs, 25 October 2019, <www.dva.gov.au/documents-and-publications/review-commonwealth-agencies-relationship-late-signaller-geffrey-gregg>.
18 Stephanie Kennedy, 'PM rejects SAS cover-up claims', ABC News, 1 June 2005, <www.abc.net.au/news/2005-06-01/pm-rejects-sas-cover-up-claims/1583498>.
19 'PM backs SAS over "souveniring" incident', the *Age*, 1 June 2005, <www.theage.com.au/national/pm-backs-sas-over-souveniring-incident-20050601-ge09s8.html>.
20 Iggulden, 'SAS soldier disciplined over Afghan action'.
21 'In the line of duty', the *Age*, 2 June 2005, <www.theage.com.au/national/in-the-line-of-duty-20050602-ge09zv.html>.
22 The ADF official statement was also included in the *Age*'s story on 2 June 2005.
23 Sergeant Andrew Russell was killed when his unprotected patrol vehicle (which was unsuitable for the operating environment) struck a landmine in the Helmand Valley on 16 February 2002.
24 Hansard, 'Afghanistan: Death of Sergeant Andrew Russell', Parliament of Australia website, 18 February 2002, <parlinfo.aph.gov.au/parlInfo/search/display/display.w3p;query=Id%3A%22chamber%2Fhansardr%2F2002-02-18%2F0084%22;src1=sm1>.
25 'The sudden death of Sergeant Russell' the *Age*, 24 February 2002, <www.theage.com.au/national/the-sudden-death-of-sergeant-russell-20020224-gdtztr.html>.
26 Antonio Giustozzi, *The Taliban at War, 2001–2018*, Hurst, London, 2019, p. 6.
27 For more details on 'night letters' see TH Johnson, 'The Taliban insurgency and an analysis of Shabnamah (Night Letters)', *Small wars and insurgencies*, vol. 18, no. 3, 2007, pp. 317–344; and T Rid and M Hecker, *War 2.0: Irregular warfare in the information age*, Praeger, Santa Barbara, 2009, pp. 172–174.
28 *Afghanistan: Opium Survey 2004*, United Nations Office on Drugs and Crime, November 2004, <www.unodc.org/pdf/afg/afghanistan_opium_survey_2004.pdf>.
29 Mark Berniker, 'Afghanistan stands on brink of becoming "narco-state"', Eurasianet, 10 February 2004, <eurasianet.org/afghanistan-stands-on-brink-of-becoming-narco-state>.
30 'Hill sees no further Afghanistan deployment', ABC News, 1 April 2005, <www.abc.net.au/news/2005-04-01/hill-sees-no-further-afghanistan-deployment/1543676>.
31 Alexander Downer, *Meet the Press*, interview transcript, 18 November 2001.
32 See Ian Hancock, *John Gorton: He did it his way*, Hodder, Sydney, 2002, p. 102.
33 Hansard, 'Transcript of Press Conference with the Prime Minister: Parliament House, Canberra: Troop deployment to Afghanistan, Telstra, Rau family', Parliament of Australia website, 13 July 2005, <parlinfo.aph.gov.au/parlInfo/search/display/display.w3p;query=Id:%22media/pressrel/8QOG6%22>.

8 DRAFTING A STORY: SELLING THE AFGHAN WAR 2005–2013

1 Jeffrey Grey, *The Australian Army counterinsurgency and small wars reading guide*, Land Warfare Studies Centre, September 2009, <researchcentre.army.gov.au/sites/default/files/wp135-as_army_counterinsurgency_jeff_grey.pdf>.
2 David Fickling and agencies, 'Australia to send troops to Afghanistan', the *Guardian*, 14 July 2005, <www.theguardian.com/world/2005/jul/13/afghanistan.australia>.

3   Owen Harries, 'After Iraq', address to the Lowy Institute, <archive.lowyinstitute.org/publications/after-iraq>.
4   Confidential Liaison Office Report produced for the Netherlands, *A Survey of Uruzgan Province – July 2006*, copy held by author.
5   Susanne Schmeidl, *The Man Who Would Be King: The challenges to strengthening governance in Uruzgan*, The Liaison Office, November 2010, copy supplied to the author by Dr Schmeidl.
6   Dan Oakes, 'General defends Afghan warlord ties', *SMH*, 7 December 2010, <www.smh.com.au/national/general-defends-afghan-warlord-ties-20101206-18mum.html>.
7   See William Maley, 'Provincial Reconstruction Teams in Afghanistan – how they arrived and where they are going', NATO Review, 1 July 2007, <www.nato.int/docu/review/articles/2007/07/01/provincial-reconstruction-teams-in-afghanistan-how-they-arrived-and-where-they-are-going/index.html>; and 'Provincial Reconstruction Teams (PRTs): Overview', Institute for the Study of War, <www.understandingwar.org/provincial-reconstruction-teams-prts>.
8   John Howard, 'Australian Contribution to a Provincial Reconstruction Team in Afghanistan', PM Transcripts, Department of the Prime Minister and Cabinet website, 21 February 2002, <pmtranscripts.pmc.gov.au/release/transcript-22134>.
9   Hansard, 'Commander of Reconstruction Task Force to Afghanistan announced', Defence media release, Parliament of Australia website, 13 June 2006, <parlinfo.aph.gov.au/parlInfo/search/display/display.w3p;query=Id:%22media/pressrel/BT0X6%22>.
10 John Howard, 'Ministerial statement to Parliament on the Australian Defence Force Commitment to Afghanistan', Parliament of Australia website, 9 August 2006, <parlinfo.aph.gov.au/parlInfo/search/display/display.w3p;query=Id:%22media/pressrel/T6IK6%22>.
11 Hansard, 'More troops for Afghanistan', Parliament of Australia website, 10 April 2007, <parlinfo.aph.gov.au/parlInfo/search/display/display.w3p;query=Id:%22media/pressrel/YDQM6%22>.
12 Hansard: 'Ministerial statements: Afghanistan', Parliament of Australia website, 19 February 2008, <parlinfo.aph.gov.au/parlInfo/search/display/display.w3p;query=Id:%22chamber/hansardr/2008-02-19/0038%22>.
13 Fergus Hanson, 'The 2008 Lowy Institute Poll: Australia and the world', Lowy Institute website, 23 September 2008, <www.lowyinstitute.org/publications/2008-lowy-institute-poll-australia-and-world>.
14 Sophie McNeill, 'Diggers under fire', *Dateline*, SBS, no date, <www.sbs.com.au/news/sites/sbs.com.au.news/files/transcripts/381295_dateline_diggersunderfire_transcript.html>.
15 International Crisis Group, *The Insurgency in Afghanistan's Heartland*, Brussels, 2011, p. 23.
16 Tom Hyland, 'Army commander takes swipe at Afghan muddle', *SMH*, 23 October 2011, <www.smh.com.au/national/army-commander-takes-swipe-at-afghan-muddle-20111022-1mduk.html>.
17 Peter Connolly, 'Counterinsurgency in Uruzgan 2009', Australian Army Research Centre, 2009, <researchcentre.army.gov.au/library/land-warfare-studies-centre/counterinsurgency-uruzgan-2009>.
18 Jesse Lee, 'A new strategy for Afghanistan and Pakistan', blog, White House website, 27 March 2009, <obamawhitehouse.archives.gov/blog/2009/03/27/a-new-strategy-afghanistan-and-pakistan>.

19 Mark Landler, 'Obama says he will keep more troops in Afghanistan than planned', *New York Times*, 7 August 2007, <www.nytimes.com/2016/07/07/world/asia/obama-afghanistan-troops.html>.
20 Ran Yosef, 'Afghanistan, Tactical Directive on the Employment of Force', IHL in Action website, no date, <ihl-in-action.icrc.org/case-study/afghanistan-tactical-directive-employment-force>.
21 'Kabul Afghanistan', Headquarters International Security Assistance Force, 29 August 2009, <info.publicintelligence.net/ISAFpartnering.pdf>.
22 Matthew C Brand, *General McChrystal's Strategic Assessment*, Air Force Research Institute Papers, July 2011, <media.defense.gov/2017/Jun/19/2001765050/-1/-1/0/AP_BRAND_MCCHRYSTALS_ASSESSMENT.PDF>.
23 Jesse Lee, 'President Obama on Afghanistan, General McChrystal & General Petraeus', blog, White House website, 23 June 2010, <obamawhitehouse.archives.gov/blog/2010/06/23/president-obama-afghanistan-general-mcchrystal-general-petraeus>.
24 'Gen. Petraeus updates guidance on use of force', ISAF Public Affairs Office, 4 August 2010, <www.centcom.mil/MEDIA/NEWS-ARTICLES/News-Article-View/Article/884119/gen-petraeus-updates-guidance-on-use-of-force/>.
25 Julia Gillard, 'Australia will not abandon Afghanistan – Speech to the House of Representatives, Canberra', PM transcripts, Department of the Prime Minister and Cabinet website, 18 November 2011, <pmtranscripts.pmc.gov.au/release/transcript-17501>.
26 Adam Bandt, 'Ministerial statements', Parliament of Australia website, 20 October 2010, <parlinfo.aph.gov.au/parlInfo/search/display/display.w3p;db=CHAMBER;id=chamber%2Fhansardr%2F2010-10-20%2F0065;query=Id%3A%22chamber%2Fhansardr%2F2010-10-20%2F0106%22>.
27 Karen Middleton, *An Unwinnable War*, Melbourne University Press, Melbourne, 2011, p. 315.
28 'Australia to take control in Uruzgan', ABC News, 31 May 2012, <www.abc.net.au/news/2012-05-31/australia-to-take-control-in-uruzgan/4045016>.
29 Emma Griffiths, 'Main Australian base in Afghanistan to close', ABC News, 26 March 2013, <www.abc.net.au/news/2013-03-26/tarin-kot-base-to-close/4594404>.
30 Tony Abbott, 'Joint press conference, Sydney', PM Transcripts, Department of the Prime Minister and Cabinet website, 16 December 2013, <pmtranscripts.pmc.gov.au/release/transcript-23171>.
31 Tony Abbott, 'Joint press conference, Sydney'.
32 Sandy Milne, 'Bang for our buck? Afghanistan and ANZUS', Defence Connect website, 20 March 2020, <www.defenceconnect.com.au/key-enablers/5784-bang-for-our-buck-afghanistan-and-anzus>.

9 SEARCHING FOR SOLUTIONS: AUSTRALIA'S LONGEST WAR 2005–2013

1 Hansard, 'Transcript of Press Conference with the Prime Minister: Parliament House, Canberra: Troop deployment to Afghanistan, Telstra, Rau family', Parliament of Australia website, 13 July 2005, <parlinfo.aph.gov.au/parlInfo/search/display/display.w3p;query=Id:%22media/pressrel/8QOG6%22>.

2   K Gillespie (Vice Chief of the Defence Force) and R Moffitt (Deputy Chief of Joint Operations), 'Presentation to Defence Watch', speech, 16 September 2005; and Chris Masters, *No Front Line: Australia's Special Forces at war in Afghanistan*, Allen & Unwin, Sydney, 2017, p. 65.
3   'ADF – Command – Afghanistan', Nautilus Institute for Security and Sustainability website, 16 August 2010, <nautilus.org/publications/books/australian-forces-abroad/afghanistan/adf-command-afghanistan/>.
4   'National Command Element – Afghanistan', Nautilus Institute for Security and Sustainability website, 8 March 2010, <nautilus.org/publications/books/australian-forces-abroad/afghanistan/national-command-element-afghanistan/>.
5   For a general discussion of command and control arrangements see *Afghanistan: Lessons from Australia's Whole-of-Government Mission*, Australian Civil-Military Centre, Australian Government, November 2016, <acmc.gov.au/sites/default/files/2018-07/apo-nid71004-15836_0.pdf>.
6   IGADF Afghanistan Inquiry report, chapter 1.01.
7   This scheme did not apply to officer entrants.
8   The most vivid and engaging account of the civilian contribution to the Australian PRT effort is Fred Smith, *The Dust of Uruzgan*, Allen & Unwin, Sydney, 2016.
9   Theo Farrell, *Unwinnable: Britain's war in Afghanistan*, Bodley Head, London, 2017, pp. 156–160.
10 Chris Masters, *No Front Line: Australia's Special Forces at war in Afghanistan*, Allen & Unwin, Sydney, 2017, p. 120.
11 'Australian Defence Force Warfare Training Centre', Australian Defence College website, <www.defence.gov.au/adfwc/documents/doctrinelibrary/addp/addp06.4-lawofarmedconflict.pdf>.
12 *Law of Armed Conflict*, Defence Publishing Service, June 2006, <www.onlinelibrary.iihl.org/wp-content/uploads/2021/05/AUS-Manual-Law-of-Armed-Conflict.pdf>, p. 1–1.
13 *Law of Armed Conflict*, p. 1–1.
14 'Practice Relating to Rule 47. Attacks against Persons Hors de Combat', International Committee of the Red Cross website, no date, <ihl-databases.icrc.org/customary-ihl/eng/docs/v2_rul_rule47>.
15 The standard explanation is that 'divulgence of these details could lead to mission failure and/or place the lives of ADF personnel in danger unnecessarily': Commonwealth, *Parliamentary Debates*, House of Representatives, 9 August 2005, p. 177, De-Anne Kelly, Minister for Veterans' Affairs and Minister Assisting the Minister for Defence. See also Peter Rowe, 'The Rules of Engagement in Occupied Territory: Should They Be Published?', *Melbourne Journal of International Law*, vol. 8, no. 2, 2007, pp. 327, 330.
16 Jon Moran, 'Time to move out of the shadows? Special operations forces and accountability in counter-terrorism and counter-insurgency operations', *UNSW Law Journal*, vol. 39, no. 3, 2016, p. 1257.
17 There are definitions of spotters and squirters, and a discussion of when they could be engaged in the IGADF Afghanistan Inquiry report, pp. 271, 28–88, 295–297, 299, 331 and 454.
18 William Byrd and Christopher Ward, 'Drugs and development in Afghanistan', Social Development Papers: Conflict Prevention and Reconstruction, Paper No. 18, December 2004, <documents1.worldbank.org/curated/en/156391468740439773/pdf/30903.pdf>.

19 Department of Defence media release, 'Afghan and Australian troops seize insurgent poppy seed cache', 7 December 2011.
20 Tom Hyland, 'Our war rhetoric is deflated by an unlikely source', *SMH*, 31 May 2008, <www.smh.com.au/world/our-war-rhetoric-is-deflated-by-an-unlikely-source-20080531-2k7g.html>.
21 Jim Hammett: 'We were soldiers once: The decline of the Royal Australian Infantry Corps', *Defender*, Summer 2007/2008, <www.ada.asn.au/assets/files/Defender/Summer2007-08/SoldiersOnce.pdf>.
22 Anthony 'Harry' Moffitt, *Eleven Bats: A story of combat, cricket and the SAS*, Allen & Unwin, Sydney, 2020, p. 279.
23 Javid Ahmad, 'An analysis of "insider attacks" in Afghanistan: An MWI report', Modern War Institute website, 3 April 2017, <mwi.usma.edu/analysis-insider-attacks-afghanistan-mwi-report/>.
24 Nicole Brangwin, Marty Harris and David Watt, 'Australia at war in Afghanistan: revised facts and figures', Parliament of Australia website, 12 September 2012, <www.aph.gov.au/About_Parliament/Parliamentary_Departments/Parliamentary_Library/pubs/BN/2012-2013/AfghanistanFacts>.
25 Krystian Frącik, 'Insider attacks as one of the main threats to resolute support personnel in Afghanistan', *Security and Defence Quarterly*, vol. 12, iss. 3, pp. 3–18, 2016, <securityanddefence.pl/Insider-attacks-as-one-of-the-main-threats-to-resolute-support-personnel-in-Afghanistan,103234,0,2.html>.
26 'Number of fatalities among Western coalition soldiers involved in the execution of Operation Enduring Freedom from 2001 to 2021', Statista website, October 2021, <www.statista.com/statistics/262894/western-coalition-soldiers-killed-in-afghanistan/>.
27 'Afghan Jirga Ends With Reported Agreement On U.S. Presence, Peace Talks', Radio Free Europe/Radio Liberty website, 19 November 2011, <www.rferl.org/a/afghan_jirga_expected_to_go_into_fourth_day/24395717.html>.
28 Brangwin, Harris and Watt, 'Australia at war in Afghanistan'.

10 RUMOUR AND REFORM: THE CROMPVOETS AND IRVINE REPORTS 2014–2018

1 AAP, 'Afghanistan veterans to be welcomed home', Nine News, 21 March 2015, <www.9news.com.au/national/afghan-veterans-to-be-welcomed-home/b55f592c-3fa2-475b-80cd-0705cf197b35>.
2 Matthew Raggatt, 'Canberra welcomes home Afghanistan veterans', *Canberra Times*, 13 October 2017, <www.canberratimes.com.au/story/6070370/canberra-welcomes-home-afghanistan-veterans/>.
3 'Operation Slipper: Parades marking end of military operation in Afghanistan held across Australia', ABC News, 23 March 2015, <www.abc.net.au/news/2015-03-21/operation-slipper-parades-welcome-home-soldiers-from-afghanistan/6337526?nw=0>.
4 'Operation Slipper', ABC News.
5 A summary of these claims, where they were reported and subsequent official statements can be found at Karen Elphick, 'Reports, allegations and inquiries into serious misconduct by Australian troops in Afghanistan 2005–2013', Parliament of Australia website, 9 November 2020, <www.aph.gov.au/About_Parliament/Parliamentary_Departments/Parliamentary_Library/pubs/rp/rp2021/Chronologies/AllegationsAfghanistan>.

6   Nick McKenzie and Ash Sweeting, 'Military in Afghan cover-up', *SMH*, 11 May 2009, <www.smh.com.au/national/military-in-afghan-coverup-20090510-az9p.html>.
7   Colonel P Short, *Inquiry Officer's report into collateral damage and allegations of mistreatment of a local national by the [redacted] in Uruzgan Province, Afghanistan on 23 Nov 07*, ADF, DoD, 21 December 2007, which is summarised in Karen Elphick, 'Reports, allegations and inquiries into serious misconduct by Australian troops in Afghanistan 2005–2013', Parliament of Australia website, 9 November 2020, <www.aph.gov.au/About_Parliament/Parliamentary_Departments/Parliamentary_Library/pubs/rp/rp2021/Chronologies/AllegationsAfghanistan>.
8   A summary of each of these incidents is set out in Elphick, 2020.
9   *Four Corners* team, 'In their sights', ABC News, 1 September 2011, <www.abc.net.au/4corners/in-their-sights/2873730>.
10 Defence statement to ABC *Four Corners* program 'In Their Sights', 5 September 2011, Department of Defence website, 6 September 2011, <news.defence.gov.au/media/on-the-record/defence-statement-abc-four-corners-program-their-sights-5-september-2011>.
11 Defence statement to ABC *Four Corners* program 'In Their Sights', 5 September 2011.
12 Defence statement to ABC *Four Corners* program 'In Their Sights', 5 September 2011.
13 Defence statement to ABC *Four Corners* program 'In Their Sights', 5 September 2011.
14 Defence statement to ABC *Four Corners* program 'In Their Sights', 5 September 2011.
15 These statements and claims were reported in a study entitled 'SOCOMD: Culture and Interactions – Insights and reflection', compiled by Samantha Crompvoets, January 2016, and available at <afghanistaninquiry.defence.gov.au/sites/default/files/2020-11/SOCOMD-Culture-and-Interactions-Insights-and-Reflection-Jan-16_0.pdf>.
16 Mark Willacy, 'The inquiry into Australian soldiers in Afghanistan is finally over. The reckoning is about to begin', ABC News, 18 November 2020, <www.abc.net.au/news/2020-11-18/igadf-inquiry-into-special-forces-in-afghanistan-is-over/12816626>.
17 In 2016 the author was given a series of documents by SOCAUST as part of an incoming brief for members of a commander's ethics advisory panel he intended to establish. This document and others were part of that briefing pack. Some of this material was made public with the release of the IGADF Afghanistan Inquiry report in November 2020.
18 Major General Jeff Sengelman, 'SOCOMD Governance Remediation – 2–15', SOCAUST memorandum AM2324225, dated October 2015. The full text is available at <afghanistaninquiry.defence.gov.au/sites/default/files/2020-11/Special-Operations-Command-Governance-Remediation-Oct-15.pdf>.
19 Samantha Crompvoets, *Special Operations Command (SOCOMD): Culture and Interaction: Insights and Reflections*, January 2016, <afghanistaninquiry.defence.gov.au/sites/default/files/2020-11/SOCOMD-Culture-and-Interactions-Insights-and-Reflection-Jan-16_0.pdf>.
20 Samantha Crompvoets, *Special Operations Command (SOCOMD) Culture and Interactions: perceptions, reputation and risk*, February 2016, hereafter *Crompvoets*

Report, <afghanistaninquiry.defence.gov.au/sites/default/files/2020-11/SOCOMD-Culture-and-Interactions-Perceptions-Reputation-and-Risk-Feb-16.pdf>.
21   All of the material provided to me in 2016 is now available under the 'Resources' tab at the IGADF Afghanistan Inquiry website: <afghanistaninquiry.defence.gov.au>.
22   *Crompvoets Report*, February 2016, p. 38.
23   *Crompvoets Report*, February 2016, pp. 3–4.
24   *Crompvoets Report*, February 2016, p. 20.
25   *Crompvoets Report*, February 2016, p. 20.
26   *Crompvoets Report*, February 2016, p. 21.
27   *Crompvoets Report*, February 2016, p. 22.
28   *Crompvoets Report*, February 2016, p. 27.
29   *Crompvoets Report*, February 2016, p. 32.
30   Andrew Tillett, 'Meet the "feminist civilian" sociologist who got SAS soldiers to talk', *Australian Financial Review*, 11 December 2020, <www.afr.com/politics/federal/meet-the-feminist-civilian-sociologist-who-got-sas-soldiers-to-talk-20201207-p56l5r>.
31   The story was still being reported as a truth in mid-2021. See Ben Doherty, 'How the "good war" went bad: elite soldiers from Australia, UK and US face a reckoning', the *Guardian*, 2 June 2021, <www.theguardian.com/australia-news/2021/jun/02/how-the-good-war-went-bad-elite-soldiers-from-australia-uk-and-us-face-a-reckoning>.
32   'Notice of possibly serious unacceptable behaviour within SOCOMD', Special Operations Command, Department of Defence, 9 March 2016, <afghanistaninquiry.defence.gov.au/sites/default/files/2020-11/Minute-SOCAUST-to-CA-9-Mar-16.pdf>.
33   'Referral of serious concerns regarding Special Operations Command', Office of the Chief of Army, 30 March 2016, <afghanistaninquiry.defence.gov.au/sites/default/files/2020-11/MINUTE-Referral-CA-to-IGADF-30-Mar-16.pdf>.
34   A copy of the Inquiry report is available at 'IGADF – Annual Reports presented to Parliament', Department of Defence, Australian Government website, no date, <defence.gov.au/mjs/reports.asp>.
35   'Inspector-General of the Australian Defence Force', Department of Defence website, no date, <www.defence.gov.au/mjs/igadf.asp>.
36   David Wroe and Rory Callinan, 'Australia's elite special forces being investigated over disturbing stories of conduct and culture', *SMH*, 17 April 2016, <https://www.smh.com.au/politics/federal/australias-elite-special-forces-being-investigated-over-disturbing-stories-of-conduct-and-culture-20160416-go7wuh.html>.
37   'Support for the International Criminal Court', Attorney-General's Department website, <www.ag.gov.au/international-relations/international-law/support-international-criminal-court>.
38   David Irvine, *Review of Special Operations Command, Australian Army*, 31 August 2018, hereafter 'Irvine Report', <afghanistaninquiry.defence.gov.au/sites/default/files/2020-11/Irvine-Report-2018-Review-of-SOCOMD-Australian-Army.pdf>.
39   Nick McKenzie and Chris Masters, 'Former spy chief heads new Defence inquiry into "war crimes"', *SMH*, 10 June 2018, <www.smh.com.au/politics/federal/former-spy-chief-heads-new-defence-inquiry-into-war-crimes-20180610-p4zkmx.html>.
40   David Irvine, *Review of Special Operations Command, Australian Army*, 15 June 2020, hereafter 'Irvine Report', <afghanistaninquiry.defence.gov.au/sites/default/files/2020-11/Irvine-Report-2020-Review-of-SOCOMD-Australian-Army.pdf>.
41   *Irvine Report*, August 2018, p. 13.
42   *Irvine Report*, August 2018, p. 14.

43   *Irvine Report*, August 2018, p. 31.
44   *Irvine Report*, August 2018, p. 33.
45   *Irvine Report*, August 2018, p. 49.
46   *Irvine Report*, August 2018, p. 51.
47   *Irvine Report*, August 2018, p. 68.
48   *Irvine Report*, June 2020, p. 35.
49   *Irvine Report*, June 2020, p. 35.

11   REVELATIONS AND ALLEGATIONS: MEDIA REPORTING 2016–2020

1   For the full text of the article see: Harold D Lasswell, 'The structure and function of communication in society', originally published in Lyman Bryson (ed.), *The Communication of Ideas*, The Institute for Religious and Social Studies, New York, 1948, <sipa.jlu.edu.cn/__local/E/39/71/4CE63D3C04A10B5795F0108EBE6_A7BC17AA_34AAE.pdf>.
2   A website maintained by the 'Boot Camp Military Fitness Institute' refers to Australia's 'Elite & Special Forces': <bootcampmilitaryfitnessinstitute.com/elite-special-forces/australian-elite-special-forces/>.
3   Ian McPhedran, *The Amazing SAS: The inside story of Australia's Special Forces*, HarperCollins, Sydney, 2007.
4   Robert Macklin, *Warrior Elite: Australia's Special Forces Z Force to the SAS intelligence operations to cyber warfare*, Hachette, Sydney, 2015.
5   Andrew Greene, 'Australian commando claims he covered up POW's execution; Supreme Court judge joins secretive Defence probe', ABC News, 13 October 2016, <www.abc.net.au/news/2016-10-13/supreme-court-judge-examining-special-forces-conduct-afghanistan/7927420>.
6   Anonymous, 'Australian special forces veteran breaks silence on "insidious, infectious" culture', ABC News, 10 July 2017, <www.abc.net.au/news/2017-07-10/australian-special-forces-veteran-breaks-silence/8453728?nw=0>.
7   McBride was later committed to stand trial in the ACT Supreme Court for the theft of Commonwealth documents. The documents were offered to at least another two journalists who separately declined to receive the material.
8   David Wroe, '"What I've done makes sense to me": The complicated, colourful life of David McBride', *SMH*, 23 June 2019, <www.smh.com.au/politics/federal/what-i-ve-done-makes-sense-to-me-the-complicated-colourful-life-of-david-mcbride-20190621-p5204h.html>.
9   Wroe, 2019.
10 Dan Oakes and Sam Clark, 'The Afghan Files', ABC News, 11 July 2017, <www.abc.net.au/news/2017-07-11/killings-of-unarmed-afghans-by-australian-special-forces/8466642?nw=0>.
11 Karen Elphick, 'Reports, allegations and inquiries into serious misconduct by Australian troops in Afghanistan 2005–2013', Parliament of Australia website, 9 November 2020, <www.aph.gov.au/About_Parliament/Parliamentary_Departments/Parliamentary_Library/pubs/rp/rp2021/Chronologies/AllegationsAfghanistan>.
12 A story posted by journalist Chris Uhlmann on 21 April 2014 based on documents leaked by McBride and a report by the Inspector General of Intelligence and Security into the matter is available at Chris Uhlmann, 'Special forces soldier pulled handgun on Australian spy during drinking session in Afghanistan', ABC News, 21 October

2014, <www.abc.net.au/news/2014-10-21/soldier-pulled-gun-on-spy-while-drinking-in-afghanistan/5828160?nw=0&r=HtmlFragment>. There are additional details at Dan Oakes and Sam Clark, 'The spy and the SAS soldier with a loaded Glock', ABC News, 11 July 2017, <www.abc.net.au/news/2017-07-11/the-spy-and-the-sas-solider-with-a-loaded-glock/8496608?nw=0&r=HtmlFragment>.

13 For further discussion, see also: Karen Elphick, 'Reports, allegations and inquiries into serious misconduct by Australian troops in Afghanistan 2005–2013', Parliament of Australia website, 9 November 2020, <www.aph.gov.au/About_Parliament/Parliamentary_Departments/Parliamentary_Library/pubs/rp/rp2021/Chronologies/AllegationsAfghanistan>.

14 Chris Uhlmann, 'Special forces soldier pulled handgun on Australian spy during drinking session in Afghanistan', ABC News, 21 October 2014, <www.abc.net.au/news/2014-10-21/soldier-pulled-gun-on-spy-while-drinking-in-afghanistan/5828160?nw=0>.

15 Nick Butterly, 'Afghanistan SAS gun-threat case resolved by Defence Department', *West Australian*, 22 September 2016, <thewest.com.au/news/australia/afghanistan-sas-gun-threat-case-resolved-by-defence-department-ng-ya-118872>.

16 David Chen, 'Chief of Army bans soldiers from wearing "arrogant" death symbols', ABC News, 19 April 2018, <www.abc.net.au/news/2018-04-19/army-bans-troops-from-wearing-skulls-death-symbols/9673242>.

17 'Chief of Army (new CDF) bans "death symbology and iconography"', Contact website, 19 April 2018, <www.contactairlandandsea.com/2018/04/19/chief-of-army-new-cdf-bans-death-symbology-and-iconography/>.

18 Chen, 'Chief of Army bans soldiers from wearing "arrogant" death symbols'.

19 Chief of Army minute OCA/OUT/2018/R33922870 dated 10 April 2018. It was distributed to the Army's senior leadership team.

20 Justin Huggett, 'Open letter to Chief of Army re death symbology ban', Contact website, 19 April 2018, <www.contactairlandandsea.com/2018/04/19/an-open-letter-to-lieutenant-general-angus-campbell/>.

21 C August Elliott, 'Death symbol ban isn't about political correctness: it's the difference between an army and a "death cult"', ABC News, 28 April 2018, <www.abc.net.au/news/2018-04-28/death-symbol-ban-not-political-correctness/9696674>.

22 Dan Oakes, 'Australian soldiers flew Nazi swastika flag from vehicle in Afghanistan; PM says diggers' actions "absolutely wrong"', ABC News, 14 June 2018, <www.abc.net.au/news/2018-06-14/photo-shows-nazi-flag-flown-over-australian-army-vehicle/9859618>.

23 Oakes, 'Australian soldiers flew Nazi swastika flag from vehicle in Afghanistan'.

24 Quoted in Oakes, 'Australian soldiers flew Nazi swastika flag from vehicle in Afghanistan'.

25 Oakes, 'Australian soldiers flew Nazi swastika flag from vehicle in Afghanistan'.

26 Naaman Zhou, 'Nazi flag on Australian army vehicle "utterly unacceptable", Turnbull says', the *Guardian*, 14 June 2018, <www.theguardian.com/australia-news/2018/jun/14/nazi-flag-on-army-vehicle-utterly-unacceptable-turnbull-says>.

27 Simone Fox Koob, 'Ben Roberts-Smith files defamation proceedings against Fairfax', *SMH*, 17 August 2018, <www.smh.com.au/national/ben-roberts-smith-files-defamation-proceedings-against-fairfax-20180817-p4zy5a.html>.

28 Nick McKenzie, David Wroe and Chris Masters, 'Beneath the bravery of our most decorated soldier', *SMH*, 10 August 2018, <www.smh.com.au/politics/federal/beneath-the-bravery-of-our-most-decorated-soldier-20180801-p4zuwp.html>.

29 'Stop the witch hunt. Support the SASR and Ben Roberts-Smith', Change.org petition, no date, <www.change.org/p/scott-morrison-stop-the-witch-hunt-support-the-sasr-and-ben-roberts-smith>.
30 Nicole Douglas and Josh Hanrahan, 'Embattled war hero Ben Roberts-Smith, 42, debuts new girlfriend, 28', *Daily Mail*, 16 January 2021, <www.dailymail.co.uk/tvshowbiz/article-9154101/Ben-Roberts-Smith-42-debuts-new-girlfriend-28-Magic-Millions-Race-Day.html>.
31 Max Mason, 'Brendan Nelson "cautioned" over association with Ben Roberts-Smith', *Australian Financial Review*, 28 June 2021, <www.afr.com/companies/media-and-marketing/brendan-nelson-cautioned-over-association-with-ben-roberts-smith-20210628-p584te>.
32 Andrew Greene, 'War Memorial boss Brendan Nelson wants speedy end to "protracted" probe into diggers in Afghanistan', ABC News, 2 November 2017, <www.abc.net.au/news/2017-11-02/afghanistan-special-forces-war-memorial-boss-blasts-inquiry/9110170>.
33 Bevan Shields, 'Call to speed up Ben Roberts-Smith probe condemned as "highly inappropriate"', *SMH*, 1 November 2018, <www.smh.com.au/politics/federal/call-to-speed-up-ben-robert-smith-probe-condemned-as-highly-inappropriate-20181101-p50dhk.html>.
34 Mark Willacy, 'Killing Field', *Four Corners*, ABC, 16 March 2020, <www.abc.net.au/4corners/killing-field/12060538>.
35 Mark Willacy, 'The inquiry into Australian soldiers in Afghanistan is finally over. The reckoning is about to begin', ABC News, 18 November 2020, <www.abc.net.au/news/2020-11-18/igadf-inquiry-into-special-forces-in-afghanistan-is-over/12816626>.
36 Nick McKenzie and Chris Masters, '"Rotten. Shameful": Surely no one can now ignore the abuses of the SAS', the *Age*, 17 March 2020, <www.theage.com.au/national/rotten-shameful-surely-no-one-can-now-ignore-the-abuses-of-the-sas-20200317-p54awg.html>.
37 Australia: Hold Special Forces to Account, Human Rights Watch website, 23 March 2020, <www.hrw.org/news/2020/03/23/australia-hold-special-forces-account>.
38 Mark Willacy, *Rogue Forces: An explosive insiders' account of Australian SAS war crimes in Afghanistan*, Simon & Schuster, Sydney, 2021.
39 Nick McKenzie, 'One last mission', *SMH (Good Weekend)*, 27 June 2020, <www.smh.com.au/interactive/2020/one-last-mission/>.
40 Nick McKenzie and Chris Masters, 'Investigation puts a name to the man whose death traumatised SAS medic Dusty Miller', the *Age*, 7 November 2019, <www.theage.com.au/national/investigation-puts-a-name-to-the-man-whose-death-traumatised-sas-medic-dusty-miller-20191107-p538a8.html>.
41 Mark Willacy and Alexandra Blucher, 'Witnesses say Australian SAS soldiers were involved in mass shooting of unarmed Afghan civilians', ABC News, 14 July 2020, <www.abc.net.au/news/2020-07-14/australian-special-forces-killed-unarmed-civilians-in-kandahar/12441974>.
42 Mark Willacy and Rory Callinan, 'The same AK-47 was photographed on two dead Afghan civilians killed by Australian soldiers', ABC News, 15 July 2020, <www.abc.net.au/news/2020-07-15/sas-soldiers-allegedly-plant-gun-on-dead-bodies-in-afghanistan/12452964>.
43 Willacy and Callinan, 'The same AK-47 was photographed on two dead Afghan civilians killed by Australian soldiers'.

44 Mark Willacy and Rory Callinan, 'The mistaken identity that led to Australian soldiers allegedly killing the wrong man', ABC News, 21 July 2020, <www.abc.net.au/news/2020-07-21/australian-sas-soldiers-killed-the-wrong-afghan-man/12472478>.
45 Willacy and Callinan, 'The mistaken identity that led to Australian soldiers allegedly killing the wrong man'.
46 Mark Willacy and Alexandra Blucher, 'Australian special forces shown posing with "Southern Pride" Confederate flag in Afghanistan', ABC News, 22 July 2020, <www.abc.net.au/news/2020-07-22/australian-soldiers-signal-with-confederate-flag-in-afghanistan/12476530>.
47 Jade Gailberger, 'Morrison lobbies Trump to keep killer Afghan sergeant behind bars', News.com.au, 10 August 2020, <www.news.com.au/national/politics/australia-lobbies-for-afghan-sergeant-to-be-kept-behind-bars/news-story/29e3509f36ab4675c9275014ab98c422>.
48 Anthony Galloway, 'Rogue Afghan soldier who killed Diggers set to be released', *SMH*, 10 August 2020, <www.smh.com.au/politics/federal/rogue-afghan-soldier-who-killed-diggers-set-to-be-released-20200810-p55ka6.html>.
49 Dan Oakes and Jeremy Story Carter, 'Australian special forces Instagram account mocks war crime allegations, calls to "Make Diggers Violent Again"', ABC News, 3 September 2020, <www.abc.net.au/news/2020-09-03/instagram-account-from-australian-special-forces-mocks-killings/12595062>.
50 Mark Wales, 'Unfocused, not fully committed, disjointed – our Afghanistan mission was always doomed', *Australian*, 7 September 2020 , <https://www.theaustralian.com.au/commentary/unfocused-not-fully-committed-disjointed-our-afghanistan-mission-was-always-doomed/news-story/18f1f0582fd95cbec59172d88018b888>.
51 Jack Waterford, 'Time to admit defeat in Afghanistan war', *Canberra Times*, 19 September 2020, pp. 26–27.
52 Nick McKenzie and Chris Masters, 'Covert war crimes inquiry compromised by former AFP chief Mick Keelty', 16 August 2020, <www.theage.com.au/national/covert-war-crimes-inquiry-compromised-by-former-afp-chief-mick-keelty-20200812-p55kzj.html>.
53 John Bale, 'Afghan message may hurt but we need to hear it', *Australian*, 22 August 2020, <www.theaustralian.com.au/inquirer/afghanistan-message-may-hurt-but-we-need-to-hear-it/news-story/971715e2224770b879e2dda3d3dc46d5>.
54 Ben Packham, 'Immunity could threaten war crimes trials', *Australian*, 25 September 2020, p. 3.
55 Nick McKenzie and Chris Masters, 'A warrior culture and the murders that followed; what went wrong with the SAS', *SMH*, 25 September 2020.
56 Brendan Nicholson, 'Army sharpens focus on ethical soldiering ahead of war crimes amid Afghan probe', *Weekend Australian*, 3–4 October 2020, p. 16.
57 Kellie Tranter, 'Different country, different rules', Pearls and Irritations website, <johnmenadue.com/kellie-tranter-different-country-different-rules/>.
58 Michael McKinley, 'A possible deep-seated flaw in the ADF's third inquiry into allegations of misconduct and war crimes', Pearls and Irritations website, <johnmenadue.com/michael-mckinley-a-possible-deep-seated-flaw-in-the-adfs-third-inquiry-into-allegations-of-misconduct-and-war-crimes/#disqus_thread>.
59 Christopher Elliott, 'The reputation of Australia's special forces is beyond repair', the *Conversation*, 30 October 2020, <https://theconversation.com/the-

reputation-of-australias-special-forces-is-beyond-repair-its-time-for-them-to-be-disbanded-148795>.
60 Greg Lockhart, 'PR spin on our alleged war crimes and "rogue SAS squad" in Afghanistan', Pearls and Irritations website, 14 October 2020, <johnmenadue.com/pr-spin-on-our-alleged-war-crimes-and-rogue-sas-squad-in-afghanistan/>.
61 'Soldier with PTSD "killed so many people"', *Canberra Times*, 20 October 2020, <www.canberratimes.com.au/story/6975852/soldier-with-ptsd-killed-so-many-people/>.
62 Mark Willacy, Alexandra Blucher and Dan Oakes, 'US marine says Australian special forces soldiers made "deliberate decision to break the rules of war"', ABC News, 21 October 2020, <www.abc.net.au/news/2020-10-21/soldiers-killed-man-who-could-not-fit-on-aircraft-says-us-marine/12782756>.
63 Giovanni Torre, 'Australian soldiers killed Afghan prisoner as only six could fit on American helicopter, US marine claims', *Daily Telegraph* (UK), 21 October 2020, <www.telegraph.co.uk/news/2020/10/21/australian-soldiers-killed-afghan-prisoner-six-could-fit-american/>.
64 'Ex-special forces commando hits back at "outrageous and false" allegations his platoon murdered an Afghan prisoner because there wasn't enough room on a helicopter', Now My News website, 28 October 2020, <nowmynews.blogspot.com/2020/10/ex-special-forces-commando-hits-back-at.html>.
65 Sally Jackson, 'Response to today's story by Jonathon Moran in News Corporation titles' ABC, 28 October 2020, <about.abc.net.au/correcting-the-record/response-to-jonathon-moran-and-news-corporation/>.
66 For the full text see: November Platoon, 2012, 'Letter to the ABC', Veteran Support Force website, <vsf.org.au/abc>.

12 MEDIA AND MISINFORMATION: THE NEW ZEALAND EXPERIENCE

1 Paul Little, *Willie Apiata VC: The reluctant hero*, Viking, Auckland, 2008.
2 Phil Goff, 'NZ's role in peacekeeping and in Afghanistan', Beehive.govt.nz website, 11 November 2005, <www.beehive.govt.nz/speech/nzs-role-peacekeeping-and-afghanistan>.
3 Jon Stephenson, 'Kiwi troops in "war crimes" row', Stuff website, 8 August 2009, <www.stuff.co.nz/national/2712026/Kiwi-troops-in-war-crimes-row>.
4 This episode was based on first-hand knowledge provided to Jon Stephenson by NZSAS personnel. See Jon Stephenson 'The price of the club: how New Zealand's involvement in the "War on Terror" has compromised its reputation as a good international citizen', p. 263.
5 John Key, 'Afghanistan review decisions announced', Beehive.govt.nz website, 11 August 2009, <www.beehive.govt.nz/release/afghanistan-review-decisions-announced>.
6 Samantha Morris, 'The contested space of post-conflict development: Reflections of New Zealand Defence Force personnel on working at the nexus of security and development in Afghanistan', Masters thesis, Victoria University of Wellington, March 2015, <core.ac.uk/download/pdf/41340382.pdf>.
7 'Death of Lieutenant Tim O'Donnell', Office of the Governor-General website, 4 August 2010, <gg.govt.nz/news/death-lieutenant-tim-o'donnell>.
8 Much of the detail below comes from a personal conversation with Dr Mapp on 15 October 2020.

9   Selwyn Manning, 'MTV Native Affairs Investigation collateral damage – independent inquiry must be initiated', the Daily Blog website, 1 July 2014, <thedailyblog.co.nz/2014/07/01/mtv-native-affairs-investigation-collateral-damage-independent-inquiry-must-be-initiated/>.
10 *The Valley: A Stuff Circuit documentary series*, <interactives.stuff.co.nz/the-valley/>.
11 Eugene Bingham, Paula Penfold and Toby Longbottom, 'The Valley: Defence Force responds to Afghanistan investigation', Stuff website, 1 September 2017, <www.stuff.co.nz/national/96425527/the-valley-defence-force-responds-to-afghanistan-investigation>.
12 Nicky Hager and Jon Stephenson, *Hit & Run: The New Zealand SAS in Afghanistan and the meaning of honour*, Potton & Burton, Auckland, 2017.
13 David Fisher, 'NZ Defence Force claims 105 errors in *Hit & Run* including false report of Taliban leader's death', *New Zealand Herald*, 21 November 2018, <www.nzherald.co.nz/nz/nz-defence-force-claims-105-errors-in-hit-run-including-false-report-of-taliban-leaders-death/FF4AICNDC36TAFFRFELILS3HXQ/>.
14 Charlotte Greenfield, 'New Zealand launches inquiry into 2010 military raid in Afghanistan over reports of civilian casualties', Reuters, 11 April 2018, <www.reuters.com/article/us-newzealand-afghanistan-idUSKBN1HI0M4>.
15 Jonathan Mitchell, 'Operation Burnham inquiry: Misleading statements and briefings come to light', RNZ website, 16 September 2019, <www.rnz.co.nz/news/national/398902/operation-burnham-inquiry-misleading-statements-and-briefings-come-to-light>.
16 Home page, Inquiry into Operation Burnham website, <operationburnham.inquiry.govt.nz>.
17 *Report of the Government Inquiry into Operation Burnham*, Inquiry into Operation Burnham website, July 2020, <operationburnham.inquiry.govt.nz/inquiry-report/>.
18 Bronson Perich, 'Ron Mark backs NZDF after Operation Burnham report', Te Ao Māori News website, 31 July 2020, <www.teaomaori.news/ron-mark-backs-nzdf-after-operation-burnham-report>.
19 *Report of the Government Inquiry into Operation Burnham*, p. 170.
20 *Report of the Government Inquiry into Operation Burnham*, p. 284.
21 *Report of the Government Inquiry into Operation Burnham*, pp. 379–380.
22 'Report of the inquiry into Operation Burnham released', New Zealand Defence Force website, 31 July 2020, <nzdefenceforce.medium.com/report-of-the-inquiry-into-operation-burnham-released-d8ad9e203f51>.
23 'Operation Burnham', *Otago Daily Times*, 3 August 2020, <www.odt.co.nz/opinion/editorial/operation-burnham>.
24 *Inquiries Act 2013*, Parliamentary Counsel Office, New Zealand Legislation website, 26 August 2013, <www.legislation.govt.nz/act/public/2013/0060/48.0/DLM1566106.html>.
25 'Court of Inquiry assembled by Major General A.D. Gawn, MBE, Commander Joint Forces New Zealand into the circumstances in which elements of TU 653.1.1 (OP CRIB) came into contact with insurgents in the vicinity of DO ABE, Bamyan province, Afghanistan, while providing in extremis support to the NDS on 4 August 2012 and the circumstances in which the remains of three soldiers were returned to New Zealand following a separate IED attack on 19 August 2012', <web.archive.org/web/20150123011224/http://nzdf.mil.nz/downloads/pdf/public-docs/2013/coi-report_baghak_redact_reopen_final.pdf>.

26 A copy of the full report can be viewed at David Fisher, 'Our faulty war: the Afghanistan report they fought to keep secret', *New Zealand Herald*, 27 March 2017, <www.nzherald.co.nz/nz/our-faulty-war-the-afghanistan-report-they-fought-to-keep-secret/KASEQM27OIATWFRQ3VRVR2Q47Q/>.

13 HISTORICAL LEGACIES AND PUBLIC OPINION: THE UNITED KINGDOM EXPERIENCE

1 The 22nd Special Air Service Regiment (22 SAS) is a Regular Army unit while the 21st and 23rd Special Air Service Regiments (21 and 23 SAS) are Reserve units.
2 In Britain, all officers join a regiment after commissioning and remain with that regiment throughout their careers until they move into senior staff appointments. A small number of officers may later transfer to the Parachute Regiment (or other regiments or corps) but this is not usual practice. 22 SAS recruits from all regiments and corps, as well as from the Royal Navy and Royal Air Force.
3 Quoted in Christian Jennings and Adrian Weale, *Green-Eyed Boys: 3 Para and the Battle for Mount Longdon*, Harper Collins, London, 1996, p. 135.
4 Luke Jennings, 'On Mount Longdon: Parachute Regiment came back from the Falklands with their reputation for bravery reinforced. But two years ago, they were accused of atrocities by one of their own. Now others are speaking out', *Independent*, 16 May 1993, <www.independent.co.uk/arts-entertainment/on-mount-longdon-parachute-regiment-came-back-from-the-falklands-with-their-reputation-for-bravery-reinforced-but-two-years-ago-they-were-accused-of-atrocities-by-one-of-their-own-now-others-are-speaking-out-2323239.html>.
5 Martin Granovsky, 'Fresh claims of atrocities in Falklands war', *Independent*, 23 August 1992, <www.independent.co.uk/news/fresh-claims-atrocities-falklands-war-1541937.html>.
6 Vincent Bramley, *Two Sides of Hell*, Bloomsbury, London, 1994, p. 178.
7 Jennings and Weale, *Green-Eyed Boys*, Harper Collins, London, 1996, p. 190.
8 'British crimes in Falkland War', Axis History Forum website, 6 September 2004, <forum.axishistory.com/viewtopic.php?t=58193&start=60>.
9 Jennings and Weale, *Green-Eyed Boys*, p. 191.
10 'Baha Mousa inquiry: "Serious discipline breach" by army', BBC News, 8 September 2011, <www.bbc.com/news/uk-14825889>.
11 The full inquiry report is at Sir William Gage, *The Report of the Baha Mousa Inquiry*, The Stationery Office, 2011, <assets.publishing.service.gov.uk/government/uploads/system/uploads/attachment_data/file/279190/1452_i.pdf>.

14 SHAMEFUL SHADOWS AND SUPERIOR STANDARDS: THE CANADIAN EXPERIENCE

1 'The Mefloquine issue', Report of the Somalia Commission Inquiry, 12 February 2007, <web.archive.org/web/20070212225529/http://www.dnd.ca/somalia/vol5/v5c41e.htm>.
2 Stephen Zhou, 'Canada's tragic legacy in Afghanistan', *Aljazeera News*, <www.aljazeera.com/opinions/2014/6/23/canadas-tragic-legacy-in-afghanistan>.
3 Stuart Hendin, 'Unpunished War Criminals, the Shameful Legacy of Canada's Military Involvement in Afghanistan', *Liverpool Law Review*, no. 34, 2013, pp. 291–310.

4   Robert Semrau, *The Taliban Don't Wave*, Wiley, Toronto, 2012, p. 172.
5   'Canadian soldier sacked for shooting wounded Afghan', BBC News, 5 October 2010, <www.bbc.com/news/world-us-canada-11478886>.
6   'Commentary of 2016, Article 12: Protection and care of the wounded and sick', International Committee of the Red Cross website, 2016, <ihl-databases.icrc.org/applic/ihl/ihl.nsf/Comment.xsp?action=openDocument&documentId=CECD58D1E2A2AF30C1257F15004A7CB9>.
7   Quoted in Michael Friscolanti, 'Summary of "Capt. Robert Semrau dismissed from the Forces"', Frontier School Division, Social Studies/Native Studies website, <ssns.frontiersd.mb.ca/SeniorYrs/Curricula9-12/Grade11/CanadianHistory/RemembranceDay/Summaries/5Oct2010.html>.
8   Tim Dunne, 'Courts martial deny soldiers the very rights they defend', *Chronicle Herald*, 10 March 2018, <military-justice.ca/wp-content/uploads/2018/12/046-Courts-Martial-deny-rights.pdf>.
9   Reported in 'Canadian Forces members cleared of Afghan allegations', CBC News, 15 December 2011, <www.cbc.ca/news/politics/canadian-forces-members-cleared-of-afghan-allegations-1.1005650>.
10 Bruce Campion-Smith, 'Special forces secrecy impeded probe of potential wrongdoing in Afghanistan, report finds', *Toronto Star*, 5 September 2018, <www.thestar.com/news/canada/2018/09/05/special-forces-secrecy-impeded-probe-of-potential-wrongdoing-in-afghanistan-report-finds.html>.
11 Christe Blatchford, *Fifteen Days: Stories of bravery, friendship, life and death from inside the new Canadian army*, Anchor, Ottawa, 2008, p. 205.

15 FACING THE FUTURE BY ACKNOWLEDGING THE PAST: THE FRENCH EXPERIENCE

1   Niall Ferguson, *The Cash Nexus: Money and power in the modern world, 1700–2000*, Basic Books, London, 2002, pp. 25–27.
2   See Jeremy Black, *Avoiding Armageddon: From the Great War to the fall of France 1918–1940*, Bloomsbury, London, 2012.
3   Rita Maran, *Torture: The role of ideology in the French–Algerian war*, Praeger, New York, 1989, p. 79; and quoting the novel by Jean-Jacques Servan-Schreiber, *Lieutenant in Algeria*, Knopf, New York, 1957, p. 22.
4   John E Talbott, 'The myth and reality of the paratrooper in the Algerian war', *Armed Forces & Society*, vol. 3, no. 1, 1976, pp. 69–86, p. 76 cited.
5   Daniel Moran, *Wars of National Liberation*, Cassell, London, 2001, p. 110.
6   Aussaresses, *Battle of the Casbah: Counter terrorism and torture*, Enigma, London, 2004, p. 17.
7   General Paul Aussaresses, quoted in *Le Monde*, 4 May 2001.
8   Jacques de Bollardiere, *The Battle of Algiers*, De Brouwer, Paris, 1972, p. 150.
9   Bollardiere, *The Battle of Algiers*, pp. 100–102.
10 Aussaresses, *Battle of the Casbah*, p. 126.
11 John E Talbott, 'The Myth and Reality of the Paratrooper in the Algerian War', *Armed Forces and Society*, vol. 3, no. 1, November 1976, p. 79.
12 David Galula, *Pacification in Algeria, 1956–58*, originally published in 1963, Rand reprint, Santa Monica, 2006, p. xxiv.
13 Galula, *Pacification in Algeria, 1956–58*, p. 269.
14 Galula, *Pacification in Algeria, 1956–58*, p. 5.

15 See for example, *Doctrine for the Employment of the French Armed Forces*, Joint Doctrine (FRA) JD-01(A)_DEF(2014) No. 128/DEF/CICDE/NP as of 12 June 2014 at <www.irsem.fr/data/files/irsem/documents/document/file/63/20140612_np_cicde_fra-jd-01a-def.pdf>.
16 Général de Saint-Quentin in Olivier Hanne and Guillaume Larabi, *Jihâd au Sahel: Menaces, opération Barkhane, coopération régionale*, Paris, Bernard Giovangeli Editeur, 2015, pp. 136, 140.
17 'French Special Forces in Afghanistan: Lessons learned', Second Line of Defense website, 30 November 2009, <sldinfo.com/2009/11/french-special-forces-in-afghanistan-lessons-learned/>.
18 'French Special Forces in Afghanistan: Lessons learned', 30 November 2009.
19 Olivier Schmitt, 'French military adaptation in the Afghan War: Looking inward or outward?', *Journal of Strategic Studies*, vol. 40, iss. 4, 2017, <www.tandfonline.com/doi/full/10.1080/01402390.2016.1220369>.
20 Philippe Leymarie, 'France's unwinnable Sahel war', *Le Monde Diplomatique*, March 2021, <mondediplo.com/2021/03/05mali>.
21 Thierry Hommel and Marc-Antoine Pérouse de Montclos, 'The French military in Africa: a bad economic investment', the *Conversation*, 25 September 2019; and Marc-Antoine Pérouse de Montclos, *A Lost War: France in the Sahel*, Jean-Claude Lattès, Paris, 2020.
22 John Lichfield, '"We are not messengers of death in Mali", says French colonel', *Independent*, 23 January 2013, <www.independent.co.uk/news/world/africa/we-are-not-messengers-death-mali-says-french-colonel-8463926.html>.
23 Kim Willsher, 'French soldier wears Nazi slogan on uniform in Central African Republic', the *Guardian*, 23 December 2013, <www.theguardian.com/world/2013/dec/22/french-soldier-nazi-slogan-uniform>.

16 TOWARDS A RECKONING 2016–2020

1 Justice Brereton was appointed to the New South Wales Court of Appeal in August 2018.
2 IGADF Afghanistan Inquiry report, para 38, p. 133.
3 Under section 10 of the Inspector-General of the Australian Defence Force Regulation 2016.
4 Inspector-General of the Australian Defence Force Regulation 2016 – REG 28A Application of This Division, Commonwealth Consolidated Regulations website, <www.austlii.edu.au/cgi-bin/viewdoc/au/legis/cth/consol_reg/iotadfr2016509/s28a.html>.
5 Barnews, *Journal of the NSW Bar Association*, Summer 2020, p. 81, <barnews.nswbar.asn.au/summer-2020-mag/LEGAL-HISTORY.html#page=83>; and Tim Barlass, '"No one does it for popularity": Justice Brereton follows in his father's footsteps', *SMH*, 13 December 2020.
6 *Commonwealth of Australia Constitution Act* – section 80, Commonwealth Consolidated Regulations website, <classic.austlii.edu.au/au/legis/cth/consol_act/coaca430/s80.html>.
7 IGADF Afghanistan Inquiry report, Part 1, p. 38.
8 Shane Wright, 'SAS inquiry: Gossip, rumours behind Army chief Angus Campbell's special forces inquiry', the *West Australian*, 26 October 2017, <thewest.com.au/news/australia/gossip-rumours-behind-army-chief-angus-campbells-special-forces-inquiry-ng-b88640172z>.

9   Wright, 'SAS inquiry'.
10 Nick McKenzie and Chris Masters, 'Special forces chief acknowledges war crimes, blames "poor moral leadership"', the *Age*, 28 June 2020, <www.theage.com.au/national/special-forces-chief-acknowledges-war-crimes-blames-poor-moral-leadership-20200628-p556z6.html>.
11 Andrew Greene, 'Findings from Afghanistan war crimes investigation will cause "distress" for some elite soldiers, judge warns', ABC News, 21 May 2020, <www.abc.net.au/news/2020-05-21/judge-warns-afghanistan-war-crimes-investigation-cause-distress/12269870>.

INDEX

9/11 terrorist attacks 28, 50, 107, 134, 136, 140–42, 144, 276, 286, 338, 350, 366, 402

Abbott, Tony 191–92, 227–28
'Abd al-Rahman Khan 32
Abu Ghraib 340–41
ADF *see* Australian Defence Force
ADF Investigative Service (ADFIS) 233, 259
Afghan files, the 257, 259–60, 263
Afghan National Army 62, 69, 146, 153, 156, 158, 184, 218, 222, 270, 288
Afghan National Directorate of Security 294, 341, 342
Afghan National Security Forces (ANSF) 342–43
Afghan State Intelligence Agency (KHAD) 51
Afghanistan
  Australian diplomatic relations with 3–4, 101–107
  Australian forces in 2–3, 4–9, 15, 19–25, 29, 144–52, 160–62, 180, 196–206, 216–24, 228–30, 233–36, 238–42, 244, 246, 247, 248, 254–56, 258–59, 262–74, 277, 280, 352, 385–86, 390–92, 394–400, 403, 406, 408–10, 413
  British colonial forces in 30–34
  Communist rule in 36, 43, 49, 60, 68
  drug trade in 19, 71, 96, 156, 157–58, 184, 215–16, 279, 367, 369
  and Pakistan 34, 42, 39, 50, 60, 62, 81, 93, 96, 99, 101, 153, 156, 171, 172, 173, 221
  politics in 27–31, 32–33, 34–45, 47–65, 89–107
  rise of the Taliban in 89–107
  and the Soviet Union 3, 34–35, 38–39, 40–46, 47–66, 67–88, 89–90, 92–93, 102–103, 152–53, 156, 162, 170, 206, 402
  and the United States 5–6, 28, 63, 64–65, 69, 78, 99–100, 107, 142–45, 158, 166–67, 170, 171, 172–73, 176, 178, 179, 180, 186–87, 188, 189, 190–91, 192, 194–95, 196, 197, 200, 202– 203, 216, 219, 221, 269–70, 279, 286, 287, 294, 304, 338, 339–41, 344, 347–48, 349, 352–53, 366, 367–68, 370, 402
Afghanistan Independent Human Rights Commission (AIHRC) 264, 315, 341
Akbar, Shaharzad 315
Akhromeyev, Sergei 55
al-Qaeda 28, 49, 140, 141, 142–43, 144–46, 147, 150, 151, 152, 156, 157, 166, 176, 186–87, 188, 191–92, 195, 370
al-Zawahiri, Ayman 145
Algeria, war in 356–64, 365, 366, 367, 368, 374, 404–405
Amanullah Khan 33, 34
Amin, Hafizullah 40–41, 42, 48, 60
Amnesty International 77, 292
Andropov, Yuri 42
Anglo–Afghan War 33–34
Ansary, Tamim 30
Anzac tradition 16–19, 24, 111, 228, 254, 351
ANZAC *see* Australian and New Zealand Army Corps
Apiata, Willie 286
Arbour, Louise 341
Ardern Government 299
Ardern, Jacinda 292
Argentina, military of 308–13
Arnold-Palmer Inquiry 292–95
Arnold, Terence 292, 293, 299, 301
Arone, Shidane Abukar 334–37
Arush, Achmed 334, 336–37

Asia-Pacific Economic Cooperation (APEC) 161
asylum seekers 103, 106, 130
    see also refugees
Aussaresses, Paul 359, 361
Australia, New Zealand, United States (ANZUS) Security Treaty 140, 142, 286
Australian and New Zealand Army Corps (ANZAC) 170, 285
Australian Defence Association 150
Australian Defence Force (ADF)
    allegations of misconduct in 1, 5, 6, 7–10, 19–26, 118, 124, 130–34, 136, 138, 148, 150–51, 177, 183, 187, 190, 192–93, 195–96, 230–31, 232–36, 238–51, 254–81, 381–401, 402, 404–14
    allegations of war crimes in 2, 3, 6, 8, 20–26, 125, 130–34, 138, 147–48, 230, 239, 244, 246–48, 251, 252, 256, 257, 260, 264, 266, 270–73, 382, 384, 387, 388–89, 391, 393, 396, 400, 402, 404, 406, 409, 410–11, 412
    Law of Armed Conflict 4, 20, 23, 118, 137–38, 162, 163, 173, 177, 192, 208–13, 229, 232, 246, 263, 274, 281, 388, 397, 400, 405, 407, 409–10
    media reports on 5, 6, 7–8, 20, 21, 23, 25, 103, 130, 131, 132, 146, 147, 149–51, 234–35, 238, 245–46, 247, 251, 252–81, 317, 374, 381, 390–91, 392, 393–400, 405, 407, 408, 409
    Mentoring and Reconstruction Task Force (MRTF) 185, 219, 221–22
    Mentoring Task Force (MTF) 185, 189, 195, 219, 222
    Provincial Reconstruction Team (PRT), Australian 4, 158–59, 161–62, 178, 203–204
    Reconstruction Task Force (RTF), Australian 179–82, 185, 195, 203–204, 219, 221–22
    Redback India 1 patrol 146
    Redback Kilo 3 patrol 146, 147–48, 150
    Royal Australian Air Force 139
    Royal Australian Infantry Corps 114, 217
    Royal Australian Navy 139, 331–32
    Royal Australian Regiment (RAR) 4, 115, 134–37, 154, 197, 222, 235, 387
    Rules of Engagement (ROE) 4, 20–21, 23, 118–19, 150–51, 162, 173,177, 183, 192, 208–11, 213, 231–33, 256–59, 275–76, 281, 293, 397, 400, 409–10
    Special Forces Task Group (SFTG) 160–62, 164, 166–68, 170, 174, 179–80, 196–98, 199–200, 202–203, 204, 205, 248, 250–51
    Special Operations Commander – Australia (SOCAUST) 5, 20, 180, 197, 235, 242–43, 286, 390–91
    Special Operations Task Group (SOTG) 2–3, 4–5, 7, 19–21, 23, 175–76, 180, 181–82, 191, 198, 207–209, 213, 214, 216, 217, 218, 219, 222, 223, 228–29, 231–33, 236–37, 241–43, 250–51, 265–66, 268, 280, 381–82, 387, 390, 400–401, 404–406, 407, 410, 412
    in Vietnam 4, 5, 116–20, 124, 139, 160, 163, 164, 167, 168, 220, 227, 285–86
    see also Commando Regiments; Inspector-General of the Australian Defence Force (IGADF) Afghanistan Inquiry; International Security Assistance Force (ISAF); Special Air Service (SAS) Regiment; Special Operations Command (SOCOMD)
Australian Federal Police (AFP) 130, 239, 245, 257, 266, 273, 381
Australian Olympic Federation 102
Australian Secret Intelligence Service (ASIS) 247, 259
Australian Security Intelligence Organisation (ASIO) 238–39, 247
Australian War Memorial 15–17, 18–19, 227–28, 262–63, 273
Azzam, Abdullah 49–50

Bale, John 273
Bali bombings 136, 173, 176
Bandt, Adam 189
Baradar, Abdul Ghani 154
Bean, Charles 17, 24
Beazley, Kim 150
Bendle, Mervyn 18–19
Biden, Joe 187
Bin Laden, Osama 49, 50–51, 97–98, 140, 144–45, 221
Binskin, Mark 228, 382
Birt, Ashley 219
Bishop, Bronwyn 24
Black Hawk accident 127
Black September 123
Black Watch 313–14
Blackman, Alexander 320–29
Bloody Sunday 'Saville' Inquiry 7, 382–83
Blucher, Alexandra 267–68
Bocharov, Gennady 80–82
Boer War 15, 52
Boland, Mark 335
Bonsor, Nicholas 312
Borneo 4, 15, 115–16, 120, 383
Borovik, Artyom 58
Bosnia 63, 338, 353
Bougainville 89, 105, 158, 286
Boyle, Jean 337
Bramall, Edwin 312
Bramley, Vincent 311
Brereton, Paul 263, 267, 382–84, 387–88, 390–91, 397
Brereton, Russell 383
Brezhnev, Leonid 40–41, 42
British Armed Forces *see* United Kingdom, military
British Commonwealth Forces 332
British East India Company Army 31
Brown, Bob 168
Brown, Kyle 335–36
Brydon, William 31
Burchett Inquiry 245
Burkhard, Thierry 373
Burnham Inquiry 292–305
Burr, Rick 247, 274–75, 392–93, 394
Bush, George W. 140, 154
Bush Administration 144, 166, 172–73

Calley, William 119
Callinan, Rory 23, 263, 269
Cameron, David 320
Camp Russell 21, 196–97
Campbell Barracks 114, 120–21, 236, 238–39, 390–91, 392
Campbell, Angus 20–21, 244–46, 260, 300–301, 381–82, 386–87, 393, 394, 407
Canada, military of 5, 7, 144, 160, 189, 205, 216, 276, 281, 287, 331–54, 367–68, 369, 376, 406, 407
Canadian Forces National Investigation Service (CFNIS) 347
Cantwell, John 175
Carey, George 323
Carrizo, Oscar 310–11
Carter, Jimmy 102
Castres, Didier 371
Chechnya 63
Chirac, Jacques 367
Chretien, Jean 337
Churchill, Winston 33
Clark Government 286–87, 302
Clark, Sam 23, 257
Clinton Administration 141
Clinton, Bill 139–40
Coalition of the Willing 153
Coleman, Jonathan 297
Collins, Matt 263
Combined Joint Special Operations Task Force – Afghanistan (CJSOTF-A) 197
Commando Regiments (ADF) 4, 7–8, 19, 21, 23, 112–13, 114–15, 121, 122, 124, 134–37, 154, 160, 162, 196–98, 199–201, 203, 204, 205, 206, 215, 216, 217–18, 221–22, 223, 229, 234, 235, 240, 241, 246, 247, 254, 255, 256, 259, 264, 265, 274, 278–79, 280, 320–21, 322, 325–26, 327–28, 352, 367, 386, 391–92, 394–95, 400, 403, 413
Commonwealth Criminal Code 384
Conine, Ernest 84–85
Connolly, Peter 185
Cosgrove, Peter 129–30, 160
counterinsurgency 165–66, 168, 185
Cramer, Jack 113–14
Creighton, Jim 190

Crisis Response Unit (Afghan) 287
Crompvoets, Samantha 5, 8, 238–44, 386, 394, 409–10

Danish Special Forces 286–87
Daoud, Khan 36–37, 38, 90, 93, 102
Darwish Khan 219
Dawe, Peter 349
De Chastelain, John 337
De Gaulle, Charles 355–56, 362, 363
De Zélicourt, Bruno 367–68
Defence Force Discipline Act (DFDA) 384, 405
Delta Force 6
Democratic Republic of Afghanistan (DRA) 37–38, 47
Desai, Morarji 123
detainees, treatment of
    by Australian military 2, 130, 131–32, 214, 229–30, 233, 256, 269, 384, 406–407
    by Canadian military 334–35, 339–42, 351–52
    by French military 364, 367, 375
    by New Zealand military 286–87, 290, 298, 301
    by United Kingdom military 320
    by United States military 5, 286–87, 340–41
Directorate of Special Action Forces, Canberra 122
Dobell, Graeme 142
Dostum, Abdul Rashid 98, 99
Downer, Alexander 159, 161–62
Drax, Richard 322–23
drug trade in Afghanistan 19, 71, 96, 156, 157–58, 184, 215–16, 279, 367, 369
Duffy, Bryce 219
Dunstan, Donald 121–22
Durand Line 34
Durrani, Ahmad Shah 30

East Timor 15, 89, 105, 128–31, 133–34, 135, 138, 139, 158, 163, 170, 173, 199, 203, 235, 239, 286, 387, 403–404
Edgar, Hector 113
Elliott, August 261
Elliott, Christopher 277

Ermacora, Felix 77
Evans, Chris 131, 133

Falklands War *see* South Atlantic war
Fallon, Michael 315
Fatah 123
Faulkner, John 223
Ferguson, Niall 355
Fiji 105, 127
Findlay, Adam 390–91
First World War 15, 16–17, 33, 111, 285, 332, 355
Fitzgibbon, Joel 182–83, 223
Folliot, Philippe 374
Force Element-Alpha (FE-A) 197, 198–99, 204, 205, 230
Force Element-Bravo (FE-B) 197, 199–201, 205, 206
Force Element-Charlie (FE-C) 197–98
Force Element-Echo (FE-E) 197
Foulkes, Charles 34
Fraser, Malcolm 102–103
Fraser Government 103, 123
French Action Service 359
French Foreign Legion 355, 362
France, military of 5, 64–65, 179, 216, 281, 331, 332, 355–77, 404–405, 407
    10th Paratroop Division 357–60, 361–63
Froger, Amédé 357
Front de Libération Nationale (FLN) 356–58, 360, 361, 364
Fullerton, John 80

Gage, William 320
Gallipoli 16, 18, 285
Galula, David 363–64
Gankovsky, Yuri 68
Gareyev, Makhmut 70
Gavin, Luke 219
Gaynor, James 245
Geneva Agreement (1988) 91
Geneva Conventions 2, 76, 132, 294, 298, 319, 321, 339–40, 345, 397
Georgelin, Jean-Louis 369
Germany 33, 64–65, 68, 143, 287, 306, 332, 338, 354–55, 364, 370
Ghani, Ashraf 32, 270

Gillard Government 191
Gillard, Julia 188–89, 223
Gilmore, 'Gus' 228
Giustozzi, Antonio 154
Gleig, George 32
Goff, Phil 287
Good Friday Peace Accords 308
Gorbachev, Mikhail 54, 55, 56–57, 58
Gorton, John 160
Greene, Andrew 23, 256
Grey, Jeffrey 165
Gromyko, Andrei 42, 55–56
GRU (Soviet intelligence) 52–53
Guest, Ken 50–51

Habibullah Khan 33
Hager, Nicky 291, 292, 296, 297, 299
Haider Khan 76–77
Hammett, Jim 217
Hanifa, Abu 95
Haqqani, Jalaluddin 50–51
Harper, Stephen 339
Harries, Owen 169
Hawke Government 103, 123, 227
Hekmatullah 219, 270
Hekmatyar, Gulbuddin 50, 92, 96
Helsinki Watch 77
Hendin, Stuart 342
Hezb-e Islami 80
Hezb-e Wahdat 92
Hezbollah 215
Hill, Robert 131, 158, 160, 185, 189, 223
Hiller, Rick 354
Hilton Hotel (Sydney), bombing of 123
Hindmarsh, Mike 180
Hollande, François 369
Holsworthy Barracks 135, 137
Holt, Harold 160
Hope, Ian 350
Horner, David 113
Houston, Angus 160, 292
Howard Government 101, 130, 139, 166, 169, 179, 181, 203
Howard, John 104, 139–40, 142, 144, 149–50, 159, 160, 171, 178, 179, 180, 196, 402
Huggett, Justin 260
Human Rights Watch 266, 315–16

Huntley, Ian 324–26
Hussein, Saddam 64, 153
Hyman, Anthony 38

Ignatieff, Michael 98–99
Incident Response Regiment (IRR) 197, 221–22
India 30, 92, 93–94, 99, 102, 106, 123
    British control of 31–32, 33, 34, 35
Indonesia 104–105, 115–16, 128, 129, 203, 285–86
Inspector-General of the Australian Defence Force (IGADF) Afghanistan Inquiry 2–3, 5, 6, 7, 8, 21, 23, 24, 245–47, 250–51, 255–56, 257, 263–64, 267, 270, 272, 273–75, 278, 280–81, 316, 329, 376, 381–401, 404–405, 407–409, 412–13
intelligence activities
    Afghan 51, 53
    Australian 5, 112, 115–16, 131, 145, 148, 150, 151, 167, 198, 199, 200, 204–205, 206, 207, 214, 215, 216–17, 229–32, 239, 247, 258, 259
    French 367–68, 375
    New Zealand 216, 338
    Pakistan 50, 93
    Soviet Union 40, 52–53, 78–79, 83, 86
    United Kingdom 216, 308, 318
    United States 140, 216
Inter-Services Intelligence (ISI), Pakistan 50, 62, 93, 99, 101
International Committee of the Red Crescent (ICRC) 103, 215
International Criminal Court 246, 292, 372, 394, 412
International Crisis Group 184
International Force East Timor (INTERFET) 128–30, 135, 139, 286, 387
International Security Assistance Force (ISAF) 4, 5, 20, 21–22, 143, 155, 157, 160, 167, 168, 172, 173, 176–78, 181–84, 186–88, 190, 196–97, 201, 202–203, 204, 206, 213, 214, 215–16, 218–20, 223, 231, 233, 237, 263, 269, 271, 288, 289, 293, 298, 299, 302, 325,

329, 338–39, 340, 342, 346, 348, 349, 353, 367, 368, 370, 375, 403, 406, 410
Iran 30, 35, 40, 41, 50, 56, 63–64, 93, 96, 99–100, 102, 145
Iraq 105, 127–28, 153, 158, 197, 291, 340, 365, 407
  invasion of 4, 15, 152, 153–54, 161, 167, 169, 170, 171, 179, 203, 205, 313, 314, 320, 321
Iraq Historic Allegations Team (IHAT) 314
Irish Republican Army (IRA) 215
Irvine, David 5, 247–51, 409, 410
Islamic Republic of Afghanistan 58
Islamic State (ISIS) 370

Jacquard, Roland 95
James, Neil 150
Jan Muhammad Khan (JMK) 175
Jaron, Gilles 374
Jeffery, Michael 122
Jemaah Islamiyah 176
Jennings, Christian 313
Jewish Anti-Defamation Commission 262
jihad 39, 49, 60, 63, 101, 155, 370–71, 372, 373
Johnson, David 223
Joint Task Force 197
Joint Task Force 2 (JTF2) 337–39, 347–52
Jones, Alan 262
Jones, Andrew 219
Jospin, Lionel 366

Kakar, Hasan Kawun 33
Kakar, Mohammad Hassan 75
Karmal, Babrak 48, 51, 53, 54–55, 70, 93, 103
Karzai, Hamid 143, 155, 158, 188, 220, 259
Keating Government 104
Keating, Tim 292, 296, 298, 300
Keelty, Mick 273
Kent, David 16–18, 24
Kerr, John 102
Key, John 287, 289, 290, 300, 302
KGB 40, 42, 51–52, 55, 69
Khalidi, Noor Ahmad 73
Khaliq, Hajii Abdul 183

Khan, Vance 292
Khomeini, Ayatollah Ruhollah 40
Killen, James 102–103
Kirillov, Alexander 86
Kolomeitz, Glenn 264
Korean war 15, 112, 221, 285–86, 332
Kosovo Liberation Army 215
Kosygin, Alexei 40
Kuwait, Iraqi occupation of 64, 127–28, 153, 365

Lacoste, Robert 357–58
Lange, David 286
Lasswell, Harold 252, 281
Law of Armed Conflict
  Australian military 4, 20, 23, 118, 137–38, 162, 163, 173, 177, 192, 208–13, 229, 232, 246, 263, 274, 281, 388, 397, 400, 405, 407, 409–10
  Canadian military 5, 338, 343–44, 346, 350
  French military 5, 373
  New Zealand military 5, 293
  Soviet military 65, 78
  United Kingdom military 5, 319–20, 322, 324, 329
  see also Rules of Engagement (ROE)
Leahy, Peter 133
Ledwidge, Frank 318–19
Lewis, Julian 314–15
Lockhart, Greg 277–78

MacDonald, Ken 318
Macklin, Robert 255
Maddison, Paul 341
Mahon, Peter 296–97
Malaya 15, 112, 285–86
Malaysia 115, 285–86
Maley, William 100, 102
Mali 370–73, 374, 375
Mambrin, Santiago 310
Manchanda, Nivi 28
Mapp, Wayne 289, 291, 297
Maran, Rita 356
Mark, Ron 294, 298
Markov, Alexei 81
Martin, James 219, 270

Mason, Tony 310
Massoud, Ahmad Shah 52, 92, 96, 98, 99, 144
Massu, Jacques 358, 360, 361, 362
Masters, Chris 8, 21–23, 231, 262, 266, 274, 390
Mataparae, Jerry 293
Matchee, Clayton 335–36
Mathieu, Carol 334
Matiullah Khan (MK) 175–76, 230, 231–32, 375
Mawlawi Sher Mohammad 269
Mazari, Abdul Ali 92
McBride, David 257–58
McChrystal, Stanley 186–87
McDonald, Kristy 292
McFarlane, Robert 65
McKenzie, Nick 23, 238, 247, 262, 266, 274, 390–91, 395
McKiernan, David 186
McKinley, Michael 276, 277
McKinnon, Stuart 320
McMahon Government 117
McMichael, Scott 87
McPhedran, Ian 254–55
media
  reports on Australian military 5, 6, 7–8, 20, 21, 23, 25, 103, 130, 131, 132, 146, 147, 149–51, 234–35, 238, 245–46, 247, 251, 252–81, 317, 374, 381, 390–91, 392, 393–400, 405, 407, 408, 409
  reports on British military 312, 314, 316–17
  reports on Canadian military 337, 352
  reports on French military 369, 372
  reports on New Zealand military 291–92, 300, 302–303
Mendès-France, Pierre 356
Mentoring and Reconstruction Task Force (MRTF) 185, 219, 221–22
  see also Reconstruction/Mentoring Task Forces (RTF/MTF); Mentoring Task Force (MTF)
Mentoring Task Force (MTF) 185, 189, 195, 219, 222
  see also Mentoring and Reconstruction Task Force (MRTF)

Menzies Government 113
Mercy, Johnny 316
Miller, 'Dusty' 267
Mills, Barbara 311–312
Milosevic, Stjepan 219, 270
Miraj, Qari 294
Mirza Khan 264
misconduct
  Australian military 1, 5, 6, 7–10, 19–26, 118, 124, 130–34, 136, 138, 148, 150–51, 177, 183, 187, 190, 192–93, 195–96, 230–31, 232–36, 238–51, 254–81, 381–401, 402, 404–14
  Canadian military 333–54, 407
  French military 357–77, 407
  New Zealand military 289, 300–305, 407
  Soviet military 52, 73, 74, 76, 79, 82–87
  United Kingdom military 309–30, 407
  United States military 5–6, 187
  see also war crimes
Moffitt, Harry 217–18
Mojeddedi, Sibghatullah 91
Morrison, David 260
Morrison, Scott 270
Mousa, Baha 320
mujahideen 39, 40, 42, 49–51, 52, 53, 55, 56, 57–59, 61–62, 64, 69, 70, 72–76, 78, 79–80, 81, 83, 86, 87, 90–91, 93, 143, 174
Musharraf, Pervez 171
My Lai massacre 85, 118–19

Najibullah, Mohammad 54–57, 63, 64, 70, 90, 91, 92, 93, 96–97, 103, 104, 153
Naseerullah Babar 99
National Islamic Front for the Salvation of Afghanistan 96
National Islamic Front of Afghanistan 80
NATO 107, 169–70, 183, 188, 190–91, 194–95, 216–17, 219, 220, 288, 332, 338, 352, 353, 365, 366, 368, 369–70, 376
Nelson, Brendan 180, 223, 262–63
Netherlands, military of 179, 180, 189–90, 196, 203, 216, 375

New Zealand, military of 5, 281, 285–305, 338
  see also New Zealand Special Air Service
New Zealand Defence Force (NZDF) 289–305
  see also New Zealand, military of
New Zealand Special Air Service (NZSAS) 128, 286–95, 298–305
Nicholson, Brendan 274–75
North American Air Defense Command (NORAD) 332
North Atlantic Treaty Organization *see* NATO
Northern Alliance 92, 96, 101, 144
Northern Ireland 7, 276, 307, 308, 313, 321, 323, 382–83, 388
Norway, military of 179, 287, 338
November Platoon (2nd Commando Regiment) 279–80

O'Donnell, Tim 288–89, 304
Oakes, Dan 23, 257
Obama, Barack 186, 220
Objective Nile (Taliban commander) 205
Ogarkov, Nikolai 43, 70
Omar, Mullah Mohammad 93–94, 95, 96, 97–98, 100, 144, 154, 156, 171, 220–21
Operation Anaconda 145, 286
Operation Barkhane 370–73
Operation Burnham 289–91, 292–93, 295–96
  see also Burnham Inquiry
Operation Eagle's Summit 206
Operation Enduring Freedom 144, 366
Operation Northmoor 314–17
Operation Nova 289, 292, 293
Operation Salam 90–91
Operation Serval 370
Organisation Armée Secrète (Secret Armed Organisation – OAS) 362

Packham, Ben 23
Pahlavi, Mohammad Reza 40
Pakistan 35, 40, 41, 49, 52–53, 56–57, 58, 63, 65, 68, 69, 86–87, 93, 94, 101–102, 103–104, 143, 144, 145–46, 154–55, 166, 191–92, 367, 368
  border dispute with Afghanistan 34, 42
  support for Afghanistan 39, 50, 60, 62, 81, 93, 96, 99, 101, 153, 156, 171, 172, 173, 221
Palestine Liberation Organisation (PLO) 123
Palmer, Geoffrey 292, 293, 299, 301
Parachute Regiment (United Kingdom) 204, 307, 308, 311, 313
Parachute Regiments (France) 362, 367, 373–74
Parachute Training School (NSW) 121, 125
Pâris de Bollardière, Jacques 360–61
Paris Peace Accords 56
Parker, David 297
Payne, Donald 320
peacekeeping missions 1, 15, 91, 127, 163, 332–33, 353, 364, 372
Pearson, Elaine 266
People's Democratic Party of Afghanistan (PDPA) 36–44, 47–49, 51–54, 56–60, 65, 68, 69, 75, 83, 94, 96
Pérouse de Montclos, Marc-Antoine 371
Perron, Jean-Guy 345–46
Petraeus, David 187–88
Plibersek, Tanya 105
Poate, Robert 219, 270
police
  Afghanistan 44, 53, 79–80, 184–85, 219, 230, 236, 340, 341
  Australian military 129–30
  Canada 337
  United Kingdom 311–14
  see also Australian Federal Police (AFP)
Politburo 38, 40, 41–42, 47, 49, 53–55, 59, 60, 67, 68, 70, 170
Pollock, George 31
Project Sand Trap 346–47, 348
Project Sand Trap 2 347–48
Provincial Police Reserve Company (PPRC) 184
Provincial Reconstruction Team (PRT)
  Australian 4, 158–59, 161–62, 178, 203–204
  New Zealand 288, 291, 293, 302
  United States 158, 388
Provisional Irish Republican Army (PIRA) 308, 323

see also Irish Republican Army (IRA)
Puzanov, Alexander 38–39

Quetta Shura 154–55

Rabbani, Burhanuddin 91–92, 96, 100
Rahbari Shura 154–55
Ratebzad, Anahita 48
Ray, Robert 103–104
Reagan Administration 65
Reagan, Ronald 69
Reconstruction Task Force (RTF),
   Australian 179–82, 185, 195, 203–204, 219, 221–22
Reconstruction/Mentoring Task Forces (RTF/MTF) 195
   see also Mentoring and Reconstruction Task Force (MRTF); Mentoring Task Force (MTF)
Red Army *see* Soviet Army
Redback India 1 patrol 146
Redback Kilo 3 patrol 146, 147–48, 150
refugees 41, 56–57, 59, 63, 64, 65, 93, 104–105, 106, 128, 146, 373
   see also asylum seekers
Rifkind, Malcolm 311–12
Roberts-Smith, Ben 235, 262, 273, 385–86
Roberts, Andrew 319–20
Rome Statute of the International Criminal Court 2, 246
Royal Air Force 285, 306
Royal Australian Air Force 139
Royal Australian Infantry Corps 114, 217
Royal Australian Navy 139, 331–32
Royal Australian Regiment (RAR) 4, 115, 134–37, 154, 197, 222, 235, 387
Royal Flying Corps 285
Royal Marines 204, 307–308, 320, 323–24, 327, 328, 352
Royal Military Police (RMP) 311, 314, 316, 318
Royal Navy 285, 306, 307–308
Royal Netherlands Air Force 203
Royal New Zealand Air Force 285
Royal New Zealand Navy (RNZN) 285
Rozi Khan 230–31
Rubin, Barnett 91

Rudd, Kevin 223
Rudd Government 182
Rules of Engagement (ROE)
   Australian military 4, 20–21, 23, 118–19, 150–51, 162, 173, 177, 183, 192, 208–11, 213, 231–33, 256–59, 275–76, 281, 293, 397, 400, 409–10
   Canadian military 5, 338, 343, 346, 347, 350
   French military 5, 365, 370, 373, 374
   New Zealand military 5
   Soviet military 70, 78
   United Kingdom military 5
   see also Law of Armed Conflict
Russell, Andrew 152, 196
Russia 30, 31, 32
   see also Soviet Union
Rwanda 89, 127, 163, 173

Saikal, Amin 34
Sakharov, Andrei 53–54
Salafists 60
Sardar, Haji 263–64, 267
Sarkozy, Nicolas 368
Sayyaf, Abdul Rasul 92
Second Anglo-Boer War 285
Second World War 4, 15, 84, 112, 285, 332, 356
Secret Armed Organisation *see* Organisation Armée Secrète
Semrau, Robert 344–46
Sengelman, Jeff 20–21, 235–38, 244–45, 246–47, 386, 390–91, 394
September 11 terrorist attacks *see* 9/11 terrorist attacks
Seward, Anthony 335
Shah, Mohammed Zahir 36–37, 90
Shebarshin, Leonid 69
Shiner, Phil 314
Shirzad, Fazi Ahmad 230
Shirzad, Muhammad Omar 230
Short, Kevin 298
Shorten, Bill 228
Smethurst, Neville 122
Smith, Stephen 191, 223
Snesarev, Andrei 34–35, 43
Snow, Deborah 132
Soldier On 273

Solomon Islands 89, 105, 135, 158, 170, 286
Somalia 64, 89, 127, 163, 173, 201
    Canadian forces in 7, 276, 332–40, 350, 353, 354, 407
South Atlantic war 308–13
South Tomi MV 130
South Vietnam 4, 51, 54, 56, 59, 116–20, 160, 164, 168, 227, 276, 285–86, 317, 332
    see also Vietnam war
Soviet Directorate of Military Intelligence (GRU) 52–53
    see also Spetsnaz
Soviet military
    40th Army 47, 51, 52–53, 54, 55, 60, 62, 65–66, 67–88, 103, 162, 402–403
    media reports on 58, 73, 84
    misconduct 3, 72–88
Soviet Special Forces 48, 52–53
Soviet Union 34–35, 38–42, 111–12, 332, 404
    intervention in Afghanistan 3, 42–43, 45, 47–56, 58, 67–88, 102–103, 162, 170
    legacy of intervention in Afghanistan 58–66, 89–90, 92–93, 152–53, 206, 402
    withdrawal from Afghanistan 56–60, 103, 156
Soviet-Afghan Friendship Treaty 48
Sox, Michael 335
Special Air Service (SAS) Regiment
    conduct of 3, 7–8, 19–23, 117–20, 129–38, 146–51, 162, 205, 223–24, 228, 229, 230, 233–36, 238, 239–44, 245, 246–47, 258–59, 262–77, 280, 385–86, 390–92, 394–97, 399–400, 403, 406, 408–409
    formation of 4, 112–15
    in Afghanistan 144–52, 160–62, 180, 196–206, 216–24, 228–30, 233–36, 238–42, 244, 246, 247, 248, 254–56, 258–59, 262–74, 277, 280, 352, 385–86, 390–92, 394–400, 403, 406, 408–10, 413
    in Borneo 115–16, 120
    in East Timor 128–38, 239
    in Iraq 153–54,
    in Kuwait 127–28
    in Vietnam 116–19, 120
    recruitment and training of 124–27
Special Air Service (SAS), United Kingdom 112, 114, 307–308, 313–14, 317, 319, 329–30, 407
Special Boat Service (SBS), United Kingdom 128, 307–308
Special Forces Direct Recruiting Scheme (SFDRS) 201
Special Forces Task Group (SFTG), Australian 160–62, 164, 166–68, 170, 174, 179–80, 196–98, 199–200, 202–203, 204, 205, 248, 250–51
Special Forces, Soviet 48, 52–53
Special Operations Command (SOCOMD) 25, 160, 171, 197, 198, 204, 217, 259–60, 274, 411
    formation of 4, 133–37
    investigations into 5, 20–21, 23, 138, 235–41, 245, 246–51, 257, 258, 275, 277, 292, 381–85, 386, 388–92, 395, 413
Special Operations Commander – Australia (SOCAUST) 5, 20, 180, 197, 235, 242–43, 286, 390–91
Special Operations Engineer Regiment (SOER) 197
Special Operations Forces Command (CANSOF), Canada 348
Special Operations Group, United States 338
Special Operations Task Force – Afghanistan (CJSOTF-A) 197
Special Operations Task Group (SOTG) 2–3, 4–5, 7, 19–21, 23, 175–76, 180, 181–82, 191, 198, 207–209, 213, 214, 216, 217, 218, 219, 222, 223, 228–29, 231–33, 236–37, 241–43, 250–51, 265–66, 268, 280, 381–82, 387, 390, 400–401, 404–406, 407, 410, 412
Special Operations, New Zealand 291, 295
Spetsnaz 52–53, 86
Starov, Yuri 85
Stephenson, Jon 291, 292, 293, 296, 297, 303

Stewart, Bob 323
Stirling HMAS 102
Stokes, Kerry 262, 273
Sukarno 115

Taliban 3, 4, 50, 93–101, 141, 142–45, 152–53, 154–57, 158, 159, 163, 164, 166, 171–77, 181, 190, 214, 215, 216, 220–21, 230, 270, 276, 277, 402–403, 404, 405
   Australian government's response to 101, 104, 106–107, 142–43, 158, 159, 170, 173, 181, 191, 192, 194, 195, 196, 228
   Australian military engagements with 3, 19, 20, 21, 22, 24, 145–47, 150, 167–68, 170–71, 174, 175–76, 183–84, 186, 189, 190, 195, 202–207, 211–13, 219–21, 230–32, 235, 242, 258, 263, 268, 269
   Canadian military engagements with 341, 344
   French military engagements with 367, 368–69
   New Zealand military engagements with 286, 287–88, 299
   Pakistan support for 99, 153, 172, 173
   United Kingdom military engagements with 320–21, 322, 325, 326, 328, 329
   United States government's response to 99–100, 141, 142–43, 172–73, 186, 194
Tamil Tigers 215
Tampa MV 130
Taraka Valley, SAS operation in 146–52
Taraki, Nur Muhammad 37–39, 40–41
Thatcher, Margaret 311
Thatcher Government 308
Thom, Vivienne 259
Thompson, Hugh 85
Tranter, Kellie 275–76, 277
Treaty of Rawalpindi 34
Trump, Donald 270
Turnbull, Malcolm 262

Ullah, Shafied 219
United Front 98, 100

United Kingdom, military 5, 6, 7, 30–34, 52, 64–65, 179, 204, 276, 281, 285, 306–30, 332, 352, 388
   see also Law of Armed Conflict; Rules of Engagement (ROE); Special Air Service (SAS)
United Nations (UN) 20, 57, 58, 60–61, 77, 85, 90–91, 92, 96, 100–101, 103–104, 105, 127–28, 129, 130, 139, 143, 153, 157, 169–70, 173, 176, 286, 332, 334, 341, 365, 372–73
United Nations High Commissioner for Refugees (UNHCR) 103
United Nations Security Council 100–101, 143, 332, 373
United Nations Transitional Administration in East Timor (UNTAET) 129, 135
United States Air Force 102, 127–28
United States Drug Enforcement Agency (DEA) 216, 279
United States military
   and Afghanistan 5–6, 28, 63, 64–65, 69, 78, 99–100, 107, 142–45, 158, 166–67, 170, 171, 172–73, 176, 178, 179, 180, 186–87, 188, 189, 190–91, 192, 194–95, 196, 197, 200, 202– 203, 216, 219, 221, 269–70, 279, 286, 287, 294, 304, 338, 339–41, 344, 347–48, 349, 352–353, 366, 367–68, 370, 402
   and East Timor 139–40
   and Iraq 4, 15, 152, 153–54, 161, 167, 168, 169
   and Kuwait 127–28
   and Vietnam 51, 54, 56, 59, 85, 116, 118–19, 168, 276, 317
   conduct of 5–6, 187, 286–87, 298, 340, 347–48, 349
United States Navy SEALs 6, 221, 352
United States, relationship with Australia 102–103, 106, 120, 139–41, 142, 159, 160, 161, 166–67, 168–70, 171, 185, 192, 194, 207–208, 222, 228, 286, 402
USS *Abraham Lincoln* 154
Ustad, Hayat 230–32
Ustinov, Dmitry 42, 70

Vietnam war

Australian military in 4, 5, 116–20, 124, 139, 160, 163, 164, 167, 168, 220, 227, 285–86
New Zealand military in 285–86
United States military in 51, 54, 56, 59, 276, 317, 332

Wahab, Shaista 27
Wahab patrol base 219, 270
Wales, Mark 8, 271–72
Walker, Michael 179
war crimes, allegations of 2, 9–10
    Australian military 2, 3, 6, 8, 20–26, 125, 130–34, 138, 147–48, 230, 239, 244, 246–48, 251, 252, 256, 257, 260, 264, 266, 270–73, 382, 384, 387, 388–89, 391, 393, 396, 400, 402, 404, 406, 409, 410–11, 412
    Canadian military 340, 342, 344, 349
    French military 358, 372–75, 376–77
    New Zealand military 298, 300, 305
    Soviet military 72–74, 77–87
    United Kingdom military 312, 314, 315–16, 318, 320–21, 327, 330
    see also misconduct
Waterford, Jack 272–73, 277
Weale, Adrian 313
Whealy, Anthony 263
Whitlam Government 120
Wikileaks 213
Willacy, Mark 8, 23, 235, 263, 265, 267–68, 269
Wilson, Charles 50
Wroe, David 257, 262

Yar, Saifullah Ghareb 317–18, 329
Yugoslavia (former) 88, 98, 350

Zimbardo, Philip 275

www.ingramcontent.com/pod-product-compliance
Lightning Source LLC
Chambersburg PA
CBHW021927290426
44108CB00012B/744